Johnny Bluenose

Brian Cuthbertson

Formac Publishing
Halifax, 1994

Formac Publishing acknowledges the support of the Canada Council and the Nova Scotia Department of Education in the development of writing and publishing in Canada

Canadian Cataloging in Publication Data
Cuthbertson, Brian, 1936-
Johnny Bluenose at the polls
ISBN 0-88780-294-X (pbk.). — ISBN 0-88780-295-8 (bound)

1. Nova Scotia — Elections — History — 18th century. 2. Nova Scotia — Elections — History — 19th century. 3. Nova Scotia — Politics — government — To 1784. * 4. Nova Scotia — Politics and government — 1784-1867. * I. Title.

JL229.A5C87 1994   324.9716'01   C94-950227-8

COVER: Electioneering against Johnny Bluenose, 1823, Almon Family Papers, (MGI, Vol 14, p56) courtesy of the Public Archives of Nova Scotia.

Formac Publishing
5502 Atlantic Street
Halifax, Nova Scotia B3H 1G4

Contents

	Preface	v
1	Electioneering Against Johnny Blue Nose	1
2	Oligarchs and Assemblymen of Halifax Town and County 1759-1830	28
3	The Triumph of Reform in Halifax 1830-1847	60
4	The Yeomen Farmers and Merchants of Kings and Hants Counties	93
	The Family Compacts of Kings County and Their Ledgers	96
	In Defence of the Gypsum Trade	111
5	Planters, Acadians and Loyalists of Annapolis and Digby Counties	129
	The Tory/Baptist Alliance and the Rise of Parties in Old Annapolis County	131
	Factions Become Parties in Digby County	158
6	Halifax Connections and the Counties of Lunenburg and Queens	161
	Foreign Protestants and Englishmen	163
	Liverpool's Two Family Compacts	175
7	Planters, Acadians and Loyalists of Yarmouth and Shelburne Counties	188
	The Reformers of Yarmouth and the Squires of Argyle	189
	The Sargents of Barrington Township	199
	Respectability, Religion and Faction in Loyalist Shelburne	204

8   The Scotch Irish, Yorkshire and Scots Farmers of   216
    Cumberland and Colchester Counties

    Upholding the Tory Cause in Cumberland   217

    The Colchester/Halifax Axis   235

9   The Scots, Loyalists and Acadians of Pictou,   247
    Old Sydney and Cape Breton Counties

    Kirkmen and Seceders: Tories and Reformers   250

    The Family Compacts of Guysborough and   258
    a Bishop & His Highlanders

    Repealers Versus Annexationists on Cape Breton   272
    Island

10 Nova Scotian Politicians and the Achievement of   288
    Reform

    Notes on Databases and Sources   311

    Endnotes   317

    Index   334

Preface

The genesis of this study of early Nova Scotian politicians was in 1984. In that year, I received a private scholar's grant from the Social Sciences and Humanities Research Council of Canada. It provided me with a year's salary to do an analysis of members of the Nova Scotian Legislative Assembly (MLAs) from 1785 to 1830. Three months into the grant, however, I left the Public Archives of Nova Scotia, where I had been the Public Records Archivist since 1974, to take up my present position with the Government of Nova Scotia as Head of Heritage. I did not pursue this study while what research time I had was taken up with writing *The First Bishop: A Biography of Charles Inglis,* published in 1987 on the occasion of the bicentenary of his consecration as bishop of Nova Scotia.

At the Public Archives, my main task was the preparation for publication of the *Inventory of Manuscripts,* published in 1976. Among the many collections I had to describe were those for election writs, surviving poll books and papers for controverted elections. When I began again to do research for this book, these sources became the focus of my attention. I also concluded that the original time frame of 1785 to 1830 was too short to provide a meaningful study of early politicians and their elections. The natural time frame was from 1758 to 1848.

In 1758, Nova Scotians elected their first Legislative Assembly. Under representative government, the executive branch of government in the form of an appointed council was not responsible to the elected representatives sitting in the Assembly, but to the colonial governor appointed by the British government. After two decades of political struggle, in 1848 Nova Scotia and the other British North American colonies gained responsible government. Under responsible government, the colonial governor could appoint to his Executive Council (or Cabinet) only those recommended to him by the leader of the political party with the majority of members in the Assembly.

The more I researched early elections, the more I became convinced that the most interesting way to present the material was county by county. After all, the foundation of representative and responsible government is election of MLAs by constituencies. Moreover, in the case of Nova Scotia, constituency boundaries in the eighteenth and nineteenth centuries conformed to those of the counties. Beginning with elections in Halifax and ending with those in Cape Breton, the book describes the electoral history of each county. The focus, however, remains on the Legislative Assembly as the forum of principal political activity for those elected from the county and township constituencies.

With the achievement of responsible government, an era lasting nearly one hundred years came to a close in which MLAs had been elected and voted in the Assembly without the constraints of party. How and why they voted is the essential part of the story of early Nova Scotians and their elections.

To deal with the mass of information accumulated on the 437 MLAs elected from 1758 to 1847, I created three major databases to allow for computer-generated analysis. These databases are described at the end of the book under NOTES ON DATABASES AND SOURCES.

As a means of providing readers with an economic and social context for the electoral history of each county, I have introduced each chapter with an account by an imaginary traveller of 1830. The sources used for the descriptions by this imaginary traveller of the inhabitants of each county, their occupations and their religious adherence, are given as well in the NOTES ON DATABASES AND SOURCES.

Almost all the research was done in the Public Archives of Nova Scotia. In 1931, my mother, Eileen Odevaine, and Sergeant Major Joseph Jessup became the first employees of the newly-created Public Archives of Nova Scotia. It was my mother, as secretary and assistant archivist, and Sergeant Major Jessup, the caretaker, who welcomed D.C. Harvey when he arrived in August of that year to take up his appointment as Provincial Archivist. His appointment ushered in an era of historical research and publication by the archives staff which is, I believe, unequalled by any other archives in the nation.

My mother's roots in Nova Scotia reach back to Richard John Uniacke (1753-1830), known as the Old Attorney General, of whom she is a direct descendant. I have a picture of my mother sitting on the knee of her great-great-grandmother, taken when she was a little girl living probably at the Bower in Halifax (for those who have read Charles Ritchie's *Appetite for Life,* she is Eileen). The four generations appearing in that picture have family ties to many of the political families I describe in this book — among them are the Wilkins, Morris, Almon, Ritchie and Stewart families. After attending Sacred Heart Convent in Halifax and Branksome Hall in Toronto, my mother went to finishing school in Switzerland. A university education was never considered seriously. Instead, she attended a Boston secretarial school before accepting a position at the Public Archives of Canada, obtained partly because of her bilingualism. The establishment of the Public Archives of Nova Scotia drew her back to her native province to become its first assistant archivist. I dedicate this story of eighteenth- and early nineteenth-century Nova Scotian politicians to Eileen (Odevaine) Cuthbertson, who died, aged ninety-two, on February 27, 1994.

The statistical underpinnings of this book made its writing an unusually complex task. I owe thanks particularly to my editor, Marjory Whitelaw, for pointing out again and again the need for clarity and for simplifying convoluted sentences. John Somers and Peter Guilford, colleagues of mine in the former Nova Scotia Department of Tourism and Culture, gave freely of their expertise and time in dealing with computer inputting and analysis. Without them, I could not have managed. Professor emeritus of political science at Dalhousie University J. Murray Beck and Professor David Bell of the Faculty of Law, University of New Brunswick, kindly read and made many helpful comments on the manuscript. The original plan was to co-publish this book with the Nova Scotia Government Book Store. Much work was done by Government Publishing on preparation of the manuscript before it was determined that the arrangement could be perceived as a conflict of interest, because of my status as a civil servant. I owe a special debt of gratitude to Susan Lucy of Government Publishing for kindly completing the computer work on the manuscript. As usual, I offer my heartfelt thanks to my former colleagues in the Public Archives of Nova Scotia.

Brian Cuthbertson
April 1994

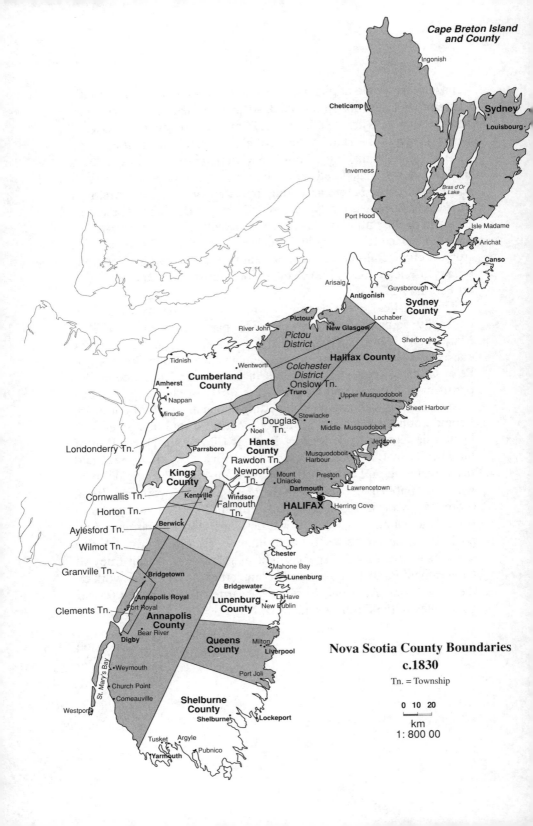

Cape Breton Island and County

Ingonish

Cheticamp

Sydney

Louisbourg

Inverness

Bras d'Or Lake

Port Hood

Isle Madame

Arichat

Canso

Arisaig

Guysborough

Antigonish

Sydney County

River John

Pictou

New Glasgow

Lochaber

Pictou District

Halifax County

Sherbrooke

Tidnish

Wentworth

Colchester District

Onslow Tn.

Truro

Upper Musquodoboit

Cumberland County

Amherst

Nappan

Minudie

Sheet Harbour

Stewiacke

Douglas Tn.

Middle Musquodoboit

Noel

Londonderry Tn.

Parrsboro

Hants County

Jeddore

Rawdon Tn.

Musquodoboit Harbour

Kings County

Newport Tn.

Mount Uniacke

Preston

Cornwallis Tn.

Kentville

Windsor

Dartmouth

Lawrencetown

Horton Tn.

Falmouth Tn.

HALIFAX

Herring Cove

Aylesford Tn.

Berwick

Wilmot Tn.

Chester

Granville Tn.

Bridgetown

Mahone Bay

Lunenburg

Annapolis Royal

Bridgewater

Port Royal

Lunenburg County

LaHave

Clements Tn.

Bear River

New Dublin

Annapolis County

Digby

Queens County

Milton

Liverpool

St. Mary's Bay

Weymouth

Church Point

Port Joli

Comeauville

Westport

Shelburne County

Tusket

Argyle

Shelburne

Lockeport

Pubnico

Yarmouth

Nova Scotia County Boundaries
c.1830

Tn. = Township

0 10 20

km
1 : 800 00

Chapter 1

Electioneering Against Johnny Blue Nose

... your petitioners lament ... the Occurrence and Prevailing extent to which the Scenes of Riot and dissipation have been carried in the late County Elections ... [and] suggest that the opening of the poll in so very few places ... Collects the freeholders from the extremes so far distant they frequently ... are compelled to take Shelter in that worst of asylums (the Candidates Open Houses) and in very many instances are rendered unfit either to demean [sic] themselves as tolerable members of civil society or to Exercise their Privilege as freeholders with anything like a judicious discrimination.
Petition of the Inhabitants of Musquodoboit, 1 March 1833

On February 7, 1758, the Board of Trade in London sent off a dispatch to Governor Charles Lawrence in Nova Scotia directing him to call into being a Legislative Assembly. Deluged with angry petitions and representations from Halifax merchants demanding an end to rule by decree of the Governor and his appointed Council, the Board had finally lost patience with Lawrence. When that dispatch arrived in Halifax in May, Lawrence sensed rightly that he could delay no longer, whatever he thought of the merchant "dram-sellers" of Halifax and their self-interested motives for demanding an elected Assembly. On 20 May, eight days before he left to command a brigade at the siege of the great French fortress of Louisbourg, Lawrence and his Council promulgated regulations for the conduct of Nova Scotia's first election. Nearly a century later, on August 5, 1847, Nova Scotian freeholders voted their first responsible government into office. In the intervening years there were sixteen general elections, but the manner of conducting them did not change significantly from that first election in 1758. For the 1847 election, however, there was simultaneous polling. Under simultaneous polling there were sufficient polling stations established in each county so that all voting could take place in a single day, instead of taking weeks, as in past elections.[1]

Governors issued the writs for elections to county sheriffs. The sheriffs acted as returning officers, being responsible for the whole conduct of elections. Some, such as William Winniet of Annapolis and David McQueen of Guysborough, became known for their flagrant displays of partiality. As returning officers, sheriffs decided the date for the opening of the polling. On the morning the poll opened, the sheriff read from the hustings the writ and the regulations governing elections. The hustings were generally no more than a raised platform, usually erected in or outside the county courthouse but sometimes in a church or a private dwelling. Two passageways led up to the platform; one was for voters to come forward to declare their vote and the other was for them to leave. On the platform stood the sheriff, his assistants, and the candidates with their inspectors. The candidates were officially nominated from the hustings and could then address the assembled freeholders.

The law required the sheriff to keep a poll book in which he listed, in running sequence as they voted, the names of electors and their place of residence. Candidates and their inspectors could question electors on their eligibility to vote. They could demand that voters swear to their property qualification. When candidates objected to an elector, this fact had to be noted opposite the elector's name in the poll book. The sheriff recorded the elector's vote by placing a check mark opposite his name in the column of the candidate or candidates named by him. Such were the strongly-held feelings for the manly old practice of open voting that not until 1870 did Nova Scotians vote by secret ballot.

From the founding of Halifax in 1749, the pattern of settlement was determined by the creation of townships of roughly twelve square miles in area, in which the first settlers, or proprietors, received free grants of land from the crown. Halifax and Lunenburg were the first townships created. With the arrival of the New England Planters in the early 1760s, the government established a further fourteen townships. In 1759 the province was also divided into counties, each consisting of one or more townships. The regulations for the 1765 election provided for freeholders in each county to elect two representatives, and in each township one representative; the exceptions were Halifax Township with two members and Halifax County with four. As the government established newer townships (such as for the Loyalists whose arrival in 1783 and 1784 doubled the population) not all these townships were given representation. This system of county and township representation meant, however, that freeholders

Halifax from Fort Needham
Drawn by Lieut.-Colonel Edward Hicks, engraved and published, London, c. 1782.

in the first settled townships could vote for their single members and also for the two county members. Those who settled later were generally denied township representation, no matter that their populations greatly exceeded those in many of the older townships. The result was a highly inequitable system of representation.

Often township and county elections were held together, with the sheriff using the same poll book to record the votes for both elections. The sheriff first recorded a freeholder's vote for one of the candidates for the single township seat. Then he accepted the votes of the same freeholder for his choice of candidates for the two county seats. In voting for county elections, however, freeholders did not have to vote for two candidates, but could vote for only one and refuse to give their second vote to another candidate. Usually this happened when electors were prepared to vote for a single candidate because he might be the only one of the candidates resident among them, or because of religious or personal loyalty. In the language of the day, such single votes were called "plumpers" (an eighteenth-century English election term for votes given solely to one candidate when freeholders had the right to vote for two or more candidates). The number of plumpers could be decisive in determining the outcome of elections, as in the case of the triumph of the Tory, Andrew Mitchell Uniacke, in taking one of the two Halifax Township seats in the 1843 election. The liberals should have easily won both seats, but many liberals voted for just one of their party's two candidates and refused to vote for the other. Uniacke was the single Tory candidate and his supporters voted only for him. As a result of so many plumpers, Uniacke managed to get more votes than the second liberal candidate. As it turned out, the Tories won the 1843 election by a majority of one seat.

In those elections where there were few freeholders, the election could be decided in a day or two of polling. As late as the 1820s, such old townships as Falmouth in Hants County or Onslow and Londonderry in Colchester had well under a hundred eligible freeholders. Moreover, for township elections, the poll seldom moved from the county courthouse; as soon as the poll closed the sheriff could declare the winner. But in such large counties as Annapolis, the poll for the county elections could move to as many as five different locations. At each new location, the sheriff erected the hustings and conducted the polling as before. In his poll book he kept a running daily total of the vote for each candidate. At the close of the final poll, he declared the victors. These county elections took weeks to complete; consequently, they were most open to every abuse inherent in the system of open voting. In the Cape Breton County winter by-election of 1832, the poll opened on November 12th at Sydney, moved to Arichat and then to Port Hood, and finally to Cheticamp, where the sheriff closed it on December 14th. As well as one of the lengthiest on record, the election was among the most violent, with the sheriff conniving openly with one of the candidates, William Young, to secure him the election.

The widespread and appalling drunkenness that accompanied many of these county elections was the result of the open houses kept by candidates. As early as the 1793 election in Halifax, candidates kept open houses, or "houses of entertainment," as they were also called. These provided supporters with lodgings of a sort, food, rum in abundance, and stabling for as long as the poll remained open. By the 1830s candidates for most county elections accepted that they had to provide open houses at each poll if they were to have any hope for success. Costs could easily be in hundreds of pounds. In some of the more fiercely contested elections we shall discuss, the cost ran into thousands of pounds. Spending was highest at Pictou and Halifax elections, but was also heavy in Annapolis County. In the 1832 Cape Breton by-election mentioned above, Richard Smith spent £3,000 in his attempt to defeat William Young. No aspect of elections in this period aroused more passionate public outcry than did the prevalence of open houses and the resulting drunkenness. The increasingly influential temperance movement became the leader in calling for their end. But attempts to legislate them out of existence failed utterly until the Simultaneous Polling Act of 1847.

At any time during the course of an election, candidates could withdraw and concede the election. As was often the case, if only one candidate appeared, the sheriff kept the poll open for the required one hour; he could then declare the single nominated candidate the winner. In fact, from the earliest elections, the cost, drunkenness and tumult associated with contests caused leading freeholders to meet before the poll opened. From among themselves they selected the candidate or candidates who would be unopposed on election day. As early as 1806, Halifax Township freeholders had the sheriff call a public meeting, well before polling day, to nominate candidates on the understanding that they should be unopposed. Elsewhere in the province, public meetings to select candidates before the polling date became a fairly common practice as a means of avoiding contested elections. Liverpool merchant Simeon Perkins noted in his diary numerous occasions when he and other leading freeholders went to great lengths to arrange matters so that the township and Queens County could avoid the evils associated with contested elections.

Where elections were fiercely contested, however, there could be much fraudulent voting, drunkenness, epic battles to gain possession of the passageways leading up to the hustings, intimidation of voters, and great expense to candidates. Not until 1847 did public pressure force the Assembly to legislate simultaneous polling "to promote the purity of Elections, and ... the diminution of expense," as the preamble to the act so singularly described its purpose. Instead of moving the poll from location to location within a county over a three- or four-week period, simultaneous polling provided for the division of each county into a sufficient number of electoral districts, each with its own polling station, so that all electors in the province could be polled in a single day. The introduction of simultaneous polling removed the evils so lamented by the petitioners of Musquodoboit, quoted at the beginning of this chapter. What the Assembly failed to deal with in a satisfactory manner was eligibility of voters.

It was a basic tenet of British parliamentary democracy that only those who held property in freehold could vote. The 1758 regulations stated that candidates and electors had to be possessed of a freehold estate within the constituency in which they voted or were candidates. In England, electors had to have freehold with an annual value of forty shillings.[2] In 1759, the Council revised the regulations to bring Nova Scotia into conformity with English practice. But how Nova Scotian electors were to demonstrate proof of their freehold and its value was another matter.

An act of 1789 allowed that eligible freehold was ownership of a dwelling house or one hundred acres of land, cultivated or uncultivated. In 1797, the one hundred acres provision was changed; at least five acres now had to be under cultivation. Furthermore, any grant or conveyance had to be registered six months before the writ was issued. The reason behind the restrictions lay in the desire to halt the scandal whereby candidates created instant freeholders. Such large landowners as Squire Jonathan Crane of Horton became notorious for having their agents make up deeds to hand to otherwise ineligible electors, who would then vote for them. Often the deeds were so worded that, in fact, the land was never transferred to the elector. An amendment in 1839 eliminated the one hundred acre provision entirely. An elector had to have freehold possession of a clear yearly value of forty shillings. This was estimated by value of agricultural or other produce, or the annual rent from buildings owned.

The whole question of voter eligibility was bedeviled by so much property in Nova Scotia being conveyed, by one means or another, without being recorded in the local registries. Registration had never been required by law. The healthy fees charged by registrars of deeds and probate discouraged registration. Generally, the male heads of households held the ownership of the family property. As sons married and established their own households, the father often transferred to them their share of the family lands. The youngest son usually accepted responsibility for the aged parents, and, in return, inherited the family homestead. Within families, land could be handed on, divided among sons or leased over generations, with few or none of these transactions officially recorded. The situation was worst in Cape Breton. In 1763 the island had been joined to Nova Scotia, only to be separated in 1784 in anticipation that many Loyalists would settle there. Few did, and it was re-annexed to Nova Scotia in 1820. Consequently, little land was granted in freehold before 1820 and licences of occupation had to be accepted as evidence of freehold. Hundreds of Scottish families arriving in the great waves of immigration caused by the Highland clearances simply squatted, and had no right or title except that of occupation. As late as the 1847 election, it seems that less than half of the heads of households in Inverness County could demonstrate eligible freehold and vote. Only with the introduction of universal suffrage in 1920 was the property qualification for provincial elections finally laid to rest.

Where elections were contested, much time could be taken up in questioning freeholders on their property qualifications. Voters could be turned away for an endless number of reasons — not having a freehold according to the terms of a will, owning land which was not paid for, holding land but receiving no emoluments from it, land that had in fact been sold, lands rented for less than forty shillings, not a legal heir, married to a widow who had no legal title to the property in question, or trying to claim as a dwelling house a building with no chimney. Candidates often demanded that electors swear that they could vote by right of the property qualification they claimed and that they had not obtained it fraudulently to qualify to vote.

By 1839 the fine for voting fraudulently was £20. The oath served to discourage from voting those who had property but could not necessarily provide acceptable evidence of its registration at least six months prior to the election. If prosecuted, and unable to pay the fine, they stood to lose their property. Those without property had nothing to lose and could be bribed with rum, tobacco or odd bits of clothing to swear the oath. Moreover, it was difficult and expensive to prosecute electors for fraudulent voting, or candidates for bribing electors. From 1758 to 1847 there are just two recorded cases of successful prosecution of candidates accused of bribing electors. One case involved a candidate supposedly bribing an elector with five shillings; in the other the sum was twenty shillings. In both cases the general view of contemporaries was that the accused candidates were prosecuted and punished unfairly. In one other case, the Assembly found a winning candidate guilty of bribery, but the House relied entirely on the evidence of the man who claimed he was bribed. In some elections we shall describe, the system seems to have broken down completely, with many coming forward to vote who had no property recorded in the county deed office but who readily who swore the oath and voted.

After the poll finally closed, losing candidates could demand a scrutiny. This entailed the re-examination of the property qualifications of all those electors listed in the sheriff's poll book and marked as "objected to" by the candidates. Where the sheriff had used the same poll book for the township and county elections, there could be endless wrangling, beloved by the lawyers engaged by both parties, over which candidate for which election had, in fact, objected to which electors. A scrutiny could last for days and be costly in fees for the sheriff to attend and for deed and probate searches. The lengthiest and most expensive was that demanded by William Stairs, the defeated candidate in the Halifax Township election of 1843. After the poll finally closed at the St. Margaret's Bay schoolhouse on 21 November, the declared winners were James McNab and Andrew Mitchell Uniacke. Stairs accused Uniacke of having brought to the hustings many illegal voters, including some from outside the township boundaries. The scrutiny dragged on for weeks until in February 1844 an exasperated Stairs appealed, unsuccessfully, to the Assembly to hear his case on the grounds that he was not enabled to force the attendance of witnesses. So adept had Uniacke's agents been in dragging out the proceedings that, of the 132 votes in dispute, fewer than one-third had been investigated. The eleven-week farce drew forth the following ditty:

> Cold Winter reigns, the mercury's low,
> And all things bound in ice and snow,
>   Around us now we see;
> The times are dull each one declares,
> But thanks to Uniacke and Stairs,
>   We'll have the Scrutiny
>   Provided both can pay.[3]

There is no record of a sheriff overturning the election of a winning candidate and declaring his opponent duly elected as the result of a scrutiny. If, however, a losing candidate wanted to petition the Assembly to have the election of the victorious candidate voided, a scrutiny had to be completed first. This was the problem William Stairs had and presumably why the Assembly refused to hear his case. Until 1821, the Assembly heard petitions on disputed elections in whole session or by select committee. In that year, it enacted a version of the English 1770 statute that delegated to a committee, chosen by ballot, the responsibility to regulate and determine trials of controverted elections.

"Trial" was the correct word for the procedures enacted, with witnesses having to be brought to Halifax at much expense. From the second decade of the nineteenth century, it became standard practice for the contending parties to engage legal counsel to the point that attendance by articling students was considered part of their training. Proceedings could continue for days, with much lobbying of members by the contending parties. In the 1830 election for Cape Breton

County, when James Boyle Uniacke was accused of lacking freehold, Uniacke's defence counsel, J.W. Johnston, took four full days for his opening remarks alone. Most petitioners claimed that, had it not been that so many unqualified electors had been able to vote for their opponent, or had it not been for the partiality of the sheriff, they would have won. Select committees could call for the sheriff's poll book and require him to travel to Halifax, sometimes at his own expense, to appear before them. After hearing witnesses and examining the poll book, the committee could strike off those votes it judged were not legal. The votes for each candidate were retallied and either the sitting member was confirmed or the petitioner given the seat. The Assembly could always call for a new election.

In the disputed 1811 election for Truro Township, won by 53 to 50 votes, the Assembly struck off two votes of the winner's total. It then had to decide if the vote of John Johnstone, who had been deaf and mute from birth, was legal. If it determined that his vote was illegal, then the two candidates were tied and another election necessary. After hearing evidence from several witnesses, on the motion of the lawyer, S.B. Robie, the House declared by a vote of 20 to 13 that Johnstone was incapable. At the next sitting, another motion called for reconsideration; it passed with the Speaker, Lewis Morris Wilkins, breaking a tie vote. In the ensuing debate the arguments of the Guysborough lawyer, J. G. Marshall, were instrumental in bringing the Assembly to reverse its first decision, on the ground that Johnstone was capable of communicating by signs.[4]

No similar debate took place in the two disputed elections in which women voted. The first was in the 1793 election for Windsor Township. In that election two women voted for the winning candidate, John McMonagle, and four for his opponent, George Monk. But as the six women had the legal property qualifications, the sheriff left it to the Assembly to decide if they could in law vote. The Assembly ruled in favour of McMonagle but deliberately avoided the question of whether women could vote.[5] In the 1806 Amherst Township election, Edward Baker had 35 votes; five of those were from women. His defeated opponent, Thomas Dixon, petitioned to have the Assembly overturn the result, partly on the grounds of the women voting, but mostly because he claimed Baker lacked the legal qualification to be a candidate. When the House refused to consider the petition, other than on the sole question of the legality of Baker's candidacy, Dixon withdrew it.[6] Although women in Nova Scotia did not vote again in a provincial election until 1920, a good marriage could dramatically forward a man's political career in nineteenth-century Nova Scotia. We shall encounter numerous men, lawyers especially, who had the good fortune to marry into local family compacts and thereby to rise in station and to benefit themselves greatly.

In 1758, when Nova Scotia's first election took place, the European population was probably no more than 3,000. As the population grew with the arrival of 7,000 New England Planters in the 1760s and some 19,000 American Loyalists two decades later, the Governor and his Council acted to increase representation from twenty-two to thirty-nine seats. But, other than two additional seats for Cape Breton Island on its re-annexation to Nova Scotia in 1820, there was no further increase or redistribution in representation. By the 1830s, when the population had grown to around 200,000, the Assembly finally felt compelled to deal with the intractable issue of redistribution.

At the heart of the problem was the distressing fact that the older townships in the western and central counties were continuing to have representation long after their number of freeholders ceased to warrant it. As noted earlier, freeholders in each county could elect to represent them two members and, in each of the older townships, one member. Freeholders in the older townships, therefore, not only elected their own member, but also voted for two members in the county elections. In essence, freeholders in the older townships had a double franchise and double representation. Hants was among the least populated counties, but it had more representatives than any other county except Annapolis, with twice its population, and Halifax, which had five times its population. These older townships defended their representation with political skill and tenacity; a redistribution that fully reflected actual population distribution was a virtual impossibility. Moreover, Scottish and Irish immigration into the eastern part of the province had given that region a much increased population that was not matched by the number of seats it had in the Assembly. The Assembly attempted to deal with the worst of the evils by a series of patchwork acts that gave representation to some of the newer townships, divided some of the larger counties, and created a number of new townships and counties. Not until 1859, however, was township representation ended, one hundred and one years after its introduction.

From 1758 through to the 1847 election, Nova Scotian freeholders elected 437 members to the Assembly. Before 1800, four-fifths of these members had come with their families in one of the incoming tides of settlers who populated mainland Nova Scotia in the eighteenth century. But after that date, three-quarters of those elected were native-born Nova Scotians. Other than this division in origin, there was a remarkable continuity in make-up among the 437 members elected over nearly a hundred years. The average age on election, for example, did not change markedly, with forty years being the norm. There were, however, few elections in which there was not a sizeable changeover of members, often nearly half or more of the sitting members being replaced. The reasons included death, infirmities, departure from the province and promotion to the bench or to the Council. But the chief cause was defeat at the hustings, or declining to enter or to continue a contest when faced with the likelihood of defeat. In fact, an elected member could on average look forward to no more than eight years in his Assembly seat. Some forty of those elected, though, served over two decades each, with John George Pyke of Halifax sitting in the House for thirty-seven years.

One characteristic of this period, noted again and again in later chapters, was the dominance of lawyers and merchants in every Assembly. Together they accounted for close to half of all members elected from 1758 to 1847. After the 1836 election, this proportion rose to over two-thirds. The remainder were divided among office-holders, farmers and such other assorted occupations as mariners, physicians, land surveyors and a few tradesmen. For those wishing to enter the Assembly, even if merchants or lawyers, it was an undoubted asset to hold local offices. One half of those elected were justices of the peace at the time of their election, or were appointed shortly after taking their seat. One third were militia officers on their election and, of these, fifty-nine were commanding one of their local militia battalions. Numbered among militia colonels elected were such prominent lawyers as Thomas Barclay and Thomas Ritchie of Annapolis and William Frederick DesBarres of Guysborough. Among the wealthiest merchants who were colonels were George Smith of Pictou, and James Ratchford DeWolf and Joseph Freeman of Liverpool. One of the few farmers who commanded a militia battalion was James Fulton of Londonderry. Moreover, one quarter of members elected could expect additional offices once they entered the Assembly, mostly appointments to the local inferior courts of common pleas. All these offices (except militia commissions) had fees attached to them and could generally be held for life.

No group sought election more for the rewards of office than did lawyers. Of sixty-four lawyers elected up to 1847, forty-five entered the Assembly after 1800. In fact, until 1820 there were never more than five to seven lawyers elected, but in that election eleven were returned. It was to these eleven lawyers that Johnny BlueNose refers (on the cover to this book) when he exclaims: *"Oh Mercy me, I'll not Swallow him* (Charles Rufus Fairbanks, the Halifax lawyer and candidate for the 1823 Halifax Township election). *Eleven of them already tearing my very guts out."* This sudden increase reflected the rapid growth in the number of younger lawyers. During the long war with Revolutionary France many young Nova Scotians had taken commissions in the army and the navy. With peace in 1815 the military life was largely foreclosed; for young men seeking to enter a profession, law now held considerable attraction. To some, such as the wealthy Pictou merchant Edward Mortimer, the profession was overrunning the country. The Reverend Thomas McCulloch, principal of Pictou Academy, thought this new breed of lawyers poorly educated for the profession. He wrote S.B. Robie, then Speaker of the Assembly and Solicitor General: "A month's Latin now prepares a boy to sweep an office and at the end of his apprenticeship he becomes qualified to turn off [sic] two more as good as himself every five years." He also told Robie that the bar ought to be purged of its "dandies, dinnersmen and dunces."[7] He could have as well commented upon their prickly sense of honour. Outside the officers of the garrison, lawyers fought the most duels, though there were more challenges than actual duels.

Until the 1820s, most aspiring lawyers gravitated to Halifax. Their growing numbers, however, soon forced many to seek practice in towns from Yarmouth to Sydney, where they connected themselves, commonly through marriage, with the local family compacts. A notable example of this pattern was Thomas Dickson, one of the Truro Dicksons, who studied his law under S.G.W. Archibald. He then opened a practice in Pictou. Shortly afterwards he married Sarah Ann Patterson, connecting himself thereby with the Patterson and Mortimer families, easily the most prominent in Pictou. Another was Samuel Fairbanks, a scion of one of the oldest established mercantile families in Halifax. He set up practice in Liverpool where he married Charlotte Ann, daughter of Joshua Newton, collector of customs, and the granddaughter of the merchant and diarist, Simeon Perkins. But the case of William Frederick DesBarres is perhaps the best illustration of how marriage into a local family compact could forward a career. DeBarres spent his early years in Minudie, Cumberland County. His parents sent him to the Halifax Grammar School before they arranged for him to study law with Lewis Morris Wilkins, a judge of the Supreme Court. After admission to the bar in 1821, DesBarres established a practice in Guysborough where he married Maria Cutler, whose father was patriarch of the most extensive family compact in the county. DeBarres became the leading politician in the county, Solicitor General in the first ministry under responsible government and a judge of the Supreme Court. For these young country lawyers, election to the Assembly followed naturally, with their average age on election being thirty-one, compared to the norm of forty years.

By the 1840s, lawyers formed a fifth or more of the elected members; in the 1843 election, for example, Nova Scotians elected fifteen lawyers in an Assembly of fifty-one members. But their influence extended well beyond their voting numbers. To start with, as the editor of the *Novascotian*, Joseph Howe, charged, they had among them nearly all the speaking talent, dominating debates and managing Assembly proceedings with an eye to their own self-interest. For all but seven sessions from 1758 through to 1847, lawyers held the office of Speaker; by the nature of his position as First Commoner in the days before party government, he was the most powerful figure in the Assembly. Of the seven lawyers who became Speaker, five were either Solicitor General or Attorney General while they presided, and five of the seven were promoted to the bench. In fact, of the sixty-four lawyers elected, twenty-nine gained judgeships and most of these promotions came while they were still in the Assembly.[8] Their dependence on government for these much sought-after offices ensured that the executive branch of government always had powerful friends in the Assembly.

If ambition and the rewards of office were sufficient in themselves to entice lawyers to enter the Assembly, the motivation of others was more varied, though not necessarily less self-interested. From the very first Assembly in 1758, members drawn from the merchant class formed on average two-fifths of those elected. This figure increased with time, rising to near half of the members returned in the 1840 election; in all probability the cause lay in the mounting costs of fighting elections, which were borne almost entirely by the merchant class. At all times merchants were by far the largest number of any occupation represented in the House. Some of this class were never more than storekeepers, but most had extensive interests in property, shipbuilding and export trading, for which the West Indian market was the most important. This was particularly true around the South

Shore for such merchant-assemblymen as John Ryder of Argyle, John Sargent and his sons John and Winthrop at Barrington, and at Liverpool Joseph Barss and his sons, James and John. Those in the agricultural western counties were usually substantial landowners, giving seasonal employment to a labouring class of quite substantial numbers in some of the older townships. In Kings County the De-Wolfs, Cranes and Chipmans were the principal families of this merchant-landowner class.

Outside of the most wealthy in Halifax, the merchants of Liverpool appear to have been the wealthiest in the province. Much of this wealth had its origin in the privateering ventures mounted by Liverpool captains and merchants during the long war with Revolutionary France and during the War of 1812 with the United States. Next to Enos Collins, who went on to found the Halifax Banking Company, Joseph Freeman was the most successful among the Liverpool privateers. Freeman's privateering ventures laid the basis for a large fortune. The ledger influence that went with it ensured that he had a twenty-six-year uninterrupted tenure in the Assembly. Nowhere was the seafaring spirit more present than in Liverpool township. Fish and lumber formed the staples of a seaborne trade that took fish from as far away as Labrador to markets in Europe, the Mediterranean and the West Indies. This trade relied on the labours of hundreds of inshore or small boat fishermen, but of this class not one is known to have been elected, or seems ever to have been a candidate in this period.

In many counties, there arose family compacts of merchants and lawyers whose ascendancy rested in large measure upon their control over local offices. Representation in the Assembly was a natural extension of such an ascendancy and was essential to its preservation. As long as they stayed on reasonably good terms with the Governor and his Council, they could expect to receive their due when it came to such local appointments as sheriffs, registrars of deeds and probate, customs and revenue officials, and coroners. But it was control over the expenditure of road moneys, and the appointment in some counties of up to seventy road commissioners annually to supervise the work, that gave them the most extensive form of local patronage. In his travels around the province in 1830, Captain William Moorsom noted that marvellously little hard cash ever found its way directly into the palms of those who laboured with pickaxe and shovel on the roads. Those employed were usually men already in debt; their pay was simply credited against their debts with local merchants, who thereby pocketed most of the hard cash that came into the county from the Assembly's annual appropriations for road work.[9]

No family compact could long maintain its local ascendancy without having available to it the influence that came with the ledger. Merchants used ledgers to keep running accounts of goods sold and credit provided to individuals.[10] Although the accounts were kept in pounds, shillings and pence, usually little coin changed hands, with payment in the form of fish or agricultural produce. These running accounts, by name of individual, were kept from year to year, normally without interest being charged and the balance owing never paid in full. Among fishermen the use of the ledger was most pernicious. A system of credit, originating in Halifax, provided fishermen with advance supplies needed for the fishing seasons. In return for repayment, local merchants received a high proportion of the catch. This system of payment in kind or truck system, as it was known, bound fishermen in perpetual debt, from which escape could only come by turning to trading and smuggling.

The most likely cause of a day of reckoning came when the merchants themselves died insolvent, or the liabilities of their estates exceeded their assets, including the amounts owed as shown on their ledgers. The usual procedure was to separate the outstanding debts into good, doubtful and bad, but their collection and the settlement of the estate could drag on for years. When William Allen Chipman, the Kings County landowner, merchant and member of the Assembly for many years, died in 1845, the claims against his estate by creditors and legatees exceeded its value, though he was owed £2,174 by two hundred and twenty-three individuals. His executors, however, could collect from just sixty-six of them for a total of £955.

Merchants could at any time call for payment of balances and sue to recover the money owed them. It was the threat to do so at election times that gave the merchants such influence over those on their ledgers. Merchants who were candidates and their agents would ride about the countryside to canvass freeholders, ledger in hand, threatening and cajoling. Promises were made for road work, for cancelling of debts or suits at law, and for minor offices in return for support at the hustings. With open voting, when a freeholder failed to fulfil his part of the bargain, a reckoning could be swift and merciless.

In succeeding chapters, we shall have cause to comment upon the small number of freeholders who voted in some of the township and county elections compared to the number of male heads of families listed in the censuses of the period. Property ownership—and with it the right to vote as a freeholder—was almost entirely restricted to male heads of households. The chief censuses of this period (1827 and 1838) listed only the name of the head of the family and his occupation, with the numbers of males and females in the family broken down into age groups. There is, however, no way of knowing from the censuses whether the family owned the property on which they resided, or, more importantly for our purposes, whether the male head could demonstrate ownership and vote as a freeholder. Consequently, only tentative estimates can be made on the proportion of family heads who were eligible and, in fact, voted. The numbers ranged from nearly every head of a household in Amherst Township voting (though even by the late 1830s, their numbers barely exceeded 200) to just one-fifth of those in the town of Halifax. Generally, anywhere between half and three-quarters of family heads voted in the township and county elections. A good proportion of those who did not vote either lacked property or were unable to demonstrate registered title.

Although generalizations can be misleading, some comments on Johnny BlueNose in the first part of the nineteenth century are in order. In his *The Old Judge,* Thomas Chandler Haliburton described Mr Blue Nose (a *sobriquet,* he says, acquired from a superior potato of that name) as a man of all work, but expert in none, knowing a little of many things, but nothing well. His Nova Scotian could often be found working on his farm and building a sailing vessel at the same time. He was not only able to catch and cure a cargo of fish but to find his way to the West Indies or the Mediterranean.[11] Haliburton knew at first hand only the descendants of New England Planters and Loyalists, but what he had to say on how these Nova Scotians made their living held true generally for the province as a whole.

The census data do allow us to gain a more particular insight into Johnny BlueNose's social and economic circumstances. With the exception of the continued Scottish immigration into Cape Breton, by the 1830s most Nova Scotians were native-born, if not of the second or third generation. The population stood around 200,000, made up of 30,000 to 35,000 households, each of six to seven occupants. The extraordinary bonding strength of kinship within extended families, formed by birth and marriage, was the most conspicuous characteristic of both new and old settlers. Nearly all these families drew part of their livelihood from the land, though this might entail among fishermen little more than the ownership of a cow and the growing of root crops, especially the potato. Others had sufficient cleared and improved land to grow hay, wheat and other grains, as well as root crops. In the Annapolis Valley most farms had orchards; some, such as those of Charles Prescott and Abraham Gesner, were of horticultural renown.

Whether they drew most or little of their sustenance from the land, nearly all able-bodied males in western Nova Scotia, and many elsewhere, sometime in their lives went to sea. Their voyaging could extend from no more than coastal trading within the Bay of Fundy and the Gulf of St. Lawrence to annual sailings to the West Indies and year-long or longer voyages to the East Indies. Shipbuilding gave employment to a good number in the more seafaring townships. In Liverpool, shipwrights, caulkers, sailmakers, coopers and other tradesmen outnumbered both farmers and fishermen. Nearly a fifth of the household heads in Yarmouth Township in 1838 listed themselves as mariners. Carpenters, shoemakers, blacksmiths and similar trades were to be found in the agricultural townships. However, probably no more than one-fifth of all farmers in the province could live comfortably from the proceeds of their farms.[12] The remainder could not sustain their families on what their farms provided, but had to labour for more prosperous farmers or find work in the woods and in the seasonal inshore fisheries.

Although there were variations in the pattern, in the first half of the nineteenth century Nova Scotian society in the counties and townships was at the top composed of a small class of merchants, lawyers and well-to-do farmers. They were usually inter-related and their families made up around five per cent of the population of their counties and townships. At the bottom of the social and economic scale was a sizeable labouring class. In the western counties this class made up ten to fifteen per cent of the population; in Windsor Township, labourers outnumbered farmers in the 1838 census. On Cape Breton Island, thousands of Scottish immigrants squatted on backlands and, to survive, had to labour for others. In between there was a middling class of farmers, fishermen and tradesmen whose economic status could vary greatly, but seldom ever approached that of the merchant class to whom they were almost all indebted, usually for their whole lives.

The ubiquitous chain of credit and indebtedness reached back to Halifax. It was the extension of credit to merchants in the outports and townships, combined with the control of the chief offices of government, that tied local family compacts to successive ruling oligarchies in the capital, composed of interrelated families of merchants, lawyers and office-holders. Moreover, because the salaries of many important officers of government were paid out of the British parliamentary grant for Nova Scotia, the Assembly could exercise little control over them. The offices were usually held for life. Incumbents treated them as a form of property to hand on to their sons. The record for inheritance was that for the surveyor generalship, held by the family of Charles Morris for one hundred and four years through four generations. A major reason why the practice was acceptable for so long was because neither the Assembly nor the crown felt any need to pay the father a pension when the son inherited an office.

Until the 1830s, the most important office-holders could expect to be appointed, by reason of their office and service, to His Majesty's Council. When presided over by the Governor, the Council formed the executive branch of colonial Nova Scotian government. With the exception of those offices paid out of the parliamentary grant or of the imperial customs service, the Council of Twelve (as it became called pejoratively) made appointments to every salaried office in the province. Furthermore, its control over the life of the colony extended to choosing almost every public official—magistrates, sheriffs, judges of inferior courts of common pleas, registrars of deeds and probate, coroners, health officers and similar officials—by whom fees could be charged in the course of their duties. When the Assembly was in session, the Council sat in its legislative capacity with the Chief Justice of the Supreme Court presiding. Except that it could not amend the revenue and appropriation bills sent up by the Assembly (it could only approve or reject these bills in their entirety), the Council in its legislative role was the constitutional equal of the elected Assembly. In practice, it seldom initiated legislation, using its constitutional power and the patronage at its disposal to check any democratic pretensions emanating from the Assembly.

The power to appoint and to dismiss magistrates gave the executive branch of government its chief means to extend its authority to the local level. When sitting in General Sessions of the Peace, usually twice a year, justices of the peace carried out the administrative responsibilities of local government and also sat as a criminal court. When sitting as a criminal court, juries decided the verdict and the justices the punishment; the lash was freely used as a form of punishment, with twenty or more lashes regularly administered for convictions of the theft of no more than a pair of boots or a small quantity of flour. They could hear as well, either singly or in pairs, actions to recover small debts. Such summary trials (that is, without a jury or lawyers involved) could take place at any time or in any locale. Most summary trials took place in magistrates' houses. They could issue summons for debtors to appear before them, make judgements on the amount of the debt owed and decree either payment or seizure of goods and property.[13] For all these actions there was a fee schedule. Those justices who made a good part of their living from such summary trials became known as "jobbing magistrates."

Justices could also be appointed to the inferior court of common pleas, which in practice acted as a county court to try civil actions, mostly for the recovery of debts. Its members were entitled to higher fees; in prestige, at least, it ranked above membership on the sessions bench. The appointment of justice of the peace was a much desired office for the respectability it bestowed on its holder, for the patronage that went with the appointments for all minor offices in a township or county, and for the fees. We have already noted that half of the members were already justices on election or received the appointment while in the Assembly. Again, the large majority of members who were magistrates were either merchants or lawyers. This increased over time; in the 1840 election, for instance, eighteen of the twenty-five magistrates elected were merchants or lawyers.

No group in the Assembly displayed greater resolve than did merchants to retain and increase the authority of justices of the peace to conduct summary trials for small debts. Four-fifths of those merchants who voted on the question were strongly in favour of justices continuing to conduct summary trials.[14] On the other hand, lawyers were almost always opposed. Such country lawyers as William Otis Haliburton of Windsor and Thomas Ritchie of Annapolis Royal voted at every opportunity against continuance of summary trials by justices. Lawyers wanted an increased local jurisdiction for the inferior and supreme courts. As they could represent clients in both, the more cases that came before these courts, the more fees to both lawyers and judges. For merchants, however, summary trials by justices provided a simple and inexpensive way to sue and collect small debts within a system largely administered by themselves for themselves. The higher the court involved, the greater the cost of actions. Where creditors had to proceed through Chancery Court (a court of equity, in which the principal business was the foreclosure of mortgages), the high fees charged were greatly resented, leading finally to its deserved abolition in 1855.

This rough and ready system of local government and administration of justice by appointed and unsalaried magistrates came under increasing criticism in the first two decades of the nineteenth century. Many justices possessed little legal knowledge and few apparently even had copies of the provincial statutes. They found attendance at the general sessions burdensome and many avoided attending whenever possible. But attempts to reform the system in 1824, by appointing three new judges to preside at the sessions and at the inferior courts, aroused a storm of opposition around the province. In one district freeholders passed resolutions to settle all future disputes by arbitration and not to resort again to the courts. The inferior courts of common pleas were finally abolished in 1841, though not without much opposition from assemblymen-lawyers.

A persistent criticism by the legal profession (which seems to have had considerable validity) was the low state of education of many magistrates. As so many assemblymen were also magistrates, this criticism by contemporaries raises the question of the levels of education among those elected in this period. Until the arrival of the Loyalists in 1783, the range of formal education among assemblymen varied little. Although three were Harvard graduates, together they served for only a total of ten years and none played an important role in House proceedings. Because nearly all of those elected between 1758 and the arrival of the Loyalists in 1783/84 would have received their education in either New England or the British Isles before coming to Nova Scotia, they likely had six or more years of formal schooling. Those who had chosen legal and mercantile careers—and they were the sizeable majority—would have served further years apprenticed to a lawyer or to a merchant. Not only, therefore, had these assemblymen received a generally sound education to prepare them for a profession or to enter the counting house, there was no significant difference in education among them.

The tensions aroused in Nova Scotian society by the arrival of the Loyalists can, in part, be attributed to the higher level of education of the leading Loyalists. Of the thirty-six Loyalists elected to the Assembly between 1785 and 1800, nine were university graduates. The Loyalists were behind the founding of King's College at Windsor in 1789 and it became the chief source of college graduates who became members. Of the seventeen university graduates who entered the House after 1800, thirteen were from King's College. But as the number of native-born Nova Scotians in the Assembly rose, the average level of formal education declined. Of the 221 assemblymen elected after 1800 (aside from the seventeen college graduates), only twenty are known to have attended grammar schools or academies in the province, in New England or in the British Isles. Within Nova Scotia, the choice was limited to King's College School at Windsor, Pictou Academy and the Halifax Grammar School. Of the twenty noted above, fourteen attended these institutions.

Most parents had to rely on what local schooling might be available. There was no compulsory taxation for schools or for any form of public education. Parents made their own arrangements with teachers, many of whom were capable at best of teaching only the very basics, while some were drunkards and otherwise undesirable characters. Others, such as the Reverend Thomas Trotter, the Presbyterian minister at Antigonish, and John McNamara in Annapolis Royal, provided their students with a sound education so that they could enter a profession. But for the large majority of Nova Scotian youth who came of school age between the 1790s and the 1820s, the best they could have expected was a few years of rudimentary schooling. We shall encounter a surprising number of assemblymen, however, who had compensated for their lack of formal education by family or self teaching. Some, such as John Homer of Barrington and Herbert Huntington of Yarmouth, were as widely read as any of their classically educated colleagues.

Aside from the advantages their training in law gave them, lawyers as a group had a far higher degree of formal education than their fellow members. Of the twenty-four members from 1758 through to 1847 who attended university, sixteen were lawyers, of whom twelve were graduates of King's College at Windsor. Another four of the lawyers who entered the Assembly attended the Halifax Grammar School and three went to Pictou Academy, where they were pupils of Thomas McCulloch (although, as we noted above, McCulloch thought little of the profession). Whatever the schooling they received, all had to serve five years in the office of an attorney of the Supreme Court preparatory to their admission to the bar. A few, notably William Blowers Bliss and James Boyle Uniacke, continued their training at one of the Inns of Court in London. As well as applying themselves diligently to the study of law, aspiring lawyers were expected to read widely in the classics and contemporary literature. A number of those elected to the Assembly could lay claim to being well-educated individuals in the enlightened sense of the term. William Young, who attended Glasgow University before articling and being admitted to the bar in 1826, remarked in his autobiography that he could read Cicero's Orations in Latin with tolerable ease, but had lost much of his ability, learned in school and university, to read in Greek. He learned French in Halifax and read such authors as Voltaire. He claimed, and there is no reason to believe otherwise, that he was acquainted with most English authors of note in the general literature of the day — Samuel Johnson, Jonathan Swift and Adam Smith, to name three quoted by him.[15]

When faced with this array of educated legislative talent, many country members, with a few years at a local school the most formal education they had received, no doubt shared the feelings of Samuel Bishop Chipman of Annapolis. He remarked during the 1841 session that "None in the House felt the want of education more than [himself]" when he looked around and saw "the great difference education made in men."[16] The great difference had come about because by the 1830s and the 1840s lawyers were, as a group, better educated than previous generations of their colleagues (with the exception of the Loyalist lawyers). However, country members like Samuel Bishop Chipman had less formal schooling than their immigrant predecessors of past Assemblies.

Nearly half of those elected to the Assembly before 1800 were Anglicans. Although the 1827 census recorded Anglicans making up no more than a quarter of the population, after 1800 they still usually accounted for two-fifths of the members elected. Moreover, when members of the Church of Scotland persuasion are added, the two nominally established churches could claim the adherence of half the members elected after 1800. The other half were mostly Dissenters—Protestants who refused to adhere to either the Church of England or the Church of Scotland as state or national churches established as such in law. The chief Dissenting denominations were Congregationalists, Baptists, Methodists and Presbyterians. Until the disintegration of Congregationalism in Nova Scotia under the double impact of the American Revolution and the Allinite Revival, its adherents had made up, after the Anglicans, by far the largest number of members in the Assembly. In the aftermath of its collapse, many Congregationalists became Baptists, but far fewer Baptists were elected, around ten per cent. A similar proportion of members were Methodists. The first Roman Catholic was not elected until 1820, though Laurence Kavanagh did not take his seat until 1823. When he did, he became the first of his faith outside of Quebec to sit in a

Legislative Assembly of the British Empire/Commonwealth. In sub-sequent elections, another thirteen Catholics took their seats. Two Lutherans and two Quakers were also elected.[17]

Presbyterians made up fourteen per cent of those elected from 1758 through to 1847. Just who, however, could be classed as Pres-byterians in this period needs some explanation. The Church of Scotland was the state or established church by law in Scotland, as was the Church of England in England, or for that matter the Con-gregational Church in Massachusetts. Quarrels in Scotland over church government had led to the creation of a Secessionist Church. Both those of the Church of Scotland (commonly called Kirkmen) and Secessionists (or Seceders) shared, however, a common doctrinal allegiance to Presbyterianism. In this book, when discussing the political consequences in Pictou County arising from the transfer to Nova Scotia of this quarrel between the two branches of Scottish Presbyterianism, we shall speak of Kirkmen and Seceders. However, most of the Scotch-Irish from Ulster in Ireland who settled in Nova Scotia were also Presbyterians. These Scotch-Irish Presbyterians shared with Seceders the same opposition to established churches. When discussing Presbyterians outside of Pictou County, we shall use the term Presbyterian to include all those Presbyterians who were not of the Church of Scotland and would have considered themselves Dissenters.

The high proportion of Anglicans elected, in relation to the general population of whom the majority were Dissenters, was partly the result of so many Loyalists and lawyers being of that faith. Of the ninety-one Loyalists or sons of Loyalists who entered the Assembly, sixty-seven belonged to the Church of England. Among the sixty-four lawyers elected, three-quarters of them were Anglicans and another seven were of the Church of Scotland. Although there was a High Church party in the Council of Twelve, Anglicans in the Assembly never formed a bloc to forward the interests of their church. As we shall see, religion could at times play a major role in the politics of this period, but there was no continuous pattern of involvement by any single denomination. Moreover, with the occa-sional exception, there was no voting along religious lines until the 1840s.

In summarizing this profile of the 437 members elected from 1758 to 1847 to the Nova Scotian Assembly, the most marked charac-teristic was the fifty percent or better chance that a member was a merchant or a lawyer. In religion, there was also an equal probability that he belonged to either the Church of England or the Church of Scotland. In many counties he was also a member of a local family compact and had behind him all the ledger influence and respectability that a compact could bring to the hustings. If not already a magistrate, he would expect to receive this appointment (and other offices) while serving in the Assembly. Almost all members who had gone to university were lawyers, and after 1800 nearly all graduates were from King's College at Windsor. By the 1830s and 1840s, there was a manifest difference in education between the lawyers elected and your average country member.

Once elected, a member could expect to attend annual sessions of the Assembly lasting from six to ten weeks. In the early years, in order to ease travelling, the House convened usually in the late spring. Later in the nineteenth century, sessions began in January or February. After 1781, members received a daily rate of payment for attendance and for travelling to and from Halifax. This greatly improved attendance. Sessions were held in rented premises until the opening of Province House in 1819. Within the assembly chamber of Province House, members sat on benches probably arranged in semicircular rows facing the Speaker's chair until the 1840s, when they were rearranged to the right and left of the Speaker on the introduction of responsible government. The governing party sat on his right and the opposition on his left. Although stoves provided some warmth against the winter cold, members wore heavy clothing. House orders, in fact, required that they wear hats and there were strict rules on when hats could be taken off and put on.

From the first session in 1758, the clerk of the House kept a journal of the daily proceedings. Not until 1784 did the Assembly agree to have freeholders admitted to hear debates, or to have entered into the journals how members voted on various issues. By no means were all votes so recorded. Moreover, no record of debates was kept. Throughout this period, in fact, members displayed a distinct reluctance to have what was said in the House reported and published in the press. However, from its first publication in 1813, the *Acadian Recorder* began reporting debates. But it was Joseph Howe's comprehensive legislative reviews in the *Novascotian* during the late 1820s and the 1830s that allowed Nova Scotians to learn, as never before, what was happening in their House of Assembly.

A visitor sitting in the gallery of Province House on the morning of 12 January 1837 would have looked down upon the opening session of the fifteenth Assembly to be elected since the introduction of representative government in 1758.[18] As Lieutenant Governor Sir Colin Campbell read the Speech from the Throne, our visitor would have been aware of a sense of tense expectation on the floor of the House and in the gallery. This Assembly was very different from those of the immediate past.

The 1836 election had been held the previous November for a new House of forty-nine members, an increase of four seats, to give somewhat fairer representation to the rapidly growing eastern region of the province. But what made this Fifteenth Assembly significantly different from its immediate predecessor elected in 1830 was the number of new members in their seats. Thirty of the forty-nine members had been elected for the first time. More significantly, close to twenty of these members were clearly for reform and most of the others would be won over to the cause. In electing Joseph Howe, William Annand, Hugh Bell and Thomas Forrester, Halifax Town and County freeholders had sent four leading Reformers to the Assembly. Elsewhere in the province, freeholders had elected candidates who proved also to be leaders in the forthcoming struggle for constitutional and financial reform — notably Gaius Lewis for Cumberland, Peter Spearwater of Shelburne and Gloud Wilson McLelan of Londonderry. These newly-elected members joined fellow Reformers who had been re-elected, such as Herbert Huntington of Yarmouth and William Young, a rising Halifax lawyer who represented Inverness. Mounting anger at the blatant use of patronage and its corrupting influence by an oligarchy of wealthy Halifax merchants, bankers and office-holders; inflated salaries for officials, especially the judiciary; severe agrarian distress in some counties; and a devalued provincial currency which had brought widespread insolvency in its wake had all coalesced to cause Nova Scotians to demand an end to oligarchic rule. In giving focus to this agitation for reform, newspapers had played a formative role. From Halifax the *Novascotian,* with its comprehensive legislative reviews and biting editorial comment by Joseph Howe, circulated throughout the province. It served as an inspiration for such country papers as the Yarmouth *Herald* and the *Hants & Kings Gazette.*

Nova Scotians in 1836 had voted for reform. They had sent a majority to the Assembly determined to reduce the costs of government and to make the executive branch of government more responsible to the elected representatives of the people. The constitutional form of that responsibility was yet to be defined. In a decade, however, Nova Scotia became the first of the British North American colonies to introduce full responsible government.

Full responsible government meant government by the party having the majority of seats in the Assembly. By the mid-1830s people were freely calling their elected members either Tories or Reformers (by the 1840s, the party names of "conservatives" and "liberals" were used interchangeably with Tories and Reformers). There were as yet, however, no formal party structures. Members continued to feel free to vote as their personal views dictated. When Reformers won the 1847 election, they formed in February of the following year the first government in which all the Executive Council were all of their party, thus ensuring the executive branch of government was fully responsible to a majority in the Assembly. Responsible government also meant that assemblymen now voted as members of disciplined parties. A political era lasting nearly a century had ended with members of successive Assemblies free to vote without the constraints of party. How and why they voted forms a major part of our story of early Nova Scotian politicians.

If the Fifteenth Assembly, elected in 1836, was determined on reform, it was in composition by no means a revolutionary break with the past. In this House of forty-nine members, merchants and lawyers held thirty-three of the seats. There were eleven farmers, a number marginally less than the usual quarter of members elected; the rest were of assorted occupations—two land surveyors, one tanner, one newspaper owner/editor and one mariner. In religion, there were eighteen Anglicans and seven of the Church of Scotland, continuing the unbroken pattern of the adherents of these two nominally established churches having around half the representation. Ten members were Presbyterians and another seven were Methodists, with four Roman Catholics and three Baptists accounting for the remainder. With the election for the first time of two Acadians—Frederick Robichaud and Simon d'Entremont—the last major cultural or religious group in the province had representation in the Assembly. Local family compacts were also well represented, with no less than twelve members owing, at least partly, their recent success at the hustings to the support received from family and ledger. Of the four university graduates in the new Assembly, all were lawyers; three of them were from King's College at Windsor and the fourth from the University of Glasgow. If promotion to the bench and imperial honours were any guide, the ten lawyers proved an illustrious lot. Six finished their careers as judges, William Young was knighted, and Alexander Stewart made a Companion of the Bath.

In past Assemblies, leadership had always come from the lawyers in the House. Professional ambition and the need to keep the favour of government had restrained any conspicious enthusiasm for major reform. We shall encounter in succeeding pages occasional lapses by assemblymen-lawyers into mild bouts of radicalism, but they were all short-lived. This pattern of lawyers as a continuous dominant minority was, however, broken with the election of Joseph Howe to the Fifteenth Assembly. At thirty-three years of age and the owner/editor of the Novascotian, the most popular newspaper in the province, Howe stood forth in Nova Scotia as the foremost representative of the awakening spirit of the new age of popular democracy. That the movement for reform in Nova Scotia should be led by Joseph Howe was pivotal for determining its direction and its success.

We shall recount in succeeding chapters, county by county, how, as Nova Scotia moved towards major reform of its political institutions, the early politicians of Nova Scotia won and lost their elections. We shall chart the rise and fall of local family compacts and of factions coalescing into recognizable political parties. In the process, we shall have cause to analyse the interplay at both the local and provincial level of family rivalries, personal feuds, religion, regional loyalties and divergent economic interests. As we read of how these early Nova Scotian politicians grappled with the great issues of their day, we shall perhaps conclude that these issues were not so much different from those of our own day.

Chapter 2

Oligarchs and Assemblymen of Halifax Town and County 1759-1830

The town and country ... are not at variance and with respect to their mutual prosperity:—on the contrary, they are one and indivisible; and the safest policy lies in uniting them.
Gentlemen, you have long tried the opposite course. To the House of Assembly, you have sent a succession of what are called resident merchants, who were to defend your individual rights, and yet you still continue to bewail that those rights have been generally sacrificed. The cause of this I think is obvious, and will exist without a change of measures. The country members, acting upon the same views, have constantly outnumbered you in voting: and your resident merchants, although true to their engagements, have but too often retired from public life, disappointed in their schemes, and with some diminution of their popularity.

John Young To The Freeholders of Halifax, *Acadian Recorder,*
May 6th, 1823

A visitor entering Halifax Harbour early on the morning of 28 May 1758, would have beheld one of the greatest armadas of ships and troops ever assembled in the New World, now setting sail to lay siege and capture the great French fortress of Louisbourg. From his vessel our visitor would have viewed a well-planned town running from the shore of the harbour up to the base of a massive hill on which a citadel was being constructed. On closer inspection, he would have found many streets still not cleared of the tree stumps and large boulders left from laying out the town nine years before at its founding. Its fine harbour and location had made it pivotal for British strategy in the struggle for North American empire. For the merchants of Halifax, the war meant military contracts and they were waxing rich. It was said that the business of one half of the town's 3,000 residents was to sell rum to the other half.

When Governor Charles Lawrence and his Council issued the writs for Nova Scotia's first elected Assembly eight days before the great armada sailed for Louisbourg, the number able to meet the property qualifications probably did not exceed 200 electors. A third of the town were Roman Catholics, who were unable to vote, and most of the foreign Protestant emigrants from Germany and Switzerland were not yet naturalized. These 200 freeholders could elect four township representatives and vote for sixteen members for the province at large. Other than Lunenburg, where 58 eligible freeholders elected two for their township and voted for the members at large, there was likely no voting elsewhere in the province. With the exception of two from Lunenburg, all the newly elected members, who convened on 2 October 1758 for the opening session of the First Assembly, were Halifax residents and were either holders of public offices or merchants. After two sessions, Governor Charles Lawrence dissolved the House, so that new elections could be held to give representation to the newly-created counties and townships, which were then filling up with New Englanders. In the Second Assembly, Halifax merchants and office-holders held twelve of the twenty-two seats. William Nesbitt was elected Speaker and would hold the office for the next twenty-four years. The founding of Halifax had opened up unforeseen opportunities for such men as Nesbitt to rise in status. Although he had little or no formal legal training, Nesbitt had progressed from governor's clerk to be the colony's Attorney General.

Another drawn to Halifax in the hopes of bettering his prospects was Michael Francklin. With backing of the most powerful merchant in early Halifax, Joshua Mauger, Francklin rose from being a dram shop operator to become the wealthiest man in the town. When the mixing of office, politics and business was accepted, no one in those years personified this entwining relationship more than did Michael Francklin. He was elected in the 1761 election, but his appointment a year later to the Council as its youngest member came as no surprise. Nor was it unexpected that his seat in the Assembly went to John Butler, who on Mauger's removal to England had become his agent-attorney. Butler, Francklin and the former Boston merchant, Jonathan Binney, formed the core of a Halifax, or Mauger, party that operated in the Council and Assembly to protect their patron's and their own business interests.[1] Others were already or would be tied to the party by reason of indebtedness and their dependence on Joshua Mauger to exercise influence at the Board of Trade on their behalf.

The most dramatic display of the influence that could be exercised by the Mauger party came when the acting Governor, Chief Justice Jonathan Belcher, moved in 1761, on instructions from London, to prevent the Assembly from extending the debtors' act for another year. In one sudden stroke, he threatened to remove the protection enjoyed by Halifax merchants from their creditors outside of Nova Scotia. A strike of Halifax members was the response and an impotent Belcher had the mortification of watching the truant assemblymen walking the streets of the town, while he could do no more than continually prorogue the House for lack of a quorum. Belcher managed to gain the authority to dismiss the delinquent members from all public offices, but appeals to Mauger to use his influence at the Board of Trade resulted in restoration of all the offices and the removal of Belcher as Lieutenant Governor. Belcher's humiliation by the Mauger party was complete.[2] The reason the Mauger party could so paralyze the Assembly was that, in practice, the six Halifax members could control the proceedings of the House. Few of the eighteen country members attended or their attendance was erratic, so that having sufficient members for a quorum was often problematical.

A weakening of Halifax control, and with it that of the Mauger party, was inevitable; by 1770 the increasing population of the colony at large required the addition of nine seats for a total of thirty. Furthermore, within Halifax there had always been opposition to Mauger's insidious influence. This showed itself in the 1765 election, when the sitting members for the two Halifax Township seats (who were closely tied to the Mauger party) either declined to face a contest or were defeated. Probably by agreement, the four county seats continued as its preserve. But this arrangement did not last past the election of 1770, in which the merchant Robert Campbell challenged the Mauger party's grip on the county seats. He took one of the four seats. But it was John Day's entrance into the Assembly, as a result of a Halifax Township by-election in 1773, that produced the major challenge to the party's control over the House. John Day was elected by the "great majority," which could mean there was a contest, or simply that the poll stayed open for an hour with no other candidate appearing.[3] The former is the more likely. As a member in the previous Assembly for Newport Township, Day already had a reputation for taking the lead in attacking the prevailing corruption in the handling of public moneys. There were many in and out of office who had good reason not to have him back in the House. By training a surgeon and a druggist, though he also engaged in commercial pursuits, Day had just returned from four years in Philadelphia. There he would have observed at first hand the rising agitation that was leading to open rebellion; this may be why he returned, for there was never any question of his loyalty. Day was most likely the author of the pamphlet *An Essay on the Present State of the Province of Nova Scotia,* in which was laid bare the appalling state into which Nova Scotia had fallen, massively in debt with no trade other than the distilling and selling of spirits: it was ruled by a "Junto of cunning and wicked Men, whose Views extend no further than their own private Emolument, and who further the Distresses of the Community in order to promote a slavish Dependence on themselves."[4]

With Francis Legge's appointment in 1773, Day had a zealous Governor who believed that he had been sent to bring order to Nova Scotian affairs. Although an honourable man, it became apparent soon after Legge arrived that he was incapable of grasping the intricate play of forces at work. He openly challenged the rule of the Mauger party that had transformed itself into a ruling oligarchy of merchants and office-holders, united now as much by ties of marriage as by a common venality. During the late autumn session, Day proved to be the most able member in trying to deal with the chronic indebtedness of the province, but the usual absence of most country members greatly hindered him; generally, only sixteen to eighteen members attended, and in December a Speaker's call for more met with no response. Between the end of the 1774 session and the reconvening of the House in June 1775, an audit committee, of which Day was a member, presented Legge and his new Solicitor General, James Monk, with the means to undertake prosecutions against such public defaulters as Nesbitt and Jonathan Binney.

Legge had removed Nesbitt from his duties as Attorney General and given them to Monk, while requesting the Board of Trade to dismiss Nesbitt on the grounds of his withholding of sums, laxity in collecting debts owed the crown (probably uncollectable), his advanced age, and general legal ineptitude. Monk had returned to Nova Scotia from reading law at the Inns of Court in London with a mandamus as Solicitor General in his pocket, and a promise that he should have the Attorney Generalship on the first vacancy.[5] The impetuous Monk had Jonathan Binney arrested and jailed, with the result that Binney became a martyr to Legge's supposed tyranny.

When the House re-assembled in June 1775, the "friends of government" led by Day gave Legge the support he desired, getting through a loyal address to the crown at a crucial moment when the rebellion to the south was starting to rage. But, by late June or early July, the majority supporting Legge evaporated, almost certainly because many country members returned home. This gave the Mauger party temporary supremacy, which it used without scruple to exonerate Nesbitt and the other public defaulters. Day was impotent to prevent the dropping of all charges against them. In any case, while taking supplies to British forces under General Thomas Gage besieged in Boston, he drowned before the next session. By birth, by education, and as a man who had to seek a living in a harsh and unforgiving mercenary world, Day did not differ from his eighteenth-century contemporaries. What separated him was his refusal to stoop to their level of venality, and even more to have a view of the public good that transcended personal ambition and greed.

Day's successor in the Assembly as leader of the friends of the Governor was Monk, a man whose conduct was governed by his desire for advancement. Monk drafted the measure presented in the autumn 1775 session that was nearly to drive the whole province to open rebellion.[6] His militia bill gave the Governor extensive powers to embody and discipline the militia, even when there was no actual invasion. Nesbitt argued the militia bill was unnecessary, impolitic, injuriously coercive and severe. The debate over the bill became so heated that the House went so far as to censure Nesbitt from the Speaker's chair for his interventions against the bill. He and others managed to secure a temporary majority against the measure on the grounds that it was the business of the province to remain "Silent." Monk, in his turn, accused members of disloyalty and of reprehensible conduct, only to be faced with the threat of expulsion. Enough members rallied to the government to have a much-amended bill passed by four votes on last reading. Nesbitt could not have been more prescient in forecasting its reception. When Legge declared martial law and called out the militia, only those at Halifax and Lunenburg, and the Acadians along St. Mary's Bay, answered the call. By now Butler and Francklin in Halifax and Mauger in London had succeeded in so discrediting Legge that an alarmed Board of Trade, fearing that Legge was driving the province to open rebellion, called him home to answer charges manufactured by Mauger.

In Halifax, war once more brought military contracts and with them political quietude. The oligarchy was again in full control, enriching itself on a grander scale than ever before. Nesbitt was back as Attorney General; Monk had been rewarded with the Attorney Generalship of Quebec. The Assembly first elected in 1770 continued from year to year, with hardly an echo of the factional warfare of past years. Nonetheless, there was a complete changeover of Halifax members. It is doubtful that any of the by-elections were contested, but all these new members were elected beforehand to be wardens of St. Paul's Church, continuing a pattern that went back to the earliest elections.[7]

The last of the old Mauger party to go was Nesbitt, who in 1784 finally retired as Attorney General and also resigned his seat. The House gave him an annual pension of £100, but when he died a few months later, leaving an indebted estate hounded by creditors, an uncompassionate Assembly refused to honour even the first installment to his destitute widow. The deaths of Nesbitt and Francklin and the retirement of John Butler to England ended the rule of an oligarchy whose roots went back to the very founding of Halifax, and which had the dubious record of having brought down three Governors.

The old oligarchy was succeeded by a new coterie of lawyers, merchants and office-holders that would take its form as a Loyalist ascendancy. Among the Loyalists arriving in 1783 and 1784 there were former office-holders and members of colonial assemblies. These men had nothing but disdain for the officials surrounding the new Governor, John Parr. A bitter struggle for offices now ensued, commencing with the vacant Attorney Generalship. It should have gone in the natural order of succession to Solicitor General Richard John Uniacke. It went instead to Sampson Salter Blowers, a Harvard-educated Loyalist, whose practice in Boston before the war had gained him an income of £400 a year, far beyond what he could expect in Nova Scotia.[8] Uniacke had to be satisfied with Parr naming him Advocate General of the Vice Admiralty Court.

Before the arrival of the Loyalists, probably never more than 200 of the Halifax populace were eligible to vote; by late 1785, when the writs were issued to elect four for Halifax County and two members for the town, there were an additional 500 to 600 freeholders. A united Loyalist party should have been able to take all six seats, but the Loyalists were not united; many were finding more common cause with the old inhabitants than with the patrician class of Loyalist best represented by Blowers. There was, however, a meeting of minds between the leaders of the two parties, who wanted above all else to avoid the expense and anticipated violence of a contested election. Whatever their personal quarrels, Uniacke and Blowers published a joint election card, along with two of the sitting members, Supreme Court Judge James Brenton and the barrister John George Pyke; they were joined on the same card by two merchants, John Fillis and William Cochran, for the town. This arrangement, which meant that only one Loyalist would be elected, was clearly unacceptable. Three Loyalists now became candidates for the four county seats: the former Boston lawyer Jonathan Sterns, the merchant Michael Wallace, and Samuel Waddington, a brewer from New York, who announced that he intended to pay his respects to every freeholder in the county. When James Brenton realized to his great consternation that his election would not be unanimous, and he would be faced with "competitors" in an election, perhaps carried on with the "Violence and contest of party opposition," he quickly withdrew. There was none of the violence feared by Brenton, and with Wallace in essence replacing Brenton, the candidates on the two joint cards were elected.[9]

In the new Assembly the Halifax members found themselves in a House much enlarged to provide representation for the Loyalists. The Loyalists had thirteen out of the thirty-nine members, and they generally voted as a cohesive bloc.[10] Still, they were a minority and accepted the need to form alliances of mutual interest, however temporary they might be. This was made easier by the generally superior leadership displayed by such Loyalists as Thomas Barclay, Isaac Wilkins and Blowers, the last elected Speaker. It was this leadership and their cohesiveness that made the Loyalists a dominant minority, who were bent on enacting measures of reform and general improvement. It was the Loyalists who got unanimous support in the 1787 session for the establishment of a committee to examine the dissatisfaction concerning the administration of justice in the province. When Chief Justice Bryan Finucane died in 1785, his two assistant judges, Isaac Deschamps and James Brenton, had attempted to carry on as best they could, though Deschamps had no formal training in law at all. Near the end of the session, the House went into secret proceedings to hear testimony on the conduct of the judges. It was, of course, the lawyers in and out of the House who gave the evidence, in some cases expecting to succeed to the judgeships if the present incumbents could be removed. Blowers, however, sat in "solemn silence" in the hopes that he would be made Chief Justice, but had to be content with the Council seat he got a few months later. Once in the Council, he "took a decided part" in

View from Fort Needham near Halifax
Drawn, engraved and published by G. T. Parkyns, London, April 29, 1801.

defending the judges from the attacks by his fellow Loyalists in the Assembly.[11]

The by-election for Blowers' vacated seat pitted Jonathan Sterns, one of the judges' chief accusers and an unsuccessful candidate from the 1785 contest, against Charles Morris. The son of Surveyor General Charles Morris, the younger Morris represented the interests and views of the old order. The poll opened on a Wednesday, and though there was considerable intimidation of voters, a total of 689 came forward before it closed on Friday evening, with Morris having 415 to Sterns' 274 votes. Morris was then carried in triumph through the principal streets, "surrounded by immense concourse of people, who filled the air with their repeated acclamations of joy"; Sterns' enraged supporters rioted and many were wounded, with one man killed.[12] Most eligible freeholders must have voted and Morris's substantial majority could only have come from a good number of Loyalists voting for him. As in the 1785 election, the Loyalist vote was divided.

The Loyalists in the Assembly remained united in their determination to impeach the two judges. In the 1790 session, they gained the support of a majority for articles of impeachment, accusing the judges of "High Crimes and Misdemeanours." The articles were sent to London with an address requesting that the judges be given a regular trial. The issue, however, lost much of its emotion with the arrival in May 1790 of a new Chief Justice, Thomas Andrew Strange, whose tact and conciliatory manner did much to bring the opposing factions to cease their warring.

On the death of John Parr, Loyalist discontent was further assuaged by the appointment of one of their own when John Wentworth assumed the Governorship in 1792. Wentworth, the last royal Governor of New Hampshire, had been living in Halifax since 1783, performing his duties as Surveyor General of the King's Woods. Through his travels and long-standing friendships, Wentworth knew Nova Scotia and her people better than any previous Governor. Although he could not immediately remove the old officialdom from their offices, they had to make their peace with the new order Wentworth set about creating, or be subject to his ruthless, secret and tenacious efforts to replace them with his own appointments.

Wentworth issued the writs for an election in the early winter months of 1793. Of the Halifax County members, Uniacke had made no effort to ingratiate himself with the new Loyalist order and vowed "he should not come into the House again." The enmity between the Loyalists and Uniacke had become so personal that in the autumn of 1791 Blowers had challenged Uniacke to a duel over a quarrel about the dismissal of a black servant. Chief Justice Strange had had to intervene to prevent the two principal law officers of the crown from fighting a duel. John George Pyke and William Cochran stood for the town and would double the vote over a single opponent in an election that did no more than sanction the continuation of the two township seats as a preserve of St. Paul's Church vestry. For the four county seats there was no shortage of willing candidates, including two Loyalist lawyers, Jonathan Sterns and James Stewart, and the Loyalist merchant Lawrence Hartshorne. The old inhabitants had as their candidates James Freke Bulkeley, Benjamin Salter, and the Londonderry Township farmer James Fulton.

Although the boundaries of Halifax County encompassed the districts of Colchester and Pictou, until Fulton no candidate from outside the capital had ever offered, nor had the poll been moved from the capital. Interest was high in the election, with the candidates using the newspapers to make personal solicitations to freeholders. Benjamin Salter saw this practice as "altogether superfluous if not impertinent." The freeholders seemed to have felt the same about his candidacy; by the second and final day of voting in Halifax, he had so few votes that he declined to continue the contest, as did Stewart. Bulkeley had the most votes with 586, just three more than Sterns who had lost so decisively in the violent 1788 by-election. Hartshorne and Wallace were behind them by about 100 votes. The *Royal Gazette* noted approvingly that the contest had not been "obstructed by the least tumult or irregularity."[13] Fulton had managed just 24 votes, but insisted that the poll move to Onslow Township, where he immediately declined. It was a symbolic gesture on his part, but one that portended an end to the exclusion of Colchester and Pictou freeholders from voting in county elections, and, moreover, to being represented solely by Halifax residents.

Joining the three Loyalists elected for Halifax County were another fourteen from around the province. From this group was to be drawn the core of what became known as the court party. Under the nominal leadership of the Speaker, Thomas Barclay, the court party could usually be relied upon to forward measures desired by Wentworth and the Council. Harmony generally prevailed between the House and the Council and it was not too difficult for the court party to secure majorities for government measures. Although a minority, they gave Wentworth a more dependable influence in the House than any previous Governor had enjoyed. Their loyalty to Wentworth was often personal, rooted in patronage already received or expected. This was especially true for Sterns, Wallace and Hartshorne, who were the most active members on behalf of government and almost always voted as a bloc.

The 1797 resignation of Chief Justice Strange offered Wentworth a fortuitous opportunity to place his own men in offices important to his government. It was accepted that Blowers should be promoted from the Attorney Generalship to be Chief Justice, but both he and Wentworth wanted to have Jonathan Sterns made Attorney General over the head of Uniacke, who as Solicitor General had every reason to expect the promotion. In his usual secretive and tenacious manner, Wentworth had carefully laid the groundwork by earlier accusing Uniacke of being "secretly connected with seditious purposes, & giving advice against the service."[14] But the nature of the vicious game Wentworth was playing was recognized for what it was by the Duke of Portland at the Colonial Office. Providentially for Uniacke, the Duke was related by marriage to Uniacke's Irish family. Portland sternly reprimanded Wentworth in a private communication, while informing him that Blowers was to be Chief Justice, Uniacke to be promoted to Attorney General and Sterns to be made Solicitor General. Much animosity remained. Some time afterwards Uniacke had a public brawl with Sterns at the corner of Sackville and Hollis

Streets; he beat him so severely that it may have been a cause of Sterns's death some months later. Blowers was so incensed that he again challenged Uniacke to a duel and the two had to be bound over once more to keep the peace. The Solicitor Generalship went to Maryland Loyalist James Stewart, who succeeded to Sterns' Assembly seat in an uncontested election.

In 1797 Wentworth also received authority to swear in Michael Wallace as Provincial Treasurer at a salary of £450. Other than Uniacke, Charles Morris, and the Naval Officer William Cottnam Tonge, Wentworth now had in every major office of government men of his own choosing who were loyal to him personally. These years of the mid-1790s were to be the high tide of Wentworth's Governorship, though paradoxically, it was the mounting surplus in the public treasury that gave rise to the first serious public opposition. This came in the form of a country party under the nominal leadership of William Cottnam Tonge. The war had brought prosperity; by 1799 the surplus was an incredible £25,000. Whether this new-found wealth should be expended on much-needed roads in the countryside or on the erection of public buildings in Halifax became the issue that divided town and country as never before. The substantial benefits to the capital from the construction of large public buildings was cause enough for the six Halifax members to take the lead in pushing through a vote of £10,000 for the erection of a new residence for the Governor.

James Fulton was in Halifax when it became known that Wentworth would issue the writs in a matter of days for an election to be held in the late months of 1799. From his experience as the sole non-Halifax candidate in the 1793 county election, Fulton and his friends had concluded that the only possible way candidates from either Colchester or Pictou could be elected was by the freeholders of these districts agreeing to vote only for their own local candidates, and not give any of their remaining votes to Halifax candidates. By this means they hoped to be able to overcome the big majorities gained at Halifax by the resident candidates. For this strategy to work, the country candidates had to be at the opening of the poll in Halifax to apply to have the poll moved to Colchester and Pictou; otherwise, the Halifax candidates would ensure the poll was closed as quickly as possible.[15] At this point, Fulton had not decided to run again, but Edward Mortimer of Pictou had made his intentions known; it was to him that Fulton looked for the leadership and the necessary organization to execute the agreed-upon plan.

As a youth of sixteen, Mortimer had left Scotland for Nova Scotia in the 1780s to be a clerk in the employ of a Scottish merchant firm trading to North America. His ship was wrecked near Pictou but he managed to reach the settlement, where Squire Robert Patterson took him in. Mortimer soon established a commercial system that provided for the exchange of imported Scottish goods for future deliveries of fish, timber and farm products; a consequence was that hundreds became indebted to him and he became the wealthiest individual in Pictou. His position within the community was further enhanced by his marriage to the daughter of Squire Patterson, the leading figure in the settlement from the earliest days. On the death in 1807 of his father-in-law, he succeeded to his role in the community, becoming the senior militia officer, a justice of the peace and a judge of the inferior court of common pleas.[16]

As early as 1775, Pictou had petitioned for its own representative, and in that year the Assembly even passed a resolution calling for an election, but this was blocked by those in Halifax who did not want to see any increase in country members. Instead, Pictou became a fiefdom of Michael Wallace, who looked after its interests with government, while maintaining control through the ruthless use of the patronage he was able to exercise as a confidant of Wentworth and as Provincial Treasurer. Another potent factor that gave Wallace unusual influence was religion; most of the Highland Scots had been raised in the Church of Scotland, with an inbred hatred towards the Secessionist Presbyterian Church. The sole minister in the area, however, was the Reverend James McGregor, a Seceder. Wallace was an adherent of the Church of Scotland and a fanatical opponent of the Seceders, of whom Mortimer was one. Both sides in the forthcoming contest knew that McGregor's stance would be a crucial factor in deciding the outcome in Pictou, and hence the final result.

Neither side was anxious to appear as a party. To Mortimer, Fulton recommended that the contest should not be so much between Halifax and the country, as between the interests of the province and the measures being pursued by the court or government party. Although the sitting county members, Morris, Wallace, Stewart and Hartshorne, with Pyke and Cochran for the town, published a joint election card, they speciously claimed there was no combination of interest and their only motive was to save the printer trouble and expense. In fact, their hope was to avoid any contest at all. On their behalf, Charles Morris wrote McGregor soliciting his interest, with the plea that "all the heats and animosities (the natural concomitants of contested elections)" should be avoided.[17] It could be only be a matter of a short time, Morris was certain, before Pictou would have its own representative (in fact, it would be another 36 years); meanwhile, he and his friends would faithfully serve the district. The Halifax merchant, James Fraser, was much more blunt, telling McGregor that for any Scot in Pictou to withhold his vote from his fellow countryman, Michael Wallace, would be the "height of ingratitude."[18]

William Cottnam Tonge also sought MacGregor's interest; he had decided not only to run again for Newport Township, but also for Halifax County. He was now resident in Halifax and had the backing of a number of merchants and other freeholders who had found themselves on the outside of the governing clique. Tonge promised that these voters would support whatever candidates freeholders in Pictou and Colchester chose, if his Halifax friends could run two of their own candidates, Tonge and one other. In short, the agreement was for two to be chosen by the town and two by the country districts, with their respective supporters giving their votes to this slate of four candidates. As it turned out, just Tonge was a resident Halifax candidate, joining with Fulton and Mortimer to stand for the county.

The poll opened at the Halifax courthouse on 18 November 1799, and polling continued for the next six days. Over 700 voted, which may have been more than the total of eligible freeholders in the township. The agents for the Halifax coalition brought in Acadian and Irish fishermen of every description, Indians and blacks. Few of them could have met the property qualification, but swore that they did. Moreover, Tonge's Halifax supporters did not give their votes to Mortimer and Fulton, but voted either for Tonge only, or divided their remaining three votes among the resident Halifax candidates. The final totals for the latter ranged from the high of 758 for the popular Morris down to 580 for Hartshorne, 388 for Tonge, and 91 and 109 for Fulton and Mortimer. Mortimer was right when he told McGregor that he and Fulton were treated as "aliens" in Halifax. The town had voted only for its own.[19]

The poll now moved to Onslow where it opened on 30 November. Almost every freeholder of the over 500 eligible to vote came to the hustings. To a man, they gave their votes to Tonge, Mortimer and Fulton, with the resident Halifax candidates together receiving a paltry total of 85 votes to be divided among them. Tonge now had the most votes, followed by Morris, Wallace, Stewart, Mortimer, Fulton and Hartshorne. The election would clearly be decided at

Pictou, where the poll was to open on 12 December. Rather than face snowshoeing across Mount Thom, Hartshorne and Stewart went home, leaving a furious and still determined Wallace and possibly also Morris to persevere. Meanwhile Mortimer, upon whom fell the full cost, sent instructions through McGregor to his friends to call in the voters and provide the necessary provisions and rum for distribution at the hustings. Mortimer took the most votes with 456, followed fairly closely by Fulton and Tonge, but Wallace and Morris were far behind. The four county seats thus went to Tonge, who led the poll with a remarkable 1,257 votes, followed by Mortimer, Fulton and Morris. Wallace was in fifth place. He immediately protested the election on the grounds that Tonge had no freehold in the county. This was widely known but mattered little; since Tonge had chosen to sit for Newport, there would have been a vacant county seat anyway. In its first session after the election, the Assembly would not, however, give the seat to Wallace, but insisted on a by-election. Wallace left nothing to chance and defeated James Kent of Stewiacke 437 votes to 7; needless to say, the poll was not moved out of Halifax. Wallace was back in the Assembly, but two years later he would resign his seat and join his friends at the Council table.

The 1799 election for the town was as exciting as that for the county, if of much less import. Pyke and Cochran found themselves opposed by Andrew Belcher, the son of the late Chief Justice. Belcher had risen from running a grog shop to becoming the chief contractor for supplying the navy. Along with his opponents, he was prominent at St. Paul's and in a few months was to be elected a warden. Belcher had at his disposal considerable ledger influence, but it was not enough, for Cochran led the poll with 404 votes, followed by Pyke with three more than Belcher. Once the Assembly was in session Belcher petitioned to have the result overturned; the House declared the election of Pyke void by a one vote margin. This time Belcher's ledger influence was very much in evidence and the rowdyism at the hustings kept many away. With half the number voting, as in the first contest, Belcher won decisively. When he was being carried through the streets in triumph, Pyke's supporters attacked the procession, knocking Belcher off his chair and forcing him to flee to his home. An unrepentant Pyke appealed to the House to void this result because of the "unwarrantable manner" in which Belcher had obtained the votes of many freeholders.[20] The Assembly dismissed the petition summarily.

For all his efforts and great expense to win a seat, Belcher attended in the House for a total of only six days before accepting a seat at the Council table. Solicitor General James Stewart had lost his seat in the 1799 election and Wentworth now saw an opportunity to put his friend back into the Assembly without a contest. Wentworth issued the writ for the by-election while John George Pyke was visiting his son in Quebec. Aware of what was afoot, Pyke's friends were at the husting as soon as the poll opened and nominated Pyke in his absence. Young Brenton Halliburton, who was articling in Stewart's office, turned up to nominate Stewart. But he was much embarrassed to have to admit he could not now do so because Stewart would not let his name stand if there was to be a contested election. The sheriff then declared Pyke the winner. On his return Pyke had a card printed, graciously thanking the freeholders for his election.[21]

After the 1800 session, disputes between the Assembly and the Council over money bills dominated. Tonge and the country party provided the leadership for the Assembly to resist the constitutional pretensions of the Council and of Wentworth's attempts to extend his prerogative. But when Tonge was perceived as being too radical, the majority began shying away from confrontations and sought compromise. In the belief that Tonge and his radical friends were finally on the defensive, Wentworth decided to issue the writs for an election in May 1806, a year before it was required. By voting with Tonge and his friends in defence of the Assembly's constitutional rights, William Cochran had raised the wrath of many Halifax freeholders. He now thought it best to run for one of the county seats. Pyke immediately agreed to stand for Cochran's old township seat, noting that he had had twenty-seven years as a representative for Halifax. He was joined as a candidate by John Howe (father of Joseph), King's Printer and publisher of the *Nova Scotia Royal Gazette,* postmaster in Halifax and justice of the peace. The lawyer Foster Hutchinson also published his card. Both Howe and Hutchinson were Loyalists from Boston. As the son of a former assistant justice of the Massachusetts Supreme Court and nephew of the last royal Governor of that colony, Hutchinson was clearly of the patrician class. Not so John Howe, who in his youth had been apprenticed as a printer. It is doubtful if either canvassed. Howe may well have withdrawn before or shortly after the poll opened, for there is no record of any voting taking place, only the return of Pyke and Hutchinson.

View from Cowie's Hill, near Halifax, N.S.
Drawn, engraved and published by G. T. Parkyns, London, April 29, 1801.

In offering for the county Cochran obviously hoped that either there would be an uncontested election, or he would have sufficient support outside of Halifax to ensure his victory. Instead, Cochran found himself in a contest facing Mortimer, the popular Halifax merchant William Lawson, and two rising lawyers, S.B. Robie and S.G.W. Archibald. When James Fulton had decided to retire to his Bass River farm, the choice of Colchester freeholders had fallen on Samuel George William Archibald for the seat that they now considered belonged to Colchester by right. A native of Truro, whose grandfather and father had both sat in the House for the township, Archibald had just completed his legal studies in S.B. Robie's office.[22] To ensure that Cochran should not again represent them in the House, a number of Halifax freeholders had met before the election and nominated William Lawson to run. Thirty-four years of age and the scion of a long-established mercantile family, Lawson was already a successful partner in the firm Prescott and Lawson, trading to the West Indies, the Canadas, Spain and Portugal.[23] These freeholders employed their considerable influence against Cochran; by the end of the Halifax poll, Lawson and Robie respectively had 156 and 162 votes, while Cochran had just 75; both Mortimer with 129 and Archibald with 97 still had more than poor Cochran.

Cochran, however, was far from beaten. At the Truro poll, with an astonishing 409 votes, he even led Archibald, but at Pictou he was again at the bottom with 88. Mortimer, who easily led the overall poll, must have thrown his influence against him, as part of an agreement with those in Halifax who were determined to have Cochran out of the Assembly. Cochran nearly had his revenge on his Halifax enemies; he paid the registrars in each of the three districts to search for any record of freehold by Lawson. All the registrars signed affidavits that they had found none. Extraordinary as it may seem that such a well-off merchant as Lawson could own no property, it was nevertheless true. What saved him from having his election voided was the discovery of some land in Dartmouth held in his wife's name, which he tabled in the Assembly. When Pyke moved that Cochran be allowed another day to be heard on his case, only two others supported the motion. Cochran had sat in the House for twenty-one years, longer, except for Pyke, than any of the then members who had just treated him so cavalierly.

War with Napoleonic France and, from 1812 to 1814, with the United States had brought prosperity on a vast scale. Nova Scotia became a thriving entrepôt for trade with the United States and the West Indies. In both legal and clandestine trading, fortunes were being made. Prize goods, worth thousands of pounds, flowed in and out of Halifax. Between 1811 and 1816, at least £318,000 in prizes were condemned in the Court of Vice Admiralty. In 1808 Wentworth had been replaced by Sir George Prevost, the first of a succession of military governors; in 1811 Prevost went to Quebec as governor-in-chief and Sir John Sherbrooke replaced him. A Peninsular Campaign veteran, where he had been second-in-command to the Duke of Wellington, Sherbrooke was an able administrator, who soon mastered the intricacies of colonial Nova Scotian politics. For the next six years general peace prevailed in the Assembly and in its relations with the Governor and Council. Lord Dalhousie, another Peninsular veteran, assumed the Governorship in late 1816. During the 1817 spring session he was impressed by the quiet, peaceful and diligent manner in which assemblymen conducted the public business. He was much less so a year later, when the House was in its last session before an election. The members, he noted, had little to do but appropriate revenue for roads and bridges; they were "more talkative than usual" and seeking "popularity" as dissolution approached.[24] Dalhousie expected a general change in representation, but in the case of Halifax County he was mistaken, for the sitting members—Robie, Archibald, Mortimer and Lawson—went back in without opposition.

The town election was a very different story from the county. An aged Pyke at seventy-five decided not to re-offer. He had had thirty-seven years in the House. By the time of his death some ten years later, he had given over half a century of service to Halifax in varying capacities: fire warden, commissioner of the jail, chief magistrate, colonel of a militia regiment, provincial grand master of the Masonic order, warden of St. Paul's, and its first stipendiary magistrate. In this last office he had displayed "great firmness, the utmost prudence, and the kindest forbearance."[25] Three newcomers came forward as candidates. The first was John Albro, who by age seventeen had been operating his own tannery; his commercial abilities soon ensured that he played an active role in the mercantile and community life of Halifax.[26] He was of New England stock, as was Henry Hezekiah Cogswell, who also decided to run.

Cogswell had gone to King's College at Windsor and from there into Richard John Uniacke's law office, with admission to the Bar in 1798. An avid seeker of office, he first sought, unsuccessfully, that of clerk of the Assembly, writing to members that he was "Just embarking on the voyage of life without Fortune and without Friends able to assist" him.[27] He soon had the necessary friends. Through Chief Justice Blowers' intervention, Cogswell secured the office of deputy provincial secretary in 1812 with an income, including fees, of £1,000 a year. As with Albro, he was involved in such ventures as the Halifax Steam Boat Company. He also served his time as warden of St. Paul's, as Albro was to do shortly. The third entrant was Richard Kidston Jr., the son of another of those Scottish merchants who had come to Nova Scotia in the 1780s, but he lacked the same degree of respectability as the other two. Kidston did well to remain in the contest for three days of polling. When the poll stood at 260 for him, a hundred votes behind the other two, he declined to continue the contest.

The prosperity of war was giving way to the great post-war depression. Its impact sharpened and widened the cleavage between Halifax mercantile interests and those of the agricultural districts. The two now clashed over how to deal with the scarcity of specie.[28] Beginning in 1812, to meet the increased expenditures caused by the war, the province began issuing a redeemable form of paper currency called treasury notes, but these proved insufficient to make up for the extreme shortage of gold and silver coin. With the balance of foreign trade against the province, the little specie in circulation was being drained away to pay for imports or settle debts. By 1818, country members were demanding a paper currency that could be used to make loans to farmers, many of whom were heavily in debt because of successive crop failures in 1815 and 1816. Lawson spoke for the Halifax merchant class when he opposed the whole idea; he believed that such paper money would never be repaid and would prove ruinous both to the lender and the borrower.[29] He did not believe there was "one sixteenth of the distress that had been talked about." The main demand for paper currency and loans was coming from farmers in Hants, Kings and Annapolis Counties. Farmers in those counties would, in fact, do "anything but farm," Lawson claimed, and if they would but emulate the industrious farmers of Lunenburg, they would be rich.

Mortimer was equally blunt, describing the idea for loan offices as a scheme for "mere speculation."[30] In the end, the House simply voted for an increase in treasury notes, but as the provincial financial situation deteriorated further, the growing friction between town and country added to the difficulties members had in allocating road moneys. This led to much bickering and, in Dalhousie's view, much "petulant" behaviour in the House in its relations with the Council and himself. From the Speaker's chair, a frustrated and irate Robie turned on the Council, calling them "a composition of Placemen & Pensioners, paid enemies of the people."[31] More and more of the Assembly's business was being done with the galleries cleared, so that the *Acadian Recorder* could not publish its daily proceedings. The paper's correspondent commented that the members spent their time "exhibiting a sense of guilt while to the public eye they fawned & flattered."[32] Matters did not improve when unofficial word came of George III's death, and with it the realization that the Assembly would be dissolved and another election held.

Unhappiness with the sitting members was general and widespread, but especially so in Halifax. A week after the writs were issued in late May of 1820, a group of Halifax freeholders met at the Exchange Coffee House to nominate candidates for the two township seats. A number of merchants engaged in private banking, and they were particularly furious with Cogswell's advocacy in the old House that banks should be chartered by the Assembly. They were able to exercise sufficient control over the meeting at the Exchange Coffee House to defeat the candidacies of Cogswell and Albro; they replaced them with George Grassie and John Pryor, the latter having been one of the representatives for the town from 1811 to 1818. George Grassie was another of those Scots who had come out in the 1780s as a young man to enter trade. He shortly afterwards married William Lawson's sister; by 1820 he was among the most successful and respectable of merchants in the town. If the factional infighting over banks within the mercantile community had not been so bitter, probably Cogswell and Albro would have withdrawn, and a contested election been avoided; instead, they published their election cards. Of the sitting members for the county, Robie initially declined to re-offer. Dalhousie had blamed him for the failure of the Assembly to provide the militia grant Dalhousie wanted and to answer special messages sent by him to the House. All of this had greatly upset Robie; moreover, his health was not good and he found the business of the House took too much of his time.

What caused Robie to change his mind was the realization that he would in all likelihood be succeeded by John Young. Young had first come to public notice as the author, under the assumed name of Agricola, of a series of letters to the *Acadian Recorder* on agricultural improvements. He subsequently became the second secretary to the Central Board of Agriculture. Young had studied theology at the University of Glasgow, where he had been a brilliant student; when, however, he decided to enter medicine instead of the Church of Scotland, his father had refused further financial support and Young went into business. What had drawn him to Nova Scotia had been the trading opportunities generated by the War of 1812. A somewhat vain man and intolerant when criticized, neither he nor his ideas were overly popular in Halifax, however acclaimed in the country districts. When a meeting of freeholders prevailed on Robie to re-offer in order to stop Young's being elected unopposed, Young then declined. He wished to avoid the "evils" of a contested election.[33]

The assumption was that the sitting members, with George Smith replacing the recently deceased Mortimer and his son-in-law, would now be returned without opposition. However, Archibald was in trouble in Colchester. He had been ambivalent in his support in the previous Assembly for agriculture, particularly in his lack of enthusiasm for farm loan offices for the district. When Young was contemplating running, he was assured of support in Colchester and his decision to withdraw was greeted there by "astonishment."[34] Archibald's opponents then turned to Samuel Tupper, an elderly farmer of Stewiacke, and nominated him to contest what was really Archibald's seat.

As election day drew near, there was mounting excitement once it was realized that there were going to be closely fought contests for both the county and the town seats. Some saw in the Exchange Coffee House nomination meetings an attempt by a "party" to exert "authority over the opinion of others, which the law does not warrant."[35] On the actual day, the crowds gathered early at the hustings to see Tupper's arrival and Archibald's reaction. Archibald met the challenge with a speech from the hustings upholding the arrangement of 1799 for two resident Halifax members, with Colchester and Pictou having one each. In entering the election, Tupper was breaking the "compact."[36] By the afternoon, the *Halifax Journal* had published a Supplement, providing its readers with the substance of Archibald's speech. It agreed with Archibald's view on the division of the county representation and gave its support to his re-election as the representative for Colchester. After six days of polling, Tupper, the outsider, stood last, but with a not-insignificant 292 votes, compared to Lawson's leading total of 1,011 and, more importantly, to Archibald's 883 votes. At Truro, with the backing of the "Radicals of Colchester", Tupper led the poll with nearly 100 more votes than Archibald, though Archibald still had an overall lead. Tupper had some support at Pictou, but he could not overcome the electoral weight that George Smith could bring to bear for Archibald; Tupper declined, leaving the sitting members the victors.

The contest for the two town seats proved much closer and far more exciting. Although the electoral alliance of Grassie and Pryor held together during the first days of polling, that of Albro and Cogswell broke down immediately; the unpopularity of the latter was such that nearly half of those voting for Albro refused to give their second vote to Cogswell. On the fifth day Cogswell declined. Albro had a lead of 39 votes over Grassie, and Pryor was within three of him. To defeat Albro, Grassie and Pryor had to hang together; instead, the election became so heated that they began competing with each other for votes, and as a result Albro increased his lead. The candidates agreed on the sixth day that the poll should finally close at sunset, to be determined by the firing of the garrison gun.

The contest between Grassie and Pryor remained so close, with the resulting noise and confusion so great, that the sheriff had to send his assistant outside to listen for the gun. He returned with the word just as one freeholder had tendered his name to vote, intending to vote for Grassie. But the sheriff closed the poll without allowing him to vote, and with Grassie and Pryor tied at 395 votes each. The *Acadian Recorder* commented that the election had been the most "strenuously and spiritedly" conducted on record in the province,

Perspective view of the Province Building from the N. E.
Drawn and etched by J. E. Woolford, published Halifax, N. S., 1819.

while noting that people were becoming "daily more independent and sensibly alive to the importance of the rights they constitutionally possess."[37] Pryor died shortly after the election. When the new Assembly opened in December 1820, the House gave the Halifax seat to Grassie.

George Grassie, however, died three years later. This precipitated the most bitter Halifax election battle since Charles Morris had defeated Jonathan Sterns in 1788. The contest brought to the fore all the frustrations felt in the mercantile community as the post-war depression continued unabated. Gross shipping tonnage to the port was at its lowest level in a quarter of a century; the exchange rate for Halifax currency against sterling was at times as high as 15 per cent; dry cod exports, the barometer of the fishing industry, were way down; and property rents had fallen drastically.[38] The economic crisis was as severe as Halifax would know in the nineteenth century. Either directly or indirectly, many of the Halifax merchant community were dependent on the fishery. In session after session of the Assembly they had watched measures to support trade and the fishing industry sacrificed to the agricultural interest, while four-fifths of the provincial revenue came from customs and excise duties paid into the treasury by them. They had tried to have the Assembly approve bounties for the importation of salt and the export of merchantable fish. This, the agrarian interests refused to concede, unless restrictions were also placed on the importation of American foodstuffs, which would have had the effect of forcing up the costs to the fishery. Finally, in the winter session of 1823, the Halifax merchants succeeded in temporarily overcoming the opposition to salt and cod bounties, but much anger and frustration remained.

John Young was among those merchants who had gone under in the first years of the post-war depression, though unlike a number of them he had avoided debtors' prison. By 1823 most of his income came from being secretary-treasurer to the Central Board of Agriculture. When Young published his election card, he realized that he would certainly be opposed and in a matter of days Charles Rufus Fairbanks let it be known that he would challenge Young. A scion of one of the oldest and most respected merchant families in the town, Fairbanks had gone to King's College at Windsor, but left before completing his degree; he said it was because he would not subscribe to the Church of England's Thirty-nine Articles as required of graduates. He then went to the Roman Catholic Seminaire de Quebec, before entering Robie's office to study law.[39] In marrying a daughter of William Lawson, he further advanced his position in Halifax society, if that was possible. As he was clearly a rising member of the bar it was natural, if not mandatory, that he should seek to succeed Grassie, who after all was a relation by marriage. Fairbanks feared that others would enter the contest, notably Henry Cogswell. It was Fairbanks' desire to know Cogswell's intentions that introduced the first nastiness into the election. John Young's son, William, was articling with Fairbanks. Fairbanks wanted William to discover whether Cogswell was going to run; this placed William in an impossible position, with the eventual result that Fairbanks accused William of revealing election secrets and of abusing his trust as an indentured student in law. William Young then left Fairbanks' office to assist in his father's canvass.

Young did have the support of some of the Halifax gentry. For one, Attorney General Richard John Uniacke was gratified that Young was offering and hoped that perhaps Fairbanks would yield without a contest. Such support, along with his popularity in the country districts, seem to have misled Young on the amount of voting strength he had in the town. He tried to overcome the antipathy of many merchants to his candidacy by publishing a series of letters in the *Acadian Recorder,* addressed to the freeholders of Halifax. By this unusual means he hoped to counter the idea that, if elected, he would favour the agricultural interest and be "hostile" to trade and the fishery. This was just what Fairbanks and his friends were saying as the two candidates and their friends canvassed the town and the St. Margaret's Bay area. Young replied through his letters that he would promote "the fisheries as well as the plough": the town and country were linked by "inseparable ties," for the former could not prosper without rural enterprise and the latter could not permanently improve without a brisk and vigorous commerce.[40] If the poll was moved to St. Margaret's Bay, the fishermen's vote would be critical. Here Fairbanks had the clear advantage because his merchant friends shamelessly and blatantly used their ledger influence. Rumours were spread among the fishermen that Young had called them "lazy" and that they "ought to eat nothing better than rye flour."[41] To the tune of "Scots wha hae" Young's supporters replied:

> Come Freeholders far and near
> At the hustings now appear
> Give your votes with conscience clear
>   Not aw'd by Bribery
>
> On this glorious day and hour
> You enjoy a Free-man's pow'r
> Scorn the boasted Ledger's glow
>   Be bold—be candid and be free![42]

As the two parties continued their canvass during August and into September, Young found that he had to reply to Fairbanks' "vilest slander" that Young was a foreigner and should not be elected because he was not a native son. Again the passionate feelings aroused found expression in election verse, this time to the tune of Yankee Doodle (originally a British Army tune):

> Come all ye foreign British boys
>   who 'cross the seas have come Sirs
> to follow fortune's faltering hand
>   Come give your votes to Young Sirs
>
> Fort George shall move to Lunenburg
>   and Dartmouth sink in the bason
> Ere we permit a British son
>   Be thrown the last disgrace on.[43]

The *Free Press* gave explicit voice to the real opposition to Young. As a salaried official of the Central Board of Agriculture, he "must coincide with the country party," which was opposed to the "commercial advancement of Halifax." At the opening poll, Fairbanks openly asked freeholders to support "a native over a stranger." But he had to defend against the strong objection to the election of another lawyer, with the specious plea that no candidate had come forward from the merchant community; otherwise, he would not have offered. He was unequivocal in stating that he considered himself the candidate for mercantile Halifax and would uphold "its just claims" against the remainder of the province.[44] After the first day of polling on a Monday, Fairbanks led with 112 votes to 101 for Young. On Tuesday and Wednesday, Fairbanks gradually increased his lead to 82 votes. On the Thursday morning, in a speech "replete with liberality and candour," Young declined.[45] The election proved so costly that some believed even Fairbanks' "pecuniary gravity" would not bear the expense.[46] Young's plea (expressed by the quote which began this chapter) that the safest policy lay in uniting the interests of town and country could not overcome the engrained belief in mercantile Halifax that they were fundamentally antagonistic.

Fairbanks became the twelfth lawyer in the House at a time when there was much resentment against this class, both in the Assembly and outside. The merchant Elisha DeWolf expressively summed up the feelings of many when he told William Young that the Assembly was "now filled almost to overflowing with those rascally saints of the law," when what was needed were men of "independent influence."[47] Fairbanks, however, was the single lawyer to vote against the bill, which Archibald and the profession barely got through, providing for the division of the province into three districts, with a judge at £400 a year salary to preside in each. Fairbanks' opposition demonstrated his political canniness, for there was furious opposition to the measure among the very Halifax freeholders who had just elected him. On Robie accepting the office of Master of the Rolls in 1826, Archibald became Speaker and Solicitor General and Fairbanks succeeded Archibald in his unofficial role as House leader. Hugh Denoon of Pictou thought of running for Robie's seat, until he heard that Lawrence Hartshorne, the merchant son of the councillor and former member of the Assembly, was offering; Hartshorne, Denoon said, had the "confidence of the friends of government," and Denoon declined to stand.[48] Hartshorne went in unopposed. After the battle between Fairbanks and Young there was little stomach for a sequel, and this feeling carried over for the 1826 election. For the first time in two decades no meetings of freeholders were held to select candidates. The sitting Halifax County members were all returned unopposed.

Albro and Fairbanks also re-offered for the town, expecting to be unopposed as well, but they were forced to fight an election when the twenty-six-year-old lawyer Beamish Murdoch decided to stand. After his father had been jailed for debt, Murdoch had been raised by his mother's family, the Beamishes, and sent to the Halifax Grammar School for his education. Murdoch was given little chance of defeating either the sixty-two-year-old Albro or the well-connected Fairbanks. But after a "severe and unprecedented contest lasting six days," the poll closed with Fairbanks in the lead by a substantial margin and Murdoch in second place, having 391 to Albro's 359 votes. Albro's unpopularity related mainly to his judgements as a long-serving magistrate. Of the 723 freeholders who voted, 210 of them only did so for either Fairbanks or Murdoch, and refused to give their second vote to the unpopular Albro. If 33 of these plumpers (voters who had voted for only a single candidate), had also voted for Albro, he would have won. Another factor favouring Murdoch was the appearance of the town's Irish freeholders in some strength; he was a former vice president of the Charitable Irish Society and a known advocate for Catholic emancipation. The *Acadian Recorder* could not remember any contested election at which there was so little of the angry or irritating feelings and the intoxication or bloodshed that had disgraced former contests. The only note of criticism came from the pen of Edmund Ward, the Tory editor of the *Free Press,* who regretted that the town was now to be represented by two lawyers and was upset by the abuse heaped on Albro from the galleries of the courthouse.[49]

Although Beamish Murdoch was the sole new member for the Halifax constituencies, he was one of twenty-one of the new members in the recently elected Assembly. The *Acadian Recorder* held the view that the rejection of so many of those who had sat in the old House was their "punishment" for previously having shown the utmost contempt and disregard for public opinion.[50] Archibald continued as Speaker, with Fairbanks resuming his leading role in the conduct of the House's business. Trade had revived and the return of prosperity meant increasing revenues for expenditures on roads and such new ventures as steam boats. Sir James Kempt was a Governor whose easy rapport with members greatly lessened the likelihood of confrontations with the executive branch. Moreover, there was little on the political horizon likely to arouse much excitement, other than the expected annual clashes within the Assembly, seeking increased road appropriations, and the Council wanting to reduce the duties paid by merchants on imports.

However, by the 1830 session, there was a noticeable hardening of attitudes in both the Assembly and the Council. There was growing resentment at the Council for using its control of patronage to gain influence in the House. Attacks on the constitutional role of the Council as an appointed body, from within the Assembly and from such newspapers as the *Colonial Patriot* of Pictou, were more radical in language than during the judges' affair, when the newly arrived Loyalists had challenged the old oligarchy's control over offices. Some sixty-five years later, Loyalists held all the principal legal offices, except those of Attorney General and Solicitor General. The senescent and quite deaf Blowers still presided as Chief Justice and as president of the Council when it sat in its legislative capacity; on the bench with him were fellow Loyalists James Stewart, Lewis Morris Wilkins and Brenton Halliburton, while Robie was Master of the Rolls. Robie, Stewart and Halliburton were also members of the Council.

At the Council table with Halliburton were his brother-in-law, Bishop John Inglis, and his son-in-law, Enos Collins, who was well on his way to becoming reputedly the wealthiest man in British North America. Competent, intelligent, but contemptuous towards the Assembly, Halliburton attributed the "fiery harangues" emanating from the floor of the House and the press to a faction playing on local and petty grievances, which required the Council to exercise a "cleansing control."[51] Michael Wallace was seldom present because he acted as administrator in the frequent absences of Sir Peregrine Maitland, Kempt's successor as Governor. His tenures as administrator gained him the epithet of "King Michael," and at eighty-three years of age he was still as revengeful as ever in the dispensing of patronage. On one occasion, after a majority in the Assembly refused to conform to his wishes on a new road, he ensured that one of the offending members was refused the authority for an advance payment to build a needed bridge, spitefully telling him that this was because of the "treatment I met with in the Assembly" during the last session, and George Smith of Pictou "has been the first to experience the effects of it."[52]

There was still no reason in the winter of 1830 to believe that the forthcoming session would be any different from previous ones. A few weeks before its opening, the *Colonial Patriot* did hold up some individual members to ridicule, while challenging Nova Scotians to show themselves an "independent spirited people" by refusing to submit to the wishes and patronage of a "pitiful would-be aristocracy."53 Early in the session the Assembly and the Council agreed on the total allocation of £25,000 for roads. But the haggling over its division among the assemblymen became unusually protracted and the Council more obstinate than ever about approving over-expenditures on the previous year's road grants. Late in the session, to resolve the issue, the House simply increased the amount for roads by £3,000. The Council agreed, conditional on the Assembly finding the additional revenue. Fortunately, or so it seemed at the time, the committee formed to examine a petition of Enos Collins & Company discovered that fourpence of a two shilling fourpence tax on brandy imposed in 1826 had not been collected for four years. An impasse, however, ensued when the Council refused to pass the revenue bills if the fourpence tax was included. Both the Assembly and the Council expected the other to back down, but neither did. The revenue acts all expired at midnight on 31 March. Such merchants as Enos Collins took full advantage and threw on the market their now tax-free goods, which infuriated the members of the House nearly as much as the actual rejection of the revenue bills.[54]

On 2 April, the House sent up a bill to revive and continue the revenue bills, with the additional tax on brandy. On the following day, the Council rejected the bill and sent notice of its rejection. Archibald left the Speaker's chair and entered into the debate with an impassioned speech defending the constitutional right of the Assembly to have the sole privilege of framing money bills. His speech and his later intervention roused the Assembly and hardened its determination. Only three members were prepared to defend the action of the Council. Within the Council, Archibald's angry attacks on it were seen as being motivated by an earlier falling out with Attorney General Richard John Uniacke and Judge Brenton Halliburton over the succession to the Chief Justiceship on the expected retirement of Blowers. On 13 April, Michael Wallace, as administrator, prorogued the session, with resulting loss of both the revenue and appropriation bills; no provincial revenue could be collected and no expenditures made.

Shortly afterwards, Sir Peregrine Maitland reassumed the Governorship. He understood that the intrigue for the Chief Justiceship had greatly exacerbated the constitutional impasse. The feeling against Archibald within the Halifax oligarchy was bitter indeed, though some like Nathaniel White were amused that "Archibald after spending 30 years in piddling down the backs of the powers that he [had] bolted off the course; hoisted the liberty cap and come out a proper man of the people."[55] For its sheer spitefulness Nova Scotians had never seen the likes of the campaign that supporters of the oligarchy now waged against Archibald. He had a large family to support and educate and was greatly concerned about his prospects. He did retain Maitland's confidence, who realized the conflicting pressures exerted on him. Maitland was in a quandary over whether he should reconvene the Assembly or have an election. The death of George IV solved his difficulty by necessitating an election and the writs were issued for August.

The Brandy Election, in 1830, was the most violent and nasty contest so far for the Halifax seats, with the Council using every means in its power to influence the result. For the first time, the press played a significant and highly partisan role. The *Novascotian* (now under the ownership of the precocious Joseph Howe), the *Acadian Recorder* and the *Colonial Patriot* all upheld the actions of the Assembly week after week, while only the *Free Press* came out in support of the Council. Copies of the *Free Press* were sent to all magistrates in the hopes of influencing opinion outside the capital. For Halifax township, Murdoch re-offered, as did Fairbanks, who had returned from seeking additional capital for the Shubenacadie Canal in England, while at the same time ensuring he should be remembered if any offices became vacant. Fairbanks' absence during the impasse over the tax on brandy meant that Murdoch bore the whole brunt of the wrath of the Council and its powerful friends. They had already been furious with him for his attempt in the Assembly to have imprisonment for debt abolished. Foremost in his mind was his father's ordeal when imprisoned for debt twenty years earlier. Murdoch had sought "to secure to the poor imprisoned debtor, a little of the light and the air of Heaven," but the measure had been "destroyed" by the Council. The merchant notability had never been enamoured with the upstart Murdoch and had never accepted him as their representative. In fact, not one of the Halifax Chamber of Commerce had ever approached him to offer advice, and had only consulted with Fairbanks.[56] They were determined to see Murdoch defeated and put up one of their own in Stephen DeBlois, well known for his opposition to reform and to any democratic pretensions by the Assembly. The fifty-year-old DeBlois was utterly disdainful of Murdoch, despising him as nothing more than an arrogant young lawyer seeking promotion.

All the sitting members for the county re-offered. In the previous election the long-standing convention of two members from Halifax, with one each from Colchester and Pictou, had again been upheld; now in 1830, with emotions so high, it was completely disregarded. As angry at Lawson as they were at Murdoch, the Council party nominated merchant John Alexander Barry and Henry Blackadar, a twenty-seven-year-old lawyer and native of Halifax, but now practising in Pictou. They were to stand with Hartshorne. In opposition to this slate were the popular candidates S.G.W. Archibald, William Lawson and George Smith, and a newcomer, Jotham Blanchard. Blanchard had been one of the first students to graduate from Pictou Academy and had gone on to study law in the office of Thomas Dickson, a brother-in-law of Archibald. He did not practise much law but spent his time as editor of the Pictou *Colonial Patriot*. In a series of editorials he attacked the Council and its ubiquitous tentacles: as "the system which prevails among the Provincial authorities to keep all the good things among themselves and their families." For Blanchard, the Assembly's upholding of its right to originate and frame money bills marked the "Glorious Emancipation" of Nova Scotia.[57] He entered the election with the radical notion, not shared by his colleagues, that what was needed was an organized party to break the hold of the Halifax oligarchy on the political life of the province. There was also an eighth candidate, John Leander Starr; at twenty-eight years of age, Starr was already achieving a leading position within the mercantile community, and Halifax society generally, for his involvement in various civic, church and Masonic activities. In 1826 he had backed Murdoch, his former classmate at the Halifax Grammar School, and now in 1830 he voiced criticism of the oligarchy, but outside of Halifax he was viewed as part of the Council's coalition of candidates.[58]

The poll opened on 13 September with the usual nominations and speeches. Only Murdoch was prepared to challenge directly and personally the pretensions of the Council and the merchant notability. He knew that the town's ledger influence was marshalled against him, asking rhetorically if it was right "by dint of wealth—by the influence of the ledger—to force men into the Assembly, who are not the free selections of the people." Although he claimed he was not alluding to DeBlois, there was no disguising it when Murdoch went on to call upon the freeholders to ask DeBlois "whether he had been trained at the feet of the Gamaliels of the constitution, or at the feet of his Majesty's Council."[59] Gamaliel, the great Jewish rabbi, jurist, and teacher of St. Paul in his pre-Christian period, had been noted for his liberal and tolerant views; such a barbed intellectual comment, coming from the upstart Murdoch, enraged DeBlois and his friends. Unwisely, Murdoch added some uncomplimentary allusions to DeBlois's Loyalist parentage. It was a courageous and forceful speech and Murdoch paid heavily for it.

It was obvious from the start of polling that the "all-powerful" influence of the major merchants was going to be used; servants, truckmen, Shubenacadie Canal workers and men from the steam boats were sent to the hustings to prevent voters coming forward for Murdoch. On the second day DeBlois read a previously prepared address, alluding to Murdoch's speech of the day before; he called Murdoch "a vain and flippant young Lawyer seeking of promotion." An infuriated Murdoch turned on DeBlois, telling him that, though he respected the character of those Loyalists who had left the American colonies from principle, many of them had fled from debts. Moreover, for years all the offices had been held to the exclusion of the old inhabitants by these "pretended Loyalists," many of whom were "the scum of the United States."[60] After that outburst, the result could not be doubted, though Murdoch tried to counter the forces arrayed against him by using the "low Irish mob." On the third day, when Fairbanks stood at 415, DeBlois at 409 and himself far behind with 326 votes, Murdoch declined. Few respectable voters had come forward, and both Fairbanks and Murdoch had fewer votes than in 1826. Almost all Murdoch's votes were "independent" ones, i.e. plumpers, and came from the middle and humble classes. Members, both of his own profession and of the mercantile community, turned against him almost without exception.[61] The election had cost Murdoch £1,500 by his own estimate.

The poll for the four county seats continued for another three days. On its closing, Hartshorne stood first with 979 votes, closely followed by Lawson; about 200 votes behind were John Barry, John Starr and Archibald; then came Henry Blackadar with 374; finally, way down the list, with each at under 300 votes, were George Smith and Jotham Blanchard. Halifax had voted first and foremost for its own. The individual popularity of the Halifax candidates proved to be a decisive factor, with only a small minority of freeholders voting for or against a bloc or coalition of candidates. Not so at Truro, where the single great issue of the day was the constitutional rights of the Assembly. Many of the oldest men, the fathers of the district known as "grandshires," came forward, some on crutches, as an example to their children. Nearly 200 men marched in from the northern part of the district with colours flying. Another large body of men came on horseback from Musquodoboit, Stewiacke and Gay's River. In all nearly 1,200 voted; of these 1,100 voted for the popular candidates as a bloc.

As in 1799, the last great contest for the county seats, Pictou decided the issue. When the poll opened there on Monday, September 27, the Highlanders of the Kirk persuasion, led by their clergy and armed with sticks, crowded into the town to cheer on Hartshorne, Starr, Barry and Blackadar, who all donned Scotch bonnets for the occasion. It soon became impossible to hold the poll inside the courthouse and so the hustings were erected in the street. Polling continued amidst much uproar and confusion. In the evening some sailors and others attacked Blanchard's open house. In the ensuing melee, one man was killed and many injured. On the following morning, the Council party seized the hustings, only to be confronted by some 800 supporters of George Smith brought in by steamer. The contest continued day by day, with there being much fighting each night, until Saturday when the poll finally closed. As at Truro there had been bloc voting, with the Council candidates gaining 150 more votes than their opponents. This was not enough to overcome the commanding lead built up by Lawson, Archibald, Smith and Blanchard at Truro, who would now take their seats in the new Assembly. Of the Council candidates, only Hartshorne had come close to being elected, and he was still 200 votes behind Blanchard, the lowest of the popular candidates elected.

Chapter 3

The Triumph of Reform in Halifax 1830-1847

[The Council's] influence ... enters and thoroughly pervades the House of Assembly, so that no man, who acts and votes contrary to their views, is exempt from their displeasure, nor ever succeeds when he applies for any appointment in his own Township or County. The moment he adopts a policy which runs counter to that of the Aristocracy, he forfeits ever after the sweet smile, the hearty shake, the elegant Card for dinner or Ball, on all of which minds, not borne up by a consciousness of native internal dignity, set a false estimate; and what is infinitely worse, he abridges, if not entirely destroys his influence in recommending the fittest persons to fill the offices ... within that portion of the Province which he represents.

To the Freeholders of Nova Scotia, Letter III, by Joe Warner (pseudonym for John Young) *Acadian Recorder,* 6 August 1836

By 1830 the population of Halifax town had grown to nearly 15,000 inhabitants. Its boundaries, however, had not greatly extended beyond those of the old town of the previous century. Most of the town's 1,500 houses and public buildings were compressed within a rectangular pattern of eight streets running parallel to the waterfront; these, in turn, were intersected by another fifteen streets. Water Street was the focus of the town's commercial life. At much expense, this street had been recently laid with paving stones; specially built side-paths had been created for pedestrians. Many of the other streets had been macadamized — a process first introduced eight years before, which involved laying successive layers of stone broken into pieces of nearly uniform size. Extensive fires had consumed much of eighteenth century Halifax. Although most of the newer buildings were still of wood, over one hundred were now of brick or stone. The newer houses and public buildings had much improved the appearance of the town. Province House was the principal public building. First opened in 1819, it was considered by some to be the best-built and handsomest edifice in North America.

Halifax was not only the capital of the colony with the full panoply of public buildings and officials, but it was also a fortified naval base with a permanent British Army garrison. Even in peace, military contracts were much sought after; payment was in British sterling, for which there was always demand because of the chronic drain of specie out the province to pay for imports and overseas creditors. But it was as the supplier of credit to the outports, and as the home port to over one hundred vessels trading chiefly to the West Indies, that generated the wealth of the merchant class; some of them, such as Enos Collins and Samuel Cunard, were indeed wealthy men for any age.

The power and influence of the governing oligarchy of merchants and office-holders was concentrated in the Council. But it was the Council's role in the dispute over the four-pence tax on brandy that had so aroused public feeling around the province. The Brandy Election of 1830, in itself, was not a political watershed, but never again would the Council so blatantly challenge the constitutional prerogatives of the popularly elected representatives of the people. Moreover, criticism of the Council continued unabated into the new decade. Its unrepresentative character, its sitting in both executive and legislative capacities, and its control over public offices became increasingly the focus of public anger and debate. The deaths of Richard John Uniacke, Michael Wallace and Charles Morris, and the retirement of Chief Justice Blowers, brought about the most change among office-holders and councillors seen since Sir John Wentworth's day. By 1834, there was a major reordering of senior appointments; Halliburton became Chief Justice, Archibald made Attorney General, Fairbanks appointed Solicitor General, and Charles Wentworth Wallace and John Spry Morris succeeded their respective fathers. The change in the Council membership was equally sweeping and of greater political import. With the addition of Samuel Cunard, Henry Cogswell, James Tobin and Joseph Allison, the weight of influence in the Council shifted decisively from office-holders to those engaged in commerce and banking. In religion, all the Council were Anglicans except Peter McNab, who was Church of Scotland, and James Tobin, a Catholic. This was at a time when the 1827 census had demonstrated that the claim of the Church of England to be the established church could not be sustained, with its adherents numbering less than a quarter of the total population. After 1830 the Council, with its membership of twelve office-holders and merchants, though more unrepresentative of the population as a whole than ever before, was more than ever prepared to use its powerful and insidious influence to thwart any democratic pretensions emanating from the Assembly floor.

Initially, economic more than constitutional issues dominated the seven sessions of the Assembly from 1830 to 1836. Another severe economic depression that began in the mid-1830s brought to the fore the continuing depreciation in the value of the provincial treasury notes. Because of their fear that the increasing volume of notes in circulation might depreciate even further, the majority of country members had refused for a decade to allow the establishment of a publicly incorporated bank. As Charles Rufus Fairbanks had rightly pointed out the province would be faced as a result of this refusal with a private bank over which the legislature would have little control. From its founding in 1825 the Halifax Banking Company, familiarly known as Collins' Bank, used its influence at the Council table and in the Assembly to thwart attempts to incorporate a competing institution. Not until 1832 did Fairbanks and his father-in-law, William Lawson, get through a bill to incorporate a public bank.[1] Among the most opposed was Jotham Blanchard, though he seems not to have been under the influence of the bankers in the Council as some thought, but was genuinely seeking greater safeguards against a bank failure, so common in the United States.[2] In the end, a hardly disinterested Council did it for Blanchard, when finally agreeing to the establishment of the Bank of Nova Scotia. Lawson became its first president and four more assemblymen joined him as directors.

By 1833 the provincial currency was trading at an appreciable discount to the English pound sterling. The Assembly was finally forced to deal with the critical need for a sound currency, and to restore the provincial credit.[3] Near the end of the session, there was agreement that both banks could redeem their own notes in increasingly worthless provincial paper instead of specie. In his legislative review for the 1833 session, an appalled Joseph Howe castigated assemblymen for being manipulated like puppets by the bankers on the Council, remarking that while "Midas, by his magic touch, turned everything to gold they with a stroke of a pen turned everything to paper."[4] This belated move failed abysmally to deal with the consequences of the mass of irredeemable treasury notes circulating in the capital and the countryside. The resulting chaos was especially calamitous for the smaller merchants and traders in Halifax, who petitioned the House on the absolute need for a sound

Province House, Holles Street, Halifax
Drawn by Wm. S. Moorsom, engraved by J. Clark, published by Colburn & Bentley,
London 1830.

currency.[5] The demand for coin assumed such proportions that in
1834 the majority passed a bill requiring the banks to redeem their
own notes in gold or silver coin, and declared the notes legal tender.
The treasury notes were left to find their own level. Widespread
financial distress followed, aggravated by two successive crop failures, the severity of the economic depression, and the outbreak of
cholera in Halifax. Furthermore, the ruthless competition between
the banks overflowed onto Assembly floor, creating "motley alliances" and "monied combinations" among members, greatly contributing to the financial mess in which Nova Scotians now found
themselves.

At the same time as the Assembly was grappling so disastrously
with the province's depreciating currency, the British government
was moving with determination to have Nova Scotia assume responsibility for paying the salaries of its judiciary and civil officers, or as
it was then called, the civil list. In return, the home government was
prepared to turn over to Assembly control of the last remaining
revenues accruing directly to the crown from coal-mining royalties
and fees for land grants. When Fairbanks moved just such a resolution, which involved his own salary as Solicitor General, it was
overwhelmingly defeated. Even his father-in-law voted against the
idea of a permanent provision for what were seen as grossly inflated
salaries. Fairbanks, as adroit as ever, then got through a bill giving

the Chief Justice a yearly salary of £850, including an amount in lieu of the detested fees being charged by his office.

Joseph Howe was furious that the Assembly would even consider laying "its independence at the feet of a grasping and ambitious profession"; the *Novascotian* became the chief forum for arousing public opinion on the issue.[6] In Halifax, angry freeholders circulated a petition protesting against the "enormous salaries" enjoyed by the judiciary, loudly proclaiming that the vested rights of officials must take second place to those of the people to be economically governed. William Lawson tabled the petition, giving vent to the mounting anger by noting that only public officials could afford to keep carriages.[7] Near the end of the session, Fairbanks moved for the passage of a bill incorporating a somewhat lower salary scale, in exchange for control of the remaining crown revenues, only to have his rival, Alexander Stewart of Cumberland, move that its consideration be postponed to the next session. This amendment passed by a single vote.

Fairbanks was bitter at the defeat of his bill and blamed the press, which he believed had misled the public on the issue. When it came time for the 1835 session, many in the Assembly regretted the defeat of Fairbanks' compromise, once they learned that the home government was determined to break the impasse over the civil list; it threatened to collect the long-dormant, but still legal, quitrents on lands granted by the crown. Although the amounts due were small, most owners of property would have to pay. Sir Colin Campbell, the new Governor replacing Maitland, told the Assembly that collection would begin forthwith, unless it agreed to contribute £2,000 a year to be applied against the civil list. When faced with even the possibility of collection of the dreaded quitrents, the majority voted to accede.

The constitutional deadlock between the Assembly and the Council that precipitated the Brandy Election of 1830 had raised the issue of the Council's ability to act in both executive and legislative capacities; in the Canadas and New Brunswick the Councils were separate bodies. In the 1834 session Alexander Stewart moved two resolutions that brought the issue to the floor of the House; the first called for the Council's proceedings to be open to the public when sitting in its legislative capacity, and the second for separate Councils. Jotham Blanchard used the opportunity to advocate the idea of half the members of a Legislative Council being appointed and the remainder being elected. In an able speech, Fairbanks went further and argued "that no Legislative Council can be formed with advantage to the public ... but upon the principle of election"; moreover, he would "sweep out of the Council those connected with the judiciary."[8]

Such a radical notion as an elected Council was exactly what S.G.W. Archibald and the acting administrator, Thomas Jeffery, wanted to avoid being discussed. Their response was to have Archibald announce from the Speaker's chair that the British government was contemplating constitutional changes for Nova Scotia, with the implicit message that any displays of radicalism were ill-advised. This certainly dampened the enthusiasm of many members, but the debate continued over some days until Fairbanks moved that there should be separate Executive and Legislative Councils and that members of the former should be "indifferently selected" from both the Assembly and a Legislative Council. This was defeated.

However, in an unrecorded vote the next day, the House approved an amended version of Stewart's earlier resolution providing for separate Councils; Jotham Blanchard then moved that a Legislative Council be elected, but this was defeated. Although Fairbanks was in the House and spoke in favour of the elective principle just before Blanchard's resolution came to the vote, he did not vote in either case, apparently discreetly withdrawing before each division. Fairbanks' little bout with radicalism was proving highly unpopular with his otherwise supportive friends on the Council and in government. He was very likely forcefully reminded by Archibald and Jeffery that he could expect no promotion if he continued to espouse such causes. Promotion was very much on Fairbanks' mind, for S. B. Robie, having accumulated a fortune of £60,000, had decided to give up his judgeship as Master of the Rolls in the Court of Chancery. As well, the office of Judge of the Court of Vice Admiralty was open. As usual the competition was intense, but Fairbanks came out on top with both offices.

Many believed that Joseph Howe would run for Fairbanks' Halifax Township seat. Earlier in the year, Howe had accused the Halifax magistracy of corruption. He had been charged with libel. In the most famous trial in Nova Scotian history, a jury found him not guilty. After his victory, Howe found that he could not go out "to shoot a Partridge in the woods, or catch a Trout in the streams, without being suspected of canvassing for the next election."[9] As usual the sheriff called a public meeting to nominate candidates. As many as two-thirds of the freeholders of Halifax attended, and the merchant Thomas Forrester took the chair. Forrester opened the meeting with an angry attack on the "wealth and interest" which in the past had decided the town's elections. What was needed was an opposition, as in England, before "the influence which now pressed upon the people could be rebuked."[10] The meeting nominated Hugh Bell for the Halifax Township seat; Howe, agreeing with the choice, declined to stand.

The Halifax Township seats had been almost entirely an Anglican preserve for more than half a century. Bell was a Methodist lay preacher, much in demand on Sundays in Halifax and in the outlying parts. His early-widowed mother had managed at some sacrifice to ensure that her son received a sound education; for a time, Bell was a school teacher before becoming a bookkeeper with a firm of brewers. He soon rose to be a partner. After making a substantial sum of money during the War of 1812, Bell struck out on his own as a brewer, and later as the owner of a soap and candle factory. He was, however, one of those merchants in the depression of the mid-1830s who were finding themselves in severe financial difficulties. In his election card, he attacked in impassioned language the "disgraceful and debasing system which has hitherto prevailed at our Elections, where the people have been made mere puppets or automata, to be, or do anything the movers of the machinery required; or to serve as stepping stones by which the ambitious and designing, from sinister motives rise to influence and power."[11] In the 1823 by-election, in which John Young had challenged the "system," Fairbanks had overwhelmed him; in 1835, the mounting agitation for an end to the supremacy of the wealthy merchant class over the town's public life resulted in Bell's election being unopposed.

As the Assembly elected in 1830 drew to the close of its natural term, there was widespread dissatisfaction with the indecision and timidity of the members in confronting the need for reform. Newspapers, of which there were now six in Halifax, three in Pictou and one in Yarmouth, had become the chief forum for expressing the rising public discontent through editorials, but also by numerous letters to the editors critical of the Council and calling for reform. The letters of Joe Warner in the *Acadian Recorder* were especially wide-ranging in their attacks on the abuses of government. Joe Warner was almost certainly John Young. His fourteen letters under that pseudonym were published during August, September, October and November of 1836 just before the election of that year. In letter after letter, Young attacked the "swelling of the Civil List," notably that for the judiciary, savagely blaming Archibald, whose "invariable policy has been, since his occupation of the [Speaker's] chair, to seize every occasion to benefit himself, and to clutch the receipts of the Treasury ... He becomes a terror to himself and is a terror to all others."[12] Young left nothing unsaid in his attacks on the "ascendancy of Lawyers" in the Assembly. Under the Speakerships of Wilkins, Robie and Archibald, they had increased the salaries and fees of the judiciary to almost £10,000 a year, and "nearly half of this by scandalous jobs, hatched and perfected by their direct agency, and the aggrandisement of the profession."[13]

On the creation of Pictou and Colchester Counties out of the old Halifax County, by an act passed in the 1835 session, Halifax County was reduced to having two members, but the township representation remained at two members. Halifax freeholders had the sheriff call a public meeting at the Exchange Coffee House to nominate candidates.[14] Its tenor was set immediately when Thomas Forrester called on the meeting to pass a series of resolutions requiring all candidates to pledge themselves to endeavour to abolish the "obnoxious and illegal" judicial fees. The sheer welling-up of resentment against the "aristocracy" who ruled "to pick the pockets of the people" carried through the meeting. Both Lawson and DeBlois, as sitting members, found themselves forced to defend their conduct in the last Assembly. After a scathing attack on him by John Young's son, George Renny, as a man who would "betray and despoil," DeBlois saw his nomination defeated by an overwhelming majority.

For the town, Hugh Bell re-offered and was unanimously accepted, as was the nomination of Thomas Forrester. A successful dry goods merchant, whose property assessment had risen from £300 in 1824 to £2,800 ten years later, Forrester had gone to the Halifax Grammar School. As "quite a stripling" he had entered the British Army and fought in the Canadian campaign during the War of 1812, before taking his discharge and settling into business in Halifax. Joseph Starr, brother of John Leander, was also approved as a candidate. The meeting, however, had nominated three candidates to contest for the two town seats. As George Renny Young sensibly pointed out, this was a practical absurdity, when the object of the meeting was to avoid controversy at the hustings for the cause of reform. DeBlois could still have run but declined, having nothing but contempt for such vulgar displays of public feeling as he had just undergone. In a letter to the Acadian Recorder he lashed out at Young, who in turn defended his remarks at the public meeting, while replying with the intellectual wit that so enraged the ill-tempered DeBlois:

"The palmy time of aristocratic dominion has passed away; and now, that you cannot be Jupiter, I am, not surprised you refuse to mingle among the 'lesser Gods'."

The Exchange Coffee House meeting served as the opportunity for Joseph Howe to enter provincial politics officially. In 1836 Howe, at thirty-two years of age, was the owner and editor of the *Novascotian,* the leading provincial newspaper, the forte of which was its comprehensive legislative reviews. Under Howe, the *Novascotian* had become a political force in its own right. In addition to Howe, the meeting nominated William Annand and Henry Gladwin to contest for the two county seats. The sons of a Halifax merchant, Annand and his brother had been sent to their father's native Scotland to be educated; on their return they had become gentlemen farmers in the Upper Musquodoboit River Valley. Gladwin was another gentleman farmer from the Musquodoboit area. For the first time candidates felt the need to put forth a platform in their election cards. In his own, Howe noted that in public meetings held at Lawrencetown, Musquodoboit and Halifax he had been nominated to run, though he had not solicited the nomination at any of the meetings. He, in fact, attacked the past practice of candidates visiting each freeholder in person "and by a system of gross flattery and mean solicitation combined with profuse expenditure in the neighbourhood of the Hustings to secure a seat, often without any higher claims than wealth and impudence can confer."[15] Annand was anxious to be seen equally concerned with the interests of town and country, while Gladwin proposed the most comprehensive reforms of any candidate, including the transfer of the post office (an imperial responsibility) to the province, and it so managed that it made a profit!

When the poll opened at the Halifax courthouse, Beamish Murdoch ill-advisedly decided to stand for one of the two township seats. Well before the poll moved to St. Margaret's Bay, he resigned with less than a respectable showing. At the end of polling at St. Margaret's Bay, Forrester and Bell were declared elected. For the county seats, Gladwin got only 45 votes at Halifax and dropped out. Although Lawson was in second place, he did not even appear at St. Margaret's Bay. The election of Howe and Annand was now certain, but to avoid any cavils, the poll moved to Musquodoboit and opened in Gourley's barn, which was jammed to the rafters. The December cold, however, soon drove them to the Presbyterian Meeting House, where the symbolic one vote was taken. After the regulation hour the poll then closed, with Howe having the remarkable total of 1042 votes, nearly twice the number of Annand who, with 100 more than Lawson, got the other seat. In both the town and county elections, the more popular candidates had won decisively.

By the time of his defeat, Lawson had served in the Assembly for thirty years. More than any other Halifax County member, he had been able to bridge the gap between town and country, leading the poll in the 1820 and 1830 elections and being unopposed in 1826. For a Halifax resident, this was the highest electoral compliment freeholders in town and country could have paid any candidate in his day. His rough, hard-living style likely appealed to many. At some time in his youth he had spent time among the native Indians. When he was drunk, he used to do Indian war dances, much to the rage and embarrassment of his society-conscious children. Unquestionably, his principal accomplishment was the establishment of the Bank of Nova Scotia in 1832, over the determined opposition of the Halifax Banking Company. As much as he hated its directors, who for so long used their membership on the Council to thwart the creation of another bank, Lawson wanted what he considered his due place at the Council table. Governor Sir Peregrine Maitland regretted he could find no such place or office for him, though he was "by no means a satisfied person" and "usually clamorous against the Measures of Government."[16] When the Council of Twelve was divided in 1837 and a Legislative Council appointed, Lawson was among its first members.

In electing three new members out of four, Halifax town and county freeholders reflected what had happened around the province. Redistribution had enlarged the House by five members to forty-nine, but still thirty-four were new members. Moreover, for the first time no lawyer was elected for a Halifax constituency. The number of new members boded well for the Reform cause, for which Howe became the unofficial leader. Although the four Halifax members were considered as Reformers, they voted as a bloc only on major constitutional questions. Even then Bell was not prepared to support resolutions too critical of members of the Council; this no doubt related to his being married to the sister of Joseph Allison of the Halifax Banking Company and a member of the Council. On the great issues of the day, seldom did Bell not call for moderation and caution so that the House not injure itself by acting too precipitately. Bell's business fortunes were improving and his connections with the wealthy merchant class through family and business were close; he was not about to hazard these on the altar of too much radicalism.

Nor did his Methodism include support for temperance; as a brewer, he consistently voted against any temperance measures. In distinct contrast, his colleague Forrester could be harsh in his criticism of the Council, telling his fellow assemblymen that if they "went into the heart of Turkey they could not find a more despotic authority than centred in H.M. Council in this Province."[17] Annand hardly ever intervened in debates and was content to follow Howe, who was on his feet on nearly every issue, sparring chiefly with James Boyle Uniacke, the ostensible leader of the Tories.

In the early part of the 1837 session, Howe introduced his Twelve Resolutions, declaiming on the unrepresentative character of the Council and the resulting injustices. Rather than face a major confrontation with the Council, he withdrew the resolutions, only to reintroduce them later in the session in the form of an address to the Crown, less much of their offending language. Howe's constitutional thinking was still in flux; he had no difficulty in dropping the idea of an elective Council and substituting the far less radical notion of separation into Executive and Legislative Councils. The Twelve Resolutions in the form of an address to the Crown bore fruit when the Colonial Secretary, Lord Glenelg, instructed Governor Sir Colin Campbell to divide the Council into separate executive and legislative bodies. Those who believed that the new constitutional arrangements meant that the majority in the Assembly would now govern were to be sadly disillusioned. Howe's reaction was to table in April 1838 a second address to the Crown, detailing the grievances under which the province laboured. The House voted on the address clause by clause. Led by Uniacke, the Tories either called for the defeat of certain clauses or their amendment, but the Reform majority held firm.

At the opening of the 1839 session, Campbell made public a series of dispatches from Glenelg upholding Campbell's appointments to the Legislative Council and refusing to reduce the salaries on the civil list. Glenelg also instructed Campbell to withdraw the offer to hand over the revenues still being paid to the crown directly, in exchange for a permanent civil list, unless the Assembly first passed a bill granting £4,700 yearly towards the salaries of the chief officers of government. The Tories were gleeful, while the Reformers were disheartened and appalled. The succeeding debate on the dispatches filled the galleries, and printed copies of the speeches were widely circulated. The exchanges between Howe and Uniacke "rank high among the oratorical spectaculars of the Nova Scotia House of As-

Halifax from the Red Mill, Dartmouth
Drawn on Stone by Wm. Eagar, lithographed by T. Moore, Boston, published by
C. H. Belcher, Halifax, July 1839.

sembly," as Howe led the attack on the dispatches. Uniacke defended
the Lieutenant Governor's actions and his right to act independently
of the majority of the Assembly.[18] But Uniacke was to abandon the
Tories in a few months and go over to the Reformers. He would do
so in the belief that a circular dispatch of late 1839 to colonial
governors by the new secretary of state, Lord John Russell, implied
a new constitutional order. The dispatch directed Governors to remove and appoint Executive Councillors as public policy dictated.

When Campbell failed to act on Lord John Russell's instructions
to remodel the Executive Council to make it more acceptable to the
majority in the Assembly, Howe moved a series of resolutions in the
1840 session in support of responsible government. Forrester's intervention in the debate took the form of a succinct summary of the
Reformer cause: "the main object of the resolutions was to introduce
the British constitution into the Colony. The Governor in the Province was now only a deputy of the Colonial Office. He was not
responsible to the people, he was surrounded by irresponsible advisers." Bell, in turn, was his usual equivocal self, suggesting that the
principle of responsibility be tried, and "if it would not work, well
they could abandon it."[19] Bell was really only interested in political
reform to the degree that it led directly to economic emancipation

from imperial control and provincial financial retrenchment. All the Halifax members voted with the Reform majority. They did so again near the end of the session for another resolution calling for the removal of Campbell as Governor because of his continued failure to implement what the Reformers believed to be a new constitutional order demanded by Lord John Russell's dispatch. The resolution for his removal brought Governor General Charles Poulett Thomson from Quebec to Halifax, with instructions from London to restore political tranquility to Nova Scotia. He did so through skilfully avoiding the whole issue of responsible government and by remaking the Executive Council into a coalition of Tories and Reformers, while enticing Howe to take a seat at the Executive Council table. The actual implementation was left to the new Governor, Viscount Falkland, who replaced the recalled Campbell. Falkland immediately appointed Howe and his brother-in-law, James McNab, to the Council.

Although Nova Scotia was dividing along party lines, Howe's entrance into Falkland's remodeled Council temporarily blurred the constitutional issues separating the liberals and conservatives, or more commonly referred to as Reformers and Tories. Although both parties supported Falkland's Ministry of Talents, the bitter divisions separating them ensured that in the 1840 election the four Halifax seats would be contested along party lines. The forthcoming struggle at the hustings was already being mirrored by the virulence of the newspaper war between Howe in the *Novascotian* and Edmund Ward in the *Times*. Parties and elections require organization and money; these were to be present on a major scale. Both parties held nomination meetings at the Mason's Hall and put management committees in place. Six hundred attended that of the liberals and it lasted seven hours. They were faced with having too many candidates; Howe, Annand, Bell and Forrester were prepared to re-offer, but if McNab were to retain his place on the Executive Council, he needed to become a member of the Assembly. Either Annand or Bell was prepared to withdraw, but if Annand withdrew then the Musquodoboit district, a Reformer stronghold, would be left without representation. Bell accordingly withdrew in return for Howe's promise that he would eventually be appointed to the Legislative Council. McNab was none too comfortable as a Reformer, and his loyalty was to his brother-in-law personally, which was why he refused to endorse the candidacies of either the mercurial Forrester or Annand.[20]

At the great public meeting at the Masons' Hall, McNab had said that he would use his influence only for his own election. The Tories believed that McNab had been nominated because of his ledger influence among the fishermen of St. Margaret's Bay which, combined with the Halifax Irish vote and the support of the farmers of Musquodoboit, would give the liberals the election. The Tories concluded that their only hope of getting one of their own elected was not by opposing two against two for the town and county seats, but by nominating just one for each. Their strategy was to rely on the individual popularity of their candidates to cause enough freeholders to split their votes by voting for one of the Reform candidates and for the single Tory, instead of giving both their votes to the two Reform candidates. Thus the single Tory candidate would gain enough votes to take the second seat. The *Acadian Recorder* described this as "vindictively" directing their forces against Howe, Annand or Forrester.[21] After some difficulty in finding the desired candidates, the Tories settled on Beamish Murdoch and the brewer, Alexander Keith. Murdoch had never reconciled himself to his humiliating defeats in 1830 and 1836. He was open to solicitations to run for the Tories, a number of whom had been his classmates at the Halifax Grammar School and were business clients. Neither at his nomination nor later at the hustings did Keith say much, though he was noted for his ability to mix with the "commonalty," leaving Murdoch to state the case of Tory mercantile Halifax. In 1836 for the first time, what Murdoch described as the large proportion of the intelligence and property of the community had been excluded from having at least one voice in the Assembly; the fear was that 1840 would be no different. It was, declared Murdoch, a principle of the British constitution that no single party should be the sole governors, a healthy opposition was needed; moreover, Halifax paid nine-tenths of the duties, but nine-tenths of this revenue was expended elsewhere. Halifax should have a larger representation and the "want of it caused the collision that now existed" between town and country.[22]

The poll opened on Tuesday, November 3, at the courthouse. There was much anticipation and excitement, with flags and banners in abundance bearing such rallying cries as "The Queen's Gift, Constitutional Government." Market Square was thronged with men of both sides as a struggle to gain control of the hustings began. The sheriff had erected the raised platform inside the courthouse, instead of following the custom of having the hustings outside, possibly because of the lateness of the season, but this made keeping order that much more difficult. The liberals had brought in their supporters from Musquodoboit and they early succeeded in gaining control over the passageways leading up to the hustings. Most of the first day was taken up with speeches by the candidates and attempts by each party to shout down the speakers of the other. By the end of the day somewhat under 150 freeholders had got through the commotion to vote, and the majority voted for the Reformers. The struggle for the passageways continued next day; as Howe remarked in the *Nova-scotian,* "the passages were anything but a pleasant site for dandies."[23] Another 200 managed to vote and nearly all their votes went to Howe and Annand. The Tory hope of Murdoch being able to divide the Reform vote was proving illusionary. But, for the two township seats there was some splitting and Keith and Forrester were nearly tied, though McNab had a good lead over both of them. On Thursday, Murdoch's supporters established themselves in the gallery, from where they showered abuse on their opponents as voters worked their way up to vote. Murdoch and Keith had their best day so far, but by now there was little hope of either of them catching their opponents. By Friday, exhaustion and the refusal of many Halifax freeholders to come forward resulted in a light vote; similarly on Saturday, when the sheriff adjourned the poll to open again on the following Tuesday at St. Margaret's Bay. As it was clear that both elections were already decided in favour of the Reformers, few voted on either Tuesday or the next day, when both Murdoch and Keith declined. Howe led the poll with 1085 votes, with Annand a few behind, but double that of Murdoch; for the town McNab had 716, Forrester 542 and Keith finished at the bottom with 355 votes.

The sheer decisiveness of the Reformer victory lay in the success of their strategy in bringing in hundreds of supporters from Musquo-doboit. This ensured that they had the manpower for the battle to control the passageways up to the hustings, and enough support to determine the county election at the Halifax courthouse. Another factor had to be the Irish Catholic vote, which may have amounted to one-fifth of the town's electorate. Although some Irish might have either given their vote to Murdoch as plumpers or split their second vote between the two Reform candidates, most probably voted for McNab and Forrester. The liberal election management committee had fifteen Irish Catholics out of its membership of sixty-three, compared to just one on the conservative committee with its fifty members. Intimidation had been present in the past. The 1840 election, however, was the first occasion when a party adopted the deliberate tactic of seizing control of the passageways leading up to the platform where the votes were taken by the sheriff, though it had been used elsewhere, notably at Pictou and Cape Breton elections. It was probably successful in deterring many Halifax Tory voters. The *Acadian Recorder,* not a friend of the Tories, noted that few Halifax freeholders could be polled until the fifth day. Perhaps not more than 700 were polled in five days, compared to an average of 850 for the 1820, 1826, 1830 and 1836 elections. The merchant, William Stairs, chaired the liberal committee of management. He must have raised the funds necessary to bring in the 300 to 400 Musquodoboit men and accommodate them in the candidates' houses of entertainment for three days; not all the wealth and property were on the Tory side by any means.

For their celebratory dinner in the Masons' Hall, one hundred and fifty-six Reformers drank eighteen toasts, including one to "the faithful and unflinching majority of the last Assembly" and to the "memory of one of the greatest Reformers of Nova Scotia, the late John Young." In numbers at least, the Reformers of Halifax were outdone by their black colleagues at Preston, where two hundred sat down to dinner: the toasts included "Our respected Representatives in General Assembly Annand, Howe, Forrester and McNab we supported them from conscientious motives, may the talent which so eminently distinguished them be guided by an overruling Providence for the benefit of their country." And "Lady Falkland and Acadia's Daughters in every circle of Society, they have ever been distinguished for their virtues and beauty."[24]

Before the next Assembly opened, S.G.W. Archibald retired as Speaker; in the new constitutional order it was no longer acceptable for a law officer of the Crown to preside as Speaker. What remained unclear was whether a member of the Executive Council could also be Speaker. Both Howe and James Boyle Uniacke believed so and both agreed to be nominated. Howe defeated Uniacke by a slim two votes, with a number of Reformers voting against Howe; Forrester, for one, held that for an Executive Councillor to be also Speaker was "adverse to the principles of the British Constitution." In the past the extensive influence and authority of Speakers lay in their being the First Commoner, as the chief upholders of the rights of the Commons, while managing the House to general satisfaction of the Colonial Office. Uniacke, Wilkins, Robie and Archibald had all proved their abilities in both regards and received their due rewards. Their ability to manage the House's proceedings was much assisted by it sitting so much of the time in committee of the whole, when another member took the Speaker's chair and the Speaker could then intervene in debates; the most notable occasion had been when Archibald had left the chair in the 1830 session and rallied the members to resist the constitutional pretensions of the Council to amend money bills. In accepting the Speakership, Howe had placed himself in a irreconcilable conflict of interest. He was the ostensible leader of a party which at least on constitutional issues formed a majority. As well he was sitting at the Council table where he and his fellow Reformers were a minority, but as members of a coalition they had to accept responsibility for measures proposed by the executive. That this impossible arrangement did not break down sooner than it did, was largely due to Howe frequently leaving the chair in committee of the whole to uphold the policies of Lord Falkland's government.

Forrester was never happy with the coalition experiment that Howe so lauded. By his time of his death from congested heart failure at fifty-one in November 1841, Forrester, with other such Reformers as Herbert Huntington of Yarmouth, had turned on Howe with a vengeance for his apparent betrayal of the true principles of responsible government. William Stairs, who had chaired the management committee for the Reformers in the previous election, now inherited Forrester's seat without a contest, though there were a good many Halifax Catholics who believed that the seat should have gone to one of their own. Forrester had inherited William Lawson's mantle as one of the few of the more wealthy Halifax mercantile community to support reform; so too did Stairs succeed Forrester. Although never business partners, he and Forrester had been classmates at the Halifax Grammar School. Stairs' widowed father had left Halifax because of his debts and moved to Philadelphia. He had sent William and his four other children to Halifax to be brought up by their uncle; Stairs never saw his father again.[25] Like Hugh Bell, Stairs had in the mid-1830s faced near-bankruptcy brought on by the currency crisis, which had turned him into a Reformer. By 1841, he was prospering in the ship chandlery and hardware business, with the time and the financial means to contest elections and enter the Assembly. He seems to have been unusually close to Howe and prepared to support the coalition experiment as long as Howe did.

The most divisive issue of the 1842 session proved to be the continued funding of sectarian colleges. There were now several: Acadia at Wolfville for the Baptists, St. Mary's in Halifax for the Roman Catholics, King's at Windsor for the Anglicans. Dalhousie, though largely under the control of the Church of Scotland, had the best claim to be non-denominational. The liberals generally were opposed to further grants and were in favour of a single non-denominational institution, while the conservatives usually supported sectarian colleges. Among many members there remained a deep-seated opposition to funding colleges at all, on the grounds that support of much-needed common schools should be the paramount concern. The issue was joined once again early in the next session, with Howe no longer in the Speaker's chair because of his acceptance of the collectorship of excise for the Halifax District. The most spirited debate took place on a series of resolutions proposed by Annand and seconded by Herbert Huntington; in summary, these called for an end to the chartering and endowing of sectarian colleges as unsound policy. The resolution charged that the policy led to bitter sectarian jealousies and resulted in the neglect of common schools, while the needs of a small population could best be met by one non-denominational institution. The debate lasted three days, finally concluding with a majority decision to withdraw support from sectarian establishments and to endow one college, which would be free from sectarian influences. The final vote saw six Reformers voting with a minority for the status quo, and four Tories siding with the majority.[26] The committee appointed to draft the one-university bill, however, could not even agree on a site.

The issue continued to fester and towards the end of the session, G. W. McLelan of Londonderry tabled a bill to end the permanent grant to King's College, dating from its founding in 1789. This precipitated another passionate debate on the whole question of funding of sectarian colleges and common schools. It went on until one-thirty in the morning of 28 March, when Edmund Dodd moved an amendment that, in essence, sanctioned continued funding of sectarian colleges. Howe realized that in all likelihood the amendment would pass. He immediately employed the parliamentary tactic of calling for a motion to adjourn, which passed by one vote, so Dodd's amendment never came to a vote.

In a series of public meetings around the province the Baptists, led by the Reverend Edmund Crawley and Attorney General James William Johnston, assailed opponents of sectarian colleges. In the process they moulded a Tory/Baptist alliance to fight the forthcoming election. By the end of the 1843 session, the college issue had become the Baptist cause. Johnston, a member of both the Legislative and Executive councils, formally assumed the leadership of the Tories. From the time the Baptists began pressing for grants to Acadia College, they believed that Howe was their chief opponent and relations soon degenerated into calumnious exchanges. Their tone can be judged from Howe's caustic remark in a public speech that some Baptists "exhibited as much ambition and persecution as Catholics, and if [we] were to have a Pope, [he] would as soon have one in Rome as at Horton, if a time of persecution was to arrive, it might as well be under solemn pontificals, as under a black coat and tights" (a reference to Crawley in his position as a professor at Acadia).[27] Although the college question played its role, Falkland's decision to call an early election in late October 1843 had its origin in his belief that this was the only means left to him to avoid having to form a party government of Reformers. Although Howe remained in the Executive Council, the failure of the coalition experiment was obvious to all.

As in 1840 the Reformers should have been assured of all the Halifax seats, but Halifax Catholics were in an uproar.[28] They were charging the *Novascotian*, now edited by Richard Nugent, a Catholic, with reprehensible attacks on Bishop William Walsh over a matter of internal church discipline. By inference, though unfairly, they held Howe responsible. The Tories did not hesitate to use the incident to make overtures to Catholic freeholders, though they later denied doing so. In response, one or perhaps two of the Halifax sitting members apparently offered to make way for a Catholic to run. But once this presumed offer was made, disagreements arose among the liberals. Most Halifax Irish Catholics were for the repeal of the hated union act of 1801, which had joined Ireland to England and Scotland under the Westminster Parliament. To some Reformers, the agitation for repeal smacked of disloyalty; they also feared too much Catholic influence over their party. These Reformers were determined to select the Catholic candidate. When this reached Catholic ears, they united in seeing it as a gross insult. Handbills began to appear, calling on the Catholics to stay aloof from the election. Consequently, the liberal nomination meeting (at which Stairs and McNab re-offered and were unopposed) was poorly attended. On the following evening, 750 Catholics gathered to be told by their leaders that Catholics had been treated by the liberals disrespectfully and discourteously; Michael Tobin Jr. alleged that Howe had offered a nomination to a Catholic, only to withdraw it. The meeting unanimously resolved that Catholics would take no part in the forthcoming elections for town and county members. In an impolitic public letter, Howe tried to justify the conduct of the Reformers, only confirming to the Irish Catholic freeholders that they were right to desert the liberals. The

Tories now followed their previous strategy of putting forward a single candidate, ostensibly independent of party. They settled on Andrew Mitchell Uniacke, the youngest son of the late Attorney General and, like his brother James Boyle, a graduate of King's College and a lawyer.

At the hustings on the opening day for the township election, McNab was nominated first and made a few remarks declaring he was prepared to try party government, but he was not a man of extreme measures. However, Stairs in his own speech made clear that he was now in favour of party government and knew he would be opposed by the influence that "commanding money" could bring to bear. He promised to fight to the end. Uniacke had some of the oratorical talent of his family and greatly outshone the other two; in his speech from the hustings to freeholders he stood before them as a Nova Scotian by birth and blood, free and independent, and though he had been stigmatized as a Tory by the liberals, his "principles were much more liberal than theirs." He played emotionally to the Irish vote, alluding to his Irish descent and the "feeling manner" that the memory of his father was noticed at meetings of Irishmen. Behind him there was as much ledger influence as could be mustered, the vote of some fifty public officers and a half dozen clergymen. Forty-two leading merchants gave their open support through a handbill listing their names.

From the first day of polling, Stairs fell well behind McNab and Uniacke; by the fifth day, McNab was comfortably in front, with Uniacke ahead of Stairs by forty-six votes. Each evening the supporters of the candidates harnessed themselves to carriages to take their candidate to his residence amid great cheering; in Uniacke's case, his carriage was turned into a boat with his supporters as oarsmen and himself as helmsman. At St. Margaret's Bay a schoolhouse served as the hustings. After the first day Stairs was within six votes of Uniacke. On the second day Stairs at one point was seventeen ahead, but the Tories had chartered the steamer *Saxe Gotha* to bring in the vote from the numerous outports and its arrival gave Uniacke the lead again. All these voters had to be fed and entertained. The reporter for the *Morning Post* visited that evening one of the candidates' houses of entertainment. His description bears quoting:

> What a motley and a jolly crowd was there! indulging in
> eatables abundant, and libations which always run freely,
> when hearts are rife with fellowship, or an election to be
> won. And what a filthy place it was too such a nauseous

scent of cheese and tobacco smoke rum and eatables, of all sorts ... But here we were in the midst of the fun, and who's green enough to turn aside for trifles, when bent seeing life at an election .... The fiddles are in the next room ... A low room of about ten feet square, crowded almost to suffocation a dim candle, unsnuffed for the last half hour, sheds its flickering light over the apartment ... while in the centre of the room two young freeholders and a pair of damsels, are footing it off in a style the mere sight of which would set a fashionable coquette into hysterics ... Suddenly a shout overwhelms the sound of music, and in comes the favourite candidate ... And then the cheering and the uproar are deafening. The dancers are thronged till it is impossible to move the candidate catches one of the damsels to keep her from getting crushed to death ... and the candidate dances till he is tired with one girl, and kisses all the rest ....[29]

When the revelry finally ended most slept in the haylofts of nearby barns, while the intrepid reporter spent a cold late November night on a bench of the *Saxe Gotha*. On the next morning, Stairs once more went into the lead, but then 100 to 150 of Uniacke's supporters arrived accompanied by a hand organ player and fiddlers, each man wearing a band of blue ribbon around his hat. By one o'clock, after a number of wagons from Halifax brought in voters for Stairs, Uniacke's lead was just eight votes. Then the *Saxe Gotha* again fortuitously arrived with enough electors to give Uniacke a majority of 17, just as the sheriff closed the poll at three in the afternoon. McNab had topped the poll at 786, followed by Uniacke with 636, and last was Stairs with 619 votes. In triumph, Uniacke was brought back to Halifax. His supporters sang an election song composed on the spot, the last verse of which went:

Three groans for Annand, Howe and Stairs;
First beaten singly next in pairs
We'll place these worthies on the shelf,
Where each may aggrandize himself
No longer at the people's cost;
And if by deep repentance toss'd
The loss of power to them be pain
Still 'tis our Country's GREATEST GAIN!![30]

Not only had the Irish Catholics stayed home, but of Uniacke's total, 436 had voted for him only, refusing to give their second vote to either of his opponents. This can be compared to the 14 electors who voted only for Stairs and another eight who did so for McNab. The Reformers had managed to muster just 581 freeholders who would give both their votes to the liberal candidates. Although Stairs obtained more votes than Uniacke at St. Margaret's Bay, probably through McNab's influence among the fishermen, it was not enough to offset the lead gained by Uniacke at the Halifax poll. If the liberal/Catholic alliance had held together, Stairs could have counted upon 200 or more votes and have won before the poll ever moved to St. Margaret's Bay.[31] If the Irish in withholding their vote did much to ensure Uniacke's victory, he also had the support of the Halifax and Hammond Plains blacks; the latter were provided with victuals and requested to stop on election day at the residence of the merchant W.A. Black for refreshments. After the election, the Halifax blacks held a dinner at which eighteen toasts were drunk, including one to "Tories of Halifax never say die," and to "Andrew M. Uniacke, Esquire our returned Member and choice of the Conservatives we know that he will never forsake his principles."[32]

Uniacke's triumphal election song had called for the defeat of Annand, Howe and Stairs first singly, as happened to Stairs, and then in a pair for Annand and Howe, a reference to the forthcoming county election. Rumours were rife that a Catholic and a Tory merchant would challenge the liberal hold on the two seats. The Catholics met again immediately Uniacke's victory was known; they nominated Laurence O'Connor Doyle and put in place an election management committee of 100 Irish Catholics. The liberals now moved quickly, with Annand dropping out to allow for an agreement on a joint Howe/Doyle election card. In perhaps a related change, Annand replaced Nugent as editor of the *Novascotian*. Although all involved were to deny it, the Catholics solicited the Tories to stand aloof so that Doyle could go in without the expense of an election; in return, Stairs was not to dispute the town result. Stairs could not be convinced and demanded a scrutiny. Still, the Tories decided to stand by the agreement on the grounds that the Catholics deserved their share of the representation. The arch Tory, Mather Byles Almon, accepted the arrangement with much reluctance, for as he wrote the former Speaker, S. B. Robie, he was convinced that for another £500 Howe could be beaten.[33] On 27 November Howe and Doyle appeared at the hustings and were returned unopposed. For the first time since DeBlois' election in 1830, however, the Reformers' hold had been broken on the four Halifax seats. Uniacke's victory turned out to be crucial for the Tories because it gave them a one-seat majority over the liberals in the new Assembly.

The difficulties that Howe and other more purist Reformers had with the Baptists were mirrored in their relations with the Halifax Irish Catholic community. In their single-minded pursuit of constitutional reform, they could not accept that both the Baptists and the Irish sought above all respectability and recognition of their due place in Nova Scotian society. For them constitutional reform could be secondary to respectability and equality. For the former, Acadia College was the means of having an educated clergy comparable to those of the Anglicans and Presbyterians. The Irish desired the social and political recognition that their numbers and growing professional class warranted in the wake of Catholic emancipation. In this, their most public leader was the eloquent and witty Larry Doyle, who in January 1843 had become chairman of the Nova Scotia Branch of the Loyal National Repeal Association.[34] A son of a Halifax merchant, his father had sent Doyle to Stoneyhurst College in England to ensure that he had a good Catholic education. He returned in 1823 to article in Attorney General Uniacke's office. There, five years later, he assisted in the preparation of the petition signed by 688 Halifax Catholics for the modification of the state oaths that would allow Catholics in good conscience to sit in the Assembly. Like many of his Halifax legal colleagues he had sought a constituency outside of Halifax and in 1832 was elected for Arichat. In 1840 he gave way to a local candidate in Arichat, and so had been available for the 1843 Halifax elections. The Tories had early approached him about running, but he, probably more than any other, had devised the strategy of withholding the Catholic vote until Howe and the Reformers accepted a Catholic candidate, and one who was for repeal. As the Tory *Times* chortled, "some of the Great Liberals have become Repealers!!"[35]

Neither Falkland nor his government leader, Attorney General J. W. Johnston, could admit that the conservatives as a party had won the election, for to do so would be to sanction the idea of party government, and with it responsible government on Reformer terms. Initially, uncertain whether or not to accept Falkland's invitation to remain on the Council, Howe, Uniacke and McNab had their minds made up for them by Falkland's extraordinarily impolitic appointment to both the Executive and Legislative Councils of Johnston's brother-in-law, Mather Byles Almon, who had never served in either branch of the legislature. All three immediately resigned. Falkland thus believed that he had been stabbed in the back by those who would strip the Governor of his prerogative to appoint the councillors he thought wise, rather than according to the respective party strengths in the House. The die had been cast for the most ferocious political warfare that Nova Scotia was ever to know. It was, as Falkland said after his painful break with Howe over the Council seats, "war to the knife." None of the newspapers any longer made the least pretence to be other than fiercely partisan, engaging in scurrilous personal attacks and lampoons with an unrestrained vindictiveness. As a result of this barbarous style of warfare, Falkland asked to be recalled, and Howe conceded the official leadership of the liberal party to James Boyle Uniacke, and with it inevitably the first premiership under responsible government in what became the Commonwealth of Nations.[36]

Although on constitutional questions the government could be assured of a majority, there were enough loose fish (as Howe so caustically named those who refused to be bound by party voting) in its ranks so that Johnston and his colleagues were not prepared to bring forward any important legislative measures. Falkland realized that if he filled up his Executive Council vacancies with known conservatives, he would be in effect instituting party government. Desperate to avoid finding himself in this predicament, he undertook through Johnston confidential negotiations with some prominent liberals. But Falkland's personal vendetta with Howe caused him to insist that Howe be excluded, in essence proscribed, from having a seat at the Council table. The crucial question became whether or not the liberals would accept appointments to the Executive Council and on what terms. In his dispatch sent to the colonial secretary and written on the information provided by Johnston, Falkland suggested that the Reformers had, in fact, agreed to come into his government without Howe, but then had reneged.

At the beginning of the 1845 session, Johnston tabled the offending dispatch. On the first day of the debate, the avenues to the lobbies were thronged with those wanting a seat in the gallery, which became so densely packed that a number of Legislative Councillors, clergy and military officers had to be seated behind the members' benches. James Boyle Uniacke opened the debate with an address lasting an hour. He "spoke in a tone of withering scorn of the Governor, who could so far forget his high position as the Representative of Royalty, as to place himself upon a level with any man in his Government that for a Governor to proscribe any individual, was to violate the

Constitution of the Country, which no free people would submit to."[37] He was followed by Johnston, who in a three-hour speech defended the advice he had given Falkland, the proscription of Howe and the tabling of the dispatch. On the following day the gallery was equally packed for Howe's four-hour reply to Johnston. And so the debate went on for thirteen days. The principals were Uniacke, Howe and Johnston, and they reviewed the whole sorry and tortuous history of the negotiations leading up to the coalition experiment, its breakdown, dissolution of the Assembly, and what had transpired in the aftermath of the 1843 election. McNab as usual said nothing, but Doyle and Andrew Mitchell Uniacke entered the debate on different days. Doyle's speech was marked by its wit and was filled with illustrations from English constitutional history, in refutation of the government's contention that Howe's behaviour, in openly lampooning Falkland in the columns of the *Novascotian,* had made it impossible for him ever again to be admitted to the Council table.

Uniacke's intervention came in reply to George Young's charge that the present administration intended to "fritter away Responsible Government." Uniacke pointed out that the tabling of the dispatch was an assumption of responsibility. He put Howe temporarily on the defensive when he said that Falkland could not have Howe back on the Council, because in 1840 "His Lordship had favored him with his confidence had conferred upon him a lucrative office; and what did Mr. Howe do? he had attacked him when gratitude should have withheld his pen."[38] Although clearly on different sides of the House, the Uniacke brothers may not have been politically very far apart. Andrew Mitchell fully accepted that responsible government was now established in all the North American colonies and that when Councillors lost the confidence of a majority in the Assembly they must retire. He claimed he could not accept party government, for if all the patronage were given to one party it would be "oppressive." This view did not, needless to say, stop him from defending the recent appointment of Tory magistrates for Halifax, on the grounds that when Howe was in the ascendant during the coalition, fifteen liberals were appointed.

In August 1846 Sir John Harvey arrived in Halifax to replace the embittered and politically impotent Falkland; his instructions were to restore the province to political tranquility. He was well-versed and experienced in British North American colonial politics, having already served as Lieutenant Governor of Prince Edward Island, New Brunswick and Newfoundland. In each he had proved able and conciliatory, unencumbered with doctrinaire views such as had led to Falkland's downfall. Harvey began by inviting to Government House the formerly ostracized liberals, but he was unable to persuade them to join with the conservatives in another coalition government. During the previous year, Howe had toured eight counties and spoken at twenty-three public meetings. He now felt confident that the liberals would win an election, and the only concession the liberals would make to Harvey's urgings was not to press for an immediate dissolution, but to await the election, which had to come in 1847. As it was, the government was only able to come forward with the simultaneous polling bill, as the single measure of any importance during the final session before the election call. Hardly had the House finished its business, when both parties held organizational meetings in Halifax. Andrew Mitchell Uniacke's capture of one of the two township seats in the previous contest had emboldened the conservatives to believe that they could also take one of the two county seats, for the first time since Lawrence Hartshorne Jr. had won in 1826 and then lost four years later in the Brandy Election. The conservatives launched a new newspaper, the *Standard and Conservative Advocate,* solely to promote the Tory cause, declaring in its prospectus: "Political and social improvement, divested of democratic taint, are legitimate features of Conservatism, and we shall advance in their path with alacrity." It sold for virtually nothing and hundreds were distributed free by hired agents and canvassers operating in the country districts.[39] The liberals were sufficiently concerned about the *Standard* that they began raising funds to distribute their own papers.

The Tories abandoned their previous strategy of putting forward single candidates for the two township and two county seats, in the hopes of them posing as independents so that they could divide the Reform vote sufficiently to allow their election. Now in this election, they put forward a full slate of two candidates for each of the town and county contests. With Andrew Mitchell Uniacke offering again for the town, they nominated as his running mate the merchant Thomas Grassie, whose father had been the town's member from 1820 until his sudden death three years later. For the county, Grassie's first cousin, William Lawson Jr., and James Gray both came forward as acceptable candidates. Lawson had never forgiven the Reformers for deserting his father in the 1836 election and voting in Howe and Annand. Both merchants themselves, and closely tied by interest and family to the merchant gentry, Grassie and Lawson were true representatives of that class; neither was to prove a particularly strong candidate. Gray, however, was a popular barrister who had been the county coroner for many years and also an assistant clerk of the Assembly. What made his candidacy of some interest was that until the 1843 election, when he voted for his friend Andrew Mitchell Uniacke, he had been considered a Reformer; moreover, he had married into the prominent Catholic family of James Tobin, though he did not convert, retaining a pew at St. Matthew's until his untimely death in 1848. In entering the contest as the Tory "Catholic" candidate, however, he was doing so at a time when the conservative *Times* had begun a virulent campaign against what it called the danger of a Catholic Ascendancy in Protestant Nova Scotia. The Catholic newspaper, the *Cross,* had replied in full measure and with equally vitriolic language. The anti-Catholic campaign of the *Times* may have been a deliberate attempt to draw off the Protestant liberal vote. Whatever the motivation, nothing was more to unite the Catholics behind the liberals than the Tory allegation that political considerations were behind Howe becoming president of the Charitable Irish Society, and his attendance in that capacity at mass on St. Patrick's Day (previous Protestant presidents, mostly Uniackes, had regularly done so).[40] To run with Howe in the county, the liberals put up Henry Mott of Dartmouth, a manufacturer of chocolate, who was in the process of making the transition from mechanic to man of property.[41] Doyle and McNab offered for the town. In religion, Mott and Uniacke were Anglicans, Doyle a Catholic, while Gray, Grassie, McNab and Lawson were of the Church of Scotland and Howe was associated with the Presbyterian Free Church.

From the moment of their nomination in early April, the conservative candidates began canvassing and holding public meetings around the county. Howe spent much of his time elsewhere on behalf of the liberals, while Doyle appears to have confined most of his electioneering to the town. The liberals could call upon far more active and committed groups of supporters than the conservatives, who previously had no organization outside the boundaries of Halifax Township and in the county proper. For the Tories, Gray turned out to be a fair campaigner, able to give good fighting speeches, as he did at a Dartmouth conservative meeting. He was most effective when challenging the liberal claim that there could never be responsible government unless the heads of government departments were members of both the Executive Council and the Assembly: "Why gentlemen, who are those whom it is proposed to create Heads of

Departments Mere clerks to count money ... the Treasurer. He is the same in fact as the clerk of a bank. Will you place him in a position to be surrounded with the temptations of elections, and the public money passing through his fingers every day? Gentlemen, it would be a dangerous experiment—these officers are not fit for Heads of Departments."[42]

At Preston the conservatives gained the support of the Reverend Richard Preston. He had been born to Virginia slaves and had purchased his own manumission. Richard Preston was proud to see his brethren coming forward to take their place on "the Conservative side of the question, and against those who were constantly disturbing the community. It was their duty to support the Government, so long as the Government did not depart from its duty to England. That great country has relieved us from American bondage." Although running for the town Uniacke also spoke at the Preston meeting, using the most effective argument the Tories had against the liberals when he said that conservatives supported responsible government but were against a government composed of office seekers. Just how defamatory the language could become can be judged from his succeeding remarks; speaking of the liberals he said, to cheers: "We are not of those who taunt you with still being capable of being bought and sold, as you were in the days of slavery" (many of those present would have been former slaves freed during the War of 1812 who settled at Preston).[43]

The conservatives were campaigning just as heavily in the St. Margaret's Bay area where McNab's ledger influence was important to the liberals. A Tory song lampooning McNab went:

And now when I go canvassing with weary toil and fear
The Fishermen speak sneeringly
   "you threatened Boutilier"
I meet no cheers along the shore no greetings at "the Bay"
The people disregard me If I threaten they can pay!
And thus I pass a weary time my hopes are getting low,
Oh how unlike the canvassing a long time ago,
Oh, the merry days of canvassing, a long time ago.[44]

By June, Tory electioneering became of some worry to the liberals and Howe returned to campaign in the eastern part of the county. Up to now, he and Johnston had not confronted each other at the same meeting. The Tories took advantage of Johnston's being in Halifax to call a meeting at Musquodoboit, where their agents had been especially active; they had moored offshore a vessel laden with rum, tobacco and other desirables, which they were distributing freely in return for promises of support. The day before the planned meeting the liberals heard of it, and immediately sent messages to their supporters and to Howe, then at Jeddore further along the Eastern Shore, to pack the meeting. By their sheer numbers, they imposed a liberal chairman and secretary on what was supposed to be a conservative meeting, turning it into debate between the rivals Howe and Johnston. Shortly after noon on the day, Howe led off and spoke for an hour. Johnston followed with a two-and-a-half-hour address. Howe had the best of it, making much of Johnston's appointment of Mather Byles Almon, his brother-in-law, to the Council. Howe recalled for his delighted followers that: "The Scripture says that he is worse than a heathen that will not take care of his own family; and in this respect the Attorney General is, I admit, better than a heathen." By six o'clock some disorder was setting in. Johnston was shouted down and an altercation between the two parties broke out. Supposedly, Howe said that it was better to stay all night rather than not hear out the Attorney General, while "winking to his bullies to encourage the disorder." Johnston, not for the first or last time in his political career, lost his temper and led his followers out of the hall.[45]

A week before the polling date was the day fixed for the public nomination of the candidates. The Tories made great efforts to bring in supporters from outside, while the liberals relied on theirs in the town. The parties took up opposite sides at the courthouse and by agreement the flags of both were carried off. The sheriff opened the day's proceedings by accepting the nominations. Then, as the day was overly hot, each candidate spoke briefly. McNab was the briefest, stating that he had never been a blind partisan; he then proceeded to defend his opponent, William Lawson, from liberal charges over his supposed improper conduct in the previous year as a Sable Island Commissioner. All had gone off peacefully until the Hammond Plains blacks were heading down to Steamboat Wharf with their Tory flag flying. Some "liberal lads" attacked them. The blacks were unarmed and to defend themselves tore up paving stones. The ensuing battle raged with stones and sticks along Water Street and up Duke Street; many were hurt, but none fatally, before order was restored. This was to be the only serious outbreak of violence during campaign, but the ledger influence available to the conservatives was present as never before. Rum, flour and tobacco were scattered like "chaff"; the intimidation of debtors and employees was blatant. Rumours were spread to destroy Mott's credit, bringing forth from an angry Mott that the commercial gentry were but "mere huxters." Definite class overtones surfaced, as contrasts were drawn between the idleness and luxury of the rich merchants and the sturdiness and industry of the middle classes.[46]

That religion was a significant factor in the town's voting could not be better illustrated than by the broadside which appeared after the election.[47] It listed alphabetically, ward by ward, for the six town wards, those who had voted conservative, and those who had done so for the liberal "opposition." Those liberal voters who were Protestants had an asterisk pointedly placed next to their names. The liberals led the conservatives in the town's voting by 51 votes. Of those 446 freeholders who voted liberal, 70 per cent were Roman Catholics, while of the 395 who voted conservative, 95 per cent of them were Protestants. Just how deeply religious feeling ran among the Protestants was revealed after the election, when John Watt of St. Matthew's found it necessary to publicly express regret in having "given offence, on religious grounds" to members of this Church of Scotland congregation by voting for a Catholic candidate. As he told William Young, also a member but married to a Catholic, that he had written such a statement to avoid a split in the congregation, so incensed were some members by his conduct.[48] The *Standard,* however, was only partially correct when it claimed that the election had been won by the Irish Catholic interest, for the liberals also led by about 50 votes outside the town.[49]

Not only in pure numbers did the merchant class support the conservative cause and demonstrate their die-hard opposition to responsible government, but the most powerful among them were overwhelmingly for the Tories. Those merchants who supported the liberals were those with no direct family or partnership connections with the merchant notability.[50] The one clear exception was James McNab, whose commitment to party and responsible government was at best tepid.

In giving the exact number of voters by name, the broadside was further evidence that only around one-fifth of the heads of families could vote, but that those who could, did so in very high numbers. The reason for low voter eligibility lay in the comparatively few families owning their own properties. In ward three, for example, the figure was 18 per cent, nearly all of whom voted in 1847. Overall in the six wards, just 22 per cent of the heads of families voted.[51]

The *Acadian Recorder* could not help but moralize on the fate of Andrew Mitchell Uniacke, describing how after his 1843 "ill-gotten" triumph he returned from St. Margaret's Bay accompanied by a happy throng; but now in 1847, he returned "All solitary and unattended by even a fagend of a Beech Hill or Hammond Plains Life Guard, he arrived in town on a jaded pony, be-spattered from head to foot with mud, and looking as if he were the most correct likeness of sorrow, disappointment and vexation that was ever exhibited in the world."[52]

In the county election, Howe and Mott won massively over Lawson and Gray, taking all thirty of the polls except wards one and two in Halifax, the North West Arm, Preston and Hammond Plains; only in the last two did the liberals lose by a wide margin, as the black vote went solidly Tory. The final totals were Howe 1,530, Mott 1,510, Gray 1,079, and Lawson 1,077 votes. With simultaneous polling in place, the liberal vote increased by half again, compared to previous elections. The 1847 election reputedly cost the Tories between £10,000 and £15,000 and the liberals probably not much less.

In electing one merchant and one lawyer in 1847, the freeholders of Halifax Township confirmed a long-standing pattern of choosing their representatives from these two professions. Although from 1759 to 1784 merchants and office-holders shared the town's representation equally, from the 1784 election onwards lawyers supplanted office-holders. After 1784, lawyers and merchants dominated the township's representation to the exclusion of all other occupations. A similar pattern generally held for Halifax County. Of the six lawyers elected from 1759 to 1847, all were able to combine their professional duties with being either Solicitor or Attorney General and at the same time sitting in the Assembly. The general unpopularity of the legal profession in the town deterred any lawyer who was also an office-holder from even running for the township. When Fairbanks, by far the most popular lawyer among the six elected for the town, became Master of the Rolls and attempted to remain a member of the Assembly, the outrage was such that he had to resign his seat. The election of Fairbanks and Murdoch in 1826 was to be the only time when the town was represented by two lawyers; otherwise, freeholders in the town chose one lawyer and one merchant or, far more often, two merchants. In the period from the Brandy Election of 1830 to responsible government in 1847, three-quarters of the town's representation came from the mercantile community, compared to just over a third for the province as a whole. For the Reform cause, it was the election of Hugh Bell and Thomas Forrester in 1836 that decisively broke the grip over the town seats held by the merchant notability. Both represented the interests of an increasingly militant middle class, which had suffered greatly in the economic depression and from the accompanying currency crisis of the mid-1830s. Bell was a Methodist and Forrester of the Church of Scotland and they, with the sole exceptions of George Grassie in 1820 and Fairbanks in 1823, were the first non-Anglicans to be elected since John Fillis way back in 1785. By the late 1830s, however, the rising importance of the Irish Catholic vote led to a significant degree of Protestant bloc voting, without regard to the denomination of the Protestant candidate.

Merchants, Reformer or Tory, were united in the belief that property gave its possessors a rightful ascendancy in public affairs. In the defence of property rights Hugh Bell zealously argued for a high property qualification in the 1841 Halifax City incorporation bill and William Stairs opposed the measure outright, as he did the abolition of imprisonment for debt. Of the eighteen merchants elected for Halifax Township, just two, John Day and Thomas Forrester, were prepared to challenge the oligarchies of their day. Of the seven lawyers elected, none (except Laurence O'Connor Doyle, who was not elected for the town until 1847) was prepared to do so. Murdoch and Fairbanks had little bouts of radicalism, but both became staunch upholders of the conservative order. Fairbanks probably had the best mind of any lawyer elected for the town. His mastery over financial detail and powers of sound reasoning were justifiably the awe of his contemporaries.

If there was a tragic figure among the thirty-two members elected for the town from 1759 to 1847, it had to be Beamish Murdoch. By his own admission a studious individual, he was in temperament ill-suited to challenge the merchant notability of his day. The imprisonment of his father for debt scarred and embittered him as a boy, and at least in part was the cause of his anti-Loyalist outburst in the Brandy Election of 1830. At the same election, however, the desertion by both his legal colleagues and merchant friends, who had so warmly supported him in 1826, astonished and hurt him deeply. In his speech after resigning from the poll in the 1830 election, he stated that he would never offer again, unless he was solicited by those who had just opposed him. By adhering to that promise and returning to the hustings as a Tory in 1836 and 1840, he suffered nothing but humiliating defeats. But in doing so, he satisfied a deep need for the respectability that only the merchant/office-holding aristocracy of Halifax could bestow.

In agreeing to uphold the Tory cause, Murdoch was no doubt influenced by the needs of his legal practice and having such clients as Enos Collins. The fierce competition for business made Halifax lawyers wary of offending any of the merchant and banking community. This was just another aspect of the pervasive influence exercised by a few wealthy men. Such an extensive degree of influence, for such a protracted period, was greatly abetted by the fact that the number of eligible voters in Halifax town proper was so extraordinarily few, compared to the total population of the town and to elsewhere in the province. In the election battle of 1787 between Charles Morris and Jonathan Sterns, 689 voted. In 1847, though the population of the town (the six wards) had increased four times from around 5,000 in 1787 to over 20,000 in 1847, only 841 voted, and this was a high turnout.[53] Although in 1787 anyone who could show some form of property ownership could have voted, the insignificant increase from the 1787 vote to that of 1847 can only be explained by the concentration of property ownership in proportionally far fewer hands.

If the merchant notability had had to deal with 3,000 rather than 700 to 800 voters, its grip over the town's elections would never have been so pervasive. As it was, it took the outrage generated by the depression and currency debacle of the mid-1830s finally to arouse the populace to challenge the oppressive control exercised by a few wealthy merchants and ensconced office-holders. In 1847, when the electorate of town and county had a clear choice between reform or reaction, they voted for the former, though the ledger influence brought to bear exceeded anything seen in the past.

Chapter 4

The Yeomen Farmers and Merchants of Kings and Hants Counties

... as you pass along through the Western Counties, the dwellings of the rich are pointed out to you at intervals of a few miles. Many, it must be confessed, are or have been Merchants, or Tavern Keepers, and this might lead us to believe that the only way to get wealth was to sell groceries and broad cloth, were it not for a goodly body of examples which you meet of men who, with industrious frugality and prudent management, have grown rich by farming alone; and who have lent the surplus profits of their industry on the lands of their more indolent and extravagant neighbours ....
Joseph Howe, Western Rambles, *Novascotian*, 11 September 1828

A traveller from Halifax, wishing around 1830 to visit the western counties, would do so by traversing the oldest and, after great expenditure, the best road in the province. He would find on his arrival in Windsor the single place that could be described as a town in the whole of Hants County, so agricultural was it in nature. As the summer residence for many of the Halifax gentry, the town had a number of respectable private residences and estates, as well as King's College. From the original three townships of Windsor, Falmouth and Newport, first settled in the 1760s by New England Planters, settlement had expanded into the interior and along the shores of Minas Basin and the Shubenacadie River, but the population of over 8,000 was still less than in either of its sister counties of Kings and Annapolis. Much of the valuable dyked lands skirting the Avon and St. Croix Rivers had early fallen into the hands of resident Halifax proprietors who had introduced a system of tenancy, with regressive consequences, which our visitor would have observed. Windsor, a township of 2,000 inhabitants, was best known for the exportation of gypsum to the middle American seaboard states for use as a fertilizer. Also much engaged in the gypsum trade, and equal in population to Windsor, was its eastern neighbour Newport Township. Falmouth to the west had a population of less than half that of Newport and Windsor, but it too was well-cultivated and its people generally in comfortable circumstances. Among the more newly settled townships, Douglas, bounded to the north by Cobequid Bay and to the east by the Shubenacadie River, had surpassed all others in inhabitants, with 2,300, and in its agricultural productions. Although its settlement after the American War was intimately associated with Scottish veterans of the 84th Regiment, Ulster Irish had early settled along the Noel Shore fronting on the Minas Basin. A mixture of New England Planters, disbanded Scottish soldiers and Irish could be found among most of the later settlements.

The Great West Road crossed over the Avon River about six miles from its mouth on a good substantial wooden bridge. It then ran through Falmouth over the Horton Mountains. From their summit, the attention of the traveller was arrested by the extent and beauty of the view that burst upon him very unexpectedly as he descended. A sudden turn in the road then at once displayed the townships of Horton and Cornwallis. In all, nineteen rivers meandered through these townships, emptying into the Minas Basin and creating tidal marshes which, when dyked, were the foundation of their prosperity. Before their deportation in 1755, the Acadians had enclosed and cultivated all the Grand Pré (or as the English were to call it, the Grand Prairie). When the Connecticut Planters arrived in 1760 to settle Horton Township, they found the dykes broken and the luxuriant meadows under water. It was not until 1810 that this extensive meadow of 686 acres was finally completely enclosed by a substantial dyke, costing £9,858. In the summer months immense herds of cattle could be seen on this marsh. A few houses existed at Wolfville and also in the more populous shiretown of Kentville. Most, however, of the slightly over 3,000 inhabitants of Horton Township lived on their farms. Their houses were reputedly larger and better-built than those our traveller had seen in Hants, with few of them without an adjoining orchard. An Anglican, a Presbyterian, two Baptist and two Methodist churches were visible witnesses to the diversity of their religious life.

Across the Cornwallis River lay the township of the same name, with the reputation of being the Garden of Nova Scotia. Its unusually fertile uplands and numerous rivers, bordered by dyked and rich intervale lands, accounted for this deserved distinction. Nowhere was this more apparent than on the lands bordering the Canard River. Although only ten miles in length, it furnished 2,000 acres of dyked

Windsor N. S. from the Barracks
Drawn from Nature and on Stone by R. Petley, printed by C. Hullmandel, published
by J. Dickinson, London 1837.

land, of which 600 had resulted from the completion of the great
Wellington Dyke in 1825. The work had begun in 1817 and in the
final stages well over 300 men and 50 teams of horses could be seen
toiling on the project on a single day; it cost in the end £21,281,
almost all of which was paid for by assessments on the farmer
proprietors.[1] The 4,400 inhabitants of the township shared the god-
liness of their neighbours, having an Anglican, a Presbyterian, a
Methodist, a Congregationalist, and no less than three Baptist
churches.

Across from Horton and Cornwallis, on the northern shore of
Minas Basin, lay the Loyalist township of Parrsborough with its
1,600 inhabitants. It could be reached by packet boat that ran twice
a week from Windsor. At its creation in 1784 it had been made part
of Kings County, but in 1840 would be divided and annexed to
Cumberland and Colchester Counties. Another Loyalist township,
that of Aylesford, lay to the west along the Great Western Road,
though it had a fair number of New England Planter descendants
from Granville and Annapolis Townships. They had sold their
cleared farms at good prices to incoming Loyalists and moved further
up the Annapolis River to begin again. To the traveller's eye, there
were still many areas not yet fully cleared, displaying blackened
remains of half-burnt forest and numerous rotting stumps. If he had

stopped to visit, he would have heard stories of land clearings when strong men with a full supply of Jamaican rum had made the heavy black logs roll about merrily, creating great piles of them ready for the blazing torch. With slightly over 1,000 inhabitants, almost all engaged in agricultural pursuits, Aylesford was beginning to make its weight felt in county elections.

In religious make-up, Kings and Hants Counties did not differ greatly, except that Baptists were the preponderant faith in Kings, but had fewer adherents in Hants than either the Presbyterians or Anglicans, but slightly more than the Methodists. The settlement of disbanded Scottish soldiers and Irish immigrants had changed the religious map of Hants dramatically from the first days of settlement. By the late 1820s the largest denomination was Presbyterian, followed by those belonging to the Church of England. Presbyterianism, including the strict Covenanter persuasion, was also the second largest faith in Kings County.

Although agriculture was the predominant occupation throughout the two counties, the importance of the gypsum trade to Hants County caused a divergence of economic interests. The members in the Assembly for Kings would always stand for agricultural protection and high duties on imported American flour; those for Hants would be at best equivocal, often favouring free trade with the United States. Freeholders in the two counties seldom elected farmers to represent them, choosing instead mostly merchants. With much property mortgaged and a significant number of their inhabitants either tenants or labourers (in Windsor Township labourers were double the number of independent farmers), the franchise was far more restricted than might be expected. Moreover, the same social conditions encouraged the extensive use of ledger influence at elections.

The Family Compacts of Kings County and Their Ledgers

Time was when Elections were decided in our County by local prejudices or preferences ... a man's principles were then not asked. But a new era has opened; we have been aroused from our lethargy, and have found that acting in this childish manner, we have, in common with other places, sent persons totally unfit to represent our views persons who have time after time betrayed their constituents, and sold themselves to work iniquity. Until the last House, we have never since our recollection, had even a majority that represented the County.

"A Reformer" to the candidates for Kings County, *Novascotian*, 15 October 1840

Seasoned soldiers from the 1745 and 1758 sieges at Louisbourg, and other campaigns of the Seven Years' War, formed the core of the early representation in the Assembly for Kings County, which incorporated what was to become Hants County in 1782. In origin they were a mixed lot. Henry Denny Denson and Winkworth Tonge were Irish, Charles Dickson and Sherman Denison were from Connecticut, John Day was likely of English birth, and Isaac Deschamps was Swiss. All were original grantees in the various townships and they generally amassed large land holdings. In Dickson's case, by 1770 he was among a very small number of grantees who together owned one-half the improvable acreage of Horton Township.[2] Denson ensured that he got for himself some of the best lands in Falmouth Township. All sought to establish large country estates, forming a squirearchy of landowners and office-holders, who for a generation dominated the political life of their townships. Winkworth Tonge served the longest in the Assembly and held the most public offices.

It was the Assembly's action in declaring Tonge's seat vacant for non-attendance that led in 1783 to the election of thirty-three-year-old Jonathan Crane. Crane's ambitions and his commanding personality were to shape the politics of Horton Township and Kings County for the next three decades. He re-offered for the county in the 1785 election and formed an alliance with the Loyalist Elisha Lawrence, who had taken up lands at the newly-established Township of Parrsborough. They were unopposed, as were Gurden Denison for Horton, and merchant Benjamin Belcher for Cornwallis. Other than Lawrence, who had raised the First Battalion of the New Jersey Volunteers in the American war, none of those now elected had seen military service. A new generation had replaced that of the old warriors of the French and Indian wars.

When Elisha Lawrence decided not to re-offer in 1793, Crane sought to create a new alliance that would give him, and two of his relations by marriage, both the county seats and the single seat for Horton Township. While Crane again stood for the county, his brother-in-law, John Allison, offered in the hopes of gaining the second county seat. This left open Horton Township for the husband of another of Allison's sisters, the Loyalist Major Samuel Leonard, who was unopposed. Crane's family-centred alliance proved highly unpopular in both Horton and Cornwallis. The Horton merchant Elisha DeWolf immediately offered for one of the county seats. In Cornwallis, opposition to Crane's scheme came from the candidacies of Benjamin Belcher and William Allen Chipman. By the time the poll opened at the Horton courthouse, five candidates — Crane, Allison, DeWolf, Belcher and Chipman — had offered for the two county seats. Within a short time, both William Allen Chipman and John Allison resigned in the face of the strength of the other three. At Crane's insistence the poll moved to Parrsborough. By then DeWolf was sure of victory, but it was a toss-up between Belcher and Crane.

Ever since the issuance of the writ, Crane had been transferring property to individuals, by executing deeds on the spot, so that they could meet the property qualification to be eligible to vote. In short, he was engaged in making freeholders, who would then vote for him. Now, at Parrsborough, he created twenty-nine such freeholders and defeated Belcher 270 to 263 votes, though both were still well behind DeWolf. Belcher protested to the Assembly this "making freeholders for voting." Crane defended the practice on the grounds that it was perfectly legal, but the Assembly decided that a stop had to put to such a tactic. It awarded the seat to Belcher. For creating his voting freeholders, Crane could draw from a pool, formed from among the two-thirds of the 194 individuals recorded in the 1791 Horton poll tax, who made their living labouring for others. These individuals likely did not own property, or were among the nearly half of those listed as farmers, who also did not own their land and presumably were tenants. All in all, probably fewer than 400 could vote in a county with perhaps 700 heads of families who could be classed as possibly eligible freeholders.[3]

Both Crane and William Allen Chipman chose to stand for the county again in 1799. For the next two decades, elections revolved around the temporary and shifting alliances created by these two substantial landowning merchants, each having as his prime objective the defeat of the other. In 1799 both Crane and Chipman took the two county seats, and the first casualty of this feuding was Benjamin Belcher. An opportunity for Crane to squeeze out Chipman came in the 1806 election. By having Joseph Allison, another of his brothers-in-law, stand with him for the county, Crane hoped to see Chipman defeated. As it turned out, Crane's influence was insufficient to ensure the election of anyone but himself. Allison was defeated, but so was

Chipman, leaving Crane and the Cornwallis merchant John Wells the victors.

In the sessions leading up to the 1811 election, there was little to cause controversy, but the election renewed the rivalry between the Chipman and Crane-Allison families. Likely believing he might again be defeated for the county, William Allen Chipman determined to run for the single Cornwallis Township seat, easily defeating the sitting member, the Loyalist physician William Baxter. For the county, he then put up his twenty-three-year-old nephew and lawyer, Jared Chipman. Crane and John Wells were again candidates for the county. Once they found they were going to be opposed by young Chipman, they formed an alliance. Sheriff George Chipman, brother of William Allen, opened the poll at Horton courthouse on 25 September 1811. The poll continued for four days before adjourning, at the request of Crane and Wells, for Parrsborough, where the polling lasted for two days. Crane led with 342, followed by Wells who was three votes behind, but 30 ahead of Chipman. In this election just half the number of heads of households voted, again suggesting a restrictive franchise in the county. Jared Chipman petitioned the Assembly, claiming that many had voted with deeds Crane had given them fraudulently, on lands mortgaged for debts owed Crane, and even on common lands of the township, which Crane had pretended to convey.[4] A select committee went through the poll book and the records from the scrutiny; it struck off 50 names as illegal voters. But when these were subtracted from the totals for each candidate, the order did not change, for Chipman lost nearly as many votes as did Crane and Wells. For all Chipman's outrage at Crane's efforts to make freeholders, Chipman was hardly innocent of engaging in the same tactic.

The deep depression after the prosperous times during the war years, and the successive crop failures of the "cold years" of 1815 and 1816 (which may have been caused by volcanic eruptions in the East Indies), forced the Assembly to deal with the extreme economic distress being experienced in town and countryside alike. In 1817 the members agreed on £8,000 to be divided up among the counties to purchase seed grain, though William Allen Chipman for one did not believe the distress was as bad as being portrayed. In reply, John George Marshall of Guysborough told Chipman that he was as ignorant of the true state of the province "as any person in it, and all his arguments terminated in this, that there is much wheat in King's County," so there could not be much distress elsewhere. Moreover,

Marshall believed that not "one farthing" of the money should go to Kings. Chipman replied that he was chiefly concerned about an accompanying bill to prevent the export of wheat and potatoes out of the province, which would be "ruinous" to Kings County, because of its substantial trade with New Brunswick. Crane was equally outspoken in opposition to the measure, but the overwhelming feeling among the members was that they could not allow food to leave the province when people were starving, and so the bill passed.[5]

It was a petition from the magistrates and others of Kings County in 1818 that precipitated the most heated debate of this Assembly. The petition called on the House to establish a paper currency as the only means to alleviate the prevailing economic distress.[6] In the ensuing debate Crane was first on his feet, endorsing as "indispensably necessary" a paper currency as a substitute for the scarcity of coin. He saw this paper currency circulating as money, loaned upon substantial security and to be repaid with interest. Not until the following year did the Kings petition bear fruit, when a bill was got through allowing farmers in Kings and Annapolis Counties to borrow money on the security of their lands from loan offices established by the government. If this measure was welcomed by the farmers of the county, another in the same session laid bare the divergent economic interests between King County farmers and mercantile Halifax. It arose from a move to allow a rebate of duties paid on American imports, which were to be re-exported to the West Indies to take advantage of Halifax once more becoming a free port. The fear among farmers was it would be a guise for smuggling in large quantities of American flour, depressing the local price. For Chipman it was nothing less than allowing the Americans "a free trade," and the "Province of Nova Scotia might just as well be given up" if it passed, which it did.[7]

When confronted by the ill-feeling shown by many members towards Kings County, rooted in jealousy of its general prosperity, Crane and Chipman submerged their personal rivalry in a common front. This new-found amity in the Assembly was translated in the 1818 election into an alliance at the hustings. It was precipitated by Elisha DeWolf's decision to stand again. This placed Crane in a quandary; the chances were slim that the county would elect two from Horton Township, and DeWolf was by far the more popular of the two. William Allen Chipman was put into a similar difficulty when Charles Ramage Prescott decided to offer for Cornwallis. A Halifax merchant, Prescott had decided for health reasons to retire early in life to the township, where he engaged in horticultural experimentation for the remainder of his days.

In defence, the erstwhile enemies now forged an alliance of electoral convenience, which saw Crane decline at the opening of the county poll in favour of Chipman, and in the process abandon John Wells, his one-time colleague in the former House. DeWolf easily led the field with 398 votes, followed by Chipman, with Wells coming a distant third. Crane then turned around and ran for Horton, building up such a lead over his two opponents, the physician Robert Bayard and the Kentville merchant William Hunt, that both declined by nightfall on the first day. Hunt had never expected to win. He had entered as a candidate to vent his anger from the hustings over the distressed financial state he and others found themselves in as a result of the post-war depression: Hunt spoke for many when he declaimed that "... we live in this land of liberty, under a glorious constitution ... [but] we are oppressed, insulted, abused, we live in bondage"; with peace, he said, had come no money and suits for debt; "We see nothing, we hear nothing ... but LAW and LAWYERS in the House of Assembly and in the Country ... They are rising like Locusts in the land of Egypt."[8] His speech caused such a stir that it was carried in the Halifax papers, but he stood no chance against the massive ledger influence Crane could bring to bear in Horton Township.

The Crane/Chipman alliance held up for the 1820 election to the extent that Crane did not stand for one of the county seats. However, his son-in-law Sherman Denison became a candidate, as did Chipman's relation by marriage, Samuel Bishop. Chipman led the poll with 610 votes, the highest individual total yet. Bishop took the second seat. William Hunt, weighed down by his financial misfortunes and greatly resenting being called a "radical," became the sole candidate for Horton against Crane. He did this once more in order to speak from the hustings against the evils of a system that failed to protect the virtuous in "his sylvan labours" from mortgages that deprived him and his offspring of the benefits of his labour. He used stronger language in his letter to Gentlemen Freeholders, calling on them to vote for those "who are not under the controul of others, nor seeking after preferment from those in authority, Men who are not ashamed to stand for the cause of their constituents." Such freeholders should make their own choice, "without being controuled by the rich and vain canvassers who are continually buzzing in our ears to their own disgrace."[9] No doubt poor Hunt had Crane very much in mind.

Crane's death in a few months brought an end to an era in which his forceful and domineering personality, combined with his unrivalled influence, had given him a supremacy for over three decades over the political life of Horton Township. Merchant, extensive landowner, judge of the inferior court, colonel in the county militia, reputed to be the wealthiest man in the county, and among the most distinguished in appearance in the province, Crane lived fully the life of an eighteenth-century country squire in Nova Scotia. Beamish Murdoch remembered him as a "tall, handsome man, with fluent speech and an amazing readiness of natural wit and illustrative power." Lord Dalhousie was much less impressed, finding him "a very harsh & illiberal landlord," as well as "one of the principal canting hypocrites" in the Assembly.[10]

On the other hand, Crane was a commissioner of sewers (dykes) from 1777 to his death. As a boy he had learned from two Acadians how to build dykes. For over forty years Crane had superintended the maintenance and the expansion of the original system upon which so much of the prosperity of the township depended.[11] Although he married into the staunchly Methodist Allison family, he did not have the mandatory conversion experience until he was on his deathbed.[12] If, while in the Assembly, he considered himself a Dissenter from the nominally established Church of England, he did not vote as one on church and state issues, always siding with the High Anglican group. Ever the believer that the king's government and his church as established in law must be upheld against any and every sign of popular democracy, the executive branch of government had no more reliable man in the Assembly than Squire Jonathan Crane.

When writs were issued for the 1826 election there were the usual conversations among tentative candidates about forming alliances. This time, however, there was a non-resident running. Although John Starr had been born in Cornwallis he had early gone to Halifax, where he had prospered greatly as a merchant and shipowner, become a magistrate and risen to be the colonel of the 3rd Battalion of Halifax Militia, a sure sign of respectability. Starr, it seems, was in England when the writs were issued and left the management of his candidacy for the county to his friends. However, the Cornwallis Township election was held before that of the county, and John Wells re-offered in the belief that he would have the vote and interest of Chipman.[13] The merchant John Morton also decided to be a candidate, and after two days of polling gained such a lead that Wells resigned. Wells blamed Chipman for his defeat, though Chipman claimed he had said that he would not give his influence to any candidate. Although he knew he had no chance, Wells sought his revenge by running for the county, which now had as candidates Chipman, Starr and Samuel Bishop.

The poll opened at Kentville, where it became apparent that the election would be decided by the second choices of electors. In the Kentville polling Wells placed last, but his supporters almost to the man gave their second vote to Starr, giving him the overall lead. Chipman not only had to contend with losing so much of his Cornwallis support in this way, but a good number of Chipman's friends also gave their second vote to Starr. The total electorate polled so far was 600. When the poll opened at Parrsborough, Wells withdrew and threw his support to Bishop; this made it hopeless for Chipman and so he resigned. In 1820 Chipman had won with 610 votes, now Starr did so with 563. Just as Chipman's overwhelming 1820 victory had been no proper gauge of his popularity, but the result of temporary electoral alliances, the same applied in 1826 to Starr's. Chipman and Wells were not the only sitting members to go down to defeat. James Harris defeated Sherman Denison for the Horton seat, leaving Samuel Bishop the sole surviving member from the last House. He was, however, to be joined in 1828 by Chipman, who now gained his revenge on Wells by defeating him in a by-election caused by the sudden death of Starr.

In the dispute with the Council in 1830 over the tax on brandy, the Kings County members were solidly with the overwhelming majority of their colleagues in defence of the Assembly's constitutional rights. When the writs were issued for the 1830 election, William Allen Chipman, in his seventy-third year, decided to make way for his son Samuel, who at age forty was in his prime and well established as a merchant, shipowner and large-scale marshland farmer. It was Samuel Bishop who was in trouble because the twenty-nine-year-old son of Elisha DeWolf (who had recently wed John Starr's daughter) decided to stand for the county, thus bringing into play the full electoral weight of the DeWolf clan. Also young Elisha DeWolf's entrance divided the Horton vote, which meant that either he or Bishop would be defeated. Either way Chipman was a sure winner.

It is unlikely that the poll moved from Kentville, for Chipman led it by 426 votes with DeWolf coming in at 373; poor Bishop was fortunate to have got 160. The real battle was for Cornwallis where William Allen Chipman threw his influence behind John Morton as the sitting member. Morton was opposed by William Campbell, a farmer and registrar of deeds. Campbell had behind him the ledger influence of Colonel Henry Gesner. There must have been a serious falling-out between Chipman and Gesner, for Samuel Chipman was married to Gesner's daughter. On the first day of polling, when both candidates made great exertions to stand first at the end of the day, Morton came out with a lead of 39 votes. He was still 35 ahead on the fifth day, at which point Campbell declined. At Horton, Harris defeated a fellow Methodist, Perez Benjamin, the owner of the single grist mill in the whole of the Gaspereau Valley.

The complacency with which the county merchant class viewed their grip over the political life of Kings was now to be rudely challenged by a farmer from the western district. Augustus Tupper was one of the farming class experiencing by the mid-1830s the severe distress caused by the shortage of cash in the countryside. Tupper had the temerity to publish a letter in the *Novascotian* announcing his candidacy for the 1836 election. He declared that, if elected, he would become the "Working Man's Representative; and that such of our Gentry as wish to trample upon the common people" would keep him out if they could. He had always abhorred the "illiberal and unjust policy which operates to enrich and aggrandize the few, at the expense of the many." His letter concluded with a clarion call: "FARMERS AND MECHANICS! If you desire wretchedness and degradation, sleep on; the same causes that have sunk us thus so far, if suffered to operate, will soon carry us to the bottom ... if you cannot wait patiently to see the chains of oppression and misrule riveted upon the slender wrists of your dear unconscious babes," now was the time to act by choosing a representative from among themselves.

He left no doubt that this was a direct attack on the sitting members, Chipman and DeWolf; he ended his letter by saying that he could not vote for either of them.[14] This radical language came from a descendant of a respected Cornwallis grantee, whose brother was the noted Baptist minister, the Reverend Charles Tupper (father of Sir Charles). The letter was soon circulating in the form of handbills. The shorter the time to polling, the less time for Tupper's letter to stir up the people, which was why Chipman in concert with his uncle, Sheriff George Chipman, determined on an early election. As well as Chipman and Tupper, Thomas Andrew Strange DeWolf came forward at the last moment in place of his brother Elisha. Tupper was the single candidate to pledge himself to reform, while an infuriated Chipman sought to counter Tupper's letter by claiming that he had done what he could to eliminate pay for militia field officers. Moreover, he had been instrumental in having a duty imposed on imported flour. Tupper, of course, stood no more chance against the influence that Chipman and DeWolf could bring to the hustings than had William Hunt two decades earlier. Tupper resigned even before the poll moved from Kentville to Aylesford. Chipman led the poll with 791 votes, the highest total so far for the county.

In the opening session of the new House in 1837, Joseph Howe tabled his Twelve Resolutions calling for the reconstruction of the government to ensure responsibility to the elected representatives of the people. It is likely that at the time none of the four Kings County members thought of themselves as either Reformers or Tories. Four sessions later, Chipman and Perez Benjamin were firmly in the Reform camp, while DeWolf and Morton were opposed to any and all attempts to introduce responsible government. DeWolf, however, had voted for Howe's Twelve Resolutions after they were reintroduced later in the 1837 session as an address to the throne. Ironically, the one part of the address that DeWolf was most opposed to called for some members of the Assembly also to hold seats on the Council. When the Council of Twelve was finally separated into Executive and Legislative Councils a year later, DeWolf was among those who accepted membership on the Executive Council, while still retaining his seat in the House. Moreover, in the dying days of the 1840 session, when the Assembly passed the address for the recall of Governor Sir Colin Campbell, DeWolf was the single member of the executive council left with a seat in the Assembly. Not unexpectedly he opposed passage. DeWolf did not even believe that he would have to resign from the Executive Council if he lost his Assembly seat in the forthcoming election. During a visit to Halifax in early September, he had a rude awakening. He was told that under the new system being introduced, executive councillors would only be selected from either members of the Assembly or of the Legislative Council. As an election was almost certain that autumn, DeWolf reportedly "began to canvass with the energy of a steam engine."[15] Just as the election was called, Morton was told that he would be elevated to the Legislative Council, no doubt as a mark of official approbation, for he too had voted against the address calling for Campbell's recall.

In 1836, John Morton had been unopposed for Cornwallis, but now, four years later, no less than five candidates came forward to contest the seat, though three of them would decline before the polling began. Among the farming class, there was a prevailing feeling that Cornwallis, "the Garden and Pride of Nova Scotia," was disgracing itself by continually choosing its representatives from a less important occupation than agriculture.[16] Not since John Morton's father, Lemuel, had won in 1806 had the township been represented by a farmer. In 1840, the battle was between two farmers, Augustus Tupper and Mayhew Beckwith. Beckwith had little difficulty defeating his opponent 291 to 176 votes; the weight and interest of the more populous and wealthy eastern district proved too much for Tupper to overcome. This was also true for the Horton election, in which Perez Benjamin went down to defeat by his opponent of the previous election, William Johnson.

The most interesting contest was for the county in which both Chipman and DeWolf re-offered; they were challenged by Joseph Crane and two lawyers, John Clarke Hall and John Whidden. The latter had married into the Chipman clan and he and Samuel Chipman were first cousins. The unpopularity of lawyers was such that Whidden's friends found it necessary to state that he received an income from landed property in the township to the amount of £90 a year, and had not made use of incessant solicitations for offices; the real point at issue was that he had been resident for some years in Halifax and was clerk of the Assembly. As far as solicitations for offices were concerned, as a personal and political friend of Howe, he would shortly receive on Howe's recommendation the deputy provincial secretaryship at £700 a year and the probate judgeship for Halifax County.[17] He likely only ran as a foil to Chipman's candidacy to draw off second votes that might have gone to DeWolf, Crane or Hall. If this was the strategy, it failed miserably; he obtained an insignificant 34 votes before resigning on the second day of the poll at Kentville. The election was not decided until the Aylesford poll, where DeWolf and Chipman easily triumphed.

As the Reformers increased their attacks on the funding of sectarian colleges, Chipman, whose nephew was an Acadia College professor, found himself in a most difficult dilemma. If he continued to support grants for Acadia and the other colleges while his fellow Reformers were opposed, inexorably he would become drawn into the emerging Tory/Baptist alliance that Attorney General J.W. Johnston was calling into being. His moment of decision came during the 1843 session in the heated debate on sectarian colleges, and its denouement at one-thirty in the morning of 28 March, when Howe proposed adjournment to avoid the passage of a resolution in support of sectarian colleges. Taking his cousin Samuel Bishop Chipman of Annapolis with him, Chipman went over to the side of his fellow

Reformers and ensured that Howe's motion passed by one vote. As an editorial in the Baptist *Christian Messenger* later lamented: "Had Messrs S.B. Chipman, S. Chipman ... fulfilled their oft repeated professions of friendship towards the Baptists and their institutions [Acadia College and its associated academy], nay had only one of them done so, even this small success would have been denied the party aiming at their ruin ...."[18] Chipman had succumbed to ties of friendship and political beliefs that on other issues bound him to the Reform cause. His decision to withdraw his support for further public funding for Acadia laid the seeds for his defeat in the forthcoming election.

When Governor Lord Falkland issued the writs at the end of October 1843 for an election, all the sitting members for Kings re-offered. Beckwith found himself opposed once again by Augustus Tupper, and Johnston similarly by Perez Benjamin. For the county, only John Clarke Hall appeared to be a candidate for one of the two seats against DeWolf and Chipman. The battle was now between parties rather than individual candidates. The supporters of Acadia fully realized that if Attorney General J. W. Johnston and his Tories won the most seats, public funding for the institution was assured. By no means were even the Baptists in the county united over Acadia. Soon after the election was called, an Educational Meeting was held at the Second Baptist Church of Cornwallis, located at Pleasant Valley in the western part of the township. Its minister was the Reverend William Chipman, brother of Samuel, and whose son Isaac was a professor at Acadia. The Chipmans, however, were badly divided over the issue, with Robert Chipman and the merchant William Henry Chipman speaking in opposition to funding. The former spoke of the "machinations of the Sectarian priesthood, the utter recklessness and selfishness of their designs." This cannot have endeared him to his relation, the Reverend William, who seconded resolutions supporting endowment of a plurality of colleges. Plurality was the correct word, for the good reverend wanted a college separate from Acadia for the Calvinistic Baptists. At Pleasant Valley, the Baptists present were not to be swayed from their opposition to collegiate funding. Most of them were first generation settlers in the western part of the township and were far more concerned with having common schools than a college. With near unanimity, they passed a resolution that the "endowment of Colleges out of the Provincial Treasury is unjust in principle, and an encroachment upon the privileges of the people."[19]

The friends of Acadia were determined to unseat Chipman. They exploited with effect the increasingly angry opposition to the entrenched influence of his family. Even before the 1843 session had ended, a letter appeared in the Halifax *Times* berating the Chipmans, sarcastically noting: "We now hold in the family almost all the offices of the county ... and furthermore claim them as a right ...." A later letter by Nimrod (presumably from Genesis 10: 8-9, "a mighty hunter before the Lord") set the tone for the election. He said that Chipman would be supported "by the Old Family Compact influence as heretofore," while referring to the fact that Samuel Chipman's nephew, William Henry Chipman, held the appointments of registrar of probate, clerk of the sessions and a number of other offices, as well as being agent in the county for the *Novascotian*. William Henry Chipman was also a merchant with extensive land holdings. Nimrod reported him as saying that he was "willing to sacrifice the blood, sinew, bones and muscles of three Horses before Uncle Sam [Chipman] shall lose."

Nimrod called another of the family the "smuggling magistrate," who had boasted that his "Ledger shall go the whole Hog."[20] The ledger influence of the family must have been extensive. At his death in 1846 William Allen Chipman alone had 223 debtors on his books.[21] The cry "old Sam must go" had behind it the full weight of the Tory/Baptist alliance. It proved too much; Chipman resigned when the poll stood at 298 for himself, nearly 100 votes behind Hall, with DeWolf far ahead with 629. The Kings County conservatives saw the defeat of Chipman and the overwhelming victory of the two Tories, DeWolf and Hall, as "retributive justice." DeWolf was especially praised for his "heroic and ... unflinching integrity," which had marked his "proud but solitary career in the perilous times of old Sir Colin [Campbell], marred and blotted with the foul scum and filthy slaver of the serpent-tongue of the Herod Joe [Howe]."[22]

The first day of polling for the Cornwallis Township election ended with Beckwith just one vote ahead of Augustus Tupper, but then on the second day Beckwith's strength told and Tupper resigned. The election for Horton was far more of a contentious affair, lasting five days before Benjamin emerged the winner by eight votes. William Johnson successfully protested the result to the floor of the House. The resulting by-election was held in March. It was after the House was well into the 1844 session, and Howe, J.B. Uniacke and James McNab had resigned from the Executive Council in protest at the appointment of Attorney General Johnston's brother-in-law,

Mather Byles Almon, to the Executive Council. Both parties rightly saw the by-election as a test of public opinion on the appointment. The whole influence of government was thrown into the contest, with a lavish expenditure of money.

The friends of Acadia needed no encouragement to enter the fray; Benjamin's opposition to public funding for Acadia made him an anathema to them. In the previous election, the Kentville merchant Daniel Moore had made an arrangement with Benjamin's supporters that he would not use his ledger influence for Johnson, if they would not oppose his friend, John Clarke Hall, in the county election; now Moore threw "the weight of his Ledger to assist Johnson." People living in Halifax, and as far away as Saint John, who had any semblance to the ownership of property in the township were brought in by the Tories, who also transferred shares held in the new Kentville Hotel to create instant freeholders. Tories were not alone, however, in creating voters, for the liberals of Horton in the end seemed to have been as good at it as their political enemies.[23] In the three days of polling, Benjamin's lead never went below 13 votes. When the poll closed, he was ahead with 200 to Johnson's 180 votes.

In triumph, Benjamin progressed to Halifax to resume his seat in the Assembly: at Windsor he was greeted by a "multitude of the inhabitants"; at Mount Uniacke, Crofton Uniacke rang the great bell to summon his domestics and labourers to give three cheers as Benjamin passed; Three Mile House outside the city was brilliantly illuminated in his honour; and once in Halifax he was greeted by hundreds and carried around the city on a specially erected platform, including a stop outside Attorney General J.W. Johnston's residence where "the air was again rent with cheers." Next day the reporter for the *Novascotian* wrote lyrically that "As Mr. Benjamin's hair is perfectly white, and as he was elevated high above the hundreds around him, he seemed like 'some tall cliff, with its summit covered with snow.' "[24]

On any issue of constitutional import, the Kings members now voted along straight party lines, with DeWolf, Beckwith and Hall upholding Johnston's government and Benjamin voting with the Reformers. In the sessions leading up to the 1847 election, Hall, the first lawyer to be elected for a Kings County constituency since John Chipman in 1776, intervened in debates fairly often; like most of the King's College graduates who entered the Assembly, he was trained to think and speak well on his feet, though also like his contemporaries at inordinate length. The *Novascotian* paid him the compliment, exceptional in the case of a Tory, of taking up its complete front page, as well as most of the second, with Hall's address in answer to the Governor's speech opening the 1844 session. It was a well-constructed speech, replete with the usual references to English constitutional history.

What is interesting in the address was Hall's full acceptance of party government. The past four years had abundantly proved, Hall declared, that a "Coalition Government is at variance with that high, honourable independent action which commands respect, and that discordant amalgamation of opposing sentiments and views of high Tory and Liberal, can only be produced by sacrifices of principles ... and the destruction or perversion of the people's rights." No Reformer could have said it better. When he launched into his attack on Howe's recent resignation from the Executive Council on Mather Byles Almon's appointment, he was at his best: "we have seen him [Howe] with ... distended cheek, raised arm, denouncing all those whose bosoms he would so fondly have clasped ... we have seen him presiding, the high priest as it were, at the altar of liberty, as he states, aye, of democracy, and having immolated his ... victims, endeavoring by his charms to wile all others into the vortex of his ambition."[25] So little was thought of Beckwith's intellectual abilities, however, that the *Novascotian* could with impunity lampoon him as a simpleton: it had him introducing a bill relating to stray cattle and had J.B. Uniacke ask Beckwith if donkeys were included, with Beckwith replying he was not prepared to say, as "It contained so many dictionary words that he hardly knew what was in it."[26]

When it finally came time for the election on 5 August 1847, which would decide the issue of responsible government, it was, compared to the previous election, an anti-climactic event in Kings County. DeWolf decided not to run again for the county; his Tory replacement was Daniel Moore, with Samuel Chipman upholding the liberal cause. Hall and Moore won fairly easily. There was more of a battle for Cornwallis, where Beckwith defeated his liberal opponent, Andrew Starrit, by 326 to 315 votes. For Horton, Benjamin did not re-offer, probably because of illness. His replacement was the best-known physician in the county, Dr. Edward Brown, and his popularity carried the day for the liberals. But he was the single Reformer from the county, for the remaining seats had gone to the Tories. Thus Kings County had sent three conservatives and one liberal to the Eighteenth Assembly, which ushered in full responsible government.

In voting for the conservatives in the 1843 and 1847 elections, Kings County had in the process given the Chipman family compact its most severe drubbing at the hustings. Among the local family compacts in the various townships and counties around the province, the Chipmans had the distinction of being the longest surviving, and the one which had been able to exercise the most extensive influence. The Chipmans were also unique among the local compacts in their consistent adherence to the cause of constitutional reform. At the same time, the family had adroitly managed for well over half a century to ensure that it retained a firm hold over nearly all the offices within Cornwallis Township and a good share of those for Kings County.

When Samuel Chipman, however, chose to stand with his fellow Reformers in opposition to further funding for sectarian colleges, he sealed his political fate. The Tory/Baptist alliance seized the opportunity to exploit the ill-feeling towards the family, while drawing to the conservative cause supporters of Acadia College. In all likelihood, if Samuel Chipman had remained a supporter for further funding for Acadia, he could have taken one of two county seats in both the 1843 and 1847 elections. But he would have had to do so as a Tory. This he was clearly not prepared to do.

In Defence of the Gypsum Trade

There is an old maxim that Hercules is known by his foot, and why cannot a man's political principles be known by the company he keeps? When we see a man the companion of Presidents and Vice-Presidents of Colleges, Judges, and Hon. delegates of the Legislative Council, we must take it for granted that man is an enemy to every reform (although he would fain try to make us believe otherwise) and is not to be trusted with our rights.

Letter to the Freeholders of Falmouth, *Acadian Recorder,*
14 November 1843, by a FREEHOLDER

The townships of Falmouth, Newport and Windsor were part of Kings County until 1782, when it was divided and Hants County established. In fact, its creation resulted in the first known contested election in the county when, in 1785, the Windsor merchant Benjamin DeWolf and Winkworth Tonge defeated the Newport farmer George Brightman. But this election was an exception to a general pattern of uncontested elections. In the case of Falmouth, for example, Jeremiah Northup was first elected in 1775, and did not have to face an opponent until 1806. Northup was extremely proud that he had enough wool and flax from his farm to clothe his entire family, servants and slaves in homespun. He would appear thus attired for the sessions. At Government House on one occasion, a Governor accosted him for not wearing proper evening clothes, remarking: "Mr. Northup, I presume you are one of the smartest men from your district"; to which Northup replied, "No Your Excellency, I am only the best dressed one."[27]

For the 1793 election the county seats were again contested. Hector MacLean, a Loyalist and the former adjutant of the 84th Regiment of Foot, led the poll. William Cottnam Tonge took the second seat. In the first session of the new Assembly, there was nothing to suggest other than harmony in relations between Governor Sir John Wentworth and the Assembly. But by the last session six years later in 1799, the early amicability was replaced by such divisiveness that a country or opposition party was called into being, with William Cottnam Tonge its unofficial leader. Tonge had inherited from his father a heavily indebted estate near Windsor, along with the appointment of naval officer. This was the official most responsible for the enforcement of the trade laws; his fees were envied by some and detested by most. In 1845, (presumably) Howe in the *Novascotian* wrote of Tonge:

> ... he was a very remarkable man with a strange combination of physical advantages and courtly fascination of manner, a fine eye and expressive features lit up by a mind stored with legal, political, and elegant literature, he made his way at the Bar, and in the Senate, with distinguished success. As a popular orator ... he had, in his day, no equal; when his arguments failed, he carried his hearers away by the charms of his manner, and a bold and captivating address.[28]

Tonge's education, family connections, Anglicanism and position as the holder of an important imperial office should have made him a natural member of the governing oligarchy. That he did not become so, or more correctly Governor Sir John Wentworth ensured that he didn't, became the most compelling drama of Nova Scotian politics during Wentworth's Governorship. It was Tonge's inherited indebtedness that caused him to approach Wentworth in 1796 for an appointment as a revenue collector, only to be summarily rebuffed. What precipitated an irreparable break between them was Wentworth's promotion of John McMonagle, the member for Windsor, to the colonelship of the 1st Battalion of Hants Militia over the head of the more senior Tonge. Tonge became Wentworth's fiercest and most unrelenting opponent. In the remaining twelve years of his governorship, Wentworth was to write nineteen confidential despatches accusing Tonge and his party of creating "disaffection" among the people, of making "revolutionary schemes," causing "delays" in the Assembly and embarrassment in the conduct of the public business, and being responsible for "agitated" elections by his "improper zeal and animosity."[29]

When the 1799 session commenced, the expectation was that the province would proceed with the construction of a building for the accommodation of the Assembly. But by the end of the session, the Assembly had abandoned this plan and approved a new residence for Wentworth. This was due to Tonge's botched attempt to trade off a government house, which Wentworth wanted, for the Council's consent to increased road expenditures wanted by the country members. When faced with the Council's outright refusal to agree to increased road appropriations, an embittered Tonge tried to have the Assembly reverse its approval for a government house, but lost the motion by two votes. Once the 1799 session was over, both parties prepared for an election in which the chief battleground would be Halifax County. As we have already seen, Tonge ran in Halifax County as part of the country party's strategy, though knowing he had no freehold in the county. He also stood for Newport Township, where he was assured of election. This decision occasioned a shuffling of candidates for the Hants seats, though none was contested. The result was the unanimous election of Northup for Falmouth, Tonge for Newport, George Monk for Windsor, and Shubael Dimock and John McMonagle for the county.

Tonge's overwhelming victory in the Halifax County poll made him the most popular member in the House. Later generations would call him the First Tribune of Nova Scotia. But this popularity could not be translated into a consistent majority for the county party, which remained with a core of under a dozen members. Of the other Hants County representatives, only Dimock could be described as a country party adherent. But Tonge and Dimock found themselves on opposite sides when the Assembly moved to prevent smuggling in the Bay of Fundy by granting £1,000 for the purchase of two revenue cutters, plus £100 for Tonge as naval officer to employ two deputies. This attempt to deal with smuggling and the resulting loss of revenue to the treasury was directed principally against the illicit trade in exchanging gypsum for American flour and other goods, which were then smuggled into the province.

Soil exhaustion had led to the use of gypsum as an unexcelled calcium fertilizer for the production of grain, the main export of the middle and southern American states. In the first decade of the nineteenth century, American imports of gypsum, valued in pounds sterling, were worth more than all other importations from British North America combined.[30] The gypsum came largely from small mining operations scattered around the Bay of Fundy, but especially from the Minas Basin area. To the supposed neglect of their farms, twice a year Hants County farmers carried in their small vessels cargoes of gypsum to the, as yet, undemarcated international boundary, or the "line," as it was called, in Passamaquoddy Bay off New Brunswick. There the gypsum would be exchanged for American agricultural products, without much fear of interference from customs officials. No doubt many of Dimock's friends and relatives were too engaged in the business for him to do otherwise than oppose the bill. Tonge was also involved in the trade, but in his capacity as naval officer he stood to gain more from the increase of fees. The fact that both the vessels and the deputies were to be under Tonge's control, and that he had "zealously" forwarded the measure in the House, were sufficient reasons in themselves to cause the Council with Wentworth's full approbation to veto the measure directed against the illicit gypsum trade.

For the 1806 election, Tonge decided to run with Dimock for one of the county seats, presumably to force McMonagle out of the House; the tactic was successful. When the Assembly reconvened in late 1806, Lewis Morris Wilkins opposed Tonge for the Speakership. There was some confusion during the taking of the vote, but Tonge won by a single vote. Wentworth saw his opportunity. When Tonge was presented for his approval, Wentworth declared to the astonished members, "Gentlemen, I do not approve of your choice," and desired that they return and elect another. The House tamely accepted this constitutional affront and elected Wilkins in place of Tonge. Wentworth had correctly sensed that Tonge was no longer the popular tribune he had once been. Tonge's dramatic fall from popular favour was related, at least in some measure, to his personal conduct. Forty years later in the *Novascotian* (quoted earlier), Howe commented that if Tonge's "prudence and moral principles" had been equal to his talents he might have prevailed, but he had not been able to refuse his glass and had yielded to "fashionable follies and plunged into the dissipation of the period."

Two months later Wentworth acted again, summarily suspending Tonge as naval officer and removing at one stroke his chief source of livelihood. Tonge gained some revenge. He was one of the first to know of the landing of Major General Sir George Prevost in early 1808, sent out to replace the aging Wentworth. Tonge immediately galloped out to Prince's Lodge where Wentworth was staying, so he could have the pleasure of announcing the arrival of the new Governor to an astounded and mortified Wentworth.

Prevost had arrived with instructions to find Tonge another office and to request the Assembly to vote a pension for Wentworth. It was the recently elected member for Windsor Township, William Otis Haliburton, who moved that a complimentary address be presented to Wentworth on his retirement. After one was prepared, with a laudatory recitation of provincial progress during Wentworth's administration, Tonge unsuccessfully tried to have inserted a phrase "although in no respect owing to acts of your Excellency." This proved to be the last clash between the two. When Prevost left to campaign in the West Indies, he took a dispirited Tonge with him as deputy commissary and there Tonge died sometime in the 1820s.

With Tonge's departure to the West Indies, William Otis Haliburton became the leading Hants member. He had learned his law in the office of the ill-fated Jonathan Sterns. Like his contemporary Thomas Ritchie of Annapolis, Haliburton became a respected country lawyer in a county shiretown, for whom entering the Assembly was a natural extension of his prominence within the community. For the 1811 election, Haliburton chose to run for the county. It was an example of one of those shifts by ambitious politicians from a township to a county constituency, occasioned by the fact that the latter carried more influence and significantly greater control over the division of road moneys. He and Dimock were easy victors.

The main preoccupation of the five Hants members in the new Assembly was to thwart the renewed determination of the majority to reduce the massive amount of smuggling inherent in the gypsum trade, with consequent loss in duties to the provincial treasury. A concerted attempt began in 1814 with a ten-shilling duty per ton, but the measure was fortuitously killed by the Council. In the following year, a bill was got through designed to prevent the contraband trade at the "line" in Passamaquoddy Bay. An even more zealous minority nearly managed to have the act amended to impose a draconian punishment on ship masters; those found guilty of smuggling were to lose their right to command for life. But as the Benjamin DeWolfs, father and son, forcefully pointed out in a petition tabled at the beginning of the 1818 session, before the passing of the 1816 act many hundreds in Hants County had been employed in 150 vessels. Moreover, the yearly exports had totalled 50,000 tons, with an estimated return of £75,000 in much-needed specie. In fact, the trade had been little curtailed and the Assembly bowed to the inevitable and repealed the act. The trade rapidly reverted to its previous pattern and the smuggling continued unchecked.

The Hants members found themselves an embattled minority again when, in an address to the Prince Regent, the majority protested against the 1818 Convention with the United States. This Convention between Britain and the United States re-opened British North American waters to American fishermen and consequently large scale smuggling. This had drawn forth the wrath of mercantile Halifax, which was behind the address to the Prince Regent. The Hants members, however, saw the Convention as no threat to the county's economic interests. On the contrary, it made all the easier the exchange of gypsum for American goods. When approval for the address came to a vote, all five Hants members opposed it; they were joined by just four others. Partly as a palliative, the British government made Halifax a free port, with the object of drawing American foodstuffs and other products to Halifax, where they could be combined with local cargoes, for re-export in British shipping to the West Indies. The Free Port Act, ironically, had the effect of giving further incentive, if any was needed, to smuggling throughout the Fundy littoral, for the only legal way to obtain American goods was to go to Halifax, purchase, pay the duties and return on the long coastal voyage to the Bay of Fundy. Thus, legally imported American goods at Halifax could not hope to compete with those smuggled. Dimock aptly, and with not a little touch of sarcasm, summed up the matter for the benefit of his colleagues in the House, when he remarked that "if the Free Port Act bears hard upon the merchants of Halifax, he did not pity them; they brought it upon themselves."[31]

When it came to Halifax, Dimock was at his scathing best. When he learned that the proposed Central Board of Agriculture, which he saw simply as a Halifax idea, had already spent £100 on agricultural books, he was livid. From experience, he knew that the "knowledge of farming could never be obtained from books: that kind of theory would never succeed in Nova Scotia." Although no one had a greater desire to encourage agriculture than he, Dimock was emphatic: he could never give his assent to a "vote of money for the town of Halifax," for the people of that town "were too profuse in spending money to have the distribution of provincial money entrusted to them."[32] Yet, frugal as Dimock certainly was, like so many of his contemporaries, he had his share of debts. He borrowed freely from S.B. Robie. He owed the Windsor merchant and former member, Benjamin DeWolf, the substantial sum of £356, though he was just one among the nearly four hundred in debt to DeWolf on his death in 1819, for the princely sum of £43,384. A vignette from Lord Dalhousie's Journal captures Dimock's sturdy countryman's character. When the somewhat pompous Earl visited him at his home, Dimock greeted him "without coat or waistcoat, just in the dress of a labouring man."[33]

Dimock was defeated in the 1820 election, though this was not related to his performance in the last Assembly; in fact, he was largely the author of it. At the Newport election, which was held first, he declared that he would not be a candidate. Then, after the county polling began, he changed his mind and went up against Haliburton and a newcomer, William O'Brien. "Squire Billy" O'Brien, of Ulster Presbyterian stock, was the grandson of the first settler of the Noel Shore. In the belief that Dimock would not be a candidate, many freeholders from Newport did not come to the hustings. The result was that Dimock ran a poor third and declined on the third day. Another factor in his defeat was the alliance between Haliburton and O'Brien to squeeze out Dimock. Their strategy lay in having Haliburton's Windsor supporters vote also for O'Brien, and those of O'Brien give their second choice to Haliburton. O'Brien's election signalled that the increasingly populous townships of Rawdon and Douglas were going to demand that henceforth a native son have one of the two county seats.

In the last two assemblies, the Hants members had found themselves as a distinct minority fighting to protect the county's economic interests. In the first session after the 1820 election, they became the leaders of a majority determined to deal with the high customs fees being charged, particularly on coastal trading. The issue had come before the House in the last session before the election, when two petitions (one was from Windsor) were received, both complaining of the high fees being taken by customs officers. Customs officers were not paid salaries, but received their income from a portion of the duties they collected. William Fraser became chairman of the committee selected to report on the petitions. First elected for Windsor Township in 1818, Fraser had established a legal practice in Windsor after graduating from King's College and probably studying in Haliburton's office. The report of his committee detailed the evils existing in the outports. Windsor was cited as an example; the deputy collector there had taken upwards of £3,000 in fees from 1816 to 1819, but the duties turned over to the treasury after he had deducted his fees had come to just eighteen shillings and ten pence.

Early in the first session of the new Assembly, with the galleries packed, Fraser introduced a resolution challenging the constitutionality of some of the fees being charged, holding that only the Assembly could impose such taxes. According to the correspondent for the *Acadian Recorder,* Fraser gave a "luminous and able speech" in support of his resolution. Fraser then moved for the establishment of a committee to bring in a bill setting forth the fees for the coastal trade, and to draft the appropriate address to the Lieutenant Governor. With Fraser, Haliburton and William Mayhew Young of Falmouth (the largest shipowner in that township) on both committees, the Hants members formed the majority on the first, and were three out of seven on the second. They were instrumental in the House approving an address laying out the constitutional arguments for the Assembly's case. Governor Sir James Kempt sent the address to London, where it reinforced the growing movement for the freeing of colonial trade. In 1825, the British government initiated a major reform of the imperial customs service, including the elimination of fees and the introduction of salaries. With the matter of the customs fees behind him, Fraser intervened with effect in the debate over the incorporation of banks, sharing with Haliburton a vehement opposition to any chartered monopolistic bank. In Fraser's view such an institution would be a "hydra-headed monster"; it would give Halifax's moneyed interests "a dangerous" and "overwhelming preponderance" within the Legislature. Even worse, it would expand the scope of ledger influence, by allowing Halifax creditors "to lay their paws upon every freeholder in the country." Fraser could not have been more blunt nor more prescient.[34]

Early in the 1824 session, S.G.W. Archibald began his manoeuvrings to create more judges to feed the "hungry profession." Initially, Haliburton reacted unfavourably to the idea. Then he did a volte face, spuriously denying that lawyers were "capable of being biased in

View of the Front Street of Windsor
Drawn and engraved by C. W. Torbett for *An Historical and Statistical Account of Nova Scotia*, Halifax 1829.

favour of their own interests."[35] After serving eighteen years in the Assembly, and having reached the respectable age of fifty-seven years, Haliburton deserved one of the three judgeships now to be handed out, however presumptuous his argument for finally supporting Archibald's bill. A man very much of his time, Haliburton was philosophically a conservative, but generally liberal in the particular: equality for Dissenters in the matter of marriage licences; the admission of Laurence Kavanagh to a seat in the House without having to swear the state oaths so offensive to Catholics; his support for grants to Pictou Academy, though he really never approved of the idea; and the expansion of the common school system, including compulsory assessment. Like his friend Thomas Ritchie of Annapolis, Haliburton, as a country member and lawyer, personified the better qualities of both endeavours, well able to defend and forward the interests of his constituents, while never losing sight of an enlarged sense of the public good or of the provincial interest.

Haliburton's elevation to the bench brought to the fore the increasing friction between the older established townships and the far more populous newly-settled eastern parts of Hants County. In the resulting by-election, the Windsor merchant Benjamin DeWolf defeated, by 124 votes, Richard Smith of Douglas. Almost certainly the poll remained in Windsor. In 1826 the question of eastern representation was still to the fore, pitting the Windsor residents Benjamin DeWolf and John MacKay against Squire Billy O'Brien of the Noel Shore. Again the poll was not moved out of the town, and O'Brien had little choice but to withdraw early. MacKay died before the House met, and a by-election was immediately called. The older townships now grudgingly accepted that one member for the county would come from the western section and the second would have to be from the eastern. As Benjamin DeWolf of Windsor already held one seat, the fight for the other sent Squire Billy up against Richard Smith.

O'Brien became the clear choice of electors from Windsor, Falmouth and Newport. He had also the support of all but one of the magistrates who voted, as well as the parade of Windsor respectability who followed suit. On the completion of the polling at the Windsor courthouse, O'Brien was ahead with 343 to Smith's 311 votes. The poll was moved to Douglas for the first time, and the freeholders of Rawdon and Douglas Townships swung the election to Smith by eight votes. Squire Billy objected to nearly every one of these votes for Smith. He claimed Smith had brought to the hustings voters without even the "colour of qualification" and had created a "violent party," while deceiving weak and ignorant persons during the "heat and intemperance usual at Elections." The Assembly dismissed O'Brien's petition without even a recorded vote. However, this was not to be the end of the matter. O'Brien hauled Smith before a special jury to be charged with bribing a freeholder by giving his wife a twenty-shilling note. Smith claimed it was for travelling expenses! He was tried and found guilty under the English statute for bribery at elections, the penalty for which was a fine of £500 sterling. This was an immense sum and Smith petitioned the Supreme Court as to whether such a penalty was in force in Nova Scotia. As late as 1832, the court had not rendered a decision and probably never did. Likely Smith never paid a penny of the fine.[36] The rivalry between the Smiths and the O'Briens became a constant and disruptive factor in Hants County politics for the next twenty years.

Elsewhere in the province, the constitutional confrontation between the Assembly and the Council of Twelve over a four-pence tax on brandy was at least a recognizable factor in the 1830 election. In Hants, local concerns entirely prevailed. Only William Henry Shey for Falmouth was returned without opposition. After his defeat in 1820, Dimock had been re-elected in 1826 for Newport. But at seventy-eight he had at last decided not to be a candidate again. He had served for thirty sessions as one of the most respected members of his day. In the traditional and best sense of the word, Dimock represented, in his personal and public conduct, the virtues associated with the yeoman farmer, independent in means and spirit, self-reliant, utterly disdainful of the town and its ways, and a firm believer in frugality when it came to the public purse. To succeed Dimock, Daniel Wier offered and was opposed by Felix Cochran. Their families were closely related. Felix's mother was a Wier, but this did not restrain Felix's father, Terence, as county sheriff from using every possible stratagem to ensure the victory of his son. First, he chose an inconvenient day for the election, giving Wier little time to canvass. He then arranged for the hustings to be set up in his own house, where he also conveniently kept a tavern, and for his son John to preside as deputy sheriff. On election day, the Cochrans kept many of Wier's voters away; just 77 were able to vote, and of these 51 gave their vote to Cochran.

For the first time in the history of Hants County elections, a non-resident, William Blowers Bliss, became a candidate. The son of a former Loyalist Chief Justice of New Brunswick, Bliss had graduated from King's College at Windsor in 1813 and from there had gone to London to study law at the Inner Temple. As a close family friend and childless, Chief Justice S.S. Blowers all but legally adopted young Bliss. Bliss was finding it exceedingly difficult to make a good living; in one term of the sitting of the Supreme Court he made two pounds. Both he and his father-in-law (Bliss had married Blowers' adopted daughter) well understood the relationship between place and practice—or as Bliss so cogently stated it in some desperation to his brother: "I should care less for place if I could get practice without it."[37] But both Bliss and Blowers knew there was little chance of place unless Bliss had first served in the Assembly. He now stood for one of the two county seats. Benjamin DeWolf re-offered, but Richard Smith declined to run again because he could not stand the expense of another contest. Squire Billy O'Brien once more came forward. Bliss led the poll with 405, followed by DeWolf with 372 votes and last as usual was O'Brien. Bliss, or more accurately Blowers, was believed to have spent close to £500 to gain the seat. No wonder Smith had declined when he heard Bliss would run.

To find a seat for another aspiring lawyer and Loyalist scion was the reason that David Dill found himself in a contest for Windsor Township. In his case, it was Lewis Morris Wilkins, grandson of the Shelburne Loyalist Isaac Wilkins. Young Wilkins was another graduate of King's College, where he had gained a reputation for a violent temper, having on one occasion attacked his roommate,

Thomas Chandler Haliburton, with a poker.[38] He had studied law with William Fraser in Windsor, and in marrying Sarah Rachael Thomas, reputedly the most beautiful woman in the province, he had married into the Windsor branch of the DeWolf clan. The election lasted three days. When Deputy Sheriff John Cochran closed the poll, Dill had a majority of one vote. The select committee that investigated the election came to the conclusion that the vote should have been tied, and the Assembly called for a new election. However, Dill had left on a voyage to Grenada and any election was postponed until, by 1833, it was accepted that he had been lost at sea. His brother, Joseph, decided now to do battle with Wilkins. A furious contest ensued over five days of polling. It ended in a tied vote, when Sheriff Charles Wilkins (brother of Lewis) closed the poll in the belief that according to the law the writ had to be in Halifax next day.

The House upheld Sheriff Charles Wilkins' decision and, moreover, determined that Lewis Morris Wilkins had the majority of votes and gave the election to him. This was notwithstanding the most "inflammatory" behaviour by his father, the former Speaker of the Assembly and now a judge of the Supreme Court. Judge Lewis Morris Wilkins Sr. appeared every day at the hustings to canvass votes for his son. On one occasion, when a freeholder was about to take the oath that he was eligible, the learned judge threatened to have the man indicted for perjury, informing him that when he came to trial, he, the judge, "would take care to be on the Bench."[39] Once in the Assembly, Wilkins' performance did not impress John Young, who in the *Acadian Recorder* portrayed Wilkins as "one of those living examples, who can harangue but not convince, can address the ear or the eye, but not the understanding."[40] Both Wilkins and Bliss could look forward to judicial promotions equal to their expectations. Bliss' came first, and unusually soon. The now quite deaf ninety-year-old Blowers, as a condition of his retirement from the Chief Justiceship, insisted that Bliss receive a judgeship on the first vacancy. The unexpected death of Richard John Uniacke Jr. in February 1834 created the necessary opening on the bench. Two months later Bliss was promoted in his place.

Bliss was fortunate. He might well have lost his seat in the 1836 election. There was as much discontent in Hants County as in neighbouring Kings, over the devastating consequences of the sudden and rapid depreciation of the provincial currency. Editorials written by E.K. Allen in the *Hants & Kings Gazette* were fanning public anger at the sitting members. Allen especially singled out the "legislating lawyers," who "Vampyre-like prey upon the vitals of the Country, leaving the inhabitants thereof spiritless and degraded slaves: rendering liberty and respectability mere shadows." He challenged every Nova Scotian to have the independence to come forward to assert: "This is my own, my native land," and sign a petition for its relief from "the oppressors grasp." Meetings of freeholders to draft a petition may have been held in Newport, Windsor and Horton, but no such petition ever arrived at Halifax.[41]

What did arrive in Halifax were petitions calling for Windsor to be made a free port. In early 1834 Henry Goudge, a Windsor merchant heavily engaged in the gypsum trade, called a meeting to petition for Windsor to be made a free port. This would allow Goudge and his merchant friends to export gypsum and to return legally with American flour directly to Windsor, where they could pay the required duties on foreign imports. During the ensuing debate on free ports, Benjamin DeWolf told the House the Hants County gypsum trade yielded more than the fisheries of the whole province. If the people wanted flour in return for their gypsum, why should they be obliged to have their vessels enter at Halifax or Saint John to pay the import duties on their cargoes? His case for the Windsor shipowners was somewhat tarnished when, as the result of someone breaking into a barn and stealing some goods, it became publicly known that the stolen goods had been smuggled. The *Acadian* at Halifax chortled that "The Windsor gents, it appears, are quite indignant at being told the truth, that they Smuggle. Bless the innocent bodies !!! To be serious, 'out of their own mouths are they condemned.' " The newspaper went on to ask rhetorically how long it had been since any of the merchants in the trade had been charged with smuggling.[42]

In the 1836 election every seat was contested. Goudge became a candidate and his entry created the contest for the two county seats. Squire Billy O'Brien, who had succeeded William Blowers Bliss in a by-election, re-offered. A Newport farmer, George MacKay, became a candidate as did Benjamin Smith, a brother of Richard, against whom O'Brien had secured a conviction for election bribery in 1829. The poll stayed open at Windsor for three days. By the time it moved to Newport, Goudge led all the candidates by a substantial margin, Smith and MacKay were tied and O'Brien was well behind the field. But after the polls at Newport, Rawdon and finally Douglas, Smith was the leader overall with 609 votes, well over 100 ahead of Goudge in second place. The more heavily populated eastern part of the country had clearly made its weight felt. This result was also a commentary on the extensive influence that the family of Colonel William Smith, father of Richard and Benjamin, was able to exercise in the eastern townships. Religion too may have played a role in Smith's substantial majority, the largest so far, for O'Brien seems to have been accused of criticizing the Church of England. The Smiths were Anglican and in Hants County this faith was the second largest, after the Presbyterians. If Anglicans had united behind one of their own against O'Brien, this would explain in part the magnitude of Smith's victory.

The Falmouth seat went to John Elder, a land surveyor and builder of the Avon Bridge. The Windsor election was a replay of the 1833 by-election, with Lewis Morris Wilkins defeating Joseph Dill. For Newport, James Allison defeated Felix Cochran. Allison was married to John Elder's sister. There was also a similar relationship between the Allisons, Hugh Bell, the Halifax town member, and Winthrop Sargent, member for Shelburne County; Elder, Bell and Sargent had all married sisters of Allison. Moreover, Joseph Allison, wealthy Halifax merchant, a director of the Halifax Banking Company, and a member of the Council of Twelve, was their brother-in-law. Family connections reinforced a natural conservatism, as Elder, Sargent and Allison were consistently to oppose attempts to bring about reform, though Allison could occasionally be found voting with the majority of Reformers. Goudge and Smith, however, proved to be steady supporters for the cause of reform. Wilkins, not unexpectedly, led the fight against it. A reward for his efforts was not long in coming as he was among those appointed to the first Legislative Council in 1838.

His successor for Windsor was Richard McHeffey, whose family had come with the Allisons in 1769 from County Londonderry, Ireland, and settled in Falmouth; in fact, the Elder, McHeffey, Smith, O'Brien, Allison and Goudge families were all of Ulster stock. McHeffey and Goudge families were also linked, since Goudge had married McHeffey's sister. In the last session leading up to the 1840 election, the determined opposition of Goudge and McHeffey thwarted the expectations of Douglas and Rawdon freeholders that at last they would have their own representatives. It was not, there-fore, surprising that Goudge demurred running again for the county. Instead, he reached an arrangement with his brother-in-law, whereby McHeffey retired and Goudge went in unopposed for Windsor. This opened up the possibility for O'Brien to offer for the seventh time (it was to be the last), with better hope of success than previously. For the county Smith re-offered and, in a replay of 1836, he was joined on the hustings by George MacKay as well as O'Brien. Likely Goudge did what he could for O'Brien, for he led the poll at Windsor, but after it moved to Newport and Douglas, he fell steadily behind the other two. Far fewer voters had turned out in Windsor than in 1836, when one of their own, Goudge, was running. Old Squire Billy did not gain enough votes at the Windsor poll to offset the support given at Newport and Douglas to the alliance of Smith and MacKay.

Falmouth was now to have the most contested election in its history. Four candidates were nominated, including the Windsor lawyer William Bowman, whose candidacy brought forth the letter to the Freeholders of Falmouth quoted at the beginning of this section. The author believed that Falmouth could readily do without the services of a "Dumb Windsor lawyer." Bowman came last with 14 votes. Payzant, the winner, had 29 votes. Eighty-one freeholders had climbed the hustings, perhaps half of those who were eligible to vote. Rawdon and Douglas combined had around 650 heads of households as potential freeholders, but at best could hope to elect only one county representative. Matters were not much better at Newport, where 173 freeholders voted to choose between Allison and his challenger, Ichabod Dimock. The election lasted less than half a day, for when Allison found himself 15 votes behind he realized he could not catch his opponent. He stepped down from his seat on the hustings, requesting that the sheriff take his vote for Dimock; Dimock did the same for Allison and the sheriff declared Dimock the winner. The result was not unanticipated because Dimock was the eldest son of the former popular long-serving member; in addition, he was married to a daughter of Colonel William Smith and had the backing of that family.

As a Reformer, Dimock was in good company for Goudge, Payzant and MacKay were all of the same mind. Benjamin Smith believed in supporting the coalition government of Lord Falkland as a matter of principle. He considered it his duty to give his support to the government unless there was a grave or serious reason for opposing it. Goudge was to be in the new House for just one session before he tragically drowned when sailing his boat to his shipyard. In the succeeding by-election the seat went to the farmer Henry Palmer. Palmer was an Anglican as was Smith, with Payzant and Dimock both Baptists and MacKay a Presbyterian. This religious admixture consistently favoured grants to denominational colleges, except curiously Payzant. Payzant was absent for the crucial vote of 28 March 1843 on further funding. His absence may well have been deliberate to avoid the dilemma of either voting with the Tories or further offending his constituents in a township where Baptists predominated. If so, it was to do him no good for his fellow Baptist, Elkanah Young, doubled the vote on him for the Falmouth seat in the general election held later that autumn. So overwhelming was his defeat that on the second day of polling Payzant did not even appear at the hustings.

For the 1843 election, Lewis Morris Wilkins resigned from the Legislative Council to run for one of the county seats. In the past he had never shown the least sympathy for the cause of reform. In the debates over responsible government, he had been one of the chief Tory defenders of the old order. He was over six feet tall; on one occasion Howe had tauntingly called him "the stately bird of Hants." Wilkins now appeared on the husting in the guise of a "Howite" liberal. The most charitable explanation for Wilkins' apparent conversion to reform was that he was running as a supporter for the continuation of the coalition government of Lord Falkland, of which Howe was ostensibly still a member. In all likelihood, personal ambition and political opportunism, both of which traits he had in ample measure, caused him to believe that as a Howite liberal he would stand a better chance to be elected.[43] Benjamin Smith also seems to have posed as a Howite liberal. They need not have worried for they resurrected the old Windsor/Douglas alliance and had little difficulty in squeezing out MacKay. They had the full backing of the Baptists, Anglicans and Methodists. At the public meeting that had nominated Smith, and at which Wilkins' name had been put forward as a running mate, it was stated that any man who was liberal on the college question (meaning favourable to sectarian colleges) could succeed with Churchmen, Baptists and Methodists so united on the issue. How Wilkins and Smith reconciled their Howite liberalism with their support for denominational colleges remains unknown, though it does not seem to have been an issue for Hants freeholders.

Wilkins could have run for Windsor Township with the absolute certainty of election, but likely decided to leave the seat open for James DeWolf Fraser. Fraser came from an impeccable Tory background; his father was a former member of the Council of Twelve and a prominent Halifax merchant, and his mother one of the Windsor DeWolfs. He won without much difficulty. The lone Reformer from the county was Dimock, though he had to fight off a stiff challenge from the Newport shipowner, Nicholas Moser.

Once back in the House, Wilkins immediately reverted to his Toryism, calling Howe "essentially a low blackguard." In the recorded votes leading up to the 1847 election, the Hants members usually divided along party lines. The single important exception was when Fraser, though an Anglican, opposed the parish bill, which Dissenters feared Bishop John Inglis was trying to foist on them as a means of giving greater legislative force to the Church of England as the established church. Wilkins was furious, but the damage was done. Smith now grasped that responsible government would mean government by parties. No longer could individual assemblymen introduce money bills; only the executive branch could do so. For him nothing could be more "fatal to the interests of the country." In the autumn of 1844, Smith and Wilkins met Howe in open debate during Howe's tour of Hants County. According to the correspondent for the *Novascotian,* Smith had to defend his political conduct, having "ratted from the ranks of the liberals." When William Mayhew Young was invited to attend a Falmouth Township meeting organized by the liberals, with Howe to be in attendance, he replied: "as respects that gentleman's public conduct, I cannot conscientiously approve of it. A man whose Electors are principally the Roman Catholics of the Town of Halifax, and who is very probably well paid for agitating and disturbing this country, such a man is unworthy of the wise and good of this or any other country."[44]

Young would have been no match against Howe in open debate in a hall packed to the rafters with liberals. Although his disdain for Howe was no doubt his primary reason, Young knew that both Wilkins and Smith had been bested by Howe in other Hants County meetings. Howe's tour had placed the Hants Tories on the defensive as became clear once the 1847 election campaign began. At a public meeting in Newport, Wilkins was beside himself in trying to defend the parish bill, when faced with explaining away the adverse legal interpretation of his colleague Fraser, which had given such credence to Dissenter fears. Wilkins and Smith found themselves challenged for the two county seats by the Newport mariner William Card and John McDougall, a farmer and son of a former sergeant of the 84th Regiment. With simultaneous polling and near straight party voting, Card and McDougall triumphed. Nor did the Hants freeholders divide along sectional lines. Falmouth, for example, voted liberal in the county election and also in that of the township, with Young going down to defeat before the innkeeper James Sangster. Newport gave a slight edge to Wilkins and Smith, but Dimock was successful in the township election by the good margin of 40 votes. One of the O'Brien clan took on Fraser for Windsor, but it turned out to be a feeble challenge. Fraser was the single Tory to escape the debacle, a complete reversal of 1843, when Dimock had been the sole Reformer elected.

The Reformer triumph in Hants County was, however, an aberration. If the Tories had not been so embarrassed during the 1847 election by the parish bill, they might well have held onto both county seats. With around 1,100 voting, Smith and Wilkins had lost by just 40 votes. Four years later in the 1851 election, Benjamin Smith and Nicholas Moser recaptured fairly easily both county seats for the conservatives. Elkanah Young also recovered Falmouth for the Tories. James DeWolf Fraser once again took Windsor; on his death a year later, Wilkins succeeded him. Only Ichabod Dimock held onto Newport for the liberals.

In comparison to Kings County in particular, but also to the other neighbouring agricultural counties, Hants displayed greater diversity in the national origins of its inhabitants and in its geographical divisions. This diversity in turn was reflected in its religious make-up, with no one denomination predominating. But it was the importance of the gypsum trade to its economic well-being that most set it apart from the other agricultural counties, causing its members in the Assembly to vote against protection for agriculture, and for free trade with the United States. Nor elsewhere was there the equivalent of Windsor, where the presence of Halifax respectability could be more directly felt. The diversity accounts for the lesser influence in Hants of family compacts, like the Chipmans and DeWolfs with their ledgers, though that of old Colonel William Smith held unrivalled sway in Douglas and had tentacles into Newport. Although Hants freeholders elected their share of merchants, it was not merchants but lawyers, like W.H.O. Haliburton, and such yeomen farmers as Shubael Dimock, who became leading members in the Assembly and upholders of the county's interests.

Chapter 5

Planters, Acadians and Loyalists of Annapolis and Digby Counties

... Hants, King's, Annapolis being Agricultural Counties—the almost contiguity, by easy Water Carriage on the Bay of Fundy to St. John, in the sister Province of New Brunswick, affords them a most advantageous Market ... which it is the great interest of Halifax to discourage, in order she may monopolize by every possible means ... And there are now resident in the three Districts of the County of Halifax, seventeen of the forty-four Members of the Commons House of Assembly. From this it must appear, that in any measure not in accordance with the views of those in the Eastern interest, the contest by those in the Westward must be a fearful odds, in fact a failure the result.

Petition by the Loyal and Dutiful subjects of the Upper District of the County of Annapolis to King William IV, 30 March 1835.

As our traveller of 1830 journeyed along the Great West Road, passing from Kings into Annapolis County, he would have observed settlements made by both New England Planters and Loyalists. The most easterly of the Annapolis townships was Wilmot. Almost all of this township's 2,300 inhabitants lived on their farms, which were laid out on successive roads, running in parallel lines back from the post road to the base of the North Mountain. This regular pattern of farm divisions was the legacy of loyalist surveyors, the flatness of the terrain, and the lack of much land suitable for dyking. Although considerably less in population than neighbouring Annapolis and Granville Townships to the westward, and its settlement later by a generation, Wilmot had more acreage under cultivation than either.

In distinct contrast to Wilmot, Annapolis and Granville had large quantities of dyked salt marsh, and this had governed their settlement patterns. At the eastern end of Granville lay the aptly named Bridgetown. Here the post road crossed from the north side of the Annapolis River and continued through Annapolis Township to the county's shiretown of Annapolis Royal. Bridgetown had not been laid out until 1822, but had grown rapidly into the most prosperous town in the Annapolis River Valley. Its twenty-five houses, three churches, twelve stores, and three inns were noted for their neatness and well-painted exteriors, together conveying an appearance of comfort and thrift. From Bridgetown, Granville Township ran westwards along the north side of the Annapolis River to the Digby Gut. Other than Bridgetown and the small village of Granville Ferry, from which a ferry went across to Annapolis Royal, the township's population of 2,500 was distributed in family farms its full length of twenty-eight miles.

In Annapolis Township a similar pattern of occupation prevailed, with nearly the same number of inhabitants as in Granville, who were also located close to their dyked and intervale lands. Both townships were noted for their orchards. Although beautifully situated on the extremity of a peninsula jutting out into the river, the extensive government lands, a large common, and glebe enclosures had curtailed the growth of Annapolis Royal. Still, the town could show visitors a handsome courthouse, a recently built academy, two churches, some attractive private dwellings, and a suitable residence for the senior military officer. There were also garrison barracks, though the fortifications were in a ruinous state.

From Annapolis Royal there ran a regular steam packet to Saint John, for it was across the Bay of Fundy that the trade of the Annapolis Valley townships flowed, exchanging agricultural products and lumber for European manufactures and West Indian rum, molasses and brown sugar. The town was also the terminus for the two-day stage from Halifax. Beyond lay the Loyalist-settled townships of Clements and Digby. Clements had been laid out in a pattern of three successive roads, or lines, running parallel to the Annapolis Basin; along the first line disbanded German Hessian troops had settled, at the second were Waldeckers, and Loyalist civilians had taken up grants on the third. Most of the population of 1,600 engaged in the fishery; in the spring and summer the herring fishery, especially, gave employment to nearly every able-bodied male.

In Digby Township it was the mackerel fishery that would have drawn the traveller's attention. The locals would have described how it was managed on a share basis; merchants furnished the schooner, salt, provisions and fishing equipment and received half the catch. The mackerel were packed in barrels and shipped to Saint John for export, mainly to the West Indies. Although in the first years of settlement many Loyalists had left Digby, demoralized by their fate and discouraged by the hardships of clearing their lands, at the time of our traveller's visit, its population of over 3,600 had stabilized and was the largest of any of the Annapolis townships. Digby town itself had its own courthouse, a number of substantial private dwellings, and in Trinity Church a fine edifice. In the summer months, a steam packet ran regularly between Digby and Saint John.

The fishery was also the chief source of livelihood for the Acadians of Clare, the most westerly of the Annapolis townships. Our traveller would have found a warm welcome from the former French royalist priest, the eminent Abbé Sigogne, at his rectory (today a provincially registered heritage property). His first chapel Ste. Marie had burned in the terrible fire of 1820 that had destroyed nearly every building in the township, but a larger church had replaced it. The fecundity of the Acadians was such that over a thirty-year period the population had doubled to slightly over two thousand. As yet, few had gone into the interior; instead, families were continually sub-dividing their lands along the shore, resulting in one long continuous village of shoreline settlement. Distinctive in language, religion, dress and customs, the Acadians had little intercourse with their English neighbours, but within less than a decade would become an important electoral force and have their own representative in the Assembly.

The Tory/Baptist Alliance and the Rise of Parties in Old Annapolis County

Sir,—Great and glorious has been the triumph of the Conservatives in the County of Annapolis. Never, since the first dawn of Radicalism in Nova Scotia have three self-styled "Liberals" been so signally defeated, or the voice of systematic boasting so effectively suppressed, as in this County. The Conservatives ... have met the force of an unmanly opposition with undeviating adherence to the principle they have adopted, and have recorded their firm and noble determination to resist, at every sacrifice and hazard, the daring inroads of Catholicism, supported by the insolence of a disappointed party.

UMBRA, Bridgetown, *Morning Post,* 11 August 1847

The day before issuing the writs for the election of Nova Scotia's Second Assembly in 1759, the Council in Halifax by order laid out the boundaries for Annapolis County. These were defined as running from Cape Forchu in the west to the dividing line with Kings County in the east. This same order established Annapolis Township as well, and gave to freeholders the right to elect two members each for the county and the township. The flood of New England Planters was still a year away and so at most there were a few dozen freeholders living in and around the fort at Annapolis Royal. Although Louisbourg had fallen a year earlier, there were still skirmishes with French irregulars and Indians. Such skirmishing did not hinder what the soldier Jonathan Hoar described, with a good touch of drollery, as "a Grand Election," in which four members were returned.[1] In the succeeding elections, from 1761 through to the arrival of the Loyalists in 1783, nearly all of those elected had their seats vacated for non-attendance. Some stability came as the American war drew to a close. In 1783 John Ritchie entered the House for the county and he attended for the two sessions before the 1785 election. Ritchie was a Glaswegian, who had first gone to Boston and then come to Annapolis, where he had established himself as a merchant. But he is most remembered as the patriarch of the principal political and legal dynasty in the county (both the late Justice Roland Almon Ritchie and the retired diplomat Charles Stewart Ritchie are descendants). A year later the Loyalist Colonel Stephen DeLancey was unopposed for the township. His election was a sure sign that the Loyalists were fully determined to play a leading role in the politics of Annapolis and of the province.

When Jacob Bailey, a Loyalist and missionary of the Society for the Propagation of the Gospel, arrived in 1782, he found Annapolis Royal a town of eighteen families. A population of some 1,500 were living in the county. Almost all of them were New England Planters, mostly from Massachusetts, who had come in the early 1760s. The first group of 500 Loyalists came in the fall of 1782 and they were housed as best could be done in the town. The 2,500 who arrived the following autumn spent a winter of dreadful hardships in tents hastily put up in the bush behind the town. Nowhere in Nova Scotia did the Loyalists establish themselves more successfully than in Annapolis County. A major contributing factor was the ability of a good number to purchase from the original settlers already cleared land or developed farms in Annapolis and Granville Townships. Those who pioneered the new townships of Digby, Clements and Wilmot fared less well, and many left. But the settlement of between 4,000 and 5,000 people in a matter of two or three years was an outstanding achieve-

Annapolis Royal
From *The Atlantic Neptune*, drawn and published by J. F. W. des Barres, London, 1777 to 1781.

ment. Annapolis had become a Loyalist county, though by no means entirely so, as the 1785 election was now to affirm.

There was no election in 1785 more controversial or more bitterly fought than that for Annapolis County. It pitted the Loyalists, as newcomers, against the first settlers, or oldcomers.[2] No doubt realizing there would be a fierce battle for the two county seats, John Ritchie decided not to re-offer, but to stand for Annapolis Township against the sitting member, Stephen DeLancey; Ritchie lost by 80 to 44 votes. For Granville, however, there was a close contest, with the Pennsylvanian Loyalist Benjamin James defeating, by four votes, Moses Shaw, an original 1761 grantee from Massachusetts. Digby had been created a township and that seat went to Thomas Millidge. Two prominent Loyalists, Thomas Barclay and David Seabury, came forward as candidates for the county. The old inhabitants, or Bluenoses, as Jacob Bailey contemptuously called them, were in a quandary. They knew that Barclay, one of the most outstanding and distinguished Loyalists to come to Nova Scotia, could not be defeated. Unless, however, they took the other county seat, they faced having no representative of their own in the new Assembly. Alexander Howe assumed the leadership of the oldcomers. On both sides (his mother was a Winniett), he was descended from old Annapolis families. He had entered the army at age thirteen; when faced by dismal prospects for promotion after the American war, he had returned to take up farming in Granville Township.

Howe determined to stand for the county, as did also the Loyalist Thomas Cornwall, who seems to have run to bring what Loyalist vote he could over to Howe. There was much unhappiness among the Loyalists over Seabury's candidacy. While the Loyalists had been making ready to remove to Nova Scotia, Seabury, still in New York, had been one of the infamous "Fifty-five," who had petitioned for large grants of land for themselves. This infuriated other Loyalists, who did not soon forget this insidious attempt to exclude them from the best lands. The poll opened on 15 November. As sheriff, the North Carolina Loyalist Dr. Robert Tucker proved anything but impartial, openly soliciting for his friends Barclay and Seabury, while making it as difficult as he could for Howe's supporters to vote. Barclay was certain of election from the beginning, but Seabury did better than anticipated and gained a fair lead over Howe. Howe then requested that the poll be moved to Digby. He hoped to gain sufficient votes there to overtake Seabury. However, Howe was mistaken about Seabury's unpopularity among the Digby Loyalists. The final totals were Barclay 422, Seabury 287, Howe 212 and Cornwall 41 votes. Howe demanded a scrutiny, while vehemently protesting Tucker's partiality. He then set out immediately for Halifax to protest the result to the Assembly, due to convene on 5 December.

On 8 December the House voted on the findings of a special committee established to hear Howe's petition; of the five members on the committee, only one was a Loyalist. A majority of the Assembly voted to void the election and called for a new writ. Barclay immediately wrote to his friends and supporters of Seabury, exhorting them to prepare for another battle. His letter became public. Great umbrage was taken with his statement that the proceedings leading up to the voiding were "irregular and unprecedented," and that the members had determined "right or wrong" to vacate the election. Barclay was required to apologize to the House, though in truth he was more right than wrong.[3] To win the by-election became for both sides a matter of honour, or as Barclay expressed it in his letter: "What a shame it will be to lose our Election and how great a right will the Province at large have to ground their opinion on, if Capt. Howe should be returned!" Seabury, as well, warned his supporters that the friends of Captain Howe were "amazingly industrious and seemed determined to carry their point."[4]

After three days of polling at Annapolis in early January 1786, Howe's majority over Seabury stood at 60. Once Tucker moved the poll to Digby, this time over Howe's fierce opposition, the contest was not in doubt as Seabury obtained 245 to Howe's 114 votes. This gave Seabury a majority of 71, with 803 having voted. The freeholders of Annapolis County had twice given Seabury victory, but this did not alter the view of the majority in the Assembly. They accepted Howe's protest that Tucker had kept an incorrect poll book, by refusing to note the location of each voter's freehold. By a two to one vote, they directed that Howe's name replace Seabury's in the returned writ, as the duly elected member. At the Annapolis Royal poll, the oldcomers had supported Howe, and the Loyalists Seabury, almost to the man. As W.A. Calnek recorded in his *History of Annapolis County*, the spirit of rivalry that these two elections created lasted until the 1830s, when death and intermarriage finally "obliterated the ancient marks of variance."[5]

Annapolis County would never again be represented by such an illustrious group of members.[6] All had served as officers in the American War. Barclay, DeLancey, James and Millidge had held commissions in provincial regiments raised from among Loyalists. Of the four, Barclay had the most distinguished fighting record, rising to command a light infantry battalion. DeLancey had commanded one of the six battalions of New Jersey Volunteers (the 5th) in which Millidge also served with the rank of major. James had begun the war as an ensign in a Loyalist corps and saw considerable active service before being made acting commissary for a brigade, a generally lucrative appointment. Both DeLancey and Barclay were lawyers by profession. After graduating from King's College, New York, Barclay had been a student in the office of the noted American jurist, John Jay. Millidge was by training a surveyor and had held before the war the remunerative office of deputy surveyor in New Jersey, as well as representing Bergen County in the colony's House of Assembly. James' appointment as a commissary points to a mercantile background, and in the Assembly he was chosen more than once chairman of the public accounts committee. Barclay, DeLancey, Millidge, and presumably also James, had had all their property confiscated during the war. The first two had been named in the New York State act of attainder, giving them no choice but to leave and begin new lives as Loyalists.

Of the Annapolis members in the Sixth Assembly, Barclay made his presence felt the most. He and Millidge were the only ones to attend all sessions from 1785 to 1792. DeLancey never attended at all. On the news of the death of his father, the distinguished Loyalist Brigadier General Oliver DeLancey, he left for England; on his acceptance of an office in the Bahamas his seat was declared vacant in 1789. In the ensuing by-election, the seat went to his first cousin, James DeLancey, who had commanded the Westchester Refugees, a unit that during 1780-82 engaged in forty-four separate actions in the New York area.[7] There was no reconciliation between Alexander Howe and the Loyalists. He was openly jubilant at his success in having the Assembly twice overturn Seabury's election; he described the Loyalists as being as "complicated a Sett of Rascals as ever Existed" in their "inordinant thirst for power."[8] They were most emphatically on opposite sides over the judges' affair, when the Loyalists sought to remove from office the Supreme Court judges James Brenton and Isaac Deschamps. It was Millidge's motion, during the 1787 session, to examine the administration of justice in the province that began the assault on the judicial competence of the two judges. Millidge's speech to the House on the occasion was long-remembered for its eloquence and the manifest ability with which it was given.

In 1789 Barclay launched the fiercest attack so far on Judges Brenton and Deschamps and against the government for not removing them from the bench. In an impassioned address, demonstrating to the full his oratorical skills, Barclay roused the House as never before. He offered to act as if a physician, and to raise his fellow members from their languor and lethargy: "The rays of science," he told them, "had hitherto shone but obliquely on this northern hemisphere; but Apollo, the Sun of Science, was now beaming his more direct rays on the hills of Windsor, and we should be cautious, lest, when we are in our graves, our more enlightened children should have cause to blush at the conduct of their fathers." Alexander Howe did his best to counter such stirring eloquence, regretting that "Proteus-like" the business of the judges kept being brought forward in different shapes, when he believed the matter had been already satisfactorily dealt with by Governor John Parr and his Council.[9] In the 1790 session, Barclay became the chief prosecutor for preparing and carrying through the Assembly the articles of impeachment against the judges for "high crimes and Misdemeanors." On a motion by John George Pyke to halt the impeachment proceedings, Barclay gave perhaps his finest speech, displaying "very remarkable skill in constitutional law, great eloquence and polished diction."[10] The burden upon the people, Barclay declared, was now intolerable: "it was our duty to attempt to shake off the oppression; and that if we should not succeed, like the giants under burning Aetna, our attempts might be known in the most distant parts of the British Empire."[11] As we have already described in a preceding chapter, the British government refused to proceed with a trial for the impeachment of the two judges. Instead, it sent out a trained jurist, Thomas Andrew Strange, to be chief justice.

For the 1793 election, Howe wisely chose not to run for a county seat, but to go up instead against Benjamin James for Granville, which he won. Barclay had moved from his Wilmot farm to Annapolis Royal, where he had established a law practice, so he could now avoid the expense of a county election and run for the township. He won the seat without much difficulty. Millidge had moved from Digby and had purchased a farm in Granville, leaving open the Digby seat. It was won by the merchant, Henry Rutherford. He had been educated in Ireland to be a Presbyterian clergyman before emigrating to White Plains, New York, and had come to Digby as a Loyalist. Millidge came forward as a candidate for the county, as did two other Loyalists, James Moody and Robert FitzRandolf. Another former officer of the New Jersey Volunteers, the tall and powerfully built Moody became widely celebrated for his exploits as a raider deep into rebel lines and for his incredible escape on one occasion when he was imprisoned, manacled and guarded by a sentry.[12] He chose to settle on lands overlooking the Sissiboo River at what came to be called Weymouth North. Millidge and Moody won, likely with ease.

With John Wentworth's appointment as Lieutenant Governor in 1792, the Loyalists began to receive the patronage they considered their abilities and loyalty merited. Both Rutherford and Millidge were made magistrates and Millidge, as well, appointed a judge of the inferior court of common pleas. On the outbreak of war with France in 1793, Wentworth was authorized to raise the Royal Nova Scotia Regiment to defend the province; Moody and Alexander Howe were commissioned captains. Howe had obviously made his peace with the emerging Loyalist ascendancy. Barclay became adjutant general of the militia. Wentworth also recommended the appointment of Barclay and James DeLancey to the Council. But after Barclay was unanimously chosen Speaker in 1793, Wentworth had his name dropped because of the value to his government in having Barclay in the Speaker's chair. DeLancey was named to the Council, but distance from Halifax and a chronic illness prevented his attendance.

In Halifax County in the 1799 election, it was a battle between the court and country parties, but there was no echo of this in Annapolis County. Rutherford went in again unanimously for Digby. Edward Thorne, a New York Loyalist who had settled as a farmer at Lower Granville, was unopposed for the township. It was a different story for the Annapolis Township seat. Phineas Lovett Jr., a second-generation Planter from Massachusetts, defeated by a mere three votes the Massachusetts Loyalist Robert FitzRandolf, one of the losers in the 1793 county election. For the county, there was also a contest in which the Loyalist Colonel John Taylor, land surveyor and mill owner living at Sissiboo, went up against the sitting members, Moody and Millidge. Although the poll was moved from the Annapolis courthouse to Sissiboo, Taylor was still able to collect only 292 votes, compared to 562 for the popular Millidge and 345 for Moody.

The 1806 election confirmed an emerging pattern of representation, in which local concerns and family relationships became the cardinal factors. As soon as the writs were issued, the shuffling of constituencies began. Rutherford decided to run for the county and Millidge for Granville. Rutherford's vacant Digby seat went unopposed to John Warwick, a native of Yorkshire who had gone out to the American colonies in 1774; a year later he took up arms "to aid and assist the king." As well as being a fish merchant, he was the postmaster and a tavern keeper. Thomas Ritchie also offered for the county. The son of the former member, the younger Ritchie had studied law in Barclay's office and taken over his extensive practice on Barclay's departure for New York in 1799 to be British consul general there. Both Ritchie and Rutherford were elected without opposition. The single contest was for the Granville seat, which pitted Millidge against Isaiah Shaw. Some years younger than the seventy-one-year-old Millidge, Shaw was the leading merchant in the district and a son of a New England Planter. Shaw did a complete canvass of the township; the election took on the shape of a straight contest between old and newcomers. Shaw defeated Millidge by 74 to 64 votes, but there was so much disputing over the eligibility of freeholders that it took three days to poll 138 electors. Millidge would not run again. A man of more than passing abilities, he was one of those Loyalists (carved on his tombstone was the coat of arms of Great Britain) whose leadership in and out of the Assembly had contributed much to his adopted land.

Millidge's son-in-law, Thomas Walker, came forward for Annapolis Township. He probably expected to be unopposed, but Edward Whitman decided to stand against him. Both candidates came from families well established before the arrival of the Loyalists. Walker and Whitman, however, came from opposite ends of the township and the consequent rivalry contributed to a turbulent contest. The poll opened on 14 July in Annapolis Royal. At the end of three days of polling, Walker had 106 to Whitman's 79 votes. Whitman took his defeat to the floor of the Assembly. His protest against the election of Walker was to produce a minor constitutional crisis. Among a number of charges, Whitman accused Walker of using bribery by promising a Jonathan Payson, if Payson voted for him, that he would discontinue a suit in the inferior court. After involved and unusually lengthy proceedings, the Assembly found Walker guilty of bribery, and declared the seat vacant. In the ensuing by-election, the Scottish-born Loyalist and merchant William Robertson was returned. A second by-election in the same year, caused by Rutherford's death, saw Phineas Lovett III and Samuel Bayard seek Rutherford's old county seat.[13] Lovett had the advantage of being Rutherford's son-in-law, while inheriting at least part of the business and the ledger influence that went with an estate of £16,664, mostly in money owed to Rutherford by 520 individuals. Lovett's marriage also gave him the needed respectability to counter Samuel Bayard's Loyalist credentials; during the American War, Bayard had won such rapid promotion that he became a major in the King's Orange Rangers at twenty-six years of age. Since the 1793 election, there had always been one member from the Annapolis/Granville area and one from Digby. As a resident of Digby, Lovett inherited this convention. The overwhelming support he received at the Sissiboo/Digby poll gave him victory with 349 to Bayard's 260 votes.

In the 1811 election, local concerns sufficed for the first time to ensure contests in every Annapolis constituency. The most spirited battle was for the two county seats. Lovett did not stand again, but Thomas Ritchie did, against two new candidates: Peleg Wiswall, a lawyer and a Digby Loyalist, and the Wilmot farmer Foster Woodbury. Ritchie's popularity was such that his 880 votes were double those of both his opponents, suggesting that most freeholders voted for Ritchie, and then split their second votes between the other two, with Wiswall receiving 41 more than Woodbury. Ritchie was now unquestionably the leading member among those from Annapolis. His influence extended throughout the county, whose population was approaching 10,000. Ritchie's success derived not only from the respect he had gained in and out of the Assembly, but also from his extensive legal practice, a consequence of the incredibly litigious nature of the county's inhabitants. Nathaniel White, who articled with Ritchie for over three years and should have known, estimated that about six hundred civil suits were instituted in the county annually. On behalf of his clients, Ritchie initiated or defended in three-quarters of these. Ritchie had built up this practice by "indefatigable application," though in White's opinion Ritchie was "without general knowledge & enlarged ideas sufficient to embellish or enforce his arguments." Although White was being his usual flatulent self, he was close to the mark; indefatigability summed up Ritchie's character.[14]

When the writs were published for the 1818 election, there was again no shortage of candidates to contest all the Annapolis seats. Warwick had held the Digby seat since 1806, but now offered for the county. Warwick and Ritchie were elected, with Ritchie leading the poll by a wide margin.

The Digby Township election battle, however, was the fiercest fought in the county since the Howe-Seabury battle of 1785. Once Warwick determined to run for the county, he and his friends settled on John Hughes to succeed to the seat; as another son-in-law to the deceased Henry Rutherford, Hughes could count upon the backing of most of the leading freeholders. He likely expected to be unopposed, but William Henry Roach also offered. A native of Annapolis Royal, where he attended the school kept by John McNamara, Roach left at nineteen years of age to take employment in the West Indies. On his way there he fell foul of a naval press gang. Through influence he was released and became the clerk on a Jamaican slave plantation. Once, when he found an overseer whipping a pregnant slave, he seized the lash and in turn applied it to the overseer.

From Jamaica he went to New York State, where he went into business, only to abandon all when the War of 1812 broke out. Because he refused to swear allegiance to the Republic, he was forced to leave. But he went to sea as a privateer during the war and got ample revenge before settling down at Digby as a successful merchant.

Roach would not have stood a chance in the election, if it had not been for the incredibly irascible behaviour of William Winniett as sheriff and returning officer. The poll lasted from a Monday through to midnight on the following Saturday. Roach brought to the hustings a good number of electors with highly questionable qualifications, but if, in Winniett's choice phrase, they "swallow'd the oath," he let them vote. Moreover, he refused to mark in his poll book that Hughes had objected to their voting. As a consequence, Hughes could not in any scrutiny challenge the right of those electors to vote. Winniett, of course, understood this all too well. He was quoted as saying: "Darn the scrutiny, I will not have any votes marked disputed in my book the candidates may mark what they please in their own Books."[15] He declared Roach the winner by 124 to 123 votes for Hughes. Every magistrate who voted did so for Hughes, for such was the antipathy towards the upstart Roach.

The contest for the Annapolis Township seat was unusual in that it was won by a farmer against a merchant. The farmer was Thomas Ritchie, a cousin of Thomas Ritchie, the county member. His opponent was the merchant James Russell Lovett, another son of Phineas Lovett junior and son-in-law to William Allen Chipman, the long-serving Kings County member. Such connections were not enough for Lovett to overcome Ritchie's popularity. At Granville, the battle was between Timothy Ruggles and James Hall. Both were from Bridgetown, but any resemblance between the two men ended there. Ruggles, a grandson of the famous Massachusetts Loyalist General Timothy Ruggles, was an Anglican and, as a merchant and agriculturist, was well on his way to becoming one of the wealthiest men in the county. In contrast, Hall was a third-generation New England Planter and farmer of no great means. Moreover, he was also a former New Light religious enthusiast; on this sole account, Thomas Millidge earlier had had no compunction in recommending against his being made a magistrate. In a continuation of the feuding between old and newcomers, Ruggles' respectability, combined with his extensive ledger influence, gave him an overwhelming victory; Ruggles received 80 to Hall's 30 votes.

When the 1820 election was called, no one was prepared to challenge Timothy Ruggles' hold on Granville, and he went in unopposed. For Digby Township, there was another replay of the Hughes and Roach battle, which the latter won again; ten of the eleven magistrates voting supported Hughes and the factional warfare continued unabated. Ritchie stood again for the county and, following the long-held understanding, he was joined by a candidate from Digby Township, in this case Samuel Campbell. Both had the good fortune to be unopposed. In Annapolis Township, however, Phineas

Lovett III, who had last been elected to the House in 1808, came forward also expecting to be unopposed. But there was some unhappiness over Lovett's candidacy, with the result that a son of the deceased Colonel William Robertson was brought out to run against him. John Robertson was another of that breed of Nova Scotians who went to sea as boys (in his case he ran away from home) and rose through sheer will and natural ability to command. His courage and presence of mind were fully demonstrated on a voyage to the East Indies, when his unarmed vessel was threatened with capture by pirates. The captain wanted to surrender, but Robertson cajoled the captain into allowing him to assume temporary command. Robertson then faked surrender, drawing two boatloads of the pirates near enough for his crew to surprise and kill them. For his action in saving the ship, Lloyd's of London paid him £500. Robertson left the life at sea soon after to enter into a mercantile business in his native town of Annapolis Royal. Lovett was expected to win the election, but because of the "extraordinary tact" with which Robertson conducted his campaign he defeated Lovett by 84 to 62 votes.[16]

The Annapolis members returned by freeholders in 1820 were as independent of manipulation by Halifax interests as any ever elected in the county. But, at the same time, they demonstrated a uniformly negative attitude to any measures designed to bring about social or economic improvements. The five—Ritchie, Ruggles, Roach, Robertson and Campbell—formed a tacit faction opposed to: the incorporation of Dalhousie College; support for the efforts of the Central Board of Agriculture; the seating of the Roman Catholic Laurence Kavanagh without his taking the oaths against Popery; the incorporation of banks; and any form of compulsory assessment for schooling. On the last, their opposition came from the distressing realization that there were "very few liberal minded persons" in the various Annapolis townships who were prepared to pay for the education, not only of their own children, but particularly for those of poorer parents, which was the practical implication of compulsory assessment.[17] The ability of many parents to pay for the education of their children was directly related to what cash they could earn on road work. Annapolis had been receiving more road moneys than any other county or district until 1820, when its allotment dropped from £1350 of the previous year to £800. Part of this precipitous decline was attributable to the reduction of revenue available for roads caused by the post-Napoleonic War depression. After its reannexation to Nova Scotia in 1820, the need to find money for Cape

Breton, however, seriously worsened matters for Annapolis. The severe decline in road moneys for distribution within the county no doubt politically inhibited the Annapolis members from supporting any but the most necessary public expenditures.

This ingrained reluctance for public expenditures accounts for the opposition of all Annapolis members (except curiously Robertson) to S.G.W. Archibald's motion in the 1824 session to accept a report of a joint committee of the House and Council for the appointment of more judges. Ritchie, in fact, led the attack on this first move by Archibald in legal gamesmanship, which called for two new judges to be appointed. The whole western district of the province was to be transferred to Peleg Wiswall, who had been elevated to the bench in 1816. Had this plan gone forward, any hopes for Ritchie's promotion would have been cut off. Archibald, sensing that Ritchie had to be placated if the measure was to proceed, put out rumours that Wiswall's delicate health and old age required that a third and new judge be appointed for a divided western district. This appeared in a revised report. It passed, with Ritchie voting with the majority. Now that Archibald had got Ritchie to vote for the report, he played the wily politician and drew him actively onside by arranging for Ritchie to be one of the committee to present Governor Sir James Kempt with a copy of the revised report. On second reading, Ritchie spoke after Archibald and gave as his reason, for waiving his former objections and now voting in favour of the appointment of more judges: in the mother country judges of courts of common pleas were learned in the law. With that said, according to John Young, a rabid critic of the whole charade, Ritchie "sank quickly on the bench, his hat was drawn forward to overshadow his eyes ... There he sat—a melancholy monument of mortification."[18] Two weeks later Ritchie was named to one of the three easy chairs at a salary of £400 a year.

Ritchie had first been elected in 1806. By 1824 he had served the longest of any member from Annapolis. In the two elections in which he had faced opposition, he had easily led the poll. He seems to have been genuinely popular and to have represented the county's interests to the general satisfaction of his constituents. As he was a typical country lawyer of his day, so too, he was equally an independent country member. He had an inbred aversion to giving his vote—and considerable influence—to measures that appeared in any way advantageous to Halifax, or entailed more than absolutely necessary public expenditure. Always a rival to Archibald, who had entered the House also in 1806 and was of the same age, Ritchie had hoped to succeed to S.B. Robie's mantle as Solicitor General and Speaker. But he let the temptation of a good salary for life overcome what ambitions he had to make a greater mark on the political stage.

Two candidates came forward for the by-election to replace Ritchie. The perennial Phineas Lovett III offered, and was opposed by the sixty-nine-year-old Abraham Gesner. A New Jersey Loyalist, whose property had been confiscated, Gesner had served in the King's Orange Rangers. He had purchased Alexander Howe's farm in Granville Township and had devoted his talents and horticultural skills to developing what contemporaries considered one of the finest and most productive orchards in the province. The county notables gave their support to Gesner, with such respectable freeholders as Timothy Ruggles and John Robertson voting for him; it was hardly surprising that Gesner easily disposed of Lovett by a margin of nearly 100 votes.[19] But Gesner declined to run again for the 1826 election, citing infirmities and the wish to spend his remaining days in furthering his horticultural pursuits. Samuel Campbell did re-offer for the county and was joined by Cereno Upham Jones. As Jones was Campbell's father-in-law, the fair presumption was that they were in alliance.

Opposition to the Campbell/Jones alliance within Digby seems to have been the reason that some of William Henry Roach's friends put him up as a county candidate, though he was out of the province and would remain so for the whole election. At what point Thomas Chandler Haliburton was prevailed upon to run is unknown, but it was certainly the result of freeholders in Annapolis being determined to have one their own elected. Although Haliburton had only come to Annapolis Royal and opened his law practice in 1821, he led the Annapolis Royal poll by a good margin, with 454 to second-place Roach's 406 votes. When the poll moved to Sissiboo near Digby, Haliburton got more far more votes, 179, than Roach's paltry 25. Moreover, Haliburton's 179 votes were only slightly less than the combined total of Jones and Campbell, who withdrew in the face of the large majorities of Haliburton and Roach.

When Haliburton entered the Assembly for the 1827 session, he found himself among the most youthful group of members ever to sit. These beardless boys, as the Halifax establishment called them, were all lawyers. Haliburton was the oldest, at thirty; the youngest was Charles Dickson Archibald at twenty-four. Haliburton's father was a country lawyer. As we have seen in the previous chapter, William Otis Haliburton had been the representative first of Windsor Township and then of Hants County. He had ensured that his son received the best education possible in Nova Scotia, sending him to King's College School and then to King's College, where he had graduated in 1815. Thomas Chandler probably articled in his father's office. His decision to move to Annapolis was likely governed by the overcrowding in the legal profession. Within two years of his arrival, he had had published the first of his literary efforts, *A General Description of Nova Scotia*, which in 1829 would be superseded by his still-useful *An Historical and Statistical Account of Nova Scotia*. Not since Thomas Barclay had Annapolis been represented by such a commanding presence, whose oratorical feats and power of ridicule were then unequaled. Although lengthy and overly wordy in delivery, a fault not uncommon in his day, his speeches in favour of Pictou Academy and for Catholic emancipation rank high among the great orations delivered in the Nova Scotian Assembly. Until Haliburton, no one had so scornfully, or so openly, chastised the Council of Twelve from the floor of the House, and by inference those of his colleagues who did their bidding:

> There are a few individuals in Halifax, who direct public opinion, and who not only influence but controul all public measures. Seated in the capital, they govern the movements of all the different parts; as they touch the springs, the wires move, and simultaneously arise the puppets in the different counties and towns, play the part assigned to them, and re-echo the sounds which have been breathed into them. The smiles of episcopacy, the frowns of the treasury, and the patronage of official interest, have a powerful effect, when brought to bear upon any one object ...[20]

Haliburton, with the other Annapolis members, continued to be wary of funding for colleges. In one of the few critical passages in his *History,* Haliburton vented his frustration at the establishment of Dalhousie, regretting that so much money had been so "injudiciously expended." One college, King's at Windsor, with the local academies already in being, was entirely sufficient for Nova Scotia and New Brunswick; he was equally disparaging about attempts to provide funding for a college at Fredericton, a creation of "sectional feelings" so peculiar to America.[21] As a *quid pro quo* for supporting a permanent grant for Pictou Academy, Haliburton got through the House a perpetual grant of £200 for the recently erected Annapolis Academy. The apparent radicalism of Haliburton's language was the result of anger at the baneful and insidious influence exercised by the Council of Twelve. It was not a philosophical commitment to constitutional reform. His Toryism was never far below the surface, even in these youthfully heady days. When his father died in 1829, and left vacant the judgeship of the Middle Division, the son had no hesitation in applying for and receiving the office, becoming the youngest judge of his day in the Nova Scotian judiciary.

With two brief interregnums since Barclay's first election in 1785, a lawyer with his practice centred in Annapolis Royal had held one of the two county seats. There was now no break in this succession; John Johnston was unopposed for Haliburton's seat, though he had been resident in the county for scarcely three years. Johnston, however, had close connections with Annapolis; his sister was married to Thomas Ritchie and his younger brother, James William, had articled with Ritchie. The Johnston brothers' parents were Loyalists who had gone to Jamaica and lived there until the death of their father, when their mother moved to Annapolis Royal. John stayed behind, trained for the bar, and seems to have come to Annapolis on an invitation from Ritchie to take over his law practice on his acceptance of a judgeship. For the 1830 election, Roach re-offered, but the real opposition to Johnston came from the candidacy of Anselm Doucett, a farmer in Clare and the first Acadian to run for the Assembly.

Thomas Chandler Haliburton had been on the most cordial terms with the venerable Abbé Sigogne, who had begun ministering to the Acadians of Clare in 1796. Haliburton's substantial victory margin in 1826 can be attributed to Sigogne's Acadians, who had become an important factor in the county vote. In 1830 at the Annapolis Royal poll, Roach easily led with 494 to Johnston's 376 and Doucett's 283 votes. Not having taken this poll by a sufficient margin to offset Doucett's strength in the western part of the county, by rights Johnston should have lost the election. When the poll moved to Sissiboo, it was apparent that most of the freeholders of Digby and Clare were going to vote for Doucett and Roach. Surprisingly Doucett withdrew, when there were upwards of 100 votes present for him and he was within 61 votes of Johnston. The best explanation of what transpired was that Peleg Wiswall and Thomas Ritchie intervened on behalf of their protégé, Johnston, to convince Doucett that he should withdraw. Both the judges were intimately involved in Johnston's campaign, even to making the arrangements for paying for his open house at Sissiboo. It had cost £55, including £16 for thirty-six and a half gallons of good Jamaica rum.[22] The nature of the agreement worked out with Doucett and the Acadian community would become apparent in the 1836 election.

Roach had played no role in the proceedings at Sissiboo, but he actively participated in the Digby Township election. He wrote letters to freeholders, claiming that the sitting member, John Morton, had been constantly in opposition to the interests of Annapolis County, had joined with members from the eastern part of the province against those from the western, and worst of all had favoured increases in salaries for judges and sheriffs. A freeholder from Digby wrote Joseph Howe at the *Novascotian* asking him whether these charges were true, to which Howe replied that "they are without foundation."[23] Whatever the intrigues, Charles Budd came forward to challenge and defeat Morton for the Digby seat. A second generation Loyalist, whose grandfather had been shot in his own doorway by a rebel, Budd had inherited from his father a thriving West Indian trading business and was married to a daughter of Peleg Wiswall.

When James Russell Lovett had won Annapolis Township in 1826, he had become the first non-Anglican elected for any Annapolis constituency since before the 1785 election. In 1830 Lovett, a Baptist, found himself opposed by another Baptist, his uncle by marriage Major (his name, not a rank) Chipman. Another son of the Kings County patriarch Handley Chipman, Major Chipman had taken up farming at Lawrencetown. He probably decided to challenge Lovett at the behest of some Baptist friends, who were accusing Lovett of changing his religious sentiments "as often as it did suit his convenience." Both candidates had numerous family connections to draw upon. The poll opened on a Monday and continued warmly until the next day when Chipman accepted defeat; he had but 46 votes, 15 of which came from his "connections."[24]

The most acrimonious contest in the 1830 election turned out to be for Granville, when James Delap challenged the hold on the seat by the sitting member since 1818, Timothy Ruggles. Delap's grandfather had come from Massachusetts to Granville as an early Loyalist in 1775, but the family became closely associated through marriage with those of New England Planters. The contest took place against the backdrop of arson and the burning of Ruggles' store in Bridgetown. At least some of his ledgers were destroyed in the fire. Ruggles was owed nearly £9,000 by about 200 individuals and the arsonist, who was later arrested, was likely one of them. Ruggles won by one vote and Delap demanded a scrutiny, which proved most expensive for the parties. It ended, as it began, with Ruggles still the winner by a single vote. The burning of his store was less a material loss than destructive of his peace of mind, for it seems to have greatly contributed to Ruggles' curious death four months later. He apparently was not a vindictive man; rather he was of a genial temperament, of generally cheerful countenance, and in the Assembly had carefully guarded the interests of his constituents. He had a good head for finance and for this had earned the respect of his colleagues in the House.[25]

In the by-election caused by Ruggles' death, Delap easily took the seat against a weak opponent, Joseph Shaw, a shoemaker by trade and without influence in the township.

After 1830, the issue that dominated all others for the freeholders of Annapolis was the division of the county. Its geographic extent, combined with roads that were generally poor and often impassable at certain times of the year, made for disorderly local administration. This had long resulted in demands for a division into two counties, each with its own shiretown. The impasse that developed lay not in the actual idea of division, but with the need to deal with the highly factious issue of representation for the proposed two new counties. Within Annapolis there was the expectation, loudly voiced, that with a division Wilmot, Clare and even Clements Township should each receive seats, with no change in the representation for Annapolis, Granville and Digby Townships. Furthermore, the demand was for the new counties in the proposed division to have two representatives each. Such an accretion of electoral strength for the western counties was an anathema to Halifax and the eastern region of the province. In 1832, the eastern members had united to provide Cape Breton with three more seats, heightening the already existing imbalance between the eastern and western counties. There was good reason to believe that next would be the division of Halifax County, with another increase in seats for the eastern region.

These "exclusive measures" for the eastern counties enraged Annapolis freeholders. They produced a petition, originated by Joseph FitzRandolph and signed, it was declared, by one thousand individuals. The petition called for the immediate division of Annapolis along the Bear River line, with an additional seat for Wilmot, where most of the signatories lived. John Johnston tabled the petition and introduced a bill for a division, incorporating an increase in representation. Greatly unhappy with the delay in moving the bill through the House, Joseph FitzRandolph organized another petition. This one went to the heart of the grievance, explaining that the demand for division and increased representation did not rest entirely on the grounds of geographic extent or increase in population; much more important was the "most pronounced differences" that existed between the western and eastern regions of the province.[26] When the Assembly enacted the tri-division of Halifax County in 1835, increasing by two seats the previous representation of the eastern region, and did not proceed with that for Annapolis, furious freeholders petitioned directly to the throne to present their grievance. In the 1836 session, the last before an election, the Annapolis members tried again to have the county divided, but opposition to any consequent increase in representation proved too strong.

James Lovett returned to the hustings for the 1836 election to face such wrath over his performance in the last Assembly that he determined not to run again for Annapolis Township. He felt compelled to write a letter to the Novascotian to explain his reasons for not re-offering and to justify his conduct.[27] Lovett's cardinal sin was that he had voted too often with the Archibald clan of Colchester County, which had no particularly friendly feelings for the western counties. In an extraordinary lapse of political good sense, Lovett had voted for an amendment that reduced Annapolis' share of road moneys and increased that of Colchester County. On election day for the township, Lovett did stand, but only to make a speech justifying his conduct. He then withdrew, leaving two first-time candidates to fight it out. Elnathan Whitman, a third-generation New England Planter and noted horticulturist, offered. For his opponent, he had the prime originator of the 1833 petitions for the division of the county, Joseph FitzRandolph. Whitman's victory by 39 votes simply confirmed the hold that the descendants of the first settlers had gained over the township seat and would continue to have through to 1847.

Lovett should have accepted that the feeling against him made the likelihood of his re-election in any constituency a virtual impossibility. But he now stood for the county, which turned out to be a five-candidate contest. The thirty-year-old eldest son of Judge Thomas Ritchie came forward as the natural successor to the recently deceased Johnston (he had also inherited the law practice that had been passed down since Thomas Barclay's day). Although the family was staunchly Anglican, Judge Ritchie had sent his son, John William, to Pictou Academy before his legal training and admittance to the bar in 1832. Young Ritchie's name, or for that matter the name of any of the Ritchie family, had been conspicuously absent from the petition sent directly to the king a year before. William Henry Roach, as well, decided to re-offer, but he had taken up permanent residence in Halifax and was much in disfavour. At one meeting called to select candidates, his name was voted down. What had got his constituents in such a rage was his acceptance of the inspectorship of flour at a salary of £500 a year. This was an office created by a bill that he had introduced in 1833, which he got the lawyers in the House to support. In exchange, Roach did a complete about-face on a cheap law bill, naturally opposed by the legal profession. Roach had made his political reputation as a populist, opposed to all forms of extravagant public expenditures, especially for offices. But he had gall and hypocrisy in abundance and published an election card promising to co-operate in every act of reform.

If Ritchie had inherited Johnston's place in the Annapolis political spectrum, so too had Frederic Armand Robicheau when he succeeded Anselm Doucett among the Acadians. A student of Abbé Sigogne's, Robicheau had left his native Meteghan and gone inland to Corberrie, one of the first settlers to clear a farm there. Instead of forming an alliance with Ritchie, which was what Ritchie counted upon, Robicheau did so with another new candidate, William Holland of Wilmot. The two extremes of the county—Clare and Wilmot Townships—came together in a political alliance to bring about the division of the county along the Bear River line, and to secure single member representation for their respective townships.[28] In defence, Ritchie and Roach, both with their strength in the geographic centre, forged their own alliance.

The county election lasted fourteen days and the poll moved to an unprecedented five locations. Ritchie led the poll at Annapolis Royal with 289 votes, but the surprise was Robicheau with 222 and his second-place standing; a chastened Phineas Lovett, with 97 votes, resigned. At Wilmot, Holland and Robicheau surged into the lead, increasing their margin at Digby, where Roach at last withdrew. Finally, at Meteghan in Clare, the totals after the first day stood 962 for Robicheau and 806 for Holland; Ritchie was so far behind that he conceded, with Robicheau and Holland having in reserve perhaps another 250 to 300 votes. As well he might, Ritchie blamed his loss on the Acadian vote. They had given Thomas Chandler Haliburton his substantial majority in 1826, and by Doucett's withdrawal, Johnston had gained his victory in 1830.

Delap and Budd found themselves in the same electoral difficulties in 1836 as their former colleagues. For the Granville seat, Delap was opposed by his brother-in-law, Stephen Thorne, whose Loyalist grandfather, Edward, had taken the constituency unopposed in 1799. As a boy, Thorne had been apprenticed to a local merchant before also marrying into the New England Planter family of James Hall. As well as such respectable credentials, Thorne had been a partner of Timothy Ruggles. He had assumed the guardianship of Ruggles' two sons on his untimely death in 1831, giving Thorne control of the extensive ledger influence still left in the estate. The contest lasted several days and was to be long-remembered for its bad blood, open houses and general brawling.[29] Thorne triumphed by eight votes. A total of 354 had voted, about half the heads of families listed in the 1838 census for the township, suggesting that many in the township could not demonstrate satisfactory legal title to the property they occupied; future elections were confirmation of a restricted franchise. A somewhat similar situation prevailed at the Digby Township election, where 407 voted when the same census listed 673 heads of families. By rights Budd should have had an easy election, but the past factional warfare was now being perceptibly translated into party conflict between Reformers and Tories, which ensured that there would be stiff opposition. It came from the merchant, James Bourne Holdsworth, who had inherited the support given in the past to John Morton. Holdsworth won in an extremely close contest by 11 votes.

In William Holland, Annapolis had elected its first Methodist. Of the five members, he was the only one not born in the county. From Ulster, he and his wife had taken passage in 1812 for New York, but a British cruiser captured their vessel and took it into Halifax. The couple chose to settle in Wilmot, where they took up uncleared land and with much labour carved out what became a profitable farm. Whitman and Robicheau were also farmers. None of the three engaged in any mercantile pursuits, relying instead solely upon their farms for their livelihood. For the only time in the history of the county, representatives who were farmers outnumbered merchants and lawyers. Moreover, it was the first election in the last fifty years (with the sole exception of 1799) in which freeholders had not sent a lawyer to the Assembly. Whitman, Thorne and Holdsworth were Anglicans, continuing the preponderance of that denomination. With Robicheau's election and that of Simon d'Entremont for Argyle Township, the two became the first Acadians to sit in the Assembly. In their attitudes and voting, the Annapolis members personified better than any of their predecessors the idealistic notion of the independent-minded yeoman country member. They were a dying breed, however, as party voting was assuming a more pervasive grip. From the 1837 session onwards, the Annapolis members divided increasingly along party lines, with Thorne and Whitman voting as Tories, and Robicheau and Holland joining the Reformers led by Joseph Howe. The most notable occasion in which all voted together was for a bill that finally divided old Annapolis into Annapolis and Digby Counties along the Bear River line. Each of the new counties got a single member, as did Clare, though not before a leading Reformer, George Smith of Pictou, nearly succeeded in having it deleted from the bill.

The 1840 election was a straight party contest for all three seats in the new and smaller Annapolis County. The first battle was for the Annapolis Township seat, where Whitman declined to stand again, but was replaced by his brother Alfred. As a young man, Alfred Whitman had served as a clerk and bookkeeper to Phineas Lovett, and now was a merchant in Annapolis town. Henry Gates came forward for the Reform cause to oppose Whitman; a blacksmith by trade, Gates had received a practical education at a local school. In addition to being a popular militia officer, he was a leading light in the town's Methodist church. Feelings ran high because the township had earlier submitted an address, signed by five hundred freeholders, approving of Lieutenant Governor Sir Colin Campbell's opposition to responsible government. Lord Durham's *Report* of 1839, with its advocacy of responsible government, had been received in the township by the burning of his lordship in effigy.

Whitman led the opening poll at Annapolis Royal with 125 to Gates' 89 votes. At Bridgetown, Gates went into a commanding lead within an hour and half of the poll opening. Desperate for votes and believing that Gates had brought forward all his support, the Tories rounded up some twenty widows to vote for Whitman, but an alert Reformer discovered what they were about. He described for the readers of the *Novascotian* what happened next:

> I gave my horse an extra feed of oats and ... I rode all
> Tuesday night and roused up every farmer; and what was
> the result, they harnessed up their horses, went off, and
> each one by 10 of the clock, was back with a widow or a
> fair young fatherless maid, to vote against the Tory
> women from Annapolis Royal. They found out we should
> outnumber them, and at last we had the satisfaction of
> seeing them return to Annapolis without voting.[30]

Whitman accepted that he was beaten when Gates stood at 201 to his 170 votes. The two candidates then retired from the hustings arm in arm, followed by their supporters, and cordially pledged to each, as the expression went, with a glass of Madeira.

The 1840 county election turned out to be a contest between James Russell Lovett and the Lawrencetown country store owner Samuel Bishop Chipman, whose first cousin was Lovett's wife. In 1830, Lovett had defeated his opponent's father, Major Chipman, for the township seat; ten years later the son was to avenge this, overwhelming Lovett after the poll moved to Bridgetown. The next election held was for Granville. It turned out to be a most nasty affair once again, between Thorne and Delap. The poll opened at Granville Ferry, and at the end of two days of polling Delap had a slight lead of 25 votes. There had been the usual sparring over voter qualifications. Delap's supporters accused Thorne of delaying the polling so that Delap's voters would be unable to vote at Granville Ferry, and instead have to go to the Bridgetown poll. There was probably some truth in this accusation because the number polled dropped from 142 on the first day to 79 on the second. Once the polling began at Bridgetown, the objections by both parties grew almost exponentially. On the last day, out of the 67 who managed to vote, just 15 were able to do so without their property qualifications being challenged. In fact, just under two-thirds of the heads of households listed in the 1838 census voted; nearly half of these had their property qualifications challenged.

Thorne's "understrappers" were certainly at work, raking up paupers and others, promising them gowns, shoes and handkerchiefs if they would take the freeholder's oath and vote for Thorne. Some were ushered in to vote, on deeds written up no more than an hour before by Silas Leander Morse, Thorne's lawyer and known as "our worthy attorney Bachelor." Delap's supporters accused Morse of placing the deeds in the hands of these voters and taking them on his arm to the hustings. The contest terminated with Thorne having 204 to Delap's 191 votes, or, as one of Delap's friends wrote the *Novascotian*, by "a majority of 14 Africans in Mr. Thorne's favour."[31] The traditional bad blood at the hustings between Loyalists and non-Loyalists seems to have continued into the second and third generations. Four times the number who could be classed as descendants of Loyalists voted for Thorne as for Delap.[32] With the victories of Henry Gates and Samuel Bishop Chipman, the Reformers had the satisfaction of having broken the hold of the "porkers," as they called the Annapolis Tories, over two of three seats in the county.

As to be expected, Thorne proved to be an out-and-out Tory, while Gates and Chipman were for reform. All three, however, united as a bloc to oppose any form of compulsory assessment for schooling. On one occasion, Chipman remarked that "None in the House felt the want of education more than himself," but that the time had not yet arrived for compulsory assessment.[33] On the college question, Gates was the single Annapolis member to support the idea of one good college, as proposed during the 1843 session by William Annand and Herbert Huntington. Chipman joined his first cousin and Kings County member, Samuel Chipman, and a majority of Tories, in opposition. But near the end of the 1843 session, when, at one-thirty in the morning of 28 March, Howe moved to adjourn—this to avoid a favourable vote on Edmund Dodd's amendment sanctioning continued funding for sectarian colleges—Chipman voted with the Reform majority for adjournment.

On the writs being issued for the 1843 election Attorney General James William Johnston resigned from the Legislative Council and sought election for Annapolis County.[34] John Johnston's younger brother, James William had been sent to Scotland for schooling and on his father's death had come with his mother to Annapolis, where he had entered into the study of law with his brother-in-law and guardian, Thomas Ritchie. After admittance to the bar, he practised at Kentville before going to Halifax and entering into a partnership with S.B. Robie. His marriage to a sister of Mather Byles Almon put him among the first families of Halifax society and his social position was soon matched by success at the bar. A powerful speaker, he was best before a jury where he could plead hardship on behalf of his client. A man quick to temper, he once challenged Charles Rufus Fairbanks to a duel over some remarks made during a trial. The duel took place near where today are the Halifax Public Gardens. Fairbanks fired first. Johnston finding himself uninjured, said: "I will stop you dancing" to his rival in society as well as the court room. Johnston then fired and hit Fairbanks in the heel. Fairbanks was lamed for life and his dancing career finished.[35] There was, however, another side to Johnston's character and it was to have significant consequences for the religious and political history of his adopted land. Johnston was an evangelical Anglican who, in the aftermath of the great disruption in 1824 at St. Paul's Church in Halifax, converted to the Baptist faith. Johnston's conversion gave Baptists the respectability and lay leadership that they sorely lacked, but greatly desired. It was Johnston who took the lead in securing the incorporation of Acadia, and he became a member of its board of governors. Johnston's entrance into public life had come on the 1837 separation of the old Council of Twelve and his appointment to both the new Legislative and Executive Councils. In 1841, he succeeded S.G.W. Archibald as Attorney General.

Johnston might never have accepted the mantle of leader of a Tory party, had it not been for the Reformers throwing their influence behind William Annand's resolutions on sectarian colleges during the 1843 session.[36] The resolutions attacked the policy of chartering and endowing sectarian colleges as unsound and called for its abandonment. This direct threat to the very existence of Acadia did not bring forth a major public response from Johnston until June when, in a rousing address to the Baptist Association meeting in Yarmouth, he attacked the "godless" system of education being sanctioned by the Reformers. He particularly singled out Samuel Bishop Chipman and his cousin, Samuel Chipman, for their support on what he argued was a crucial vote for continued funding for Acadia—Howe's motion to adjourn in the early hours of 28 March. Johnston declared that it had been "Mortifying ... to see on that side which was led by the bitter and avowed enemies of Acadia College, and on a question so deeply affecting its interests, the names of gentlemen representing large Baptist constituencies: But two of these gentlemen having up to that period professed themselves its friends, there was a right to expect they at least would have voted in conformity with their professions."[37] Johnston had skilfully portrayed the two Chipmans as apostates to church and college. For the Baptists of Annapolis County, there was only one election issue, continued public funding for Acadia; for the Tories there was also a single issue, no party government. Nowhere was the Tory/Baptist alliance to be more effective than in Annapolis County.

The natural constituency for Johnston was Annapolis Township, where the Ritchie family influence would stand him in the most stead; by now the Ritchies, Johnstons and Almons were so intermarried that they were really one extended family with branches in Annapolis and Halifax. Gates intended to re-offer, but was in such severe difficulties with his Baptist followers that he had felt it necessary to write a letter to the Baptist *Christian Messenger*. The letter was a forlorn attempt to refute charges of having in the past Assembly been "in opposition to the feelings and interests of the Baptist Denomination."[38] Although Gates could truthfully show that he had consistently supported funding for Acadia, he had given his vote on one occasion for the idea of a single non-denominational college. He had done this, he claimed, solely as "an expression of opinion" that it was unwise to go on incorporating more colleges when their funding would have to come from that for the road service and common schools. Worse still, he had also voted for Howe's adjournment motion of 28 March. As he readily admitted, the Baptist vote had given him his margin of victory over Alfred Whitman in 1840; now in 1843, to paraphrase Job 1:21, what the Baptists had giveth, they could taketh away; blessed be the name of the LORD. They now made it clear that was what they intended to do. Gates withdrew his candidacy rather than face certain defeat. Johnston could have had Gates' seat for the taking, but probably reached an arrangement with his fellow Tory, Alfred Whitman, for him to have the seat, while Johnston took on Samuel Bishop Chipman for the county. In the case of Granville, the Tory Stephen Thorne was unopposed.

Until that fatal vote of 28 March, there had been no more stalwart supporter of Acadia and the Baptist cause than Samuel Bishop Chipman. It was to do him little good in the forthcoming election against Johnston, in what was as nasty and furious a struggle as the county had ever seen the likes. Johnston campaigned from one end of Annapolis to the other. The Reformers attacked him for being a "lawyer" and a "non-resident," reminding Anglicans that he was an "apostate" from their church and telling Baptists that he was an "interested convert" and insincere in his profession of faith.[39] An Annapolis letter-writer to the Novascotian, reputedly a Tory and an Anglican, described Johnston as "an apostate from our church," who had recently acted a "deceitful part" in an attempt to destroy King's College and establish the Baptist college at Wolfville, "regardless of all others."[40] There was much rowdyness. At one election meeting, a heckler became so outraged that he threw a piece of granite at Johnston and almost killed him.[41] Johnston's campaign was well-financed by his Halifax friends— he had a dozen strategically located open houses—and he had the full backing of every Baptist pulpit. At the close of the Annapolis Royal poll, Johnston had a lead of 383, at Bridgetown this increased to 400 and Chipman resigned shortly after the poll opened at Lawrencetown. The final poll was 669 for Johnston to 292 for his opponent. The last word on the election came from the *Times* in Halifax, which patronizingly asked why Chipman, knowing from the second day of polling that he was destined for defeat, had put "Mr. Attorney General to expense and his friends to some needless trouble."[42]

Annapolis County had sent to the new Assembly one lawyer and two merchants, all declared conservatives. Johnston struggled to avoid another election that could lead to a government of Reformers determined to introduce full responsible government. He also began touring the province to rally support for the conservatives. More and more, he and Joseph Howe each assumed the role of leaders of disciplined parties, preparing for a decisive battle. With the encouragement of Lieutenant Governor Sir John Harvey, Johnston made one last attempt to form a coalition government; on its failure he secured a dissolution, with an election to be held with simultaneous polling on 5 August 1847. Johnston had to spend much of his time campaigning outside Annapolis, but was present at a huge bi-party rally held at Bridgetown, where he delighted his audience by quoting the more extremist statements from the Catholic press.[43] Johnston used with effect the cry of a Catholic Ascendancy in Protestant Nova Scotia in rallying support to the conservative cause. His opponent once again was Chipman, about whom during the campaign he once remarked jocularly that he believed "Mr. Chipman canvasses in his sleep, and sometimes gives his wife a shake of the hand, imagining that he is addressing an elector."[44] This time around Chipman did much better, reducing Johnston's victory margin from 427 in 1843 to 267 votes. Annapolis and Granville freeholders also returned both Whitman and Thorne. Once more, as the quote at the beginning of this section on old Annapolis County gleefully trumpeted, the conservatives had triumphed in the county.

The overwhelming nature of the conservative victories of 1843 and 1847 was, however, a significant departure from previous elections in Annapolis. In the 1836 and 1840 elections, freeholders had displayed a decided preference for Reform candidates. The single exception had been those of Granville, but in that township the ledger influence of Timothy Ruggles and, after his death in 1831, that of his partner, Stephen Thorne, had proved too much for the Reformers to overcome. It was James William Johnston's decision to run in 1843 for the single Annapolis County seat that turned Annapolis into a Tory bastion. He moulded into an effective alliance the traditional support given members of the Ritchie family and that of the Baptists. If Johnston had had to depend on only one of these bases of support, it is highly doubtful that he could have won. In Annapolis, Baptists and Anglicans were not only roughly equal in numbers, but more importantly their adherents combined made up around four-fifths of the population. It was Johnston's position as the leading Baptist layman in the Province, as much as support for Acadia College, that united the Baptist vote so solidly behind him as nowhere else in the province. Still, Johnston could not have won with the Baptist vote alone; he needed the Tory vote that came with his connection to the Ritchie family. For Johnston in 1843 to have defeated Samuel Bishop Chipman by nearly a three to one margin, he must have had the support of a substantial number of Anglicans. In its religous composition, the Tory/Baptist alliance in Annapolis was a union of Anglicans and Baptists. The alliance put together by Johnston would give the Tories all the seats in the County not only in 1843, but would do so for the elections of 1847, 1851 and 1857.

Factions Become Parties in Digby County

But the Acadians desired a member from their district. Mr. Holdsworth fearing two Liberal nominees would ensure [the] choice of the Conservative candidate, gracefully retired, and Francois Bourneuf was chosen instead.
        A Geography and History of the County of Digby.

In the 1840 election for the three seats in the new county of Digby, the sheriff, fortunately as it turned out for James Holdsworth, called for the holding of the Digby Township election first. Sheriff Jacob Roop, a recent Tory appointee, called the election for as soon as the law allowed, knowing that Charles Budd and his Tory friends had already canvassed the township, while Holdsworth had hardly begun. Polling began on a Monday morning and continued fairly evenly until noon the next day, when the weather turned boisterous. This deterred Holdsworth's country supporters from coming to the hustings. Budd's friends were not idle, however, and brought in voters of doubtful eligibility from Weymouth, who all being "well primed" swore the freeholders' oath and voted, giving Budd a lead of 34 votes. By Friday, Budd feared that he was falling behind and had his inspectors so delay the polling that only 19 individuals were able to vote. At one point during the day, the poll had to be closed because of the raging disorder; a magistrate friendly to Budd threatened one voter with prosecution for perjury if he took the oath and voted for Holdsworth. Budd's supporters used the forced delay to bring in more voters. The deputy registrar of deeds seems to have been the most successful, returning from "scouring the forest" with

View of Digby, Nova Scotia
Drawn from nature and on stone by M. G. Hall, lithographed by Pendleton's
Lithography, Boston, 1835, published by John Hooper, Saint John, N. B.

some Indians, supposedly never seen before; their votes were accepted by the sheriff for Budd.[45] Supporters of Holdsworth were not immune from accusations of the same practices. When the poll closed, they were in the process of bringing fishermen to vote on shares in a beach where they landed their catches. Budd had triumphed by 30 votes. Holdsworth now turned around and won with little difficulty the single county seat.

Until Holdsworth's defeat at the hands of Budd, Robicheau had intended to run for the county seat, but gave way to his fellow Reformer, Holdsworth, in the expectation that he could easily win Clare; after all he had been more responsible than anyone for the township having a seat. However, Anselm-François Comeau, who up to that point was the sole candidate, refused to withdraw. Comeau had received some schooling from an itinerant school master, but otherwise seems to have been entirely self-educated; as clerk for the township, he wrote with uncommonly accurate spelling in both French and English.[46] In addition, he was postmaster and engaged in such mercantile ventures as lumbering. The mass of the Acadian vote was along the coast where Comeau's influence was greatest. The Comeau family was probably the most extended in the township, and this gave him a substantial advantage. When he gained a lead of

188 to 119 votes, Robicheau conceded. As in the Annapolis elections, the Reformers had taken two of the three seats.

When the writs were issued for the 1843 election, the freeholders of Digby County could have no doubt that Comeau and Holdsworth stood for reform. Equally, Budd's credentials as a Tory could not be questioned, though he had not bowed to the pressure to support Acadia College. For the Digby Baptists, this proved not to be such a sin as to cause them to oppose his re-election; he went in unopposed. Comeau was equally fortunate in being unopposed. Not so Holdsworth, who found himself besieged on both sides with Colin Campbell standing for the Tories and, unexpectedly, François Bourneuf for the reform cause. Bourneuf was not a native Acadian. He had been a sailor in a French merchantman during the Napoleonic War and had ended up a prisoner at Halifax. He escaped captivity twice and on the second attempt reached Pubnico, where he taught school for some years, before going to Clare and taking the oath of allegiance administered by Abbé Sigogne. A man of education and ability, he soon became prominent in the social life of Clare as a successful merchant and shipbuilder. His candidacy in the 1843 election was motivated by the desire of Acadians to control one county seat in addition to that of Clare. The poll opened at Meteghan. Bourneuf early doubled his total of votes over the other two, but Holdsworth realized that when the poll moved into the entirely English areas of the county, the Reform vote could be so split that Campbell would be elected by default. Although ahead of Bourneuf by 15 votes, Holdsworth resigned the poll to ensure a liberal victory. The Reformers thus maintained their hold on two of the three Digby seats in an election where the sizeable Baptist vote refused to join the Tory/Baptist alliance.

In the new Assembly, the three Digby members voted along party lines on all issues of constitutional moment. Budd continued to be opposed to funding sectarian colleges and was joined in this by Comeau and Bourneuf. But when Huntington of Yarmouth moved for the repeal of the perpetual grant for King's College, Budd, an Anglican, voted with the majority of one in opposition to the motion. In 1847, all three were returned with little or no opposition, so Digby was to be represented by one Tory and two liberals.

Chapter 6

Halifax Connections and the Counties of Lunenburg and Queens

I had Served many years, & had been able to do Some Service by my Connections in Halifax ...
Simeon Perkins, Tuesday, 3 December 1799

Although the national origins of the first settlers in Lunenburg and Liverpool Townships were decidedly dissimilar, their coming derived from the same imperial policy of colonization. It was a policy designed to populate Nova Scotia with loyal Protestant subjects to offset the then preponderant Acadian French and Catholic population. From the settlement of Halifax in 1749, Governor Edward Cornwallis called for the emigration to Nova Scotia of foreign Protestants—the name given the thousands of French and German- speaking central Europeans, who crossed the Atlantic in the eighteenth century to seek economic betterment and freedom from religious persecution. Although Cornwallis was no longer Governor, his policy came to fulfillment in 1751 and 1752 when some 2,500 foreign Protestants arrived in Halifax. Under the supervision of Colonel Charles Lawrence, 1,500 of these immigrants in 1753 settled at Lunenburg.

Six years after Lunenburg's founding, Charles Lawrence, now Governor, issued the proclamations that would bring hundreds of New Englanders to the province, including seventy families to Liverpool. Located at the head of the Mersey River, Liverpool had the advantage of a well-protected harbour, with sufficient pasturage for family cattle and a plentiful supply of accessible timber. Just as fish was an international commodity, so would these transplanted Massachusetts families continue to be part of an international economy, divorced from any natural hinterland. Theirs was a littoral economy dependent on a perishable commodity and the vagaries of distant foreign markets.

By 1830 in Lunenburg town itself, there were upwards of 230 houses, stores and other buildings, including four churches, and a large commodious courthouse. Within the harbour our traveller could have seen any number of the one hundred or so vessels employed in foreign trade, coasting and the fishery. Yet, if he travelled beyond the town into the interior, he would have discovered that for many of the 10,000 inhabitants farming was still very much their chief occupation. At the much less populated New Dublin Township bordering on the La Have River, there was the highest concentration of saw mills anywhere in the region, in total thirty, the wood products of which were finding a ready sale on the British market.

Liverpool was generally acknowledged to be the best-built and neatest town in the province. Its spacious, pleasingly painted houses numbered one hundred and fifty; as well there were another fifty stores and warehouses served by twenty-six wharves. Although our traveller would have observed less shipping in the harbour than at Lunenburg, he would have noted that many vessels were double in tonnage, visible evidence of the town's substantial shipbuilding capacity and emerging world-class merchant marine. For public buildings there were three churches, all handsomely finished, a courthouse and jail, and what must have been the largest school in the entire province, capable of receiving two hundred students. Other than Liverpool, the single other place of any size in Queens County was Mill Village, the site of seven saw mills preparing lumber for the export trade.

By 1830, Lunenburg County had double the population of Queens. Successive generations of the first settlers of both counties had migrated either into the interior, or had filled up the numerous coves and small harbours of this coastline with a succession of fishing villages. From the very beginning in Lunenburg, however, there were greater variations in national origin; its settlers were a mixture of French-speaking Montbéliardians with Swiss and Germans from various principalities. There were also a few Englishmen, who were to play a disproportionate role in the political life of the township.

With a substantial majority of those foreign Protestants who settled Lunenburg being of Germanic origin, Lutherans formed the largest religious denomination. Anglicans were a close second in numbers, followed by Presbyterians, Baptists and Methodists. By the end of the first quarter of the nineteenth century within Queens County, out of the Congregationalism of the first generation of settlers, there had emerged a religious pluralism. Methodists vied with New Light Congregationalists to have the largest numbers of faithful. Adherents of the Church of England also had a strong presence and there was a small number of Baptists, mostly in the Northern District of the county.

The livelihoods of the inhabitants of both counties were tied to a dependence on the fishery, which, with lumber in the case of Queens and agricultural products in that of Lunenburg, provided their essential staples. From the first days of settlement, their populations were drawn into a natural connection with mercantile Halifax. More than any other factor, this would shape the political consciousness of their local oligarchies.

Foreign Protestants and Englishmen

Lunenburg, Nov. 21, 1840

GLORIOUS NEWS ... the radicals defeated ... This must certainly teach friend Joe [Howe] that he had not yet conquered the loyalty of this County, whatever influence he may have over the crocodiles of the United States; ... and we have triumphed over them, and completely substantiated the principles of our address to our late highly respected and meritorious Governor Sir Colin Campbell, who was not treated by the radical majority of the late House of Assembly with that courtesy that English gentleman would shew to his black footman. It would appear also from information received from our neighbouring counties, that the radical stars and stripes are about setting in everlasting darkness there, (we hope) to be chained for a thousand years.

POP GUN

A Note to the *Times,* 1 December 1840, giving election results

In Governor Charles Lawrence's struggle with the New England mercantile community in Halifax over the calling of a Legislative Assembly, he or his friends enlisted the aid of the foreign Protestants of Lunenburg. They agreed to sign a petition against convening an Assembly. Their fear was that such a body under the control of Halifax merchants would end government provisioning of the nascent settlement, which Lawrence had instituted to ensure its success. Moreover, in their complaints to the Board of Trade in London the New Englanders wanted the Lunenburgers totally excluded from voting for members in a new Assembly, arguing that they should not be classed as freeholders, but as persons subsisting on "charity." In the most outlandish falsehood of all, these Halifax merchants described Lunenburg as settled by "Swiss Roman Catholics" and "Old Soldiers in the French Service." What really lay behind this slanderous opposition was the calculated fear that, if the Lunenburgers had the vote, their numbers would allow them to dominate the election of members for the province at large. And worse still, they would elect representatives of Lawrence's choosing.[1]

Few of the foreign Protestants had, in fact, been naturalized; most had not been resident in a North American colony for the required seven years. By the time the election for the First Assembly was held in 1758, at most half the adult males qualified for naturalization out of around 250 heads of households. Of these, 58 voted on 31 July for two township representatives, and presumably the same number for the sixteen members elected for the province at large. With the 1759 division of the province into five counties, that of Lunenburg incorporated all the south shore around to and including much of what later became Yarmouth County. The electors of Lunenburg could now elect two for the county and two for their township, which they proceeded to do for the Second Assembly on 31 August 1759, using St. John's Church as the hustings.

Although greatly differing in national origin, those elected from Lunenburg in these first years had much in common with their colleagues in Hants, Kings and Annapolis. They were part of the great eighteenth-century migration of peoples to colonial America and, as in the case of the New England Planters and later the Loyalists, within it. Sebastian Zouberbuhler, Philip Knaut and Joseph Pernette had left their European homelands to seek better prospects in the New World. Zouberbuhler was one of those well-educated natives of Switzerland—others included Isaac Deschamps and J.F.W. DesBarres—who had found themselves in Nova Scotia as much by chance as by design. After service at Louisbourg, Zouberbuhler had come to Lunenburg as a government agent and magistrate (he spoke English, German and French); he easily mixed official duties with his commercial ventures, and prospered.[2] Probably from Saxony, Knaut had come out with Edward Cornwallis in 1749. His occupation as a furrier drew him naturally into the fur trade and once at Lunenburg he pursued it highly successfully.

Joseph Pernette had seen service in the French army before finding employment as an agent for the transportation of one of the shiploads of foreign Protestants. After his arrival, he was commissioned to serve as a lieutenant in a ranger company recruited to end the threat of

Indian attacks on settlements. For these services, he received 20,000 acres on the west side of the La Have River, including present-day Bridgewater. New Dublin Township became his political fiefdom, which he passed on at his death in 1807 to his Loyalist son-in-law, Garrett Miller. The fourth individual, who with Zouberbuhler, Knaut and Pernette formed a compact either to have themselves elected or to choose who would be, was an Englishman, John Creighton. A former British army officer on half-pay who had accompanied Cornwallis to Halifax, Creighton had come to Lunenburg as commander of one of the six divisions of its settlement.[3] Creighton was in easy enough circumstances that he was able to send his son, John, to England for his education, and then to purchase a captaincy for him costing £950. Creighton could and seemingly did content himself with performing his many duties as the government's most trusted official in the settlement.[4]

From the first election in 1758, officials and merchants resident in Halifax shared nearly equally the Lunenburg representation in the Assembly. For fourteen years, the deputy provincial secretary and clerk of Assembly, Archibald Hinshelwood, sat for a Lunenburg constituency. On his death in 1773 another Halifax resident, Otto William Schwartz, succeeded to his seat. He had served a seven-year apprenticeship in the fur trade in Riga, Latvia. After many travels, he had come to Halifax with Cornwallis, where he had renewed his business as a furrier. When Philip Knaut died in 1781, after serving for twenty-three years in the Assembly, the choice fell on Casper Wollenhaupt, who had earlier removed from Lunenburg to Halifax to establish himself as a merchant there. In fact, his election meant that until 1785 all three Lunenburg members were resident in the capital.

The principal families of Lunenburg saw their interests as being tied to those of official and mercantile Halifax. It was not initially the fishery and the West Indian trade that drew the emerging local oligarchy into a Halifax embrace; it was as suppliers of firewood and provisions to the capital. Each autumn small coastal vessels made two or three trips each with loads of cordwood, vegetables, sheep, butter and other produce. Thus, these Swiss and German settlers, who had never even beheld an ocean before their voyage across the Atlantic, first went to sea in Nova Scotia.

The 1785 election for the two county seats and the single township seat was noteworthy only for the fact that for the first time a candidate from Chester appeared. Although settled mostly by New Englanders, the township's contiguity to Lunenburg had led to its incorporation into Lunenburg County. Jonathan Prescott was another veteran of Louisbourg and a surgeon by profession with close ties to official Halifax. But in challenging the grip held over the three seats by the compact of Lunenburg town families, he stood little chance. He was easily defeated for the county by the merchant John William Schwartz, son of Otto William, and by Dettlieb Christopher Jessen. Jessen led the poll with 357 votes, nearly 100 more than Schwartz, and this substantial margin may be ascribed to his genuine popularity among the settlers. As an exceptionally conscientious justice of the peace, he refused to use his office to enrich himself and endeavoured to "mitigate between neighbour & neighbour" without taking any fees.[5] Nonetheless, Jessen was no more prepared than his colleagues to have any candidate elected from either Chester or New Dublin. During a debate on an election bill in 1789, he spoke for all the sitting Lunenburg members when he was emphatic that there was no requirement to move the poll from the town of Lunenburg to any other part of the county.

Among the few Loyalists who came to Lunenburg was a former surgeon in General de Riesdesel's Hessian Regiment. A native of Mageburg in Germany, John Bolman married the widow of Philip Knaut shortly after arriving in the township where he soon rose to social prominence. Another Loyalist was Lewis Morris Wilkins, the son of Isaac and the Shelburne Loyalist elected to the Assembly in 1785. Before the American War Lewis Morris had gone to King's College (later Columbia University) in New York. He likely studied law with an uncle in Shelburne before deciding to practise his profession in Lunenburg.[6] It was a wise decision, because there was not to be another lawyer in Lunenburg for many years; he was able to develop an extensive practice not only there, but also increasingly in Halifax and Pictou. Wollenhaupt declined to re-offer. Both Wilkins and Bolman seized the opportunity to run for the single township seat. Bolman was nearly twice the age of the youthful Wilkins and this was likely in his favour, though Bolman did not win by a large margin, the vote being 164 to 123.

The county election also had its Loyalist in Edward James, but one a good many Lunenburgers wished had stayed away. He was a half-pay officer from his service in the navy and then with the King's Orange Rangers during the American War, in which he had seen extensive service and had been severely wounded. Undoubtedly as the result of his marriage to a daughter of Philip Knaut, James had settled at Lunenburg. He was already known for his violent temperament. While in command of troops at Liverpool during the war, he had had an altercation with another man, and had sent his soldiers to beat up the individual, while he had stood by with drawn sword to prevent any interference. Now at Lunenburg James refused to pay the poll tax levy for 1792, threatening to shoot constables sent by Wollenhaupt and Jessen to collect the tax; James called the latter a "vile hypocritical poltroon" in a letter to John William Schwartz in Halifax. Official Halifax became much alarmed by James' conduct. He quickly decided to pay the tax, writing the provincial secretary that he only wanted to show his disapprobation and not cause "tumult."[7]

The ladies of the Knaut and Pernette families must have been among the most attractive and eligible in the province. Charles Morris III had married another of Joseph Pernette's daughters. In the riotous Halifax by-election of 1788, Morris had defeated Jonathan Sterns, but now in 1793 he declined to face another such contest for the seat. Presumably with the active encouragement of his father-in-law, he stood for one of the Lunenburg County seats. He lost by a wide margin to the sitting members, John William Schwartz and Edward James.

The ghost of Philip Knaut returned to the floor of the House in 1793. Bolman was married to his widow, and James to a daughter, Sarah. Bolman joined with those members who formed the nascent county party, nominally led by William Cottnam Tonge. Bolman, Schwartz and James would likely have been returned in the 1799 election with no difficulty, if the genuinely popular Casper Wollenhaupt had not decided to run again, though this time for the county. As a result, Schwartz thought better of re-offering for the county, and went up against Bolman for the township seat. Another factor in his decision may well have been a determination to bring about the defeat of Bolman because of his active role in the county party. Schwartz, with his close ties to Governor Sir John Wentworth's circle, would have had its encouragement and backing. If so, it did him little good, for Bolman defeated him. An embittered Schwartz then accused Bolman of unduly and illegally influencing the election, and moreover declared that he was an alien, thereby disabled from being elected; the Assembly dismissed the petition out of hand. The popularity and public standing of Wollenhaupt ensured that he would have one of the county seats. The contest for the second was between Edward James, the merchant Christopher Rudolf and Lewis Morris Wilkins. After his appointment in 1798 as sheriff of

Halifax County, Wilkins had moved to Halifax and his non-residency should have caused him difficulties. But he had recently married a daughter of John Creighton and he had that family's influence to count upon. Wilkins also made promises of entertainment to lure a good number of Chester freeholders to the hustings at the Lunenburg courthouse, and this seems to have been a major factor in his taking the second seat.[8]

Even as a non-resident, Wilkins was still certain of holding one of the two county seats in the 1806 election. It was left to Edward James and Garrett Miller, a Loyalist and son-in-law to Joseph Pernette, to vie for the second. James' temper had not improved with age. Although a justice of the peace, in 1804 he had been cited as a common disturber of the peace. Moreover, he had become the main "jobbing" magistrate in the county, prepared for the sake of the fees to determine any causes that came before him, instead of putting a stop to the "licentious disposition of the present young generation." Or so Pernette believed. Miller felt forced to decline during the contest because of the "most turbulent and riotous manner" of James' supporters. After little debate the Assembly dismissed Miller's petition, suggesting considerable exaggeration on his part.[9]

When the House reassembled after the election in November 1806, Wilkins was unsuccessful in opposing Tonge for the Speakership. As already described, Governor John Wentworth refused to accept Tonge as Speaker and shortly after dismissed him as naval officer. Although there were five other lawyers besides Wilkins in the new Assembly, four of them had just been elected for the first time, leaving only Simon Bradstreet Robie as a possible contender to Wilkins for the Speakership. Both were in their late thirties and fully understood the importance of this office to their future legal careers, but Wilkins seems to have made a far stronger impression on the Assembly than Robie. Wilkins was unanimously elected Speaker. Like such other Loyalists as John Sargent and James Moody, who had seen extensive service in the American War, Edward James was not enamoured with Wentworth, who had spent most of the war in England. It was James who moved that Wentworth should not receive a pension from the Assembly. Moreover, both he and Sargent supported Tonge's motion to insert an insulting phrase in the Assembly's address to the retiring Wentworth. In an otherwise quiet five sessions leading up to the 1811 election, the single occasion on which Wilkins had to break a tie vote was when he voted for an additional Supreme Court assistant judge, thus increasing the likelihood of his own elevation to that august repository for ambitious lawyers. His day came in 1816. Edward James replaced Wilkins as the leading Lunenburg member in the House. James' earlier errant behaviour was now forgotten, or at least forgiven. He had recently been made a warden of St. John's Church and shortly would become chief magistrate for the county. His new respectability probably accounts for him being unopposed in the 1818 election. But, the day in Lunenburg politics when a local oligarchy in the town of Lunenburg could arrange matters with hardly a ripple of opposition was now to be seriously challenged.

Not since the 1761 election had a candidate from either New Dublin or Chester been elected. In 1818 Charles Lott Church of Chester determined to stand as a candidate for one of the two county seats. Church's parents had come as Massachusetts Loyalists, first to Shelburne before settling at Chester. Church's father had refused to take up arms against the king, though the rebels had offered him a commission as a naval officer. Moreover, he had declined to submit a claim for his losses because he would not add to those already sustained by the British government. The son inherited this sense of loyalty. In marrying the granddaughter of Timothy Houghton, the leading name in the Chester Township grant, Church had gained a degree of respectability not readily apparent for one who had chosen to cut out a farm deep in the interior of the township. Church seems to have been largely self-educated and was acknowledged to be widely read in the literature of the day. For the 1818 election, Church faced the combined opposition of the shipowner John Heckman and the merchant Francis Joseph Rudolf. The friends of these two Lunenburg candidates spread rumours that Church would, if elected, attend only to Chester and ignore the rest of the county. Church lost, but he and his friends had learned that if Church were to stand a chance next time, they must ensure all their Chester supporters appeared at the Lunenburg town poll. Their strategy was for the Chester freeholders to vote only for Church, while he gained enough second votes of Lunenburg Township electors to give him one of the two county seats. An alternative strategy was to make an alliance with another candidate, with supporters of each giving their second vote to the other candidate.

When the death of George III occasioned another election two years later, Church stood again. Both Heckman and Rudolf re-offered and a fourth candidate came forward, John Oxner. From the hustings at the Lunenburg courthouse, Church made an able speech, though somewhat righteous in tone, as when he promised that he would never apply one penny of revenue to his private use. He must have brought a strong contingent of Chester freeholders with him, for he led the poll on the first day with 192 to Oxner's 165, Heckman's 89 and Rudolf's 54 votes. On the second day, Oxner took the lead by one vote, but both he and Church were still ahead of Heckman, and by a wide margin over Rudolf. At the opening of the poll on the third day, Rudolf declined and threw his support to Heckman. The lead then passed to Heckman; throughout the day the poll fluctuated between Oxner and Church, until Heckman told his supporters to use their second vote for Church. Oxner knew he was beaten and resigned the poll. Just why Heckman acted as he did remains a mystery, but it does not seem to have been the result of an alliance with Church, but rather a decision of the moment. At least 800 freeholders had come forward.

The day of quiet elections had passed for Lunenburg County. When the writs for the 1826 election were issued in April, a note appeared in the *Nova Scotia Royal Gazette* saying that a violent election was expected in Lunenburg. What precipitated this comment was the decision of two scions of the most influential families in the town to run for the two county seats. William Rudolf at thirty-five years of age was already a highly successful West Indian merchant, justice of peace and militia officer. Three years younger than Rudolf, John Creighton III had become heir to the Creighton family interest on the death of his father a few months before. After studying in the office of his relation by marriage, Lewis Morris Wilkins, Creighton had been admitted to the bar in 1815. The entrance of Rudolf and Creighton as candidates placed Heckman in a dilemma. He solved it by standing for the township against the aging James, who no doubt had fully expected to be returned unopposed as in the past two elections. Although he must have known that he stood no chance, Garrett Miller decided once more to stand for the county. However, his decision further divided the Lunenburg Township vote, which in turn favoured Church, because the more the Lunenburg vote was split, the more likely his Chester support would give him enough to hold one of the seats. In fact, although Church protested that one hundred of his supporters were deprived, as he said, of voting for him in an "ungentlemanly" scheme to oust him, after five days on the hustings he led the poll with 416 votes. Rudolf was second at 388, then Creighton with 240; last was Miller, who had done well to gain 179 votes. Church saw his victory as evidence that the people were no longer swayed by family connections, sinister motives and false principles.[10] Heckman's decision to run for the township was fully justified since he won 194 to the aging James' 32 votes.

Creighton's defeat taught him that he needed to form an alliance with a Chester candidate, in the hope that supporters of each would give their second vote to the other. He acted on this strategy for the 1830 election and reached such an arrangement with Joseph Wells, a retired naval officer on half-pay, while further cementing his support in New Dublin.[11] This alliance got Creighton elected, but not Wells. It also split the Chester vote and Lott Church went down to defeat. For first time since Church had won in 1818, two Lunenburg town residents, William Rudolf and John Creighton, represented the county. Heckman went in unopposed for the township.

The significant role that the fishery, shipping and the West Indian trade by now played in the economic life of Lunenburg could not be better illustrated than by the bloc voting of its members through the sessions from 1830 to 1836. They consistently voted for measures advantageous to the fishery, while opposing those designed to benefit agriculture. Lunenburg County was as dependent on imported flour as the other coastal townships. Its representatives could be relied upon to vote for any measure that exempted American flour from duties, and naturally for Lunenburg to become a free or warehousing port. Close commercial and political ties between the leading Lunenburg families and the ruling oligarchy in the capital had always been present. As the movement for reform gathered momentum, a natural alliance of commercial interest now became a common political front. In the last session before the 1836 election, Heckman, Rudolf and Creighton all voted against the Assembly taking up the question of reform of the Council of Twelve.

The Rudolf and Creighton families formed the core of the town's establishment. They were absolutely determined to keep the two county seats within the town's fold. To ensure the re-election of Creighton and Rudolf, they had to make certain their opponents, who turned out to be Church and Miller, received few votes when the poll was at the Lunenburg courthouse. Whether or not there was a formal alliance between Church and Miller to have each other's second votes, it worked out that way. During the three days of voting at Chester, Church led with 184, followed by Miller's 149. Way behind were Creighton and Rudolf with 37 and 22 votes respectively. When the poll moved to Lunenburg, every form of violence was used to force freeholders to vote for Creighton and Rudolf, and to keep supporters of Church from voting. The "rabble," as Lott Church described them, were led by the legal fraternity in the town, abetted by the principal merchants and shopkeepers. The most outrageous behaviour was that of Heckman, whose countenance at one point became "so distorted with rage that he appeared more like a fiend than a human being." The open houses of Creighton and Rudolf provided rum laced with the molasses used in the making of spruce beer, much increasing the potency of the rum. Among the "shameful stratagems" employed was to tie up a dog, so that its hind leg was fixed in the crack of a door to make it howl when the door was closed on the leg, thus drowning out Church's attempts to address the freeholders. The confusion was such that at one point a boxing match took place on the courthouse floor.

After five days of polling Rudolf stood first with 480 votes, followed by Miller with 363 and Creighton nine votes behind him. Church was well back at 314. The final round was fought out when the poll moved to Petite Riviere. As was to be expected, Miller took the most with 120 votes, with his supporters giving their second vote, not to Church, but to Rudolf, who seems to have had extensive ledger influence in New Dublin Township; just 28 freeholders gave their votes to Creighton and another 22 to Church. Church used the columns of the *Novascotian* to decry the failure of Sheriff John Henry Kaulbeck to conduct a peaceful election. He petitioned the Assembly, but to no avail as the committee who heard Church and his witnesses saw no reason to overturn the election. Nor did the full House.[12]

With Heckman's easy victory in 1836 over the eighty-year-old James, Lunenburg had returned three conservatives to an Assembly bent on constitutional reform. Rudolf remained a member for only one session before Governor Sir Colin Campbell appointed him to the Legislative Council. His departure created the opportunity for Creighton to return to the Assembly, but not before he had to do battle with two of the chief leaders of the "rabble" who had so beset poor Lott Church, the barrister Charles Bolman and Edward Zwicker. One favourable consequence for Creighton of this feuding within the local oligarchy was that he was able to continue his strategy of developing a following in Chester, which was to stand him in good stead in the future. As usual the Lunenburg members had little to say on the floor of the House. Having finally got there after two attempts, Garrett Miller found it a "motley Assembly" with much jealousy among the members. He proved to be an arch Tory, consistently opposing all moves to reform. On the last recorded vote before the 1840 election, Creighton, Heckman and Miller were among the minority of sixteen who opposed the address to Queen Victoria calling for the removal of Sir Colin Campbell as Governor.

The Reformers did not hold out much hope of taking any seats in Lunenburg, but nonetheless put up the Chester shipbuilder Daniel Dimock. For the first time there were candidates from Bridgewater, when James Waterman and George Fancy offered, though they were to receive so few votes that they need not have bothered. To run with Creighton, the Tories put up none other than the merchant Edward Zwicker, who had opposed Creighton three years earlier. Heckman once again re-offered for the town and was opposed by the blacksmith Peter Langille, who did well to get 165 to Heckman's 342 votes. Attention was centred on the county poll and how well the liberal Dimock would do. It opened at Chester. From the hustings there developed a nasty exchange between Creighton and some freeholders from New Dublin Township over the expenditure of funds obtained by Creighton for the rebuilding of the La Have bridge. Behind this accusation lay the charge that Creighton and the other members had got road moneys appropriated to districts they favoured, while leaving the improvement of the roads in others to statute labour. Creighton told one of his accusers that, if he should show his head in Lunenburg town, Creighton would make him remember the present election as long as he lived. The poll likely did not move to New Dublin, but finished at the Lunenburg courthouse where Creighton led it with 661, followed by Zwicker at 499 and Dimock with 348 votes.

With the occasional exception, Lunenburg representatives had never been disposed to support public funding for colleges, sectarian or not. In the session of the Assembly after the 1840 election, this changed. It began with Creighton voting for funding of Acadia College, and also, somewhat surprisingly, for compulsory assessment for schools. But it was Zwicker who really first broke ranks on the issue. During the votes for providing grants to Acadia, Saint Mary's and Dalhousie in the 1842 session, he voted with the majority. A year later, with the collapse of Governor Lord Falkland's coalition experiment and the emergence of a Tory/Baptist alliance under the leadership of Attorney General J.W. Johnston, Heckman abandoned his earlier opposition. He now voted with his fellow conservatives to uphold the principle of funding sectarian colleges. By the time the 1843 election was called, the liberal strength in Lunenburg was at such a low ebb that the real contest was among three conservatives—Creighton, Zwicker and the lawyer Charles Owen—for the two county seats. For the liberal interest Daniel Dimock re-offered. Creighton's strength at Chester told once more and he led the poll there, followed by Zwicker, Dimock and Owen in that order. At the close of the Lunenburg poll, Dimock was so far behind that he resigned, leaving the three conservatives to battle it out at New Dublin. By then, Creighton was leading by such a wide margin that his return was certain, but it proved close between the other two, until Owen decisively moved ahead of Zwicker. For the town Heckman had the satisfaction of not even being opposed.

In the sessions leading up to the 1847 election and the institution of responsible government, Heckman, Creighton and Owen were solid supporters of what was a conservative government under Attorney General J.W. Johnston. If the overwhelming Tory victories in past elections for the Lunenburg seats were any guide, there was every reason to believe that 1847 would be no different. It was not to be. The reasons for the conservative collapse are not entirely certain. Mostly, however, it can be attributed to Joseph Howe's determined campaigning in the county, bitter personal feuding among the Tory candidates and the introduction of simultaneous polling with increased voter turnout. Howe had been told that it was useless to come to Lunenburg because "the Germans loved not free discussion—they could not understand me—that they were deeply prejudiced— and that they venerated Tories as some heathen nations venerate the Ape ...." He found, instead, that there was no county in which his popularity was "higher or more universal than in Lunenburg."[13] In their strategy to take the Lunenburg seats the liberals were much aided by the outbreak of ferocious Tory infighting, which had a history and rationale all its own. It was said that Owen hated Creighton, while Creighton hated Heckman and Owen. Zwicker could not make up his mind whether to run and eventually did not, but his son, Benjamin, entered the fray. The liberals saw their opportunity; they recruited George Ernst, who was married to the daughter of the deceased Edward James. A merchant, sawmill operator and innkeeper, Ernst was the first Lutheran to run for the Assembly since the 1770s. No one else seems to have come forward for the Reformers and so the liberals put up the Halifax merchant and alderman Henry Mignowitz. John Kedy, a sawmill owner, went up against Heckman, who was engaged in his eighth election, having been first returned in 1818. It was to be Heckman's last, for he went down to defeat by 159 votes. A similar fate awaited Creighton and Zwicker, though they lost by smaller margins. The liberal triumph had ended the Tory "reign of terror" in Lunenburg.

From the first Lunenburg election in 1759 to the middle of the next century, two extended families — the Philip Knaut family connection (Bolman, James and Ernst), and that of the Rudolf, Schwartz and Creighton connection — remained a formidable presence in the political life of township and county. One reason for this lay in the marriages that drew in new blood, notably those of Bolman, Wilkins and also James for all his early sins. Moreover, St. John's Anglican Church in Lunenburg was the church of both these family connections; and, in fact, the church of all but two of the town and county members elected between 1759 and 1847. However much these two family connections quarrelled among themselves, they were united in their determination to keep control of the town and county representation within the town itself. The same policy applied to the local offices and to their general opposition to reform. Other than Wilkins, none of the Lunenburg members sought to play a leading role in the Assembly. In session after session, they were content to vote as their economic interests and conservative instincts dictated.

Liverpool's Two Family Compacts

It has been long my decided opinion to choose all Our Representatives among Ourselves, for one reason among Others that when gentlemen in Halifax set themselves up for candidates it creates parties and makes such disturbance in this place ... Mr Hart had Introduced the Business Some months before the Election, and we found he had so much influence with the people, we gave up the idea of choosing them all here.

Simeon Perkins to Attorney-General Blowers, 13 March 1793

In 1759, at the urgings of Governor Charles Lawrence, the Plymouth, Massachusetts, mariner and merchant John Doggett journeyed through New England, gathering settlers to take up lands along the Nova Scotian south shore whence they could better prosecute the fishery. Most of the first grantees were from Nantucket and Cape Cod. They arrived in their own fishing schooners, bringing with them stock and the workings for three saw mills. By the spring of 1760 seventy families had settled in the township, which for the 1761 election was given two representatives. When the Halifax merchant, Benjamin Gerrish, successfully sought the nomination for one of the seats, a pattern was set that would see at least one Halifax merchant always sitting for the township or county, through to the first decade of the next century. The cause lay partly in the fact that the members elected within Liverpool had the worst Assembly attendance record in the province. But it was mostly because no merchants in the townships were more dependent upon credit provided from Halifax than those of Liverpool. Gerrish's successor was William Smith, whose election for one of the county seats in 1765 was arranged by the leading figure in the township, Simeon Perkins. Smith became the conduit for official and business correspondence. He accepted consignments from Perkins and other Liverpool merchants and disposed of their fish or lumber at best prices, while paying bills for them and sending on their mail. Because neither Perkins, the other member for the county, nor the township member Elisha Freeman seem ever to have attended a session, having Smith in the capital ensured that the township's interests were looked after. The arrangement proved satisfactory until the government became doubtful about the loyalty of Liverpool, as the American colonies to the south moved to outright rebellion. Smith was accused of disloyalty and temporarily dismissed from all his offices for refusing to handle a consignment of tea.

When in 1775 the Assembly vacated the Liverpool Township seat for non-attendance, the government seized the opportunity to try and impose Jonathan Prescott of Chester. Freeholders came under much pressure to offer the seat to Prescott, who had close links to the Halifax oligarchy and whose loyalty was not in question. Perkins called a meeting at which it was unanimous that the next member should not be an outsider. This decision of Liverpool to refuse Prescott was almost certainly what led to the introduction of a bill during the 1775 summer session to dismember Queens County. The plan was to annex Liverpool to Lunenburg County and move the inferior court of common pleas to Yarmouth. The need for friends in Halifax to counter the bill became paramount. Perkins and others equally concerned settled on the Halifax merchant Thomas Cochran, a long-time associate of theirs; but there was still a contest, with Cochran just defeating an opponent by 28 to 22 votes. After the election, friends of Perkins raised funds so that he could attend the Assembly as well. Cochran's influence was instrumental in having the bill for annexation deferred. At the next session all three Queens County members were present and the bill was not reintroduced.[14] For Perkins, it was a lesson on the importance of having the right Halifax connections and one he never forgot. As lieutenant colonel of the militia, proprietors' clerk, chief magistrate, judge of probate and soon to be deputy registrar of the vice admiralty court, Perkins' services to government were much appreciated; in return, he could call on his Halifax connections when his own and Liverpool's interests required it.

The election of Benajah Collins in an 1784 by-election, as one of the county representatives, presaged a compact involving the Collins, Barss and Taylor families. Except for a brief period in the 1820s, this family connection would always have at least one member sitting for one of three seats through to 1851. Benajah Collins, the progenitor of this family compact, was typical of many of his contemporaries who went to sea as circumstances demanded as captains, shipowners, traders and privateers. Collins, with Perkins, agreed to stand again for the 1785 election, the latter for the town and the former for the county. The choice for the second county candidate was left undecided. Two Halifax merchants and Loyalists, Philip Marchinton and Samuel Waddington, offered their services, as did George William Sherlock. The writ for the township arrived before that of the county. On election day for the town, there were only eight freeholders present to vote and they all did so for Perkins. The poll was then adjourned for an hour, while Perkins swore in Collins as judge of the inferior court of common pleas. Then the despatch arrived authorizing the division of Queens County and accompanying it was the writ for electing two county members.

With the creation of Shelburne County, Queens now incorporated only Liverpool Township. County members would not be faced with representing the interests of thousands of demanding Loyalists. On this news those present persuaded Perkins to run instead for the other county seat, which he agreed to do. Then Captain Ephraim Dean, who ten years earlier had contested Thomas Cochran's candidacy because he was from Halifax, proposed Philip Marchinton; this met with the same opposition as before and so Dean accepted the nomination himself, with all 25 freeholders present immediately voting for him. Four days later the county election was held. Both Perkins and Collins stood, but were unexpectedly opposed by the resident Congregational minister, Israel Cheever, whose support turned out to be limited to the votes of the other two candidates.

When Ephraim Dean suddenly died of an epileptic fit in 1787, the Liverpool seat became the object of much contention, not in the town, but in Halifax. Alexander Brymer, the wealthy merchant and member of Governor John Parr's Council, was determined to put his young cousin of the same name into the Assembly. For this he enlisted the support of the Attorney General and Speaker of the House, S.S. Blowers, the lawyer Jonathan Sterns and the Collector of Customs, Henry Newton. George Sherlock once more offered. Sherlock had the support of Thomas and William Cochran and the firm's long-standing business associations with Liverpool. Sherlock also had the backing of a number within the Halifax governing clique who were determined to curb Brymer's growing influence over the colony's government. Neither of the candidates appeared in Liverpool. They fought the election through their commercial connections and by sending letters to prominent freeholders requesting their support. Benajah Collins acted for Brymer. Their relationship probably went back to the war years when Collins engaged in privateering, and Brymer was an official for condemned prize ships and their cargoes. Sherlock chose the mariner and trader Robert Callahan as his agent, presumably also because of past business relations. Both the agents gave dinners for their candidates' supporters.

Party spirit ran high before the election. After the first day of polling Brymer had a majority, but 16 votes given to him had been objected to, as had 7 for Sherlock. When the poll opened on the second day, disputes broke out again over contested votes and whether electors who were not given their freehold title until the day of the election could vote. On the advice that at the last election in Halifax such freeholders had been allowed to vote, the sheriff agreed to receive their votes. Sherlock's friends then came forward with enough freeholders, created that day, to give him the lead. Collins was so furious that he told Tinkham he did not care if the poll was closed, thus ceding victory to Sherlock. After the poll closed there was a scrutiny and the final totals stood 73 for Sherlock and 66 for Brymer. Tinkham, however, was so uncertain about the disputed votes that he refused to declare Sherlock the winner and said that the Assembly would have to decide. As Perkins wrote in his diary for the day: "There appears Some Hart Burnings &c."[15] The Assembly declared an undue election. In the ensuing by-election Sherlock defeated a local candidate, Joseph Taylor, by a wide margin of 68 votes. The extensive amount of credit the Cochran brothers made available in their business dealings seems to have been the major reason that their chosen candidate, the outsider Sherlock, could so triumph.

When it came time to choose representatives for the 1793 election, there was another rush of mail from Halifax to Perkins, Collins and others from prospective candidates and their backers. Sherlock, the naval contractor Andrew Belcher, and the Loyalist merchant Samuel Hart all offered. Some fifteen Liverpool freeholders now met to arrange matters in the hopes of avoiding what had happened in 1787, when "Gentlemen from Halifax Setting up as Candidates ... in opposition to each other, had thrown the place into confusion."[16] Perkins and Benajah Collins agreed to stand again, if all the members were from the county. Perkins nominated Benajah's brother, Hallet, for the township seat and the election business seemed completed. It was not, for Samuel Hart had sufficient ledger influence in Liverpool to impose his candidacy for the township seat and sent his clerk to arrange matters, very much over the opposition of most of the leading freeholders. An English Jew, Hart had gone to Philadelphia before the American War and joined the Tory cause there. He came to Halifax in 1785 with the Loyalist migration. He prospered, but yearned for respectability, which he sought to gain through entertaining and generally ingratiating himself with fashionable Halifax. Although their resistance to an outsider remained strong, too many were so "intangled with Mr. Hart by promise or encouragement" that when Major Nathan Freeman nominated him, those unhappy with his candidacy had no choice but to accept it. The unpalatable alternative was to face a contested election, which they wanted even less, so they bowed to the inevitable.

Although already nominated for the county seats, Perkins and Benajah Collins were so upset that they no longer wished to stand, but in the end were prevailed upon. Perkins had already ordered the rum. He and Collins then did the expected by telling a tavern-keeper before they went home that the "people could have what grogg they wanted." Perkins wrote propitiatory letters to Halifax (a quote from one of which begins this section), explaining that Hart had been able to force himself on the town. Perkins had wanted neither an outsider, nor especially a contested election, because it created parties and "besides we git enemies in Halifax."[17]

The attendance record of the Queens County members was worse in the 1790s than it had been in the previous decade. This was not as great a concern to freeholders as might be expected. Seaborne trade, especially with the West Indies and the American states, was the economic lifeblood of Liverpool. The regulation of trade rested with the British government, though some authority to allow certain enumerated articles to enter from the United States was delegated to the provincial Governor and his Council. Other than putting on additional duties to raise revenue, the Assembly could do little that directly affected the trade of Liverpool. The policy followed by Parr, and more particularly by Governor Sir John Wentworth after the war with France began, was to allow the importation of increasing amounts of American foodstuffs and other articles to meet the growing demand caused by the war. This was opposed by the agricultural interests, who claimed that the province was now producing plentiful quantities of all that was needed. During the 1797 session, a short-lived coalition of agricultural interests and some Halifax merchants introduced a bill with the ostensible aim of preventing smuggling, but containing clauses that would have crippled the trade of Liverpool and other outports. In particular, all vessels coming from the United States would be restricted to entering for customs clearance at the ports of Halifax, Shelburne, Digby and Parrsborough. This would have forced Liverpool captains, at great expense and inconvenience, to go first either to Halifax or to Shelburne.[18] After much debate the bill went forward to the Council, where it was rejected. An amended bill by the House was left on the Council table when the session prorogued.

Perkins was understandably greatly disturbed by the threat to Liverpool's trade. When, in 1797, Benajah Collins' removal to the United States made it possible to choose a successor for the county, he seized the opportunity to arrange for Attorney General Richard John Uniacke to be elected without opposition, so as to have "a man of Such abilities on our side" of the House, if another attempt were made, which he was certain would be the case.[19] As in the past with William Smith and Thomas Cochran, there was a mutual interest. As Advocate General of the Court of Vice Admiralty in this period, Uniacke was able to be of considerable assistance to Perkins and others in Liverpool when they were disposing of prizes from their privateering ventures.

When Perkins arrived at the hustings for the 1799 county election, he anticipated that he and Uniacke would go in without opposition. Instead, he had to defend not only his failure to attend sessions with any regularity, but also his support for Uniacke's nomination. Both his son-in-law Joshua Newton and Colonel William Freeman came to his support, but Perkins himself made the strongest case when he argued that he had been able to serve Liverpool well because of his Halifax connections. The poll was then taken for the county seats and the vote was unanimous for Perkins and Uniacke. However, the sheriff did not then declare them elected, but went on to hold the vote for the town's representative. For the first time there was a contest between two local candidates, when Colonel William Freeman and Joseph Barss agreed to stand. Barss easily defeated Freeman in the voting and when the poll closed Perkins resigned his, as yet unofficial, county seat. The next day George Collins' brother-in-law, James Taylor, was unanimously chosen for the county. Taylor had come with his Loyalist parents to Shelburne. Shortly after his marriage to a daughter of Benajah Collins, he had removed to Liverpool, where he became a mariner with shares in trading vessels and privateers.

Now sixty-five years of age, Perkins desired more than ever to withdraw from public life. He had been a member of the Assembly from 1765 to 1799 (except for the years 1768 and 1769). Although he had attended only eleven out of the forty sessions, he believed with justification that his Halifax connections had served Liverpool well. According to the Methodist leader William Black, though Perkins was "slow to speak," he was said to have "manifested great wisdom and integrity" in deciding upon questions of importance.[20] It was a fair comment. Black had been the means of Perkins' conversion from the Congregationalism of his upbringing to the Methodism of his later years.

In January 1801 the thirty-year-old Taylor died after a lingering illness. As soon as the writ to elect a successor was issued, the recommendations started to arrive from Halifax. The most sustained pressure came from William Cochran. Because of the lengthy and soon fatal illness of his brother, Thomas, William was assuming responsibility for the son, Thomas Jr. The twenty-four-year-old graduate of King's College at Windsor was studying law at Lincoln's Inn and waiting to be admitted to the English bar. The youth was well known to Perkins and others in Liverpool. William Cochran wrote to twenty freeholders in his attempt to secure the seat for his nephew. Perkins discussed the matter with his friends, who were unanimous that they should have one of their own; they felt it would be something of a "disgrace" to have both county seats held by outsiders. Perkins recommended Captain Snow Parker and he succeeded to Taylor's seat without a contest.[21] This attempt to impose young Cochran's candidacy on unwilling freeholders was the last by Halifax interests.

A new generation was taking over from the likes of the aging Perkins. They were of the second or third generation that had grown up in an increasingly confident and prosperous Liverpool. They were no longer prepared to defer to the wishes of Halifax. Moreover, their much greater wealth, derived chiefly from privateering and West Indian trading, made them far less dependent upon Halifax for credit than had been Perkins and his generation. Snow Parker was a case in point. He was another of those remarkably versatile seafaring men of the time, inured to hardships, who engaged in seaborne trading, shipbuilding and privateering. At the time of his election, Parker was reputed to be the wealthiest man in Liverpool, due to his privateering ventures. Another was Joseph Freeman, who in 1811 defeated Joseph Barss for the township seat by 60 votes, a substantial margin for Liverpool. As one of the most successful privateer commanders and as a merchant extensively involved in the West Indian trade, Freeman was amassing a small fortune. At his death in 1836 his estate came to £21,400. Undoubtedly, he was owed by many in the town; upon this ledger influence he could draw at election times. Moreover, he had had the support of Snow Parker, whose daughter he had married as his third wife. Joseph Barss was not devoid of that necessary influence, for when his son-in-law and fellow member George Collins died in 1813 he was owed £2,955 by 141 individuals. The family alliance of Barss and Collins simply could not match that of Parker and Freeman. Barss was not to be entirely outdone, because his son John succeeded to Collins' seat. It helped also that John Barss was married to Collins' niece.

Parker, Freeman and Barss were men hardened by years at sea, long experienced as traders, confident in their business affairs, and wealthy beyond the imagination of previous generations. They expected and received the usual marks of respectability of their day. Parker and Freeman were made judges of the inferior court of common pleas. All three had grown up as Congregationalists, became New Lights in their youth during the Allinite revival, and now in middle age joined the Church of England. For the 1818 election all three went back in without a contest. Then, in 1820, Freeman decided not to be a candidate for the township seat, but to hand it over to his son-in-law, James Ratchford DeWolf, while he would ally himself with Parker to oust Barss for one of the county seats. Freeman led the poll with 306 votes. Barss had half that number and came last. Control of all three seats was now in the hands of the Freeman-Parker compact. This lasted only until the next election in 1826, when

Parker decided to retire and John Barss replaced him, with Freeman and DeWolf going back in, all without opposition.

In their Assembly voting, Freeman, Barss and DeWolf were fairly predictable and were almost never found on different sides of a question. Of the three, and as a graduate of King's College at Windsor the best educated, DeWolf intervened the most in Assembly debates. In a debate over a bounty for salt, DeWolf informed the House that nineteen-twentieths of his constituents were fishermen and that this form of encouragement was a "shadow without substance." It went directly into the pocket of the merchant, not to the poor fisherman. What would happen, he prophesied, was that once the price was set the Halifax merchants would purchase all the salt that came on the market and monopolize its sale. They would then only sell it if the fishermen purchased their supplies from them at inflated prices. DeWolf reiterated his long-standing argument that a tonnage bounty on merchantable fish would be of the greatest benefit to the industry, but he accepted that the majority were set against it. Instead of a salt bounty, he therefore proposed a tonnage bounty on the general catch; it was, he assured the House, the most popular of various proposals and most of it went into the pockets of the fishermen. It was they who furnished the "grand source" of the provincial revenue. To opponents of bounties to fishermen, such as the Kings County member William Allen Chipman, he replied that the fishermen were entitled to assistance, for was not the farmer encouraged by bounties and large appropriations of road money? Surely, the poor fishermen had a right to demand the same.[22]

The deference members showed to Freeman was most unexpectedly challenged in 1829 when John Barry, the member for Shelburne Township, implicitly charged him with smuggling. From the day he had entered the House, Barry began an agitation for a change in the militia law that allowed boards of officers to fine those individuals who were warned for duty but failed to appear. During this session, Barry presented a number of petitions from those complaining of harsh treatment from militia officer boards, including one from the Liverpool merchant Patrick Gough, who claimed exemption from duty because of ill health. The fact that Gough had gone to Barry, and not to any of the Queens County members, was sufficient reason for DeWolf to rise in a fury and move dismissal of the petition; Gough, DeWolf said, could throw a fifty-pound weight as far as any man in the county. Besides, he was a notorious smuggler. In his reply, Barry implied that, if Gough was a smuggler, so was his former partner, who was none other than a sitting member and a colonel of the Queens County militia—Joseph Freeman. After many charges and counter-charges (as we shall describe in more detail in the next chapter), the House put Barry in jail until the session ended for refusing to apologize to Freeman. When Gough discovered that DeWolf had called him a smuggler, he sent an open letter to DeWolf in which he accused both DeWolf and his father-in-law of being his "schoolmasters" in that "branch of trade called SMUGGLING." He enclosed a testimonial to his "industrious, steady, sober and peaceable" character, which had as its signatories Hallet Collins and Snow Parker. In a final mocking sentence Gough took his leave of DeWolf as his "old Friend and PARTNER."[23]

When the writs were issued for the 1830 election, DeWolf likely sensed that he might have some difficulty if he ran again for the town, so he allied himself with his father-in-law for one of the two county seats. Whether prearranged or not, John Barss did not run again and his brother, James, offered for the single town seat. He was unopposed. Not so Freeman and DeWolf, who had to face a challenge from Caleb Seeley, the business partner of Patrick Gough. Zenas Waterman from the Northern District also became a candidate. In background, occupation and religion, Waterman could not have differed more from his opponents. His father was a soldier, who had fought on the rebel side in the American War. His mother had insisted that the family move into the wilderness of the Northern District to avoid having any of her sons join the privateers or be pressed into the Royal Navy during the long war with France. In religion, the family was Congregationalist. Waterman was a new breed of politician for Queens County. He had gone into the timber trade and prospered by shipping lumber to Britain. In an election noted for its orderly conduct, Freeman and DeWolf easily triumphed, but there was a 33-vote difference between Freeman and his son-in-law, a sign that the compact was weakening in its ability to hold the family's vote.

By the time of the 1836 election, Freeman was seventy-one years of age and had just a year to live, yet he still led the poll for the county with 354 votes. But, he could not carry DeWolf with him, who fell behind him by 100 votes and lost the second seat to Samuel Prescott Fairbanks. Zenas Waterman came in fourth, but doubled his 1830 total. From an established Halifax family, Fairbanks had gone to King's College (and may have been there at the same time as DeWolf), before studying law. Afterwards he had come to Liverpool to practise his profession, and had married a daughter of Liverpool's collector of customs, Joshua Newton. She was the granddaughter of Simeon Perkins. DeWolf had the opportunity to re-enter the House in a by-election caused by the death of his father-in-law but, curiously, let Zenas Waterman have the seat.

Fairbanks was now launched on a major career as a conservative politician. On the critical constitutional votes leading up to the 1840 election, Fairbanks and Waterman were on opposite sides, with the latter clearly in the reform camp. Waterman's reformist views—and no doubt also his adherence to the cause of temperance—did not endear him to the Liverpool establishment. In 1840, he found himself facing a conservative alliance of Fairbanks and DeWolf. The latter had retired from business so that he could devote his full time to being a magistrate, judge of the inferior court, colonel of the militia and a member of the Assembly. DeWolf led the poll with 522 votes, followed by Fairbanks with 448. Waterman was well behind with 204 votes, most of which was accounted for by the 184 farmers in the Northern District; probably three-quarters of the electorate voted, the largest proportion so far. The *Novascotian* attributed Waterman's defeat to the combination of two parties in the town of Liverpool, who, though they had no love for each other, would rather have divided power between them, than share it with the farmers of the Northern District.[24] During the attempt by Lord Falkland to govern from 1840 to 1843 through a coalition of conservatives and some Reformers, the three Queens County representatives could be counted upon to shore up the Tory cause. However, all three divided over the contentious issue of support for sectarian colleges. Both Fairbanks and DeWolf gave their votes for grants to Acadia College—a foretaste of the cementing Tory/Baptist alliance. Fairbanks took the position that the various denominations would never agree to a single college, Dalhousie or otherwise, so the best course was to continue providing grants to sectarian institutions. When he moved a series of resolutions to that effect, they were defeated, but he correctly forecast that attempts to draft a one-university bill would fail.

For the 1843 election, DeWolf made way for his brother-in-law and son of Joseph Freeman, the lawyer Snow Freeman. Fairbanks went in unopposed. There had been no contest for the town since 1820, and William Taylor was re-elected unanimously once again. In 1845, however, when Fairbanks resigned to accept the provincial treasurership, John Campbell easily defeated Edward Barss, a recent graduate of King's College, who had the presumed advantages of being the son of the former member, and a nephew of Enos Collins. Campbell's victory was not as surprising as it appeared. The son of the former member for Shelburne for many years, Campbell had come to Liverpool as a young man and married a granddaughter of old Joseph Freeman. He proved an enterprising businessman, engaging with success in the lumber trade and the fishery. In the 1820s he was clerk for Trinity Church Parish, but by the time of his election was an ardent Methodist. With his election he was launched, as had happened to Fairbanks a few years before, onto a career as a conservative politician and as an Executive Councillor that would last until Confederation. Campbell's election continued the pattern of Tory allegiance of the Queens County members, who never wavered in their support of Attorney General J.W. Johnston's conservatives in their opposition to party government. When it came finally to the 1847 election, for the first time in twenty-seven years both the county and town elections were contested. Freeman and Campbell doubled their vote on their opponents, Freeman Tupper and poor Zenas Waterman, who came last as usual. William Taylor tripled the vote over James MacLeod, a boat builder from Brookfield. Two-thirds of the electorate went to the polls. The majorities for Campbell, Freeman and Taylor would have been greater if many fishermen had not been out in their boats on polling day.

The electoral history of Queens County can be summed up in the control exercised over the three seats, first by Simeon Perkins and Benajah Collins until 1799, and then by the Barss-Taylor and Freeman-Parker family connections. The latter two compacts so dominated from Perkins' retirement, in 1799, to 1847 that the only outsiders who managed to be elected were Zenas Waterman from 1838 to 1840 and John Campbell from 1845 to 1847. In the case of the former he was unopposed, but in the elections where there was a contest he never did better than last. The combination of being a Reformer and a personal friend of Joseph Howe, while being from the predominantly farming and lumbering Northern District, meant that he could never succeed in garnering enough votes in Liverpool Township proper even to come close to a victory. Campbell, of course, was as conservative as both the Halifax and local Tory establishments could wish.

The commercial imperative to maintain good Halifax connections turned a natural conservatism among men who followed the sea into a political creed, as the Reformers moved to challenge the ruling oligarchy, to which Liverpool had such close ties of interest. What was surprising and somewhat baffling was how little these former New England Puritans cared when their two leading family compacts converted to Anglicanism. In the 1820s, the vestry of Trinity Church had among its members Joseph Freeman, John Barss, James Ratchford DeWolf and William Benajah Taylor.

Chapter 7

Planters, Acadians and Loyalists of Yarmouth and Shelburne Counties

[Fishermen] are the main staff and support of the commerce of their country, they are the greatest source of revenue; for their labours originate the principal article of exportation; their hard earnings have helped to enrich many of those who are engaged in commercial pursuits, and have served to aggrandize their country. But they themselves, although they compose a large proportion of the population are literally in a state of bondage ...

John Homer, *Acadian Recorder*, 24 March 1827

When our traveller arrived in Shelburne on his 1830 tour around the coast from Lunenburg to Yarmouth, he would have found that the Loyalist township had matured into a small, stable community. Shelburne was the home of the finest shipbuilding oak in the area and the town had gained a deservedly high reputation in that industry. Most of its 3,000 inhabitants lived close to the shores of the numerous small harbours and coves that gave them ready access to the fishery. As the seasons dictated, they divided their time between fishing and farming.

Although Barrington Township's population was nearly equal to that of adjoining Shelburne, it was more widely dispersed among the many small harbours of the heavily indented coastline. Its inhabitants were almost all descendants of the Massachusetts fishermen from Cape Cod who had settled there in the early 1760s. Most of its able-bodied males still found their employment in the fishery. Further along the coast at Argyle, a similar economy prevailed; there was, however, greater cultivation, especially by the Acadians who also had good stocks of cattle. Argyle was the most diverse in origin, with a mixture of New England Planters, returned Acadians and New York Dutch Loyalists. Next to Lunenburg, Yarmouth was the most populous of these south shore counties. It also ranked after Lunenburg for the most land under cultivation. Although considerably smaller than either Lunenburg or Liverpool, Yarmouth town boasted a subscription library and the only newspaper west of Halifax.

The adventurous and enterprising seafaring spirit, so manifest at Liverpool, was less present elsewhere among these south shore townships, though each had merchant families engaged in the West Indian trade: in Argyle it was the Ryder and Hatfield families; at Barrington, the Wilsons and Sargents; and at Shelburne, Gideon White and his sons. Dozens of small vessels with fish for sale or exchange went annually from the numerous harbours within easy sailing distance of New England, returning with flour and manufactured goods; smuggling was simply an integral part of this trading system. To a lesser degree, the same pattern prevailed in Yarmouth Township, but there were no powerful families who exercised such pervasive commercial control as elsewhere in this region. By the 1830s, the economy of Yarmouth gave evidence of considerable diversification, including such varied trades as chairmaker, coachmaker, hatter and printer. All in all, our traveller would have been most impressed by what he had observed in Yarmouth. This growing town best combined social and economic progress. Not without reason would Yarmouth be a bastion for the cause of reform.

The Reformers of Yarmouth and the Squires of Argyle

... the struggle is between Toryism and POPULAR FREEDOM ... Nova Scotia expects every man to do his duty! ... Let the Freeholders of Yarmouth exhibit to the world that they have too much sagacity to be deceived by counterfeit friendship or by diabolical falsehood—that they have too much spirit to be intimidated by threats—and too much honesty and self respect to be seduced by the promise of prospective rewards.

The Herald, Yarmouth, 2 August 1847

In the first years after Yarmouth's settlement in the 1760s, the difficulties of travel and the expense forced the township's freeholders to look to Halifax for their representation in the Assembly. Not until 1785 was this dependence on Halifax for representation finally broken. The election that year of Samuel Sheldon Poole began a nearly unbroken half-century reign by him over the township seat. A Harvard graduate, Poole had failed in New England to obtain a Congregational pulpit. After his arrival in Nova Scotia in 1774, he would have accepted a ministerial call, if any congregation had been prepared to pay him a regular and decent salary, but none was. From his farm at Chebogue, he traded moose skins to Boston and invested in shipping and trading ventures as opportunity offered. He was a man of intense, if somewhat eccentric, individualism; his religious perambulations were a fascinating illustration of this aspect of his character. After the disruption and upheaval in the Chebogue Congregational Church, caused by the Allinite religious revival during the American War, he first purchased a pew in the Baptist Church in 1789, but four years later he was listed as one of the proprietors for the first Anglican church in Yarmouth. By the end of the 1790s he had apparently returned to the Baptist fold. The 1827 census listed him as a Presbyterian, though one year later the Methodist records showed him as one of theirs. It is, however, certain that he withdrew from the Methodists in 1833 and went over to the Church of England, in which faith he died two years later in full communion.

Within months of his election in 1785 he was made a justice of the peace; in 1796 he became chief magistrate and presided over the general sessions of the peace for the next thirty years. As the years passed his conduct as a justice became legendary. Once when his house was broken into by a neighbour, as sole witness he lodged the information with himself, issued the warrant as sheriff, returned it to himself, served it as constable, arrested the party, brought him to his house for examination, tried him before himself as justice, found him guilty, convicted and sentenced him, and lodged him in his own cellar for lack of a jail.[1] Such a confident display of summary justice reflected Poole's belief in the local admininstration of justice by such magistrates as himself. Needless to say, he was adamantly opposed to county inferior courts of common pleas with higher jurisdiction than justices of the peace.

No one came forward to challenge Poole's candidacy for the 1793 election, but in 1799 the merchant and recently appointed justice of the peace and collector of customs, Nathan Utley, stood in opposition to Poole. Utley was owed money by about seventy individuals; it is, therefore, not surprising that he defeated Poole 78 to 59 votes.[2] Utley died two years before the 1806 election and Poole was victorious by 18 votes over an unknown opponent. In the 1811 election, he went down to defeat at the hands of the Loyalist merchant and leading shipowner in the township, Samuel Marshall. Poole ascribed his loss to the "innumerable multitude of Crosbys" (one of the largest family connections in the county) being in the opposing camp.[3] When Marshall died two years later, Poole succeeded him and was unanimously elected in 1818, 1820 and 1826. By 1830, Poole was seventy-nine years old and had become, as Governor Sir James Kempt called him, "Father of the House."[4] He used to ride the over two hundred miles to attend the sessions. When his old horse finally died, he petitioned the House for a grant to purchase a new horse; the Speaker respectfully suggested funds for an oat mill might be more appropriate, to which the members readily agreed.

Poole's old age probably accounted for him being opposed in the Brandy Election of 1830. His opponent, Reuben Clements, was at sea when the election was held, but still won by 227 to 224 votes. Poole protested the result and took his case to the Assembly. He argued that he should have the seat by right of long possession, and with more legitimacy, because Clements had not taken the candidate's oath.[5] Clements made no effort to dispute Poole's petition. The House, therefore, simply amended the writ in favour of Poole. In 1835, during his thirty-sixth year in the Assembly, Poole died. Later generations remembered him with affection as "a man of quick temper, of great integrity, of great simplicity of manner, and of an unblemished moral character."[6] In the resulting by-election Clements was the unanimous choice.

If the freeholders of Yarmouth could sort matters out among themselves in such an amiable manner, those in neighbouring Argyle were not so fortunate. Both townships had been incorporated into Shelburne County, when it had been carved out of the old Queens County to satisfy the thousands of newly-arrived Loyalists. Because Yarmouth had its own member, there was initially little interest in the elections for the two Shelburne County representatives. Not so for the freeholders of Argyle, who were virtually disenfranchised if the county poll were not moved from the Shelburne courthouse to Argyle.

For the 1799 election, a number of leading freeholders determined to force the issue by entering candidates and requesting that the poll be moved to Argyle. On the first day of the poll at Shelburne, Colonel Ranald MacKinnon was nominated. The leading figure in Argyle Township, he had settled with his family and slaves in 1765 and given the township its name after his Scottish ancestral home. James Lent also sent word he wished to run. A Loyalist of New York Dutch descent, Lent, with his young family and slaves, had settled at Tusket where he engaged with success in the fishery and the West Indian trade. He was known as Squire or Judge Lent. As a justice of the peace, he exercised his authority with a severity not unusual for the times. On one occasion, after finding a number of men guilty of stealing, he had the culprits fastened to a tree and soundly whipped.[7] The sheriff refused to accept Lent's nomination because he was not present at the hustings. In high dudgeon MacKinnon withdrew, thus allowing the two Shelburne residents to be elected without opposition.

Such men as Ranald MacKinnon and James Lent were not to be denied for long. They insisted that in future one of the county representatives had to be from Argyle. This arrangement held for the next two decades. Lent shared the county representation with his fellow Loyalist from Shelburne, Jacob Van Buskirk. They were never opposed. When they retired, they handed over the seats to Van Buskirk's son-in-law, James Bingay, and to Lent's son, Abraham. Shelburne's hold on even one seat, however, was no longer acceptable to Yarmouth freeholders, who were now double in number those of Shelburne. In 1826, both the Shelburne County seats went to candidates from Yarmouth and Argyle. For an 1828 by-election, no candidate from Shelburne appeared.

This 1828 by-election was won by the Yarmouth lawyer John Forman over Herbert Huntington. Although the loser on his first attempt to enter the Assembly, Huntington, at twenty-seven years of age, was set upon a political career that would lead to his becoming one of the foremost Reformers in the forthcoming struggle for responsible government.[8] Of Connecticut Loyalist descent, he had been mostly educated within the home. For a time as a young man, he taught school in the town and became the first librarian for the Yarmouth Book Society. But he chiefly made his living assisting his father as the district land surveyor; later, he also farmed and invested in shipping. In religion, insofar as particular doctrines mattered to him, he seems to have been a Presbyterian. What actively drew him into politics was his revulsion at the inefficiency and rank partisanship of the Yarmouth justices of the peace. Because they were all appointed by the Halifax oligarchy, he became convinced that reform of the whole system of government was the only way to rid the province of the misgovernment under which it laboured.

Huntington stood again in 1830. As well as confirming the solid hold that Yarmouth had gained over the two county seats, the election demonstrated that moving the poll could dramatically affect the results. At the opening of the poll at Shelburne courthouse, Forman, Huntington, and the Barrington surgeon James Geddes stood as candidates. The Shelburne electors gave their votes almost evenly to Forman and Geddes. They presumably hoped that Yarmouth freeholders would reciprocate, and thus one of their own, in Geddes, would have one of the two county seats. After the poll moved to Argyle, however, Geddes received so few votes that he resigned in disgust. The final result saw Forman lead the poll with 800 votes. Huntington came second with 486, but 458 of his votes had come from the polling at Argyle. This was the last election in which Yarmouth candidates were obliged to travel to Shelburne. In the last days of the 1836 Assembly session, there was finally agreement to divide Shelburne County by creating Yarmouth as a new county, to consist of Argyle and Yarmouth Townships.

Yarmouth freeholders shared the general unhappiness throughout the province with the Assembly's failure to undertake such needed reforms as reducing the number and salaries of the judiciary. Moreover, there was much anger aroused by the nefarious role the two Halifax banks had played in the currency debacle of 1834. Huntington voiced the view of most in Yarmouth when he said: "Banks were a curse instead of an advantage to every Country where they existed—they only throve by a species of gambling."[9] Still, Huntington was not immune from the general feeling among the Yarmouth populace that the sitting members had come too much under the baneful influence of the Council of Twelve. A number of his constituents told Huntington that the House of Assembly was useless.[10]

For some time, Huntington remained undecided about running again, but after the reflection decided to become a candidate for the single county seat. If the election should be contested, the expense to him would be little compared to former elections, when he had to travel to Shelburne. Huntington still felt the need to speak his mind from the hustings on the difficulties he had faced in the last Assembly. He admitted that the efforts to reduce the salaries of officeholders had been fruitless because: "Those in power had their friends and connections in the Assembly, constituting—if not at all times a majority—a powerful and talented minority, backed by the Council."[11] On the other hand, Huntington pointed out that he and his colleagues had been successful in having Yarmouth made a free port. They had also insisted that the Supreme Court hold an annual sitting in Yarmouth. Furthermore, the Yarmouth members had got Yarmouth created as a single county. But it was Clements, also unopposed for the township, who pointed out that Yarmouth had finally got its fair share of road moneys. In the past, Yarmouth members had been unsuccessful in having a distribution of road moneys on the basis of population. However, in the last session before the 1836 election, Huntington had got passed a road scale that closely reflected population by county.[12] To achieve this, he had masterminded approval of such a scale by confining its opposition largely to the eastern part of the province, while maintaining sufficient support for a comfortable majority in the remainder of mainland Nova Scotia.

Under the old Shelburne County arrangement, the MacKinnon and Lent families had held sway in Argyle Township. With Argyle now having its own representation, the Acadian vote became a crucial factor. An Acadian could now run with some possibility of being elected. It was, therefore, no great surprise when Simon d'Entremont published his election card. He was descended from Philippe Mius d'Entremont, who had been granted a seigneury in the Pubnico area in 1653. As well, he was the son of Benoni d'Entremont, who had led the Acadians back to Pubnico after the expulsion. Almost entirely self-educated, he had taught himself to read and write French and to speak and read English; he had also learned Latin and Micmac. Although like most of his compatriots he was a farmer and a fisherman as the season dictated, he was also known in the fish trade as a "good businessman."[13] Through his marriage to the daughter of John Larkin, the son of one of the original New England Planter grantees for the township, he had a connection to the English of the township, when religion and language kept the two groups distinctly apart.

Matthew Jeffrey decided to oppose d'Entremont. A blacksmith by trade, Matthew Jeffrey was the son of a Scottish soldier who had taken his discharge at Halifax at the end of the American War and then had settled in the township. Within Argyle the English outnumbered the French by half again; in fact, there were more Baptists, of whom Jeffrey was one, than there were Roman Catholics, nearly all of whom were Acadians. In the four days of polling d'Entremont led on each, building up an increasing lead. When the poll closed, he had a comfortable margin of 188 to his opponent's 160 votes. With Frederick Robichaud's victory in Annapolis County, he and d'Entremont became the first Acadians elected to the Assembly.

However, d'Entremont was unable to hold the seat in the 1840 election, losing to John Ryder. There was nothing in his conduct in the Assembly to suggest he had done other than as his constituents would have wished. Like his neighbour, the former member James Lent, he had voted consistently against any assistance for agriculture. In the 1840 session when there was a bill to re-establish a central board of agriculture, he amused the House with the remark that "he had always been able to raise potatoes, and thought the best manure for them was plenty of butter ... and wanted the aid of no central board."[14] On the constitutional issues of the day, he had voted as a Reformer. Ryder also portrayed himself as a Reformer. Squire John Ryder was a third generation New England Planter whose family had long been in the West Indian trade. In 1817 at age twelve, he had inherited the family business; by the 1830s, John Ryder was the wealthiest man in the township. For himself and "Mrs. Squire Ryder," he built an imposing house with part of it used as his general store. His schooners (five or more) took fish regularly to the West Indies, returning with molasses and sugar which he sold from Pubnico to Yarmouth, mostly on credit. Moreover, he owned the only grist mill in the township. The number who were in debt to him in 1840 could have been well over a hundred, perhaps one in five freeholders in Argyle. With such potential ledger influence thrown against him, it is astonishing that d'Entremont lost by only 11 votes.

During the Assembly sessions from 1836 to 1840, Huntington won a commanding position for himself by the force of his intellect, the sincerity with which he held to his convictions and his legislative skill. With the division in 1838 of the old Council of Twelve into separate Legislative and Executive Councils, Huntington was the only Reformer appointed to the latter. Because of an administrative error, he served only a short time. A year later Governor Sir Colin Campbell offered him another seat, but Huntington refused it. He could not see how his acceptance could forward the cause of reform; later he remarked that a seat on the Council "was no better than that of a woodcutter."[15] By then, Lord Durham's *Report* had convinced him that in responsible government lay the solution to the constitutional impasse facing all the British North American colonies.

Both Huntington and Clements were unopposed for the 1840 election, and again both spoke from the hustings on the issues of the day. In Clement's view, the creation of separate Legislative and Executive Councils meant an improved constitution had been conceded. People now had a voice in the councils of the country, one that justly belonged to them as British subjects. Clements believed that the province could now anticipate harmony and mutual confidence between the government and the people. Huntington was far less sanguine. He told the assembled freeholders that unless the members of the Executive Council were removed, when they no longer could find a majority in the House to approve their acts, then matters were just as they had been before.[16] He made no mention that the new Governor, Lord Falkland, had offered him a seat on the reconstituted Executive Council, and again he had refused the "king's wine." Once back in the Assembly, in spite of repeated offers to re-enter the Executive Council, Huntington spurned the "inglorious coalition" put together by Falkland. His unyielding opposition to the coalition and his belief in party government brought upon him charges of intransigency and disloyalty by the *Novascotian,* but he stood firm against all entreaties.

Huntington had a deep and sincere belief in the value of education. During the debate in the Assembly over compulsory assessment of freeholders for the establishment of common schools, he stated that "the difference between barbarous countries and civilized, consisted in the different degrees of education."[17] Both he and Ryder voted for a limited degree of compulsory assessment for schools, but Clements remained resolutely opposed; Clements likely reflected the view that predominated within Yarmouth County. In 1841, all three voted for the incorporation of Acadia College in Wolfville and St. Mary's in Halifax, though Huntington, especially, was unhappy with their sectarian character. Henceforth, he held to the view that one public institution, open to all, and not connected with any one denomination, was what Nova Scotia needed.

When Attorney General J.W. Johnston gave his impassioned address in June 1843 to the Baptists gathered in conference at Yarmouth, Huntington was present. When Johnston demanded that members from constituencies with substantial Baptist populations support sectarian colleges, no one there could have been in any doubt that Huntington, particularly, was being singled out. Huntington received permission to speak in defence of his conduct. He denied that on any occasion had he ever spoken disrespectfully of the Baptists. Otherwise, he was unrepentant, reiterating his opposition to funding sectarian colleges, when all that Nova Scotia needed was one college.[18]

When the Yarmouth County and Township polls opened on 23 November 1843, the foremost issue was the question of support for sectarian colleges. Clements had not intended to run again. But because he and Huntington were being so "severely censured" over their opposition to further funding of Acadia, he felt a duty to offer again and have his conduct justified by the electorate. He was especially incensed by the charges that he and Huntington were supporting not only the repeal of the act incorporating Acadia, but also the completion in Halifax of a great and costly building to house Dalhousie College. These "side blows" had their origin, he was certain, in Halifax from a party "who are striving for political ascendancy." Clements was no doubt correct in attributing the agitation to J.W. Johnston and the Tory/Baptist alliance, which was likely behind having Captain Caleb Cook stand in opposition to Clements. A former sea captain and now a farmer, Cook, a Baptist, ran from "the duty I owe to the denomination with which I am connected," and in favour of funding for sectarian colleges.[19] Presumably, the alliance was unable to find anyone willing to challenge Huntington, because he was unopposed. Although the township was mostly Baptist and Clements a Methodist, Cook stood no chance. He resigned when the poll stood at 307 for Clements and 30 for himself. Baptists were also the largest denomination in Argyle. There, John Ryder, who had voted against a grant for Acadia, faced greater opposition. He managed to defeat d'Entremont by just seven votes. The Baptists of Yarmouth County did not follow their brethren of the Annapolis Valley into the Tory camp. Whatever agitation the Tory/Baptist alliance was able to create on the college question in the county, it could not overcome the popularity of Huntington and Clements, or the ledger influence of Ryder, who was already moving to the Tories anyway.

When the election that would decide the great issue of responsible government was called for 5 August 1847, Huntington and Ryder offered again but Clements declined. All three seats were contested for the first time. For Clements' old seat, the battle was between the rising merchant and shipbuilder Thomas Killam, running as a liberal, and the mariner John Sanders. E.W.B. Moody, commission merchant, shipowner and Lloyd's agent, upheld the conservative colours against Huntington. In Argyle, it was again Ryder and d'Entremont. Three days before the election, the Yarmouth *Herald* set the tone: "NEXT THURSDAY Will be the most eventful day that ever dawned upon Nova Scotia. It will smile upon a constituency that will prove that it is either composed of individuals deserving of free institutions, or that the constitution conceded to N.S. in 1840, was committed to the trust of a people, who are too servile or too ignorant to appreciate and preserve the immunities [sic] which it confers." The paper urged every sound-hearted liberal to be at his own polling place and to give "three cheers for HUNTINGTON,-KILLAM AND D'ENTREMONT."[20]

For Yarmouth Township, Killam swamped his Tory opponent 522 to 198 votes. There was clear party voting as totals for Killam and

Huntington were nearly identical. As a result, Huntington gained a wide margin over Moody in the Yarmouth Township polls, which was sufficient to overcome his losses to Moody at the Argyle polls; the final totals were 660 to 410. Again Ryder triumphed over d'Entremont, and this time by the widest margin so far, 214 to 149 votes. The Acadians deserted d'Entremont and went over to Ryder, reportedly because they believed the conservatives that the liberals would introduce direct taxation and were anti-Catholic. The *Herald* accused these Acadians of accepting a "mess of pottage" and selling their "birth-right."[21]

In the 1847 election nearly 1,100 voted, or two-thirds of the heads of families in the county. Temperance principles prevailed and the day's voting was orderly throughout. This seems to have been true for all past elections in Yarmouth County; there is no evidence of disorderly and drunken behaviour, or even of houses of entertainment, that plagued so many other constituencies. In good measure, this can be attributed to the fewness of contested elections. In Yarmouth Township only one election was contested from 1766 through to 1806, none in the following period to 1830, and only three from then to 1847. For the county, Huntington went in unopposed from the 1836 election until party lines were clearly drawn in 1847. The plaintive petition by Poole in 1830 against the victory of Clements was the sole disputed election for the whole period.

Of the occupations of those elected, merchants were in the majority, but the combined total of eighty years that Poole, Clements and Huntington served in the Assembly meant any mercantile influence was minimal, especially when compared to other New England Planter constituencies. Squire John Ryder at Argyle was the sole exception, and his elections were the only occasions when ledger influence was a decisive factor. The successive, predominant roles played by the MacKinnon, Lent and Ryder families were also an exception within the county, having no counterpart in Yarmouth Township. The religion of candidates never seems to have been a factor; the failure of the Baptist, Caleb Cook, to unseat Clements, a Methodist, was a case in point. Nowhere in the province than in Yarmouth was there more consistent opposition to public assistance for agriculture, the establishment of banks and the funding of sectarian colleges. In its politics, Yarmouth unwaveringly (Squire John Ryder excepted) supported the cause of reform.

The Sargents of Barrington Township

I have never yet known among my constituents one solitary instance of a man getting beforehand by fishing and fishing only; those who own vessels or parts of vessels did not earn by fishing; they earned them in better times, by sailing coastwise, carrying plaster of paris, etc. ....

John Homer, *Acadian Recorder*, 4 March 1827

It took Yarmouth from 1766 until 1785 to elect one of its own who could attend sessions of the Assembly. In the case of Barrington, it was to be yet another seven years and only after a riotous contest between two outsiders. In the 1785 election, the single township seat had gone unopposed to the Shelburne Loyalist and lawyer Joseph Aplin. Two years later, Aplin left the province to become Solicitor General of Prince Edward Island. The ensuing by-election matched the Shelburne Loyalist and merchant Captain Gideon White against Richard Gambould, another Shelburne merchant. White's agent in Barrington, Heman Kenny, kept an open house, with the result that there was much drunkenness and fighting. With all 94 freeholders voting at the poll held at the Meeting House, White won by 62 to 32 votes.[22] For White it proved a Pyrrhic victory; the community determined never again to have such behaviour at the polls. White did not re-offer for the 1793 election.

The belief that Barrington should have one of its own in the Assembly was at long last satisfied with the unanimous choice of John Sargent. From long-established Salem, Massachusetts, families on both sides, John Sargent was reared within the Standing Order of the Congregational Church, while receiving a common school education before becoming a merchant apprentice. By the outbreak of the American Revolution, he was already much involved in the West Indian trade. His eldest brother took an active part on the rebel side while John followed his step-brother, Colonel Winthrop Browne, in becoming a steadfast Loyalist. When General Thomas Gage came to Salem searching for cannon stolen by the rebels, Sargent assisted him and just escaped from the attentions of the Salem vigilance committee of the Sons of Liberty. During the evacuation of Boston in March 1776, the Sargent brothers fought on opposite sides. After going to England for a period and receiving an annual allowance of £100 as a refugee, John Sargent returned to America. He was commissioned a lieutenant in the King's American Regiment and fought in numerous engagements around New York and in the southern colonies. While serving in the West Indies in 1781, he was appointed an assistant commissary, and he probably finished the war in this coveted office.[23]

At the coming of peace, Sargent came to Halifax well-recommended for his loyalty and military service. Governor John Parr immediately made him a customs official for the Shelburne District, and two months later a justice of the peace. Sargent then spent the summer of 1783 in travelling to find a suitable location for the mercantile business he intended to establish. He finally fixed on Barrington, perhaps because it had been entirely settled by Massachusetts families. He arrived with sufficient capital to purchase a house, wharves, stores and other property. His former experience in the West Indian trade made it possible for him to enter immediately and successfully into that business by building schooners and exporting fish, while importing rum and other goods. At a cost of £300 he constructed the only grist mill in the township. By the early 1790s, John Sargent was by far the wealthiest individual in the township. His election in 1793 to the Assembly was a natural extension of the influence he had among the 200 or so freeholders.

Sargent was opposed in the 1799 election, but that was to be the only time before he handed over his seat to his son in 1818. Whether because of a recurring illness or other reason, Sargent had the worst attendance record of any member during the time he sat in the House. One of the few sessions he attended was in 1808. In that session he was one of five who voted for William Cottnam Tonge's resolution to insert an insulting clause into the Assembly's address to Governor Sir John Wentworth on his retirement. Wentworth never mentioned Sargent in his correspondence, but there must have developed a deep dislike between them for Sargent to have sided with Tonge. Sargent's long absences from the Assembly had meant the practical disenfranchisement of Barrington freeholders. He had probably held onto the seat until his thirty-one-year-old eldest son, William Browne, was ready to inherit it. In returning the writ to Halifax for the 1818 election, the sheriff noted that the "poll continued by agreement," which could have meant a contested election, or simply that the poll continued open for the regulation one hour before the sheriff declared the younger Sargent elected; in the 1820 election he was certainly unopposed.

The degree of political control the Sargent family could exercise can be judged from the fact that at his death in 1834, John Sargent was owed nearly £7,000 in a community of 362 families. Moreover, no attempt was made to collect these debts. They became part of the estate to be divided among his sons and one daughter; in this way the sons succeeded to the ledger influence formerly held by their father.

Other than in 1824, William Browne Sargent was present for the entirety of most sessions. Although a Methodist, he voted for a grant to the completely Anglican-controlled National School in Halifax, and was against a permanent one for Pictou Academy. On the seating of the Roman Catholic Laurence Kavanagh, he voted with the minority in opposition. After eight undistinguished years in the House, Sargent chose not to run in the 1826 election. John Homer was the unanimous choice.

John Homer's grandfather had come to Barrington around 1772 to engage in the fish trade. His father had been John Sargent's clerk and bookkeeper. As a boy, John Homer attended, together with William Browne Sargent and his younger brothers, a school run by Samuel Osborn Doane and later apparently by his widow. However he achieved it, John Homer became an educated and widely-read individual. He was responsible for the first public lending library in Barrington; in his personal library the titles ranged from Adam Smith's *Wealth of Nations,* through *Letters written by the Earl of Chesterfield to his son, Philip Stanhope ...* to *Letters of Agricola* and *Anecdotes of Peter the Great.* For his livelihood he followed the sea. At seventeen he had gone to the United States, where "to answer commercial purposes" he became a citizen.[24] When the War of 1812 broke out, he returned to Barrington with his family and took the oath of allegiance. From Barrington he began sailing with cargoes of fish to the West Indies, purchasing rum and other products, selling or exchanging these cargoes for flour and breadstuffs before returning home. In 1818, when the Americans temporarily closed their ports to Nova Scotian shipping, he hired himself out, ostensibly as a pilot for Boston-owned vessels, but actually as their master. He also traded to Holland, Denmark, Norway and Sweden. Either before or shortly after his election in 1826 he abandoned the sea and took up farming.

Homer's voting in the Assembly followed the pattern expected of a member from a constituency whose economic life was tied to the fishery and trading to the West Indies. While chairman of the fisheries committee, he got the House to approve a bounty on vessels going into the Labrador fishery. Such a bounty would, he believed, stop men from Barrington and Argyle from crewing for the masters of American vessels who were themselves receiving substantial bounties for going to the Labrador fishery. The Council, however, rejected the bill. Although much disillusioned, Homer re-offered in 1830 and was again unopposed.

Homer was apparently among those personally affected by the devastating depression and currency debacle of the mid-1830s. He came to believe, with all the fervour of a religious convert, that the extreme shortage of specie had its origin in the fact that the province was not self-sufficient in wheat. As a consequence, specie was being drained to import flour and without it trade stagnated. In a provocative pamphlet he published in 1834, he advocated that the legislature act to aid the growing of wheat and establish a granary system centred in Halifax. Moreover, he recommended strict regulations for the manufacture and barrelling of flour to ensure its quality, so that domestic consumption could compete with imports.[25] If these views given by a representative of constituents entirely engaged in the fishery could be considered as "singular," he argued that the local interest must give way to the general good. Furthermore, he was of the opinion that spending the whole of public moneys on the road service was not necessarily the best purpose to which it could be applied.

Homer was against the establishment of grammar schools, because it would build up a "privileged class" and produce nothing but teachers of Latin and Greek, while what the country needed were men of industry. He held that every man had a "right to his portion of public money," and the measure would deprive the poor of what they might otherwise receive.[26] When debating the salaries of office-holders, he was equally adamant that he would vote against making any increases: "Was it consistent with justice and human rights," he asked, "that any one man should receive 69 times as much in a public office as a labouring man could earn?" Homer was one of the most active and thoughtful of the members of his day; regrettably, he died unexpectedly, in middle age of a pulmonary disease while attending the 1836 session. He also died insolvent, owing over £1,200, and leaving an estate one-twentieth that of John Sargent. Still, he and his family had lived in comfort, owning numerous pieces of quality mahogany furniture and good china. He lies buried in St. Paul's Burying Ground in Halifax, where his tombstone can be seen and his epitaph read. It states that as an assemblyman he had "honestly and Steadely Advocated the rights of the people."[27]

For the 1836 election, the Barrington freeholders decided to follow the increasingly common practice of gathering well before the polling began to nominate a candidate. They settled on John Sargent, younger brother of William Browne. The merchant, John Lyle, then came forward to force a contest. This overt challenge to the Sargent family's tenure on the seat was not favourably received, especially after Sargent learned that the single physician in the township, Thomas Geddes, was apparently canvassing for Lyle on Cape Sable Island. At a township meeting, Sargent publicly charged Geddes with canvassing. This brought forth the denial of the allegation by Geddes, who feared the "present state of public excitement" was calculated to have injurious consequences for his practice. Sargent refused to disavow the charge. In turn, Geddes once more accused Sargent of being either the author of the "lie" or too ashamed to admit it.28 With the support of the principal freeholders and the backing of his wife's family, the Doanes (five of his nieces would marry Doanes), Sargent was unbeatable and Lyle declined before the poll opened; for the seventh successive election there was no contest. The little contretemps with Geddes put all on notice that those who presumed to challenge the Sargent family could not do so with impunity. Once in the House, Sargent gave his vote in the 1837 session to Joseph Howe's Twelve Resolutions, but thereafter he was firmly in the conservative camp, opposing any move to responsible government.

For the 1840 general election, John Sargent declined to re-offer. For the fourth occasion in the history of the township there was a contest. Three stood as candidates: the merchant John William Homer, son of the former member; another merchant, Paul Brown; and Samuel Watson, a cordwainer of Loyalist descent. After the first day of polling, it appeared that Brown would be the winner over Homer. Homer's friends then rallied the vote for him and he went on to win by 81 votes, a healthy margin for a township of less than 600 heads of families. Previously, Barrington had sent to Halifax a conservative in John Sargent. Now it had a Reformer, John William Homer, though he was no more friendly to sectarian colleges or support for agriculture than the Sargents had been.

When the poll opened for the 1843 election, Homer found himself opposed once again by Brown and also by Paul Crowell, a merchant, justice of the peace and a member of the largest family grouping by far within the township. Crowell was a Baptist. Although Baptists were the largest denomination in the township, they still numbered hardly more than a third of its inhabitants. That no religion predominated explains in good measure why religion had never played a role in past elections. It did not do so now, as there was near-unanimous opposition to sectarian colleges. Crowell triumphed by 50 votes. Crowell did not run in 1847 and John William Homer went in by acclamation.

Over the years, little controversy surrounded elections in Barrington. Up to 1793 it sent non-residents and during that time it had two elections that were contested. However, for the succeeding twelve elections there were but three contested, the smallest number for any constituency in the province. The Massachusetts merchant families of Sargent and Homer so dominated the electoral process, that Paul Crowell's four years in the Assembly was the only time from 1793 through to 1847 that a member of those two families was not a representative for Barrington. When John Sargent did not run in 1840, it proved to be the twilight of the extensive influence that this Loyalist family had been able to exercise. His successor, John William Homer, moved Barrington into the liberal party. His uncontested election in 1847 was conclusive evidence that Barrington favoured constitutional reform, though in the 1851 election it would return to the conservative fold.

Respectability, Religion and Faction in Loyalist Shelburne

... to assist us in passing off some the gloomy hours of this winter, doubly so in this unsociable Town which I think is worse in that respect at present than I ever knew it, you will then say it must indeed be bad; as it was always famed for disagreements & a great deal of form and ceremony among the inhabitants; the Society is small, but might be very pleasant were it not for the Ridiculous party spirit that prevails.

Rebecca White (Mrs. Gideon Jr.) to her brother-in-law, Cornelius, 13 January 1818.

Although as many as 8,000 to 9,000 Loyalists had come to Shelburne in 1783, many, disillusioned by its prospects, had already left by the time of the 1785 election. For the 6,000 or so remaining the continual turmoil and anguish of settlement ensured that the elections would be fiercely contested. Four candidates stood for the two county seats:

Alexander Leckie, merchant and mill owner; Major Charles McNeil, who as a disbanded field officer of a provincial regiment had received a large grant of 1,000 acres at Sable River; Robert Ross, another merchant; and the Honourable Henry Stanhope, the senior Royal Navy officer on the Shelburne Station. The election for the single township seat saw Joseph Brewer, a storekeeper, oppose Isaac Wilkins.

Wilkins was a former representative for Westchester County in the General Assembly of New York. By marriage he was connected to the wealthy and politically influential New York family of Morrises (his brother-in-law had been a signer of the Declaration of Independence). Wilkins had stayed loyal and attempted to organize resistance in Westchester County, as well as becoming a Loyalist pamphleteer of some note. Wilkins considered himself among the most respectable of the "real Loyalists." Governor John Parr early appointed him a justice of the peace and then first justice of the inferior court of common pleas. But most importantly Parr made him president of the board of agents for the distribution of land to the Shelburne Loyalists. Wilkins and his friends fervently believed that the Loyalist cause demanded that Shelburne be represented by respectable men of education, good manners and proper breeding with characters of proven and unqualified loyalty. Leckie and McNeil formed a temporary alliance and Brewer may have joined them; they called themselves the "Blues" to distinguish themselves from the "Greens," though Wilkins, Ross and Stanhope did not forge any close compact to fight the election.[29] They were not parties, but factions created for the moment.

On election day, the streets were so crowded it was said that you could walk to the hustings on the heads of voters. The alliance of Leckie, McNeil and Brewer held together remarkably well. Leckie and McNeil easily captured the two county seats by a margin of nearly 100 votes. It was considerably closer for Brewer, who just managed a victory over Wilkins by 456 to 434 votes. Wilkins refused to accept his defeat and took his case to the floor of the Assembly. Solicitor General Uniacke and other oldcomers were determined to uphold Brewer's election and keep Wilkins out of the House. If unable, then they intended to force a new election. They lost on both counts, with enough non-Loyalist members siding with all the Loyalists to declare Wilkins the winner. The writ had been returnable at 10 o'clock in the morning on 1 December. At that time Wilkins had been ahead and the majority in the Assembly believed that Sheriff James

Clarke should have then closed the poll. Clarke had continued the polling because freeholders were still coming forward to vote.[30]

Once in the House, Wilkins, as feared, proved one of the most aggressive of the Loyalists in challenging the hold on government offices by the pre-Loyalist office-holders. During the debate on whether two judges of the Supreme Court, Isaac Deschamps and James Brenton, should be impeached, Wilkins moved that an address should be made to Governor John Parr "to remove from his Presence those evil and pernicious Counsellors," who had advised Parr that the judges should be exonerated of charges made against them in the Assembly.[31] Those around Parr charged that such language smacked of rebellion. This may be why Wilkins never received further offices and did not re-offer for the 1793 election. In fact, none of the sitting members stood again; all either had joined the general exodus from Shelburne or would do so shortly.

By the early 1790s, Shelburne's population had dwindled to around 2,000. The passions aroused in those first traumatic years of settlement had waned with the massive exodus. The 1793 election passed without a contest. For the county were elected Stephen Skinner, one of the merchants to survive the exodus by engaging in the fish trade to the West Indies, and James Humphrey. By the time of the election Humphrey had discontinued his newspaper, *The Nova Scotia Packet and General Advertiser*, and was eking out a living as a merchant of some sort. The township was now to be represented by the lawyer Colin Campbell. By the 1799 session, Humphrey had left the province and Skinner did not re-offer when the writs were issued for an election in the late autumn. George Gracie and James Cox came forward for the county.

Both Cox and Gracie were merchants who had gone into shipbuilding, while successfully engaging in the West Indian trade. Gracie was to be the first and only blind member of the Nova Scotia Assembly. On his way to the 1805 session, Gracie tragically fell overboard and drowned in Halifax Harbour. In the ensuing by-election, Jacob Van Buskirk was unopposed. A former officer of the New Jersey Volunteers and on half-pay, he was now reduced to earning his living by running a general store, selling everything from women's shoes to codlines. As we have earlier described in this chapter, Van Buskirk and his son-in-law, James Bingay, were successively to be the resident Shelburne member for one of the two county seats for the next three elections. Colin Campbell was also to be unopposed as the township representative through to 1818, when he resigned on acceptance of a senior customs office in New Brunswick.

As his successor, Campbell had in mind the young and ambitious lawyer Jared Chipman, son of a former member for Cornwallis Township and nephew to William Allen Chipman, the sitting member for that constituency. Chipman was among that bevy of lawyers in Halifax desperate for business and advancement. Once Campbell determined that Chipman would be acceptable to the "principal Gentlemen," he had Chipman write Gideon White offering to become a candidate; he went in as intended without a contest.[32] Although in 1820 he was opposed, Chipman's opponent resigned when he managed just 23 votes to 363 for Chipman.

Since 1806, Shelburne had shared the county representation with Argyle. When James Bingay and John MacKinnon, son of the old Colonel Ranald, stood as candidates, there was every expectation that the amicable arrangement would continue. However, Yarmouth Township freeholders put up Robert Huestis to challenge the hold on the two seats by Shelburne and Argyle. Polls were only held at Shelburne and Argyle and so Huestis did well to obtain 368 votes to Bingay's 600 and 534 for MacKinnon. There was apparently a good deal of wrangling among the Acadian and Yarmouth freeholders over who should get their votes. Jared Chipman, for one, believed that the zeal and spirit displayed by Shelburne and Argyle electors would "put an end to the further attempt of Yarmouth agt. Shelburne."[33] With Chipman's elevation in 1824 to one of the three *easy chairs* as the judge for the eastern division at a salary of £500 a year, he could afford to forget such concerns. The by-election to replace Chipman turned out to be not only the first real contest since 1785, but more significantly an open challenge to the control exercised over the politics of the township by the leading families, all Anglican or the Church of Scotland or Kirk.

Although there was definite voting along religious lines, the underlying issue was whether or not "respectability" would continue to hold sway. The challenge came from the family of Robert Barry, who, as a Methodist and non-American-born Loyalist, had never been accorded the deference granted to such families as those of Gideon White, Jacob Van Buskirk or Colin Campbell. The son of an English merchant of Portsmouth, Barry reputedly arrived in colonial New York as an impressed seaman; he escaped and entered into a trading partnership for the duration of the war. His fervent Methodism came from his association with the John Street Methodist

Chapel in New York. In his religious inclinations, he was much influenced by Charles (later Bishop) Inglis, rector of Trinity Church, where Barry regularly took Holy Communion. He came to Shelburne with the great migration and survived the commercial decline as a merchant in the fish trade. Sometime before 1820, however, he went to Liverpool in search of better trading opportunities. As well as having been the chief lay leader of the Shelburne Methodists, the marriage of his son, John Alexander, to Mary, the daughter of "Bishop" William Black, cemented a religious and also commercial alliance. A son of the Methodist leader, Martin Gay Black, was a Halifax merchant and a founding member of the Halifax Banking Company presided over by Enos Collins.

On election day Thomas Crowell, formerly of Saint John and a merchant who dealt extensively in mortgages, was nominated and seconded by his fellow magistrates, Jacob Van Buskirk and Colin Campbell Jr. Crowell and Van Buskirk were two of the four judges of the inferior court of common pleas, while Campbell managed to combine the offices of collector of light duty and of impost and excise, with being judge of probate and the single lawyer practising in the town. Crowell and Van Buskirk were Anglicans and Campbell a member of the Kirk. Next nominated was Nathaniel White. His candidacy was followed by Robert Barry's nomination of his son, John Alexander, which was seconded by the Anglican merchant, Charles Roche, a business associate of the Barrys.

Both Barry and White were second-generation Shelburne Loyalists in their early thirties, though resident in Halifax. But there the similarities ended. Barry had received his early education in Shelburne before entering his father's (or a fellow merchant's) business as an apprentice. He later moved to Halifax, where he set up on his own. Not so Nathaniel Whitford White, son of the Massachusetts Loyalist Captain Gideon White, officer on half-pay, merchant, deputy naval officer, former member for Barrington, justice of the peace and judge of the inferior court of common pleas. Initially, Gideon White sent his children to Halifax and then to Boston for their education. It was a painful decision to send his children to be educated in the United States, and only his determination to see them properly instructed caused him to do so. At the time, he wrote his good friend John Sargent at Barrington that he could never become a "subject of any Republican Government and I hope my boys will never—no there is not One Drop of Republican Blood in their veins."[34] When, however, he found the expense more than he could bear, he established a grammar school in Shelburne. More than likely John Barry attended with Nathaniel and his brothers. When it came time to send Nathaniel to university, a fortuitous legacy from an uncle paid for Nathaniel to attend Harvard. After graduating from Harvard—he was the first native Nova Scotian to do so—Nathaniel articled with Thomas Ritchie at Annapolis Royal before seeking to earn his living in Halifax; there he entered into society as a rising young man for whom offices would no doubt be found in due course. For Nathaniel, Anglican and social insider, a seat in the Assembly was no more than the accepted means for an aspiring lawyer to pay his dues to the governing oligarchy, with the certainty of rewards to come. For John Barry, the outsider, it offered the opportunity to gain the respectability that White already had by breeding, education and religion. His own background, and particularly his father's commercial and religious influence in Shelburne, made it the best prospect Barry had for political success and advancement in life.

There was an amateurish air to White's candidacy, and he received a paltry 28 votes and deserved no more. The real battle was between Crowell and Barry; with the former having all the weight of respectable Shelburne behind him, he came out victorious 155 to 135 votes. Barry took 80 per cent of the Methodist vote and nearly all the Baptists supported him. The Anglicans and their fellow establishmentarians of the Church of Scotland formed the two largest denominations; 80 per cent of the former and nearly 70 per cent of the latter voted for Crowell.[35] The only way that Barry could have won would have been for White to have taken more of the Anglican and Kirk vote; the very fear that White could have split this vote likely explains why not even his family voted for him.

Barry and his Halifax friends were bitter at the support given Crowell by the "magistracy & gentility of Shelburne." Nathaniel White wrote his brother Cornelius about how, under the "venom" of the "treacherous tongue" of Barry's faction, "Church & state were both suffering ... 'Tis now quite plain to me that Barry has been urged on by the canting crew to make this determined stand & that radicalism in religion & politicks ... mutually beget each other."[36]

This pattern of religious voting continued for the 1826 general election. Crowell declined running again and gave his support to Nathaniel White against Barry. Both sides went to great lengths to bring forward voters, many of doubtful eligibility. During the six days of polling, little separated the totals until, near the end, White pulled ahead, winning 162 to 159 votes. White had the support of the magistrates, the clergy of the two established churches, 80 per cent of the Anglican vote and one quarter of the Methodist.[37] The change from 1824 was in the Kirk vote, which before had gone 70 per cent to Crowell, and was now more evenly split, though still favouring White. This time Barry took his defeat to the Assembly floor. A select committee decided many of White's voters were ineligible and the House gave the election to Barry.

Once in the Assembly, Barry could never make up his mind whether or not he really wanted to challenge the established order. As a result his behaviour became erratic and tempestuous. His place in Nova Scotian politics rests entirely on the "Barry Affair" of 1829 when, as already described, he insinuated that Joseph Freeman, a member for Queens County, was a smuggler. Although called by the House to apologize to Freeman, Barry insolently refused and consequently was not allowed to continue in his seat. Barry now became a popular hero, particularly after he published letters in the *Acadian Recorder* highly critical of the Assembly's sitting with the galleries cleared, so its proceedings could not be reported. The affair took on the aura of a struggle for constitutional liberty, not against the executive branch, but against the representatives of the people, to the open amusement of Tory Halifax.

Barry was cited for high contempt and sent to jail at the Assembly's pleasure, though all the sergeant-in-arms did was to put Barry in the custody of his wife, Mary, in their own home. Meanwhile, in Shelburne the contest between Barry and the Assembly generated feverish excitement. Five petitions, signed by 256 freeholders, were sent to the Assembly supporting Barry's stand. The very violence of Barry's language, however, and his penchant for indulging in personal attacks in the newspapers against individuals he disliked, stiffened the resolve of the House. By resolution the Assembly expelled him and jailed him until the end of the session. This gave rise to the ditty, aptly entitled "Parody," of which the second and last verses went:

> We imprisoned him early at morning's hour
> The malice of members sating;
> With Speaker's warrant of doubtful power,
> And the Sargent-at-Arms in waiting.
>
> Lastly the business of vengeance was o'r,
> And he shut fast in the second story—

We turn'd a large key, we lock'd up the door,
And we left him in jail with his glory.

FUN[38]

Barry was determined to redeem himself and have his revenge by being re-elected in the by-election which had to be called. After much procrastination in Halifax, a writ was issued and the sheriff gave out that the date would be 1 June. For a time John Tottie determined to oppose Barry but declined before polling day. By early morning on the day, schooners and shallops began arriving loaded with freeholders and onlookers. At 10 o'clock, preceded by a band and a display of colours, Barry set out for the courthouse with the company of friends and a large number of followers. At the courthouse door he was received by a discharge of cannon, accompanied by much cheering. Alexander Robertson, one of the oldest and most respected of the inhabitants, proposed Barry as the only fit person to represent the town. With great emotion he proceeded to read out, from an original list, the first 250 heads of families who had settled in Shelburne, many of whose descendants were gathered before him. He did this in reply to Tottie's claim that he had been requested to run by "many RESPECTABLE freeholders." Robertson went on to regret that Tottie and his supporters were not there that day, so that he "might have the fair opportunity of judging of the respectability which they claimed, but the possession of which he denied them, ascribing it to those alone who stood before him, the descendants of those honest men who had been his contemporaries at the first settlement ...."

Although no one opposed Barry, the polling continued most of the day until Barry was satisfied he had a majority of votes in the township and allowed the poll to close. To the acclamations of the populace, his friends placed him in the usual victor's chair and carried him through the streets to the residence of Charles Roche, where he was staying. The band played God Save the King and Rule Britannia and Barry then shook the hands of all present. On the following day, an address was presented to Barry which spoke of his "manly and patriotic conduct" and to which Barry made a suitable reply before boarding the ship *Castor* for Halifax to the salute of seven 12-pounders from shore, which the *Castor* answered with nineteen rounds.[39] No election since 1785 had seen such excitement. "Respectability" had been dealt a defeat from which it would never fully recover.

What Barry desired, however, was respectability. This became abundantly evident in the dispute with the Council of Twelve during the 1830 session over the tax on brandy. Barry was one of the three members who sided with the Council. The ensuing election saw him abandon Shelburne to run with the three other Council candidates in Halifax County, where he finished second to last. He did not even stay until the end at Pictou, but rushed back to Halifax, with the intention of regaining Shelburne where the election was still to be held. But the realization that he could not win there, and the mounting displeasure of the Black family over his erratic behaviour, decided him on the wisdom of staying in Halifax. He turned to Charles Roche, who had nominated him in two previous elections and was now in Halifax apparently as manager of Barry's business. Barry prevailed on Roche to run against Nathaniel White.

Ever since the dispute over the tax on brandy had plunged the province into political turmoil, Nathaniel White had been dreaming that now the "clearest heads & the stoutest hearts" must come forward to save the province from floundering. He longed to "shake off the film of sloth & buckle on the armour and fight a good fight."[40] White stood no chance against Roche, who easily defeated him. Although White expected a judgeship for his political services, such as they were, he had to settle for registrar of the chancery court, which came to him in 1832.

In the last session before the 1836 election, when the Assembly had created Yarmouth County it had reduced Shelburne's representation to its township seat and one county representative. As soon as the election was called, the freeholders of Barrington put forward John Sargent's brother, Winthrop, to run for the single county seat. They requested a meeting with the freeholders of Shelburne. Sargent's nomination was most favourably received by such respectable citizens as Thomas Crowell and his fellow merchant, Joshua Snow, who were prepared to propose and second his candidacy. It was obvious that Sargent needed only to make a fair showing in Shelburne, and then rely on his family's influence in Barrington to overcome any opponent's lead. It thus proved difficult to find anyone to oppose him. At a specially called public meeting, the fish merchant and shipbuilder, Gilbert McKenna, was nominated. But McKenna declined to run, and Hugh Huston, a carpenter by trade, agreed to stand. For the township Peter Spearwater offered. As Spearwater later told the House, he was without a liberal education and had to earn his livelihood following the plough, hauling the fishing line and navigating his own vessel. Spearwater's opponent was another farmer, Alexander Hamilton.

After four days of polling at Shelburne courthouse, Huston had a commanding lead of 184 to Sargent's 74 votes, while Spearwater won the township by nearly the same margin. In fact, five-sixths of freeholders who voted for Huston also did so for Spearwater.[41] Moreover, most of those who supported Barry in 1826, and now voted in 1836, gave their vote to Huston and Spearwater. The Shelburne electorate was dividing along party lines, but this was not yet true of Barrington where the poll now moved. In three days of voting at the Meeting House, Sargent obtained 216 votes and Huston but 20, giving the former a healthy overall margin of 88 votes. In sending the Sargent brothers, John and Winthrop, and Peter Spearwater to the Assembly, the freeholders of Shelburne County for the first time gave their vote to three Methodists, of whom two were staunch Tories and one a Reformer. Although the Sargents and Spearwater were with the overwhelming majority in voting for the 1837 address to the throne, requesting constitutional reform, the brothers became more and more uncompromising in their resistance to any reform measures. In the debate in the last session before the 1840 election on Joseph Howe's resolutions calling for the remodelling of the constitution and responsible government, Winthrop Sargent exclaimed that "he would be willing ... to suffer the loss of his right hand rather than sanction such a system."[42]

In the 1840 election, the independent yeomen of Shelburne finally overthrew a faction made up of a "few selfish men, who for the sake of personal aggrandizement and sectarian feeling" had controlled elections. According also to the *Novascotian,* these men had in the past sacrificed the intellectual and political interest of the province and of Shelburne.[43] The party of respectability, however, might well have held on for another election, if both the Sargents had not declined to run again. Gilbert McKenna now had no hesitation in accepting a nomination for the single county seat. Alexander Cocken, though McKenna's brother-in-law and an old Barry supporter, decided to stand for the conservative cause. For the township, Spearwater was again a candidate and Augustus Vernon opposed him.

The poll stayed open for five days at the courthouse, during which there was nearly complete voting by party. Entirely absent was sectarian voting along the previous lines, when Kirkmen and Anglicans had united to oppose the political pretensions of Dissenters. Vernon gave Spearwater much more of a battle than had Hamilton in 1836. Spearwater won, but his margin was drastically cut. In the 1836 county election, Huston had led Winthrop Sargent by 108 votes when the poll closed at Shelburne, only to be swamped once it removed to Barrington. The conservative Cocken was now able to reduce the liberal lead to 48 votes, but Sargent's former majority in Barrington evaporated, with McKenna out-polling Cocken 114 to 49 votes there. The seed of McKenna's victory lay in his ability to hold the vote of four-fifths of the electors who had supported Huston in 1836, and who voted again in 1840.[44]

The old Barry faction of the 1820s had become a political party that could count upon a solid core of supporters from election to election. As an anonymous correspondent from Shelburne informed the readers of the *Novascotian*, the day of "undue and improper influence has gone forever."[45] Shelburne would now be represented by three "staunch Reformers," in Spearwater and McKenna, and in John William Homer for Barrington Township. If John Alexander Barry had justified his father's faith in him, and not allowed ambition and his desire for social acceptance to have so unbalanced his behaviour, the overthrow of respectability could have come as early as Barry's election in 1826.

Aside from their stand as Reformers on constitutional issues, McKenna and Spearwater followed their predecessors in actively opposing any assistance for agriculture and to sectarian colleges. When it came time to nominate for the 1843 elections, Spearwater was unopposed, but McKenna faced Alexander Cocken again and the Barrington merchant Obediah Wilson Jr. In what was a replay of Winthrop Sargent's victory over Huston in 1836, Wilson triumphed over the other two by 64 votes, with McKenna retiring from the fray fairly early. In the critical constitutional votes leading up to the 1847 election, Wilson, along with his Shelburne County colleagues, Spearwater and Paul Crowell, was firmly for responsible and party government. Spearwater, for one, spoke forcefully for heads of government departments having to be in the Assembly, otherwise it would "strike a death blow to Responsible Government." He referred caustically to the "a superabundance of Gentlemen" in Halifax "waiting for a fat office to be bestowed," while he lived quite retired and distant from the capital and the "fountain from whence those lucrative offices flow."[46]

Wilson did not re-offer in 1847. The contest was between McKenna and none other than John Alexander Barry, who took the Shelburne town poll by a three-to-one margin, but McKenna won so heavily at Barrington that he had a 100-vote majority. In the township election, the respectable families showed once more their influence, when they put up the merchant and long-standing conservative, Joshua Snow. In a fairly close contest, marked by unusual violence caused by a Tory mob, Snow took the town poll by nearly a four-to-one margin, and the township as a whole by a majority of 33 votes.

The extraordinary ascendancy exercised by a few Loyalist families, who saw themselves as guardians of the honour and integrity of the "real Loyalists," was the most striking characteristic of early Shelburne elections. They did this not only through their dominance of offices and the magistracy, and ledger influence, but also by their use of religious voting to deny election to any who had the temerity to dissent from the established Churches of England and Scotland. This was possible in Shelburne because of the preponderance of those two faiths. All politics was subordinated to upholding the cause of respectability. However, once the battle was joined between reform and the continuation of oligarchic rule, the continuing ascendancy of respectability was compromised, but not fatally; the victory of Snow in 1847 was ample evidence of that.

Chapter 8

The Scotch Irish, Yorkshire and Scots Farmers of Cumberland and Colchester Counties

... your Petitioners view with deep and continued alarm the yearly decreasing value of Agriculture Produce occasioned by the want of protective Legislation sufficient to enable the Colonial producer to meet the foreign importer on remunerating terms in the markets of the Province ... Protective enactments are his only shelter from pending ruin ....
Petition of Farmers residing in the County of Colchester, c.1842.

At the confluence of the Shubenacadie River and its tributary the Stewiacke, a generally passable side road turned off to the east and ran through the Stewiacke Valley, some of the most fertile intervale lands in Colchester. This had drawn such a number of the second generation settlers from the adjoining townships that it was now, next to Truro, the most populated part of the county. Where twenty years earlier, nine-tenths of the people in the valley were living in small unhewn log houses, by 1830 there were only timber framed houses. Further on at the head of Cobequid Bay lay the townships of Truro, Onslow and Londonderry, which had been largely settled in the early 1760s by Scotch Irish Presbyterians.

Truro was the chief and only town within these townships. It had, as well as seventy dwellings, a Presbyterian Meeting House, a beautifully proportioned Episcopal Church with a spire and bell, and a Masonic Hall. As benefitting a shiretown, the principal street ended in a square, around which were located the courthouse and a number of substantial two-storied private residences. Opposite Truro, on the south side of the Shubenacadie River, was the finest tract of land in Colchester, inhabited by its most prosperous farmers. Across Cobequid Bay in adjoining Onslow Township, the farms were largely found on cleared upland and not as productive. Of the three townships, Londonderry had the most diversified economy; shipbuilding, export trade in board and planks to the West Indies and Europe, and numerous saw, grist, oat and carding mills. Almost all the 10,000 inhabitants of Colchester drew their livelihoods from their farms, with Halifax the primary market for surplus productions. It was usual for Colchester farmers to send to Halifax annually such quantities as 100,000 pounds of pork and an equal amount of butter, as well as driving hundreds of cattle to the capital's market.

The post road from Truro to Amherst would not see a stage coach until the early 1840s. This road passed through the watersheds of the two major rivers that drained the still densely forested interior of Cumberland County. Of the two, the Wallace River had the best intervale lands and the township was the most populated of any part of the county. The lumber trade, rather than farming, had become the chief occupation of many of its inhabitants. This was equally true along River Philip; by mid-century the largest concentration of saw mills anywhere in the province could be found at River Philip.[1] It was, however, when our traveller of 1830 came in sight of the widest expanse of marshlands he had yet beheld that he knew he had un-questionably entered some of the most productive lands in Nova Scotia. From Amherst Ridge he would have been able to see huge stacks of hay, many substantial farm houses and numerous herds of cattle. The marshlands were not farmed; instead, they were used for grazing of cattle. It was common for Cumberland to drive 600 head overland to the Halifax market annually, as well as sending large amounts of butter and cheese. An observer of the Cumberland scene would have been astonished by the pronounced disparity in wealth between the older and more established inhabitants of the marsh-lands, and that of the later and less fortunate settlers to the east. It was a division of history and geography, and one that was a pivotal factor in Cumberland politics.

Upholding the Tory Cause in Cumberland

After all the Radical's [sic] lies and boasting about this County and notwithstanding the wholesale manufacture of votes ... the increasing growth of Conservative principles in this County has enabled us to send Three Conservative Members to take their seats in the next House. This is a glorious triumph in the cause of peace and order,

*and you may rely upon it, our opponents have been taught a lesson
that will not require to be repeated. In haste, yours,*
A CUMBERLAND CONSERVATIVE
Morning Post, 11 August 1847

In 1758 the Halifax enemies of Governor Charles Lawrence were as
opposed to having Cumberland County send any representatives to
the first House of Assembly as they were to Lunenburg doing so, and
for the same reason: they feared the election of some of the Governor's "creatures." As it turned out, the dozen or so freeholders living
off and around the garrison at Fort Cumberland on the Isthmus of
Chignecto may not even have had the opportunity to vote in the
election for First Assembly in 1758. They did so a year later in the
1759 election, but then were quietly excluded from the 1761 writ.
Within a year, however, hundreds of New Englanders arrived to take
possession of the lands left vacant since the expulsion of the Acadians in 1755. They settled in the newly-created townships of
Sackville, Cumberland and Amherst, formed from the three parallel
ridges of upland running west to east, neatly trisecting the isthmus,
with each ridge sloping gently upwards from the adjoining salt
marshlands drained by tidal rivers. A good number of these New
Englanders did not stay long, soon selling their partially cleared
upland farms and marshlands to Scotch Irish moving up from the
Cobequid Townships and to incoming Yorkshiremen. Of the Yorkshiremen, the first shipload of these experienced farmers from the
north of England arrived in 1772. They sought to escape the rising
high rents being demanded of them, in the wake of the enclosures
and consolidations brought on by the revolution in agricultural production sweeping Britain. In all, nearly 1,400 Yorkshiremen arrived
from 1772 to 1775. Many families came with sufficient capital to
purchase farms in the three townships. Others took up lands fronting
on the tidal Nappan and Maccan Rivers that also found their outlets
into Cumberland Basin.

At the onset of the American Revolution, Cumberland was scene
of the only act of open rebellion in Nova Scotia. Among those elected
to the Assembly before the rebellion, and forced to flee for their part
in it, were its leader Jonathan Eddy himself, John Allan, Samuel
Rogers and Robert Foster; another, the old Indian fighter Benoni
Danks, was captured and died from his wounds on the way to Halifax
to face a trial for treason. The bitterness between those who turned
rebel and those who stayed loyal during the Cumberland Rebellion

lasted into the next century.[2] After the war as many as three hundred Loyalists came to Cumberland. Few of them had the means to purchase cleared upland farms or marshland. Some took up grants in the densely forested wilderness along the summit of the Cobequid Mountains. Others settled the alluvial lands of the Wallace River which drained into Northumberland Strait.

With the creation of New Brunswick, Sackville Township became part of the new province. For the 1785 general election, Cumberland now sent two representatives for the county and one for Amherst Township. There was, however, both discontent and confusion over the boundary line, resulting in two of the three elected having their elections voided, because they were declared to be residents of New Brunswick. The upshot was that Cumberland was represented by three Halifax merchants. But, when it came time for the 1793 election, none of them re-offered; in future, Halifax merchants and lawyers seeking seats looked elsewhere than Cumberland. In what appears to have been two uncontested elections, Thomas Lusby went in for Amherst, and for the county, Samuel Embree and William Freeman. Whether by agreement or by chance, Cumberland was now represented by a New England Planter in Freeman, a Yorkshireman in Lusby and, in Embree, a Loyalist who, as a lieutenant, had served in Colonel James DeLancey's Westchester Chasseurs. According to tradition, Lusby would set out on snowshoes from his farm near Amherst to attend those Assembly sessions held during the winter, first going to River Philip and then across the Cobequid Mountains down to Halifax.

With the 1799 election Cumberland politics entered a new era; in future, most elections for the two county representatives were to be contested. Up to now ledger influence had not been present. This changed when the Fort Lawrence Ridge merchant Thomas Roach became a candidate. Roach had been born in Cork, Ireland. As the result of having been trained for the priesthood (though never ordained), he was well-educated and reputed to have spoken a number of languages. From Ireland he had gone first to New York and had then appeared as a late Loyalist at Fort Lawrence in 1790. He likely arrived with some capital, for he was soon much involved in merchandising and shipbuilding. His place in the community was further enhanced by his marriage to a daughter of Charles Dixon of Sackville and his conversion to Methodism. His opposition came from a second-generation Yorkshireman, George Oxley of River Philip, and from Henry Purdy, another of Colonel James DeLancey's former officers. When the poll closed, Roach led with 135, followed closely by Oxley with 128. Purdy was well behind with 98 votes; but after a scrutiny demanded by Purdy, the totals stood 78 for Roach, 63 for Oxley and 60 for Purdy. For the totals of Roach and Oxley to be halved meant that those struck off lacked eligible freehold. Roach may well have engaged also in making freeholders because many were indebted to him and open to such a practice. Certainly, for the next four elections Roach with his ledger was an ever-present factor in the county contests.[3] It was no doubt through Roach's influence and encouragement that, on Thomas Lusby's death, Thomas Law Dixon, Roach's close relation by marriage, succeeded unopposed to the Amherst Township seat in 1802.

Even with Roach's backing, Dixon's hold on the Amherst seat proved short-lived. For the 1806 election, Edward Baker came forward to challenge Dixon. Up to this election, there had never been a contest. Baker was the son-in-law of the deceased former member, Thomas Lusby. In forcing a contest, Baker was reclaiming the Lusby/Baker family interest. Baker had an advantage in that his father was register of deeds. While polling was in progress, Baker Sr. refused to determine if certain deeds were registered. Some of Dixon's supporters, therefore, could not take the freeholder's oath in good conscience. Still, the result was close with Baker defeating Dixon 31 to 24 votes (it was in this election that five women voted as discussed in Chapter 1). Of Virginian origin, the Baker family had arrived in the area in 1768 and had the good fortune to inherit 1,000 acres of rich marshland. The family soon received the usual offices; that of registrar of deeds was to remain in its possession for nearly half a century. In the 1811 election, Baker was returned unopposed for the township, as were Roach and Purdy for the county.

There now emerged, however, a movement to defeat Roach.[4] It seems to have had its origin in his about-face on the Assembly's attempt to curtail the smuggling inherent in the gypsum trade, in which Cumberland merchants and farmers were heavily engaged. After opposing any such measure, Roach apparently succumbed to pressures exerted by such influential members as the Speaker, S.B. Robie, to support the 1816 bill that imposed severe penalties for illegal trading. The poll for the 1818 election opened on 1 July at River Philip, with Roach, Purdy, George Oxley, and Andrew Forshner of Wallace as candidates. Purdy was the leader in the attempt to defeat Roach; he turned up with twenty or thirty freeholders from Amherst who proceeded to vote for him, but reserved their second vote until they could see whether Oxley or Forshner had the best chance of overtaking Roach. By the time the poll moved to Amherst, Purdy and Oxley were both ahead of Roach by five or six votes, while Forshner was more than 20 behind the leaders.

At Amherst, the battle was now between the first three contenders. Roach's strength and ledger influence lay in the Amherst area and he soon pulled well ahead of Oxley, but not Purdy. In a last attempt to have Oxley come from behind to pass Roach, Purdy called on his supporters to give their second vote to Oxley. Roach, in turn, demanded that the sheriff administer the freeholder's oath on the grounds that once having voted they could not return to the hustings and vote a second time. Whether he was correct or not in law, this proved a sufficient deterrent to most voters. The poll closed with Roach standing at 201, followed by Purdy with one less and then Oxley a further 30 votes behind. The lawyer, James Shannon Morse, was one of those who had had no reservation in using his second vote against Roach, such were his feelings against the man. One reason for his confidence on this occasion was that he had just been unanimously elected for Amherst.

The attempt to defeat Roach continued into the 1820 election. This time Purdy, at seventy-five years of age, decided not to re-offer, and threw his interest to Oxley and to William Baker, brother of the former member. Oxley led the poll throughout. But Oxley could not carry Baker with him, as the voters in River Philip and Wallace voted overwhelmingly for him but refused to use their second vote in favour of either Roach or Baker because they were from Amherst. It proved to be worse than a Pyrrhic victory; Oxley died before the first session of the new House opened.

In the sessions of the Assembly after the 1820 election, further definite signs appeared of the deepening division between the western and eastern districts that would bedevil Cumberland politics for decades. One of the most contentious issues was the altering of the place for holding the Supreme Court, when on circuit in Cumberland, from Amherst to River Philip. This was rightly seen as a first step in River Philip replacing Amherst as the shiretown. That such a measure should be contemplated lay in the increasing population of the eastern part of the county, embracing the Loyalist and Scottish settlements of Wallace, Wentworth, River Philip and Westchester. These newer settlements were receiving numerous Scottish emigrants and now had equalled the population of the older settlements fronting on the tidal marshlands and the Bay of Fundy. The issue of the location of the Supreme Court's sittings was first joined in 1816 when the Assembly passed a bill to extend the court circuit within several counties and districts; probably at the instigation of the Oxley family, River Philip was substituted for Amherst as the location for court sittings. None of the three Cumberland members seem to have noticed the change, or at least objected. In 1820 both sides petitioned the Assembly, especially after George Oxley sent in a draft bill for selling the courthouse in Amherst and for erecting another at River Philip. The bill made it through third reading, but the Council let it die. Thus River Philip held onto the sittings of the Supreme Court, and Amherst did the same for those of the inferior court and the general sessions of the peace; in practice, Cumberland had two shire-towns and two courthouses.

The decision of the thirty-two-year-old Amherst lawyer Alexander Stewart to offer in the 1826 election for one of the two county seats not only sealed Roach's political fate, but also dramatically altered the shape of Cumberland politics. Stewart was not a native of Cumberland; he had been brought up in Halifax by his widowed mother, where he had attended the Halifax Grammar School with such schoolmates as Beamish Murdoch.[5] His early success in the commission and auction business during the War of 1812 made it possible both to apprentice himself to James Shannon Morse and to marry his sister. Although he finished his legal training with Morse, there was a bitter falling-out between the two, though the cause is unknown. Apparently easily irritated, Stewart had a violent temper, which not for the last time in his life turned friend into enemy. His angry break with Morse forced Stewart to enter legal practice, as he later told a grandson, with "tenpence in my pocket" and a family to support. A man of marked ability and ambition in his chosen profession, Stewart soon had a substantial practice both in Cumberland and across the border in New Brunswick. By 1826, he could well afford to take the natural step followed by most in his profession and seek a seat in the Assembly. In his legal practice he had gained the respect of many of the leading inhabitants who now supported his political ambitions. But it was his Scottish inheritance that stood him in the greatest stead. As the offspring of a Church of Scotland minister, and as one who loved and spoke the poetry of the Scottish bards, he would have the loyalty of the hundreds of Scots at Wallace and elsewhere along the Gulf Shore. From the opening of the poll at River Philip, it became obvious that "Sandy" Stewart was the candidate to beat. From the first, he led both Roach and Joseph Oxley, the brother of George and of Stephen Oxley, who had married Stewart's widowed mother. The poll then moved to Wallace where Stewart led it with 178 votes, but Roach had a mere 40 votes. At Amherst, Morse decided that his enmity towards Stewart exceeded his former ill feelings for Roach; Morse threw his considerable influence to Roach. Roach polled more than either of the others, but still ended well behind in third place. Out of the 445 freeholders polled, a remarkable total of 378 had given their vote to Stewart.

Stewart was among the "beardless boys," with Thomas Chandler Haliburton and Beamish Murdoch, who were prepared to criticize the Council of Twelve in a manner not seen before. If Haliburton could do so with wit, Stewart could speak as a man well-read in constitutional history and precedents. The appointment in 1830 of the Halifax merchant Samuel Cunard to the Council especially upset Stewart. Stewart called for the agricultural interest to be represented; for members to be selected from those who "resided beyond the sound of the gun on George's Island" in Halifax Harbour. Previously, Morse had been an opponent of Pictou Academy; now he completely reversed himself on the issue, while Stewart became as determined in his opposition as Morse had ever been. Stewart gave as the reason for his opposition the "improper tone" assumed by the trustees of the academy before the House, but this was almost certainly specious. As a staunch Kirkman, Stewart had an inbred contempt for the Secessionists who had left the established Church of Scotland. The Reverend Thomas McCulloch did not let Stewart's opposition pass unnoticed in the Pictou *Colonial Patriot,* commenting, with the acerbity of which he was a master, that Stewart had "descended from the august character of a Senator, to that of a third rate attorney; and however he may be extolled by the partizan rabble, he [was] irrecoverably sunk in the estimation of men of sense and integrity."[6] In Morse's case there was probably no other reason for his turn-about than the continuing bad blood between the brothers-in-law. When, however, it came to the vote on increasing judicial salaries, their ostensible professional duty caused them to vote together with the other lawyers in sanctioning the measure. Professional reasons no doubt lay behind their voting for the Supreme Court to return to Amherst and for the recently constructed courthouse in River Philip to be sold.

Next to S.G.W. Archibald, Stewart was the most forthright in condemning the Council over its rejection of the tax on brandy in 1830. The dispute with the Council, however, found little echo in

Cumberland, where the continuing feud between Morse and Stewart remained the focus of attention. For the first time since 1785, enough candidates came forward to contest both the county and township elections. This came about as the result of electoral alliances between Morse and Roach, and more significantly between Stewart and Robert McGowan Dickey, a well-to-do West Amherst farmer.

What had immediately precipitated matters was Dickey's decision to begin campaigning to unseat Morse even before the writs were issued for the 1830 election. Morse had never been opposed since first entering the House in 1818; he seems to have taken great umbrage to Dickey's visiting nearly every freeholder in the township in pursuit of votes. It was obvious to all that this had Stewart's blessing, as Dickey's son, Robert Barry, was studying law with Stewart. Morse's reaction was to prevail upon Roach to enter the fray and go up against Stewart and Oxley. Morse likely had to pay Roach's election expenses, for Roach was heavily in debt to Enos Collins (and went to his grave so); in a few years he would be also forced to borrow £950 from Morse.

Roach should have stayed out, for he had no chance. This became clear as soon as the county poll opened at River Philip. It then continued at Wallace where Stewart and Oxley built up a massive lead. Roach did much better in the three days of polling at Amherst, but in the final count Stewart and Oxley had double the number of votes. Stewart's popularity was such that his supporters in the Amherst area were prepared almost to the man to give their second choice to Oxley, while Roach had to rely on plumpers. It was a much closer battle for the township, which lasted four days and Morse barely managed to win over Dickey by 67 to 59 votes.

In the new Assembly, Stewart continued to be the leader in attacking the defective character of the Council of Twelve because of its combining in one body both legislative and executive powers. Stewart believed the only constitutional reform necessary was the establishment of two separate councils and beyond that he was not prepared to go, though this was not so obvious at the time. He was denied the much-coveted silk gown and the appointment as a king's counsel because of his increasingly sharp criticism of the Council. Nowhere was this more telling than in the debate over free ports. As the leading exponent of free ports, Stewart won such confidence from the Assembly that in 1834 it sent him to plead the case in London. On his return he tabled a series of resolutions on foreign trade, entailing the extension of free port privileges to the outports. He was scornful of the Council for the "illiberality" and "impropriety" of its opposition to the measure. Many members in the Assembly feared smuggling would increase if American vessels were admitted to the outports. Stewart replied to them that it was impossible to prevent smuggling in the Bay of Fundy. Furthermore, people smuggled now as much as they would if American vessels were freely admitted. He called the restrictions on the outports "cruel," pointing out that in one year alone were shipped £12,000 worth of grindstones from Cumberland, yet they could not import a single barrel of flour directly. Was it, he asked rhetorically, "astonishing that the people of Cumberland land flour clandestinely to give to their starving children, when they are not permitted to bring back a single barrel of flour in return for the produce of their industry?" Moreover, try and force the people of Cumberland to purchase their flour from merchants in Halifax, and: "You might as well attempt to make them hewers of wood and drawers of water for you. They will never be satisfied ... till they get rights given them, which they are as well entitled to as the highest and wealthiest merchant in this Town." [7]

Such passionately anti-Halifax speeches should have ensured that Stewart's popularity would continue into the 1836 election, but it did not. In 1832 there had been a devastating crop failure throughout much of Cumberland. Stewart had secured from the Assembly £100 in the spring 1833 session to provide desperately needed seed for grain and potatoes; he had personally subscribed money for farmers in the Wallace area. The currency debacle of 1834 had similar consequences in Cumberland as those we have seen for Halifax, Hants, Kings and elsewhere, further deepening the prevailing acute agrarian distress. Well before the writs were issued for the 1836 election two candidates came forward on behalf of the "farming interest," determined to unseat both Stewart and Oxley. Of Ulster stock, fifty-six-year-old Andrew McKim had worked in previous elections on behalf of Roach and now stepped forward on his own account. [8] A farmer, who also was a shoemaker, McKim had become a Scotch Baptist and then had taken up lay preaching around Wallace Bay, though with little apparent success. His fellow candidate was Maccan farmer Gaius Lewis, a second-generation Loyalist and a Methodist.

McKim and Lewis printed a joint election card in the *Novascotian* laying out their reform credentials: an elective council, reduced salaries, greater encouragement for agriculture and manufactures, members to be required to travel every road in their constituency before taking their seats, and all acts of law to be simplified so that men of common education could understand them. The last reflected among the farming class the widespread hostility towards lawyers in general, and in particular Stewart. Stewart had moved to Halifax in 1834 in furtherance of his career; for this he was portrayed as having "prostituted his legal knowledge, and legal abilities, for personal ambition." To make matters worse for Stewart, Morse, though an arch Tory, threw his interest behind McKim and Lewis; this gave to them the respectability that up to now their canvassing had lacked. It was this lack of respectability that Stewart, Oxley and their friends attacked the most: at best Lewis was a "quiet, harmless farmer." McKim was called one of those "kissing Baptists," a "half Dipt Cobbler" and "a man of obscure origin and mean education, by profession a mechanic, without the least personal influence." A ditty on McKim as no more than a simple, uneducated Baptist lay preacher was circulated by the Tories:

> McKim who had lived for forty years
> A zealous class leader, of heaven quite sure
> Found a flaw in his creed, I am sorry to tell
> Which nothing but salt water dipping would cure.[9]

It was the unordained preacher McKim's becoming a candidate that brought out the respectable clergy to oppose him. After the poll opened in Amherst on 24 November 1836, the Reverend Alexander Clarke showed how nasty matters had become, when to the merriment of the Tories in the crowd, he called on McKim to display his erudition, by quizzing him about his views on GENICOCKNICAL government (he meant gynaecocratical)—government by women or, in the language of the day, "petticoat government." Alexander Clarke was so irate over McKim's candidacy that he broke a cardinal tenet of his Covenanter faith and voted for Stewart and Oxley, as did Stewart's future son-in-law, the Anglican Reverend George Townsend.[10] But the Church of Scotland minister, Hugh MacKenzie, gave his vote only for Stewart. None of the Methodist ministers voted, almost certainly the result of a deliberate and concerted decision, though in numbers the Cumberland Methodists were nearly double all other denominations combined. It was, however, the behaviour of the Baptist minister, Charles Tupper (father of Sir Charles), that drew the most comment, mostly derisory. Tupper apparently suppressed knowledge of a letter he received from a prominent Halifax Baptist, likely the Reverend Edmund Crawley, calling on Cumberland Baptists to support Stewart "as an advocate of civil and religious liberty."

It early became clear that Stewart was not holding his Amherst vote, with many going over especially to Lewis. Furious about this unexpected turn of events, Stewart in a violent temper initiated a rancorous altercation with Morse from the hustings over the "unnatural alliance" between the otherwise Tory Morse and the Reform candidates, McKim and Lewis, (the alliance had an intriguing aspect as McKim was indebted to Morse). The Amherst poll ended with Lewis and McKim having a good margin over Stewart and Oxley. This margin increased somewhat in the polling at River Philip. It was at the end of polling there that a much-embittered Stewart called out, "Wait until we get over Wallace Bridge." This was the very bridge for which in the last Assembly Stewart had secured £750 for its rebuilding in stone. He was right, for his fellow Scots did not fail him. Although he could not catch Lewis with his 405 votes, he managed to surpass McKim by the bare margin of 376 to 371 votes.

For all the commotion over clerical interference, there is little evidence that in this election religion played a significant role at all.[11] Anglicans divided their franchise almost evenly between the two parties, while the Methodists, with one of their faith a candidate for each of the parties, gave their votes by a substantial margin to the Reformers. The Presbyterians did go overwhelmingly for Stewart, but this was because they were Scots and clannishly loyal to Stewart, a man of their own nationality and faith. If Reverend Alexander Clarke's Covenanters had adhered strictly to their faith, they should not have voted at all; as it was, they divided nearly equally between the two parties. The crucial factor was that freeholders in the east of the county showed a definite preference for Lewis, giving him double the number of votes that they gave Stewart. Neither Lewis nor McKim were natives of Amherst, but their decisive out-polling of Stewart can be mostly attributed to the influence of the Tory Morse and disillusionment with Stewart. A total of 746 freeholders had come forward to vote, out of 1,236 heads of households recorded in the 1838 census. The high number of heads of households who apparently lacked the freehold qualification can in part be accounted for by the substantial number of tenant farmers in the Minudie, Maccan and Nappan area. Not one Acadian voted, and the supposition must be that they were all tenants, mostly of Amos "King" Seaman. At the Wallace poll, an unusually large number of voters were objected to and sworn, suggesting that many of the Scottish immigrants could not as yet demonstrate good title to their lands.

It was another battle royal for the township seat. Morse decided not to re-offer and fight another election against Dickey. His successor was his friend, Thomas Logan, who may also have belonged to Alexander Clarke's congregation.[12] What is extraordinary about this election is that 250 voted, but only 204 were recorded as heads of households in the township. Although the figure of 204 may be suspect, the vote reflected both the high degree of freehold tenure in an old township and the efforts of both parties to get every freeholder to the poll. About a dozen of the voters even came from New Brunswick to vote on property held in the township. Dickey won 127 to Logan's 123 votes. However, neither the county nor the township election was over. In the belief that a scene of corruption, splitting of freeholds and other irregularities would be uncovered, the losers petitioned the Assembly. A campaign to raise funds needed by McKim to pay for the costs began immediately. Morse headed the list with a subscription of £100. But it was the young and politically aspiring student in his office, Jonathan McCully (later a Father of Confederation and a senator), who managed matters for McKim. His opposite number acting for Stewart was Robert Barry Dickey, who as his former student had taken over Stewart's Amherst practice (Dickey also became a Father of Confederation and entered the senate with McCully in 1867). The Assembly found in favour of Robert McGowan Dickey's election for Amherst Township. Matters did not go well for Stewart and it began to appear that he would have more bad votes than McKim, leaving McKim with the most good votes. Then in a coincidence of timely good fortune for Stewart, he and Morse were appointed to the Legislative Council in 1838. Stewart's supporters wanted a new election for the now-vacated seat, but McKim petitioned successfully to be seated in Stewart's place.

With McKim's entrance into the House, Cumberland was represented by a member who in education, background, religion and ambition could not have been more different from Alexander Stewart, his immediate predecessor. Neither McKim nor his friends ever denied that in his early life his education had been much neglected, and in the Assembly his want of it was an embarrassment. But he was gifted with a rich and sonorous voice and a readiness of reply, delivered in the broad and vernacular accent of his native Ulster, easily employing racy, humorous language that seldom failed to bring laughter from all sides of the House. He was, as his friends fondly called him, a real Radical Reformer, and there was never to be any doubt where he stood on lower judicial salaries, commutation of quit rents and constitutional reform. He even urged the payment of salaries to Legislative Councillors, so all classes could be appointed to that body, though he noted "it was a misfortune to the country, that the richer people grew, the more inclined they were to toryism ...."[13]

When Stewart parted from his Reformer friends to enter the Tory ranks, Dickey followed. What precipitated Stewart's departure was his opposition to the whole notion of making the Council responsible to the Assembly. He was unequivocal in denouncing this constitutional innovation as containing "a principle dangerous to liberty"; it would "destroy the political institution by which that liberty is preserved," and would "substitute for the high-minded independence of Englishmen the low grovelling subserviency of democracy."[14] As he had always done, Stewart believed the only reform of the Council needed was its separation into legislative and executive bodies. When this was achieved in 1838, he considered it all the reform that was wise or necessary. Later he declared that the idea of responsible government in a colony was nothing more than "responsible nonsense" and could only mean independence.

Stewart saw his 1838 appointment to the Legislative Council as a promotion due him for his legal attainments and service in the Assembly. This was true even more when he entered the Executive Council in 1840, which he viewed as an honourable mark of confidence in his abilities on the part of the British government, and a further advancement of his personal career. In this and his opposition to responsible government, Stewart was no different than such others of his legal colleagues as S.G.W. Archibald, S.B. Robie, C.R. Fairbanks and Beamish Murdoch. But in Stewart's case, the rupture with the leading Reformers was far more bitter because they had believed him to be as committed as themselves to major reform. His appointment took place while he was in England to oppose Assembly representations for constitutional reform. Rumour of his likely promotion to the Executive Council caused Joseph Howe to table a resolution in the Assembly that there were "few men in Nova Scotia who enjoy so little of their confidence, and they should regard his appointment as a direct insult to the House."[15] The vote on the resolution came near the end of the 1840 session, with just twenty-nine of the forty-nine members in their seats; it passed eighteen to eleven, with McKim and Lewis voting with the majority and Dickey opposing. Whether it would have passed with the full House present is doubtful, but it certainly reflected the violence of feeling of most

Reformers towards Stewart. This unprecedented action by the Assembly came after all the angry debates on the call by the Reformers for Governor Sir Colin Campbell's removal, and the knowledge that an election was certain within a few months.

The Parrsborough Shore had been united with Cumberland County; by statute the county poll now had to be held in Amherst, Parrsborough, River Philip and Wallace. The dates for opening the poll rested with Sheriff Joshua Chandler. Probably in league with Dickey, Chandler called for the county election to take place before that of the township. Dickey was determined to run for one of the two county seats in the Tory cause, but if unsuccessful wanted to be assured that he could still stand for his old township seat. Both Lewis and McKim re-offered; the latter was indefatigable in his canvassing, for which he created very complete lists of freeholders and their voting intentions. A fourth candidate came forward. Stephen Fulton of Wallace was a thirty-year-old lay leader on the Wallace Methodist Circuit and a rising shipowner and merchant. He avoided any adherence to a particular party, but seems to have been prevailed upon to run against McKim as alternative candidate from Wallace and to draw off his support there.

After three days of polling in Amherst, Lewis led with 259, followed by Dickey with 243 and McKim with one less than that, while last was Fulton. Such closeness made the Parrsborough poll of crucial importance. Lewis had the advantage of having been born and brought up in Parrsborough. His great fear was that its freeholders would vote along sectional lines by supporting him and then giving their second vote to Dickey, instead of to McKim; he plainly told them that if they gave their second vote to either Dickey or Fulton, they would be, in fact, voting against him. McKim could not be at the Parrsborough poll because he was lying dangerously ill in his Amherst lodgings, but Jonathan McCully spoke on his behalf. McCully had no hesitation in calling upon the Parrsborough men not to let themselves be beaten by those of the Gulf Shore. Whether because of sectional loyalty or as supporters of the Reformers, Parrsborough freeholders went over solidly to Lewis and McKim, giving Lewis a substantial lead and putting McKim ahead of Dickey by 60 votes. The polling continued at River Philip, where McKim still continued to lead Dickey. Then came the news of McKim's passing from a chill received during the Amherst polling. Just before his death a friend had told him victory was nearly certain; McKim had warmly replied, "I die a martyr to my Country."[16] Victory,

Parrsboro' from the water, 1836
Drawn by Miss A. A. Jeffery, on stone by B. F. Nutting, lithographed by Jenkins &
Colburns, Boston 1836.

however, was not as certain as believed at the time of McKim's
death. At the Wallace poll, whether as Tories or because of sectional
loyalty, the freeholders of the Gulf Shore voted massively for Fulton
and Dickey. Desperate to stop Dickey's election, the Reformers
called upon those prepared to vote for Lewis to give their second
choice to Fulton. Enough did, so that Fulton led Dickey by just 12
votes, with Lewis topping the poll with 552 votes.

Dickey was not overly upset about coming last, for he had good
reason to feel he would be easily returned for the township. His
opponent proved to be Jonathan McCully, who was not able to put
up much opposition to Dickey's re-election. This meant that Cumberland had returned one Tory and one liberal to the new House with
the party allegiance of Fulton an unknown. The *Novascotian* assumed that he was a Reformer, but was to learn otherwise on the first
day of the 1841 session. A debate ensued over whether the official
chaplain for the House would continue to be from the Church of
England, or whether clergy from other denominations would also
officiate. Both the Covenanter Dickey and the Methodist Fulton
stood with the minority, mostly Anglicans, in favour of retaining a
single Church of England chaplain. Lewis, a Baptist, voted with the
majority in support of five different clergy. The Cumberland mem-

bers also divided over the far more controversial issue of denominational colleges. There was almost no support in Cumberland for a "multiplication" of colleges. In complete disregard of the party loyalty they displayed on other issues, Fulton and Dickey opposed the incorporation of any colleges. Moreover, they voted with the majority of Reformers against the principle of further funding, while Lewis went with mostly Tories in supporting it.

There is no direct evidence that Lewis' support for Acadia and other denominational colleges was a factor in the 1843 county election, but from the opening of the Amherst poll he fell behind Fulton and Dickey. At Wallace the Tory vote left no doubt as to the winners. Dickey led the final poll with 594. Fulton was in second place, with Lewis some 58 votes further behind. Once word reached Amherst of Lewis' defeat, his friends tried to prevail upon the perennial candidate, Thomas Logan, to withdraw from contesting the township seat and to make way for Lewis. Logan refused and in three days' polling he defeated the surgeon Elijah Purdy by 14 votes. There was so much in-fighting among the liberals that there was little party voting. Logan never declared any party affiliation, though he did support the principle of a coalition government, and the Tories assumed that he would support an administration headed by Attorney General J. W. Johnston. The conservatives were elated by their victories; as one wag, called Nantucket, put it: "I calculate that uncle Joe's Radical party never got such a tarnal flogging afore. They could no go it no how!"[17]

A year later in October 1844, Joseph Howe decided to challenge the Cumberland Tories on their own ground. Buoyed up by successful political meetings in Hants County, he crossed over to Parrsborough, accompanied by the vitriolic and partisan Richard Nugent as a correspondent for the *Novascotian* and the *Morning Chronicle*. Probably by chance, Howe fortuitously arrived on the day that Dickey had called a meeting of his constituents. Howe seized the opportunity to address it and press the liberal claim that Attorney General Johnston's administration should be dismissed because it lacked the confidence of the country. Dickey, as he freely admitted, was no match for Howe in debate and Howe had everything his own way. Dickey believed that even liberals would not approve of Howe's going among the people "secretly," trying to make them dissatisfied with their members. The next day Howe addressed another meeting at Maccan, the strongest base for the liberals in the county. It was also the home of Gaius Lewis, the flower of Cumberland, as the liberals called him. Here they had the backing of Amos "King" Seaman, who presided over the area as a feudal baron. At Seaman's house they determined on holding a public meeting in Amherst the following day in the knowledge that it was the date for the marriage of Alexander Stewart's daughter to Robert Barry Dickey. The plan concocted was to give short notice for a meeting to be held in the courthouse. The meeting was to begin at two in the afternoon, with Howe to speak first, leaving little time for Stewart to reply before the marriage ceremony at five. The liberals packed the courthouse with "Maccaneers" and "Amherst Raddies," but even on such short notice the Tories marshalled a good number. Howe spoke for two and a half hours and Stewart followed, but when the wedding carriages came into view it was agreed to adjourn until noon next day. This gave the Tories further time to rally their forces. After Stewart had addressed the reassembled meeting for three hours, and Howe for another two, old Squire John Bent, on behalf of the liberals, proposed a resolution condemning Attorney General Johnston's administration. He admitted, however, that the wording had been handed to him; moreover, he had not made up his mind on the whole question of party government. For the Tories, Squire William White Bent (they were brothers) amended the resolution to read that the meeting disapproved of the attempt to agitate and excite the people of the county against the government, which had their implicit confidence. Both sides disputed who won the vote of the supposedly up to 600 present, but probably the Tories did. The Tories loudly proclaimed that they had sent "Howe down the river,/ With a spike in his liver," while the liberals boasted of their great enemy Stewart that they had "Bearded the Lion in his Den/ The Douglass in his Hall."[18]

The conservatives believed that in the last election Cumberland had sent three good Tories to Halifax. From the opening of the 1844 session, however, this turned out to be completely mistaken. Logan proved to be one of the liberal party's most dependable supporters. Dickey and Fulton were equally so for the conservatives. All three were Dissenters, but Dickey, in total contradiction to his Covenanter beliefs, was as High Church in his politics as the Anglican Bishop John Inglis could have desired. At the opening of the session, he went so far as to move to restrict the House chaplain to ministers of the Church of England. He carried a majority with him, only to have the vote rescinded the next day, but it took the Speaker's vote to do so. Both Dickey and Fulton, however, joined with most liberals in opposing further funding of sectarian colleges as "improvident and unwise," while advocating more for common schools. Otherwise, on the great constitutional questions, there was never any doubt that Dickey and Fulton stood with the conservatives in opposing the principles of responsible and party government, while Logan was an out and out Reformer.

Logan's liberal credentials meant that he would be strenuously opposed in the 1847 election. His Tory opponent was the merchant Squire William White Bent, who won handily 212 to 172 votes, with the numbers voting under simultaneous polling up by one-third from the 1840 election. Both Dickey and Fulton re-offered. In what the Tories called "an unnatural junction," Gaius Lewis and the Wallace farmer John McFarlane, stood for the liberals as "farmer candidates." The liberals called on the farmers of Cumberland not to be influenced by ledgers, but to act as free Britons and elect two farmers. In a display of quite singular lyrical prose, farmers were told that their day was now at hand: "its glimmering light is plainly gilding the sky of our rights, and soon we shall behold that sun which has been darkened for many years by the odious and noxious mists of Toryism, and we shall not only behold, but we shall also feel, his genial rays, similar to those which were disseminated in years which have glided into eternity."[19] Presumably this last bit of effusive religious imagery harked back to the days when Lewis and McKim had sat in the House as upright sturdy yeomen. Far more prosaic, but likely more effective, was the call to vote along class lines to defeat the Tories. As one writer noted, in Cumberland every office of emolument was filled with a Tory, of the magistrates two-thirds were Tories, all the lawyers except McCully were likewise, and three-fourths of the merchants could be classed among the conservative ranks, along with "almost all the fashionable idlers who throng our thoroughfares." In an attempt to deal with the "pecuniary influences," which in Cumberland's case were much related to the credit system used in the lumbering trade, the liberals promised that if any freeholder was sued as the result of having voted Reform, the party would come forward to protect him. In fact, as the liberals acknowledged, increasing competition among merchants was making it less and less likely that they would use their ledgers at election time.

These liberal appeals to the farming and labouring constituency can be contrasted with the likelihood, though there is no direct evidence, that the Tories used the cry of a Catholic Ascendancy if the liberals were elected, with good effect among the class of predominantly Methodist and Presbyterian farmers. In near straight party voting, Dickey and Fulton triumphed by 100 votes. In this election, there could be no question but that the Tories had got three of their own elected; two of them were Methodists and one a Covenanter. The local conservative oligarchy could also take comfort in the knowledge that their sister county of Colchester had returned to the Tory fold.

The Colchester/Halifax Axis

Truro sends a member of great influence, because he brings with him the members for Londonderry, and Onslow ... If a Speaker were to be chosen, where was he to be obtained, for the last 20 years, but there? If a government leader were wanted, who but his honourable friend the Attorney General was appointed? Why? Because he brought three township members to the House, and, by being backed by three or four votes, he could turn the scale on important occasions and therefore government could not pass him by.
From Beamish Murdoch's Speech at Mason's Hall, *Novascotian*,
29 October 1840

As the thirteen colonies to the south moved to outright rebellion, after Cumberland the Cobequid townships of Truro, Onslow and Londonderry were the most disaffected. When Governor Mariot Arbuthnot visited the district in 1776, he described its inhabitants as "a strong, robust, industrious people, bigoted dissenters and of course great levelers," but they gave him every evidence of their loyalty. Later, when they showed their rebellious spirit by sheltering American privateers and sending men to assist the rebels besieging Fort Cumberland, he could only lamely complain of their "duplicity."[20] Both Samuel Archibald, the member for Truro, and Charles Dickson for Onslow, refused (as did all but five individuals in Cobequid) to take the oath of allegiance demanded by the government in the aftermath of the Cumberland uprising, for which the Assembly unanimously denied them their seats. The division of loyalties that took place in Cumberland and left such a bitter legacy was not present in Cobequid. A return to loyalty came readily; this was apparent when Charles Dickson got back his Onslow seat without the least recrimination from government. Moreover, for the 1785 election no Halifax residents appeared to offer their services as candidates. None of the elections for the three township seats were, in fact, contested. James Smith went in for Londonderry, Matthew Archibald for Truro and once again Charles Dickson for Onslow. All three were farmers. Their opposition to American agricultural imports became the distinctive hallmark of all Colchester members, for whom protection of the farming interest was always to be their overriding interest.

The 1793 election passed as quietly as had its predecessor, with all three sitting members being re-elected. In the seven sessions of the new Assembly, however, a pattern began emerging in which dependence on the Halifax market to take the agricultural surplus of the Colchester townships was being translated into a political relationship. This alliance temporarily broke down under the stress created by the determination of the nascent country party to break the hold of Halifax residents over the four Halifax County seats. As we have already seen, Colchester played a decisive role in the overwhelming victory of the country party candidates. The election of the Londonderry farmer James Fulton ensured that henceforth Colchester would always have one of the four Halifax County seats. In the same election, the freeholders of Truro settled on the twentynine-year-old lawyer Simon Bradstreet Robie, who had recently moved from Halifax to the township in search of practice. There were also contests at Onslow, which returned the farmer Daniel McCurdy, and at Londonderry, where the merchant Samuel Chandler triumphed. Fulton was the first to desert the country party and generally become, in the Assembly, a reliable supporter of Sir John Wentworth's government. McCurdy and Chandler followed Fulton, as the Colchester/Halifax axis or alliance of the previous decade, rooted in the economic self interest of Colchester farmers, re-asserted itself.

Chandler was the only Colchester sitting member to be returned in the 1806 election. Robie had moved back to Halifax, and gave up his Truro seat to run for Halifax County. His successor was one of the very few Loyalists to settle in the Cobequid area. Colonel Thomas Pearson was a native of South Carolina; he had been among the first in the southern colonies to rise for the British and had held a commission in Lord Rawdon's Regiment. With others of the regiment he had been granted land at Rawdon in Hants County, but in 1796 removed to Truro where he had established himself as a merchant. In Nathaniel Marsters, the freeholders of Onslow elected Colchester's first and only Baptist (and former New Light) representative in this period.

But what significantly altered the whole course of Colchester politics was the election for one of the county seats of Samuel George William Archibald. He was the son, grandson and nephew of former members, as well as being son-in-law of the deceased former member, Charles Dickson. Also through his wife, Elizabeth, he was related to Thomas Pearson. At twenty-nine years of age, after articling with Robie, Archibald had taken the first step in a political career which lasted nearly four decades. More importantly, he was to be unrivaled among his contemporaries in his wily and masterful management of Assembly business to forward both his own personal ambitions and the interests of Colchester and neighbouring Pictou. He achieved this while generally maintaining the confidence of both a majority in the House and of successive Governors, no mean feat. As a protégé of Robie, who continued to sit for one of the Halifax County seats, Archibald's re-election in 1811 further cemented the alliance between Colchester and Halifax interests.

With the 1818 election the Colchester/Halifax axis entered its most influential phase. Three of Archibald's brothers-in-law now became candidates. Robert Dickson defeated Nathaniel Marsters, the sitting member since 1806, by 53 to 40 votes to take Onslow. William Dickson, Thomas Pearson's son-in-law, took Truro. Archibald may well have had a hand in Thomas Dickson's election for one of the two Sydney County seats; his brother-in-law's victory meant the Guysborough lawyer John George Marshall's defeat and the temporary removal from the House of a rival to Archibald. With Robie in the Speaker's chair, and as well the election for Halifax County of the Halifax merchant William Lawson and of George Smith of Pictou, Archibald could through family connections, common interests and long-standing friendships bring to bear a powerful combination of members. In the incessant bargaining that took place to gain majority support for desired measures, this combination had no rival. Just what this accretion of influence over proceedings in the Assembly could mean in practical politics became obvious in the distribution of road moneys. In both 1819 and 1820, Archibald moved the scale for the allocation of road moneys to be expended in the forthcoming year within each county and district. In each case, Colchester not only received a larger amount than Shelburne and Lunenburg, both of which greatly exceeded it in population, but also there was included a substantial allocation for the Great Eastern Road as it passed through Colchester. He had so arranged matters that on each occasion his motion for the road scale passed with good majorities, leaving most of the members from the western counties furious, but impotent. The Archibald/Dickson connection continued unchanged after the 1820 election. William Dickson easily disposed of a challenge from Edward Blanchard, and Robert Dickson again defeated Marsters. Archibald and his brothers-in-law voted as a bloc on nearly every issue of substance between 1820 and 1826. Archibald continued to gain acceptance for a road scale highly favourable to Colchester.

Archibald, however, got himself into difficulty with Colchester freeholders for his role in creating the three new judgeships in 1824. As elsewhere in the province, the freeholders of Colchester were equally irate over the judgeship bill and the general complacency of their elected representatives. In the 1826 election all three sitting township members went down to defeat. John Crowe easily disposed of Robert Dickson by a wide margin of 74 votes to take Onslow. John Wier was able to take Londonderry by four votes. But the most dramatic contest so far pitted Archibald's twenty-four-year-old son, Charles Dickson, against a sixty-year-old farmer, William Flemming, for the Truro seat. After the first day of polling, Flemming had 57 votes with Archibald a few votes behind him. On the second day, only 30 freeholders were polled and Flemming's margin over Archibald went down to a single vote. After 13 more votes were taken by the close of polling on the third day, they were tied. On following day, Flemming could manage at most to bring forward one elector to Archibald's four. Likely nearly every eligible freeholder was brought to the hustings. Still, this number accounted for only around half the heads of households in the township, evidence of a sizable non-propertied labouring class.

After studying in his father's office, Charles Dickson Archibald had been recently admitted to the bar. In now entering the Assembly, he was adhering to the traditional pattern for young and ambitious lawyers. But unlike his father, or such youthful contemporaries in the Assembly as Thomas Chandler Haliburton, Alexander Stewart, Richard John Uniacke Jr. and Beamish Murdoch, Charles Dickson demonstrated no ambition to make his mark. This was not from want of ability, but from a genuine lack of interest in the political game. Even the Council's challenge to the constitutional rights of the Assembly, which made for such political difficulties for his father, did not cause Charles Dickson to run again in the 1830 Brandy Election. Instead, he accepted an appointment as chief clerk and registrar of the Newfoundland Supreme Court. Two years later he had the good fortune to marry an English heiress and spent the remainder of his life comfortably in England.

In the 1820s, S.G.W. Archibald had nurtured and sustained a Halifax/Colchester alliance by using his influence in the House to find compromises over such divisive town and country issues as bounties for the fishery. In the next decade, this alliance broke down completely. Archibald seems to have been impotent to maintain even a semblance of the old relationship between Colchester and Halifax members. The sitting Colchester members—Alexander Archibald, John Wier and Robert Dickson—showed no disposition for compromise in their calls for higher duties on imported flour and shipbuilding materials, in opposition to increasing demands for exemptions for the fishery. This hardening of attitude towards Halifax mercantile interests nearly lost Colchester its three township seats when, in 1835, the House debated the bill to make Colchester and Pictou Districts separate counties. The Halifax Township member, merchant Stephen DeBlois, moved that Colchester County should have two representatives, but that the three townships combined should be able to elect only one member; the motion was lost by the narrow margin of two votes. Just how disproportionate the act establishing Colchester left matters can be judged from the population distribution within the county itself, with its 2,050 or so households; of these more than half lay outside the boundaries of the three townships. Thus, a sizable majority of freeholders could at best participate in the election of the one representative for the county. Those residing within the townships, however, could not only vote for the single county representative, but also they could elect a member for their respective townships. In the case of Onslow, for example, as few as 150 freeholders continued to have the privilege of electing their own member.

S.G.W. Archibald's electoral strength lay throughout the county and unless he was prepared to challenge one of the sitting township members, he had little choice but to run for the single county seat in the 1836 election. In 1830 he had had the vote of 1,200 Colchester District freeholders, but he had been at the height of his popularity. Six years later he found himself the most vilified politician in the province as John Young, writing as Joe Warner in the *Acadian Recorder,* charged him with the principal guilt in the swelling of the judiciary and with "exalting the lawyers on the ruins of his country," while seizing "every occasion to benefit himself."[21] Certainly under the influence of Young, if not at his instigation, Isaac Logan became a candidate and proceeded to canvass, using the Joe Warner letters. He was a deacon and some of the Presbyterian clergy seemed to have given him considerable support. In his election card, Logan declared he was running as a Reformer; Archibald never mentioned reform in his, but stood on his past service. Archibald's supporters burnt Joe Warner in effigy in front of his house. There was never any doubt that in reality the election was between Archibald and his arch, but distant, tormentor.

By the morning of the second day of polling Archibald had amassed 577 votes to Logan's 179, which must have been a record for any single day's polling before the introduction of simultaneous voting. Now vindicated, Archibald delivered a speech from the hustings denouncing "Deacon Logan," whose gospel was the lies of Joe Warner. But Logan would find, Archibald said, "with all his outfit of iniquity, that he has walked with vanity and his feet have hastened after deceit." Archibald's final words were directed specifically at Young (who had retired to his farm outside of Halifax), when he said "My name shall remain and stand connected with Colchester, when the name of Joe Warner shall be as rotten as his compost, and stink like his dung hill."[22] John Young's response came immediately in a long letter to the *Novascotian,* in which he retorted that he expected "no clemency from the man who has always loved himself too well, to extend compassion to any one who has crossed the path of his ambition, of his lust for power, and his avidity for the people's money."[23] In 1830 the attacks on Archibald's character and place in the political spectrum had come from the Council of Twelve; in 1836 they came from a leading Reformer. Much had changed in Nova Scotian politics and in those of Colchester too.

If the Reformers, however, could do no more than vilify Archibald, they had, in the Londonderry merchant and shipbuilder Gloud Wilson McLelan, a candidate who was destined to become both one of the leading Reformers and among the most idiosyncratic of members. McLelan, defeated James Flemming for the Londonderry seat by a single vote. Flemming and his supporters petitioned the Assembly to overturn the result and thereby shield the township from "the confusion and distress" of another election. They accused McLelan of smuggling, of being an unpopular individual, and of having "acquired a character which whether true or false was at any rate in those circumstances certain to operate against him." This most extraordinary petition continued that the "wholly unanticipated" support given to McLelan had been founded not only on the "willful misrepresentation" of Flemming's character, but also on McLelan's ledger influence, which had been used with "rigid severity." Moreover, the good name of the township required that Flemming, an individual of independent intelligence and respectability, be returned in the place of an individual "unfit by education and unworthy by character," who had been chosen by the "paltry majority of one to fill an office of such trust and responsibility."[24] After a minute examination of the poll book and deducting votes from the totals of each candidate, a select committee determined that McLelan was still the winner by a single vote.

Once in the Assembly, McLelan proved to be a member whose "extraordinary liberties" with the English grammar and uncouth language gave him the honour of causing more laughter in the House than any other member. A tall, portly man, he made a practice during the sessions of sitting on the benches bare headed with slippers on, in full expectation of remaining there for the day as comfortably as possible.[25] On the other hand, his sturdy independence and manly common sense well expressed the character of a member noted for taking his responsibilities far more seriously than most. A contemporary once said of him that he had often hewn out of rough material valuable ideas which had been later polished into shape by other members of the House.[26]

In the last session before the 1840 election, McLelan remarked that many members might be re-elected with very small majorities. But he was certain that for a candidate in his part of the country, whose principles were known to be opposed to reform, to carry an election "would be just as impossible as to make a feather fly against the wind."[27] He was correct. However, except for S.G.W. Archibald, who went in by acclamation, there were contests for each of the three township seats. The Tories circulated a story in the back settlements that the last Assembly had proved so troublesome to Queen Victoria, and had so insulted her Lieutenant Governor, Sir Colin Campbell, that she had given up "Nova Scotia to its own destruction, just, as ... the Lord gives up sinners to their evil ways"; worse still, she was moving all her soldiers out of Halifax and the Americans might come and take it whenever they liked for all the Queen cared. The story's moral was that since the old Assembly had "completely ruined the country," it ought not under any consideration be sent back.[28] In McLelan's case, John Wier was his opposition and while McLelan announced from the hustings that he was for "Reform, Responsibility and Lord Falkland's Administration," Wier contented himself with

242 Johnny Bluenose at the Polls

declaring he was neither Reformer nor Tory, but favoured a middle course. In what the sheriff described as an election in which there had never been so much good order and "discretion," Wier retired after he fell behind his opponent 106 to 131 votes.[29] At Onslow, Alexander Upham managed to defeat John Crowe by 92 to 86 votes. Nor did Alexander Lackie Archibald have an easy contest, needing 114 votes to 105 to overcome William Flemming. In 1840 Colchester sent to the Assembly in Alexander Upham, A.L. Archibald and Gloud McLelan three unequivocal Reformers.

But the fiercest contest was to take place a year later in the by-election necessitated by Archibald's succession to the office of Master of the Rolls. Archibald's brother-in-law and former member for Sydney County, Thomas Dickson, came over from Pictou to stand for the Reformers. His opponent was also originally from Pictou. John Ross had moved in 1836 to Truro, where he had taken up farming as well as being postmaster; it was this appointment that singled him out as a likely Tory, though he denied that he was either "Tory" or "Foreigner" and said he was a liberal. It was an election marked by "drunkenness, perjury, bribery and corruption," with accusations that clergy were actively participating on both sides; it was said that one clergyman paraded the streets of Truro "hurrahing" for Ross.[30] Dickson won 712 to 684 votes for Ross. The closeness of the result was attributed by contemporaries to the widespread feeling that the "Dicksons have reigned long enough for all the good they have ever done, and it was time to try some one else." [31] His candidacy was reputed to have cost Ross and his friends £600. As his reward for upholding the Reformer cause in Colchester, Dickson was made collector of customs for Pictou shortly after the election, which presumably his friend Joseph Howe secured for him.

After thirty-five years in the House and fifteen as its Speaker, Archibald's elevation to the bench came at a time when he was finding himself distinctly out of sympathy with the reforming majority in Assembly. He was the last of a succession of lawyers, stretching back nearly a century to William Nesbitt through the likes of Blowers, Uniacke, Wilkins and Robie, who thought and governed their conduct according to the eighteenth-century notion of the complete separation of the executive and legislative branches, with each having their prerogatives determined by immemorial usage. Archibald proved to be a superb practitioner in making an eighteenth-century colonial constitution work. In return, he expected and did receive for himself and his sons the rewards of office that were an inherent and essential aspect of that system. He also sought office because of the increased legal practice it brought with it. Although highly successful at the bar, Archibald had a large family to educate and provide for (one son was knighted and another became baron of the exchequer in England). A remarkably handsome man, with polished manners and full of wit, he was an amiable and not a vindictive man, though he could never forgive John Young for the vilification heaped upon him in Joe Warner's letters. In 1846 he would die of a massive stroke. His passing marked the death of the old and the birth of a new colonial constitution in a more democratic age.

Although Colchester members were all staunch Reformers, it did them little good when it came to the division of road moneys. One of the leading Reformers, Herbert Huntington of Yarmouth, completely excluded Colchester from a coalition of eastern and western counties that he put together. Other than vote against the road scale for the years 1837 through to 1840, the Colchester members had been powerless to form any new alliances to challenge the control gained over the distribution of road moneys by Huntington's coalition. In the first session after the 1840 election, the Colchester members renewed their efforts to increase Colchester's allocation of road moneys. As far as Herbert Huntington was concerned, if Colchester wanted more for roads, then their members should not advocate needless and expensive measures for supporting agriculture. On one occasion when McLelan complained in debate that Yarmouth needed to be wakened up about the importance of agriculture, Huntington lashed back, telling him that: "The inhabitants of the County of Yarmouth, poor as it is, could buy Colchester all up, together with McLellan's shipbuilding establishment at Londonderry"; to which McLelan retorted the inhabitants of Yarmouth "could not support themselves three months of the year by agriculture. [It was] covered with fog most of the time."[32] Politically, McLelan very much spoke for his constituents, who were becoming greatly disturbed by the decreasing value of their agricultural produce, which they attributed to the want of sufficient protection against imports. In the petition sent to McLelan for presentation in the Assembly, and part of which is quoted at the beginning of this chapter, the farmers of central Colchester protested that "one cargo of fish caught by those living upon the production of our own soil, yield more advantage to the country generally than ten cargoes exchanged for foreign produce."[33] The simple yeomen of central Colchester could not have been bettered in their summation of the fundamental dichotomy underlying Nova Scotian economic life in the first half of the nineteenth century.

Huntington and McLelan were, nonetheless, at one on the issue of denominational colleges. In the 1841 session, McLelan had given his vote to a grant for Acadia, but it was the last occasion that he supported funding for denominational colleges. In the 1843 session, McLelan's bill to withdraw the permanent grant of £400 a year from King's College forced the Assembly to debate the first principles of supporting denominational schools and colleges. At the great public meeting held in the Onslow Presbyterian Meeting House on 9 October 1843, McLelan made clear that the basis of his opposition to sectarian colleges was "because they would tend to form a union between Church and State—the most dangerous union that can take place; and because they will be the fruitful source of bickerings throughout the country."[34] From the beginning, A.L. Archibald had been opposed, first to the incorporation of Acadia and then to its funding, but Dickson did not oppose funding of denominational colleges until the Reformers took a definite stand against the policy. Until his death in 1841, Upham had been a strong supporter of grants to Acadia and in this he was followed by John Crowe, his successor as member for Onslow. If the great public meeting at Onslow was a true indication of feeling, Onslow Township particularly and Colchester in general were with the Reformers and opposed to funding sectarian colleges. Yet, in the 1843 election, Crowe, the one Colchester member to be a consistent supporter of funding, went in without opposition. Presumably, his personal popularity outweighed any other considerations freeholders may have had. A. L. Archibald's Reform credentials did not help him withstand another challenge from James Flemming, who won handily by 82 to Archibald's 52 votes. For Londonderry, McLelan won again over Wier by much the same margin as in 1840. But the real battle took place for the county seat, pitting John Ross against another of the Dickson clan, Joseph Dickson, a Truro merchant. Apparently another Dickson was not what the freeholders wanted, for from the opening of the poll at Truro to its close at Portapique on the Parrsborough shore, Ross led all the way; when Dickson finally gave up Ross had 650 to his 467 votes, a most decisive victory.

In 1840, Colchester had sent three Reformers. Three years later the same freeholders sent three Tories in Ross, Flemming and Crowe, and in McLelan, a single Reformer. The reasons for this complete reversal are not easy to determine. There were so few Baptists in

Colchester that the Tory/Baptist alliance could not have been a factor. Moreover, popular feeling was as opposed to funding sectarian colleges as could be found anywhere in the province. The most plausible explanation is that the great issues of the day simply played little role in the four elections, with each dominated by local concerns. In the case of the county and Truro, the anger against the Archibald/Dickson family compact was so intensely felt that A. L. Archibald and Joseph Dickson were defeated, rather than Flemming and Ross winning. In the case of Crowe, he was sufficiently popular that no one came forward to contest his re-election.

When the 1844 session opened, for the first time in the memory of most there were no Archibalds or Dicksons in the House. When Huntington tried to reduce the duty on imported salted pork, all four Colchester members united in opposition to such an act of sacrilege; otherwise, they voted along straight party lines. Ross's tenure in the Assembly should best be remembered for his advocacy of the founding of an experimental farm. What the liberal press thought of Ross can best be described by quoting from the Yarmouth *Herald;* during the 1847 election campaign the paper told its readers that "Johnny Ross makes an ass of himself (we ask pardon—Nature saved him the trouble)."[35] On 7 August 1847, when the freeholders of Colchester went to the polls established under the simultaneous polling act, the great issue of responsible government seems not to have weighed heavily in their judgement. They proceeded to defeat a leading Reformer in McLelan, but also the Tory Ross, while re-electing Flemming and Crowe, both Tories. McLelan's defeat at the hands of John Wier by 14 votes can be attributed in good part to the difficulties in which he found himself over the distribution of road moneys. Although the full story is impossible to unravel, Ross, as the county member, had got control of management of most of the road money for Londonderry. He used it to embarrass McLelan to the extent that McLelan even petitioned Lieutenant Governor Sir John Harvey to intervene. McLelan's explanation for his loss lay in his failure before the election to get more deeds recorded than had Wier, for old men, persons in debt and the underage, involving leases for a single room, part of a building or whatever else could be arranged.[36] Ross was a political maverick, if not something worse, and his wildly erratic behaviour finally proved to be too much for Colchester freeholders. He went down to defeat at the hands of Samuel Creelman, a political newcomer from Stewiacke. A. L. Archibald came within three votes of upsetting Flemming and protested the result to the Assembly, but to no avail. Isaac Logan also lost by three votes to Crowe. The 1844 election had not been an aberration. In 1847, Colchester had once again returned three conservatives and one liberal in Creelman. S.G.W. Archibald would have heartily agreed with this decision by the freeholders; they had returned to the old Colchester/Halifax axis.

The Scots, Loyalists and Acadians of Pictou, Old Sydney and Cape Breton Counties

I'm not surprised that I'm sorrowful
As my habitation is behind the mountains
In the middle of the wilderness at Barney's River
Without a thing better than bare potatoes.
Before I make a clearing and raise a crop there
I must uproot the savage forest
With the strength of my arms; I will be exhausted
And in a short while an invalid before my children grow up.

The Gloomy Forest, Verse 3, Bard John MacLean

Thank God I am well pleased for coming to this county as I find myself quite easy, having occupied land called my own ... no soul living forces me to do a turn against my will, no laird, no factor, having no rent, nor any toilsome work but what I do myself.

Donald Campbell of Big Bras d'Or Lake to a friend in Scotland,
7 October 1830

A traveller journeying from Halifax to Pictou in 1830 would most likely have travelled as a passenger of the Eastern Stage Coach Company. The most populous town after the capital, with its 1,500 or more inhabitants, Pictou had grown without plan up a fairly steep slope from the water's edge. As well as its unplanned appearance, it differed noticeably from other towns in the province, for a good number of the town's two hundred or so houses were of stone, the work of Scottish stonemasons. Since the arrival of the 180 passengers who had bade farewell to Scotland in early July 1773 to cross the Atlantic in the celebrated ship *Hector*, Pictou had been a chief port of entrance for thousands of immigrating Scots. Those on the *Hector*, and those who came later, had been led to expect a land of already cleared farms. Instead, they were greeted by such impenetrable forest as they could never have imagined. It was, in the words of the most renowned Scottish bard to come to North America, a "place contrary to nature." Bard John MacLean settled at Barney's River in 1819. In his *Song to America: The Gloomy Forest,* he poured out the sorrow and disillusionment he felt at having succumbed to the "tempters" of emigration and their "fables" of life in Nova Scotia.[1] However, as the second quote that introduces this chapter is evidence, thousands of Scots who came to Nova Scotia found the land and the independence that had been closed to them in old Scotland.

There developed, nonetheless, a marked differential in the levels of economic progress between the earliest arrivals, who obtained the best lands, and those who came later and found little fertile soil left. Furthermore, those who came before the fateful clearances began in earnest did so willingly to better themselves, often being relatively well-off tenant farmers who arrived with some capital to begin their lives anew. Those who came after them, and they were the majority of emigrating Scots, had been forced out of their homes in the Western Highlands and Isles. Many arrived destitute, to be relegated to squatting on unproductive back lands and labouring for others. When the Cape Breton potato famine of the mid-1840s put an end to further immigration, at least 25,000 Scots had settled in Nova Scotia; of these some 17,500 had done so on Cape Breton Island.[2]

Most of the twenty thousand inhabitants of Pictou County lived on fourteen hundred or so farms.[3] By the 1830s its farmers had become the most productive wheat growers in the province. They had early developed a substantial export and carrying trade with Newfoundland, the French Islands of St. Pierre and Miquelon, and the North Shore of New Brunswick.[4] But what awed observers was the growing industrialization. It was centred on coal mining and on the construction of steam vessels, the most famous of which was the *Royal William* (in 1833, it became the first steam-driven vessel to cross the Atlantic). Pictou had the first newspaper, the *Colonial Patriot,* and shared with Yarmouth the distinction of having the first public subscription libraries outside of Halifax. In its academy, presided over by the doughty Reverend Thomas McCulloch, Pictou had an institution of learning that, for all the controversy surrounding it, provided its students with as good an education as could be found anywhere in the province. However, no matter how short his stay, no traveller could have left Pictou without being amazed, if not horrified, at the sheer violence of the quarrelling between those of the Church of Scotland, or Kirkmen, and those who had seceded from it, known as Seceders or Secessionists, which overbore every facet of life in Pictou.

The post road continued eastward from Pictou to the small town of Antigonish, which consisted of one principal street extending half a mile in a serpentine course. In the Roman Catholic Church, erected in 1828 by Bishop William Fraser and able to accommodate eight hundred, the town had the largest building in the eastern part of the province. By then four-fifths of the near 8,000 population were Catholic Gaelic-speaking Highlanders, and nearly all lived on a thousand or so farms. Averaging around 200 acres with about a fifth of this cleared, the farms of Antigonish yielded sizeable surpluses for export.[5] As in Pictou, little was shipped to the generally glutted Halifax market; instead, the farmers sent horses, cattle, sheep, butter, pork and grain overland to Pictou or Guysborough for export to markets around the Gulf of St. Lawrence.

From Antigonish whether a traveller's horse took the right fork of the road to the small village of Sherbrooke, a creation of the timber trade, or the left that led to Guysborough town, he would have found little good agricultural land. In what would become Guysborough County in 1836, the population of around 6,000 was almost entirely of Loyalist descent and gained a living from the fishery and the forest. Those adhering to the Church of England outnumbered Presbyterians three to one, with other faiths sparsely represented. The town of Guysborough itself was a growing community of thirty to forty dwellings and numerous stores, barns, wharves and outbuildings of various sorts.

Ever since Cape Breton had been reunited with Nova Scotia in 1820, more than £10,000 had been expended on the island's roads, but they had remained a challenge to the hardiness and patience of visitors and local inhabitants alike. No one in 1830 could have estimated with any confidence the true population of the island, as the flood of dispossessed Scots continued apace. By the time the 1838 census was taken it exceeded 35,000. Scottish immigrants now predominated over not only the descendants of the English, Irish and Loyalists of the towns and environs of Sydney and Louisbourg, but also the Acadians at Isle Madame on the Atlantic side and those at Cheticamp facing the Gulf of St. Lawrence. The Scots had come as agriculturalists and by 1830 had gained possession of the best land on the island, settling mainly along the fertile valleys of the Mabou, Margaree, Middle and Mira Rivers and around Bras d'Or Lake. They devoted much of their improved acreage to livestock, for which they found a ready market in Newfoundland.

Much of this trade to Newfoundland went through the port of Arichat on Isle Madame. But Arichat's commercial growth was coming primarily from the fishery, which gave employment to almost the entire adult male Acadian population. The management of the fishery was firmly in the hands of a few Jersey Island merchants, who exported the annual catches to markets in Spain, the Mediterranean, the West Indies and Brazil. Although Arichat was the larger in population, Sydney town had remained the administrative centre for Cape Breton after re-annexation to Nova Scotia in 1820. But the massive expenditures of the General Mining Association in the Sydney area were dramatically changing a rural economy into an industrial one.

All in all, an observer of the Cape Breton scene in 1830 would have concluded that the island was a decade behind the mainland. If, however, he could have returned in the 1840s, he would have been made pleasantly aware of a cultural awakening permeating life on the island. The titles of two new newspapers captured the spirit of the awakening: *The Cape Breton Advocate* and *The Spirit of the Times and Cape Breton Free Press.*[6]

From Pictou through to Sydney, the massive Scottish immigration had given this region a unity in race and culture but, let it be said immediately, not in religion. Furthermore, it was set apart from the rest of the province by its industrialization, founded on coal mining, and by its export trade in agricultural products within the Gulf of St. Lawrence littoral. The region's economic lifeblood was thus largely removed from the tentacles of mercantile Halifax. The exception to this had to be Guysborough, where the fish merchants were beholden for their credit to Halifax bankers and merchants. Still, this region was to have more Halifax lawyers and merchants descend on it seeking seats than anywhere else in the province. The story of their success or failure forms a vital and integral aspect of the region's emergence from political adolescence to a maturity roughly on a par to that found in older settled regions of the province.

Kirkmen and Seceders: Tories and Reformers

Ere the publication of the next number of our periodical, this community will ... be drawn into a state of most violent excitement,

*by the jarring and conflicting elements of political warfare .... We
anticipate that the artifices that have been resorted to on previous
contests will characterize the present, and that the cry of "Kirkman"
or "Antiburgher" [Seceder] will be raised and piped most furiously
by the minions of Toryism.*

Mechanic and Farmer, Pictou, 4 November 1840

In its 9 November 1836 issue, a Pictou newspaper, with the engaging
title of the *Bee*, directed public attention to the propriety of having
the sheriff call a public meeting to select candidates for the forthcoming election. By this means a contested election could be avoided
and a "total cessation of party animosity," with a saving of £1000 in
election expenses to the county. Pictou had not forgotten the drunkenness, bloodshed and violent party spirit of the Brandy Election of
1830. In that election, the divisions between Kirk and Seceders had
turned into vicious party warfare. Now in 1836, with Pictou a separate county, at stake there were two county seats and a single township seat. If one Kirkman and one Seceder were nominated at a public
meeting and unopposed on election day, the evils of another contested election for the county could be avoided. Adherents of the
Kirk, however, formed three-fifths of the population and they were
mostly Tories. Most Reformers were, in turn, Seceders. By advocating a no-contest agreement, the Reformers assured themselves of one
county member in the face of the distinct possibility of gaining none
of the three Pictou seats. This also meant the unopposed re-election
of George Smith, who had sat since 1819 for one of the four old
Halifax County seats.

Many Tories believed that they should have all three seats. No less
than six Tories came forward as candidates for the two county seats,
all of them of either the Kirk or Anglican persuasion. But in reality,
John Holmes and Lawrence Hartshorne were the only serious contenders. Hartshorne had gone down to defeat in 1830 as an upholder
of the Council of Twelve; in 1836, he made it clear that he would
not run again in a contested election or go to any expense to be
elected. When he threw his influence to Holmes, all the others withdrew. On election day, Holmes and George Smith were returned
without a contest. There was a contest for the single township seat.
In two days of polling, Henry Hatton overwhelmed Abraham Patterson by 311 to 94 votes. Hatton had the Kirk behind his candidacy,
but many were also beholden to him from his extensive dealings in
lumber and in the mercantile trades.

An 1838 by-election showed just how intertwined religion and politics had become in Pictou County. George Smith's appointment to the Legislative Council left vacant one of the county seats. This time there was no agreement between the two parties that would have allowed a Reformer to have Smith's seat without a contest. With the candidacy of Kenneth John McKenzie, a fierce contest was inevitable. As a rabid minister of the Kirk, McKenzie had refused to associate with Secessionist ministers, but instead had adopted a policy of divisiveness, and become a leading opponent of Pictou Academy. Although considered a man of superior talents, contemporaries believed that in his personal life he did not manifest a high standard of ministerial character. Whatever may have been the cause of this opinion, there was sufficient unhappiness within his congregation of St. Andrew's in Pictou for him to leave a few months before the by-election. His opponent was Thomas Dickson, brother-in-law to S. G. W. Archibald, and under whom he had studied law before setting up practice in Pictou. In marrying Sarah Patterson, Dickson had connected himself with one of the oldest and most respected families in the county. Dickson was narrowly the victor with 1035 to 989 votes for McKenzie. The expenses, amounting to £150, for Dickson's victory were met from subscriptions raised from the mercantile community. The single exception was the Reverend Thomas McCulloch, who gave £14 to see his arch enemy defeated.[7]

There could not be any doubt about the politics of the three Pictou members; Holmes and Hatton were Tories and Dickson a Reformer. At age thirteen, Holmes had come with his family from Scotland. Although he first learnt land surveying, his chief occupation was his East River farm. Once in the Assembly, he led the opposition to any exemption to the import duty on flour. On the issue of reform, he left the House in no doubt where he stood; he saw no purpose or good in constitutional change, and from that position he never wavered. His fellow Tory, Henry Hatton, spent the sessions "in silent indifference." Holmes and Hatton did show some activity in having Abraham Patterson removed, just before the 1840 election, as a magistrate and judge of the inferior court. They succeeded also in having five new magistrates appointed, all known Tories. Patterson protested that these new appointments were calculated to "disturb the peace and quiet of the county," and made solely to promote political objects and electioneering intrigues.[8] George Smith intervened with the government on behalf of his fellow Reformer. He pointed out the personal affront and embarrassment caused to Patterson, but the

Pictou from Fort Hill
Drawn by Wm. Eagar, on stone by B. Champney, lithographed by Thayer, Boston, published by C. H. Belcher, Halifax, July 1840.

Tory-controlled Executive Council was unmoved by such considerations.

The hope of the Reformers was still for a renewal of the 1836 agreement that would put Dickson and Holmes back into the Assembly without a contest. Before the 1840 election, both parties held meetings of delegates from throughout the county. The Reformers passed a resolution calling for an agreement to allow each party to nominate a single candidate for the county, while leaving open the township seat to be contested. The conservatives, however, already had determined to put up Henry Blackadar as a second candidate to Holmes. A native of Halifax, Blackadar had set up a law practice in Pictou some years before. By marrying the daughter of the Reverend Archibald McQueen, he had established his religious credentials with the Kirk. The Tories replied they were in favour of an uncontested election, but the two candidates had to be Holmes and Blackadar. Accepting the inevitable, the liberals nominated the New Glasgow merchant James McGregor to run with Dickson. But the Reformers had little stomach for a contest. This became evident from the opening of the poll in Pictou when, without any resistance from their opponents, the Tories gained control of the hustings. At the end of four days of polling, Holmes and Blackadar led McGregor and Dickson by a hundred votes. The liberals had nearly 200 supporters unpolled, but had chosen not to force them into the hustings; for this they were chastised for "unaccountable lukewarmness."[9] After two days of polling at New Glasgow, the liberals conceded the election. One reason that the Tories had been able to defeat the liberals so decisively lay in the success they had in creating freeholders. They had pursued a policy of having their supporters divide and subdivide their farms into one-acre and sometimes half-acre lots so that sons could vote. The liberals were equally unprepared to do battle for the township seat, though they put up the lawyer Alexander Peter Ross to oppose Hatton. The night before the poll was to open the Tories brought in their Highlanders or, as they were more picturesquely described by the liberals: "the deluded sons of the Mountain, true to the order of their gods, were flocking into the town; and at daybreak they were as thick on the streets as the stars in the firmament of heaven." Ross withdrew and Hatton went in unopposed.[10]

For the 1843 election, if the liberals were to elect even one of the three members, they had either to reach an agreement with the conservatives, or somehow to divide the Kirk vote so that one of their own could take a county seat. For any member of the Pictou Kirk to run for the Reformers was simply out of the question, so George Smith called on George Renny Young to come from Halifax and offer for the liberals. Smith also resigned from the Legislative Council to stand for the township. At the time of his decision, George Smith was facing financial ruin. His problems dated back to the mid-1830s depression. So serious were his business failures that by 1838 he was forced to mortgage all his property in return for a £5,802 loan from Samuel Cunard. Although initially able to meet his annual repayments, in 1842 Mather Byles Almon (who had purchased the mortgage from Cunard) began suit in the Court of Chancery for the remainder owing. Moreover, other creditors were suing for a further £4,290. In entering the 1843 election Smith was courting bankruptcy, but the passions aroused by party in Pictou County overrode any notion of sensible self-interest.[11]

As the son of the late John Young, George Renny Young's credentials as both a Reformer and a member of the Kirk could not be questioned. Moreover, he had attended Pictou Academy, over, it must be said, the objections of his elder brother William. At the Academy, George Renny had had Thomas McCulloch as his teacher, and had found him, despite "all his peculiarities of character ... a man of profound & accurate knowledge."[12] Afterwards Young had gone to Britain to study law, and on his return had gone into practice with his brother William. Young opened his canvass at Barney's River with an address laying out his reform principles, while making a plea for an equitable compromise between the two great parties in the county. The Barney's River meeting passed resolutions advocating a policy of compromise, to be tendered at a meeting of Kirk/Tory delegates at New Glasgow. Most delegates at New Glasgow were not anxious for a contest, but a determined group held that since the Kirk was in the majority in the county, all three seats should be theirs. With some misgivings, the delegates gave their blessings to Holmes and Blackadar. A satisfactory arrangement was still possible, because George Smith was prepared to withdraw from his township candidacy and leave the seat open to Blackadar. All chances of compromise, however, fell apart when Martin Isaac Wilkins virtually imposed on the Tory party his candidacy for the township seat.

Another son of Judge Lewis Morris Wilkins, King's College graduate and a lawyer, Martin Isaac had come to Pictou in the late 1820s to set up a legal practice. Although an Anglican, he had taken on the editorship of the *Pictou Observer*, to forward the cause of the Kirk and the Tory party. He had his full share of the nasty, partisan streak that marked the character of the male members of the Wilkins family, underlaid as it was by an overweening personal ambition. His candidacy ensured that it would be "Turk against Turk."[13]

At the opening of the poll for the county election the conservatives played heavily with Young's non-residency, with his being a "Sham Kirkman" and committing the sin of holding a political meeting on the Sabbath. By the end of the polling at Pictou town, Holmes held a substantial lead, but had been unable to carry Blackadar with him. This left Young in second place. This pattern continued through the New Glasgow and Merigomish polls. Young was able to defeat Blackadar by 90 votes, because four-fifths of the 1,394 freeholders who voted for Young then refused to give their second vote to either Holmes or Blackadar. But nearly one-fifth of the 1,583 who voted for Holmes also voted for Young, instead of for Blackadar.[14] The liberal strategy of dividing the Kirk vote had succeeded. The total cost to both parties was rumoured to have been £3,000. Much of this sum came from Halifax, where both parties viewed the Pictou battle as an extension of that taking place in the capital.

With Wilkins and George Smith running for the township, a brawl rather than an election could have been expected. This is what happened. Wilkins' High Anglicanism came under fierce attack from the

Seceders. He was called a member of a denomination that would "prostrate" Presbyterians to the level of "heathens," while restoring the Church of England to its "former tyrannical dominion." Freeholders were told that on no account should the township be represented other than by a Presbyterian.[15] Smith defeated Wilkins by 725 to 690 votes, but the Assembly insisted on a new election because of the violence used by Smith's supporters. A major contributing factor to the violence, however, was the decision of Sheriff John Harris to erect a gangway up to the hustings in a manner that made it impossible for him to observe the entrance to it. Most of the violence arose from the fighting between the parties to control the entrance. The party that gained control could then push their supporters forward, while making it impossible for those of their opponent to mount the hustings and vote. What further drew the ire of the Assembly was that neither the sheriff nor the magistrates present had used their full powers to ensure order.

How much the 1843 election cost Smith personally is unknown, but it, and the expense of previous ones, must have greatly contributed to the desperate financial straits in which he now found himself. Mather Byles Almon was relentlessly pursuing through Chancery his suit for the outstanding amount on the Cunard loan. Smith seems not even to have been able to afford a lawyer to defend him in the case. On his death in 1850, all his remaining property was sold by Chancery order for £600, about one-third of the sum still owed Almon. He died intestate, leaving his widow with an estate of £52, when once he had been the wealthiest man in Pictou County. It is perhaps pointless, though intriguing, to speculate whether the Tory Almon purchased the mortgage held by Samuel Cunard as a means to push Smith into bankruptcy and out of politics. If so, he succeeded. After the 1843 contest, George Smith declined to run again. In his place the liberals chose the Pictou druggist James D.B. Fraser (who in 1848 administered chloroform to his wife in childbirth, being the first to use it for this purpose in British North America).

For the by-election, Sheriff John Harris determined this time to separate the warring parties by having constructed a barrier of planks, ten feet high, stretching completely across the street right up to the hustings. But the most controversial part of his plan was to receive the votes alternately from the electors of each party. Fraser and his committee protested, with foresight, that this would result in all probability in a no-return election. Sheriff Harris persisted with his plan and declared that the poll would open on Monday, 17 March

Pictou from Mortimer's Point
Drawn on stone by Wm. Eagar, lithographed by T. Moore, Boston, published by C.
H. Belcher, Halifax, July 1840.

1845. On the first morning of polling, the two parties mobilized their
forces. Down the street came Wilkins' forces, led by a piper and
Hugh Ross, one of the magistrates who had taken the greatest umbrage when the Assembly had censured his and his colleagues' conduct at the previous election. When they met Fraser's forces, the
command was given in Gaelic to produce their hidden cudgels. One
of the first blows against a Fraser supporter was struck by Magistrate
Ross. A riotous fray ensued and many were severely injured. Once
a degree of order was restored, polling commenced and went forward
without major incident until Thursday morning. At this point some
of Fraser's supporters went over to Wilkins' side of the barrier and
claimed the right to vote. When the sheriff was unable to convince
them to return to the alternate voting system, he closed the poll.
Although the poll then stood 456 votes for Fraser and two less for
Wilkins, he did not declare a winner. The Assembly ordered another
by-election to be held.[16] The election had cost the liberals at least
another £200 and the Tories probably more.[17] The parties had already spent thousands of pounds in the previous contests. Probably
neither party had the money for another expensive battle. When the
Tories proposed Blackadar, the Reformers did not oppose his nomination. After three bitterly fought elections, with by far the greatest
expenditures yet seen in the province, Pictou had Holmes and Young

for their representatives for the county and Blackadar for the township — the very individuals that had first been proposed before the negotiations for their uncontested election had broken down before the 1843 election was held. The chief loser was Wilkins, who more than anyone else had forced the elections on the county.

A dispute within the Church of Scotland in Scotland over clerical patronage caused a similar division in Pictou County. Most Church of Scotland ministers returned home to occupy vacant parishes, leaving the Kirk in Pictou bereft of ministerial care and greatly weakened as an institutional force. A number of congregations joined the newly-formed Free Church. In a shrewd move, the liberals for the 1847 election again put forward Young, but reached an agreement with the Free Church to support Andrew Robertson as the second candidate for the Reform cause. For the Tories Holmes offered once more, but his colleague, Robert Murray, was also Free Church. In near straight voting along party lines, Young and Robertson triumphed over Holmes and Murray by nearly 100 votes. For the township, it was much closer, with the Tory Blackadar just managing to defeat Robert Patterson Grant by 36 votes. Neither Young nor Holmes had been in favour of simultaneous polling, holding that having twenty different polls on the same day in the county would not work.[18] In practice, it could not have worked better, with only one minor incident of reported intimidation of voters. Moreover, an extraordinarily high number voted, around 3,200, out of roughly 3,600 heads of households in the county.

If divisions within Scottish Presbyterianism were the source of party in Pictou, in the adjoining Sydney County it was the seemingly unnatural conjuncture of Scottish Presbyterians and Catholics, intertwined with the rivalry of two Guysborough family compacts, that underlay its politics, and to which we now turn.

The Family Compacts of Guysborough and A Bishop & His Highlanders

During the month or more preceding the day appointed for commencing the election ... I travelled on horseback through the greater part of the County, calling at private dwellings, and attending public meetings .... My brother ... was Adjutant of the battalion of Militia, of which my father was Colonel, and as the

*meetings of that force were taking place at that time ... at the close
of exercises, addressed the people on the subject of my visits.*
John George Marshall from his *Personal Narratives ...*

*[The Bishop] told the people 'an attempt had been made to separate
him and his flock to cut the cord that held them together', that Mr.
Young was his favourite candidate, 'he would now stand or fall with
him, and would let them see what his influence was, and called upon
his people to support him'.*
Novascotian, 28 December 1836

Sydney County was one of two new counties created in 1785 to
provide for Loyalist representation. Within its boundaries, it incorporated what we know today as Guysborough and Antigonish Counties. A few Loyalists settled at Antigonish Harbour, but most took
up lands in the Guysborough area. The rivalry that developed from
the beginning between two Loyalist families—the Cutlers and the
Marshalls—became for the next fifty years the most constant factor
in the politics of Sydney County. The patriarch of the Cutlers was
Thomas Cutler, a graduate of Yale College and a lawyer by profession. He had joined the British forces at the outbreak of the American
Revolution, serving first as a captain in the New England Volunteers
and later as an assistant barrack master.[19] The "Cutler Compact" at
its peak of influence embraced nineteen family members, who held
no less than fifty-seven commissions from the government, as well
as numerous local offices.[20] Of Ulster birth, Joseph Marshall had
settled in Georgia. He had fought through much of the Southern
Campaign in the Carolina King's Rangers. On his arrival in Guysborough, he took up lands on the eastern side of the harbour.[21] Early
made a justice of the peace by Governor John Parr, he was, however,
so offended when Parr made Thomas Cutler lieutenant colonel of the
local militia regiment that he refused to serve under him as a major.

For the 1785 election, neither Cutler nor Marshall was prepared to
stand and two Halifax officials represented the county. In 1793 Cutler
was elected, but attended only three sessions; he was never again a
candidate. Marshall had a better attendance record after he was elected
in 1799; he also played an active role in the House, generally siding
with William Cottnam Tonge and the country party.

In these early elections, the poll did not move from Guysborough
to Antigonish. For the 1806 election, leading freeholders reached an
agreement that both avoided a contested election and allowed for

Antigonish to have one of the two county seats. Guysborough free-holders settled once more for Marshall; those of Antigonish chose the merchant Edward Irish who, however, died during the first session of the new Assembly. When a by-election was called after Irish's death, William Allen Chipman, who had just been defeated for a Kings County seat, convinced Antigonish freeholders to support his candidacy. Some in Guysborough, however, resented having an outsider as one of the county members. They prevailed on Captain John Legget, the Country Harbour merchant and Loyalist, to oppose Chipman. For the first time a poll was held at Antigonish. Few of the Gaelic-speaking Highlanders would have been present at an election before. They refused to vote until one of their own, whom they called Adjutant MacDonald, arrived and could tell them which candidate to support. MacDonald looked at both the candidates, turned to the Highlanders and, pointing to the sixty-three-year-old Legget, asked them: "How will that old man be able to crawl through the snow every February to represent the county in Halifax? Vote for the young man" (though at 50 years of age Chipman was hardly young).[22] This turned the election in favour of Chipman, but Legget protested the result to the floor of the Assembly, whereupon Joseph Marshall convinced the members that the sheriff had irregularly conducted the election. In the succeeding by-election, the seat went unopposed to the brother-in-law of Edward Irish and the merchant John Cunningham; in the end Antigonish got a resident as its own member.

For the 1811 election, Joseph Marshall desired to pass his seat on to his son, John George. The younger Marshall had attended the Halifax Grammar School and after studying law with Lewis Morris Wilkins had established a good practice in Pictou. However, Thomas Cutler wanted the second seat for his son-in-law, John Ballaine. The unknown factor was the sitting member, John Cunningham, who did not reveal his intention to be a candidate again until the morning the poll opened at the Guysborough courthouse. Immediately, discussions took place on how matters should be arranged to avoid the evils of a contested election at all costs. It was decided that the two sitting members, the elderly Marshall and Cunningham, should once more be returned. A disconcerted John George returned home to give vent to his frustration in the presence of his mother, the matriarch of the Marshall family compact. She sent him back to the hustings to offer as a candidate, where he persuaded his brother to nominate him. He made a speech to the astounded assembled freeholders and demanded that the poll be removed to the next place, once voting was completed in Guysborough. Removal of the poll required that the sheriff give ten days' notice, but the writ was returnable in less time. The sheriff then declared that he would have to send to Halifax for a new writ.

The delay gave John George Marshall the opportunity to canvass the county. His description of his campaigning leads off this section. When the poll opened for a second time, both John George and Ballaine stood as candidates. Cunningham again came over from Antigonish intending to run, but saw that he had little prospect of success and withdrew. Once in the Assembly, John George Marshall entered freely and often into the debates, advocating especially bounties for fishermen, because they put cash directly into the pocket of the poor fishermen. But it was his opposition to funding for Pictou Academy that brought Marshall into the most prominence at this time. There was a zealous, moralistic streak in Marshall's character. On education, it took the form of a distrust in the cultivation of literature and classical knowledge, as inimical to public and private virtue. Not that he opposed education, but he believed that refinements in literature should not be promoted to the neglect of the interests of the lower classes of society, of those who constituted the wealth and strength of the country. For that reason, he held out for common schools in every county and no assistance whatever to Pictou Academy and similar institutions.

Marshall moved to Halifax to pursue his legal career. When he returned to Guysborough for the 1818 election, he found himself facing two strong opponents: the thirty-three-year-old son of Thomas Cutler, Robert, and another lawyer, Thomas Dickson. As we have noted when discussing Pictou County elections, Dickson had established his legal practice in Pictou. Through his legal work, he had developed political connections in Antigonish and, most importantly, also with Thomas Cutler. Dickson and Cutler agreed that if Robert Cutler's supporters at the Guysborough and Country Harbour polls would make Dickson their second choice, Dickson's supporters at Antigonish would give their second votes to Cutler. The alliance worked so well that Marshall got only single votes and ran a distant third.

By the time of the 1820 election Marshall had learned his lesson. Moreover, this time there were four candidates—Marshall, Dickson, Simon Fraser of Pictou, and the Halifax merchant John Steele. All were non-residents and so their local alliances were crucial for their success. Marshall, of course, had his own family. Its influence and his own popularity in the town gave Marshall 278 of the 280 votes polled at the Guysborough courthouse. When the poll moved to Country Harbour and then to Antigonish, Dickson was able to outpoll Marshall by a wide margin, but he could not overcome Marshall's lead from Guysborough. Marshall won with 621 to 518 votes for Dickson.

But the greatest surprise of the election was the polling by John Steele of 463 votes, though his candidacy had been opposed by both the Marshall and Cutler families. Steele, however, had the full backing of Halifax mercantile interests, notably the Almon and Cunard families. These Halifax interests provided much of the credit needed by Guysborough merchants and fishermen to pursue the West Indian fish trade. Steele had had at his disposal a substantial ledger influence, whose origin lay in the capital.

In 1823, Marshall accepted the appointment of the single Cape Breton judgeship; in his view another of those providential occurrences that he believed marked his whole life.[23] What now transpired was to be a replay of the Halifax by-election of 1823. In that election, John Young had gone down to defeat at the hands of C.R. Fairbanks, with the full weight of the Halifax oligarchy thrown against him. Young offered to succeed Marshall and had the support of Thomas Cutler, but this could not be enough to ensure victory, because the election would be decided at the Antigonish poll. The ties of Scottish nationality proved stronger than the divisions of religion, as Young made an alliance with the recently arrived priest, William Fraser, for the vote of his Catholic Highlanders. Highly thought of by his church for his work as a parish priest in his native Scotland, and for his academic ability, Fraser had gone first to serve in Cape Breton for two years before coming to St. Ninian's parish in January 1824.[24] Young's opponent was John Steele, whose candidacy, as before, was orchestrated from Halifax. A third candidate was the first lawyer to settle in Antigonish, John Thomas Hill. Because Hill resigned in favour of Steele after obtaining no more than six votes, it is more than likely that he ran at the behest of the same Halifax connections backing Steele, and with the expectation of future favours.

The aging Thomas Cutler was absolutely determined to see Steele defeated. He acted not only as inspector for Young at the hustings, but also as assistant to Sheriff David McQueen. With good cause, Steele objected to this highly irregular arrangement, but McQueen rejected his protest. In the 1820 election, Steele had accused McQueen of partiality. An unwell McQueen had had to walk to

Halifax in mid-winter to attend at the bar of the Assembly, which found that he had not acted either "corruptly or wickedly." Steele had also sued McQueen for a sum of money. McQueen was now to have his revenge. McQueen's partiality was as blatant as any by a sheriff in any election of this period. On the first day of polling at the Guysborough courthouse, what contemporaries described as a riot broke out, though it mostly consisted of pushing and shoving with the free use of fists; at the centre of it was Robert Cutler, who, according to which witnesses were believed, was either trying to restore order or was the instigator. As inspector on behalf of Young, Thomas Cutler objected to many of Steele's voters; then as assistant to McQueen, and with his connivance, insisted that they take the freeholder's oath or pronounced them not eligible to vote. Cutler was registrar of deeds, so he could use this office to substantiate his objections with little fear of contradiction. Still, Steele got through the poll with 90 votes and this put him close to Young, but after the poll closed at Sherbrooke village, Young had a fair lead.

The Antigonish poll opened on a Monday. Steele and Hill united in an attempt to catch Young, but at the end of the day Young had a commanding lead with 190 to Steele's 154 votes. Hill now resigned, but not before McQueen threatened to imprison him for disorderly conduct and from the hustings declared that any who voted for Steele "ought to be damned." On Tuesday some freeholders arrived from Arisaig, led by their priest, Colin Grant, and the sound of the pipes; they made, in Young's words, a "noble charge their phalanx gave us the majority" for the day. Young had sent his son, William, off to the Acadian settlements and on Wednesday with the assistance of the Reverend William Fraser's brother, he brought in more votes. When the count stood 352 for Young and 218 for Steele, the latter resigned.[25] There were around 2,000 heads of households in the county and of these a quarter had voted. This was about half the number who had voted in 1820, suggesting that by one means or another, many had been prevented from voting, particularly at the Guysborough polls. Others did not have freeholder status; this was especially true among the Highlanders. Even though Catholics now greatly outnumbered Protestants in Antigonish, 100 Protestants had voted, compared to around 175 Catholics. Of the Protestants just 3 had voted for Steele, but 98 of Fraser's flock had given their votes to Steele.

It was this revealing breakdown by religion that allowed the Antigonish Protestants, led by the Presbyterian minister Thomas Trotter, to refute accusations by Steele's friends that the Catholic clergy had induced their people to vote for Young against their own will and inclinations. Trotter and the others readily admitted that Fraser had given his interest to Young and saw no shame in this.[26] As he would in a short time become a contributor of editorials to the Pictou *Colonial Patriot,* Trotter was politically at one with Young. He and Fraser, with the few other educated Scots in Antigonish, were bound together by ties of friendship and nationality. It could well have been Trotter who convinced Fraser to support Young. The petition by Antigonish Protestants, rejecting Steele's accusations against the Catholic clergy, failed to convince the Assembly; it voided the election without even a recorded vote. In the ensuing by-election Young easily triumphed, defeating Steele 260 to 95 votes. As an indicator of his popularity, however, Young's margin was illusionary. In a frank letter before the 1826 election, Thomas Cutler warned him that the clear preference in the county was for a resident member. His own hopes were for his new son-in-law, William Frederick DesBarres, but DesBarres felt he was too young; moreover, he had just been admitted to the bar and feared that he would make enemies to the detriment of his fledgling legal practice.[27] Once Thomas Dickson announced he was re-offering and John Thomas Hill again became a candidate, Cutler gave his reluctant support to Young. The natural alliance was for Young and Dickson, as the sitting members, to unite against Hill; instead, they quarrelled and the election became a three-way contest. Cutler had warned Young to keep on friendly terms with Fraser, within a year to be consecrated a bishop. This Young did, for he topped the poll, with Dickson not far behind.

The falling-out between Dickson and Young may well have been over Pictou Academy. As one who had been educated to be a minister of the Kirk, Young had lost none of the disdain which that church held towards the Secessionists. He would go as far as supporting annual grants to Pictou Academy, but steadfastly refused to sanction permanent provision. As a result, the Pictou *Colonial Patriot* characterized Young as a literary pilferer, known for his "selfishness, and instinctive tendency to underhand dealing, and pitiful intrigues," which had "totally destroyed all confidence in his disinterestedness and integrity."[28] Still, as both Young and Dickson had opposed the Council of Twelve's constitutional pretensions in the dispute over the tax on brandy, they could with reasonable confidence return to the hustings for the 1830 election. For the fourth time in succession, John Thomas Hill stood as a candidate, thus forcing an election. This time Young and Dickson stood together. When faced with their combined strength, Hill withdrew.

For John Young the sessions of the Assembly that followed the Brandy Election were ones of mounting frustration. He had become utterly obsessed with the need for retrenchment in public expenditures. His attacks on the self-interested character of the legal profession and the baleful influence of its ascendancy in the Assembly were as pointedly direct, and as virulent, sparing none, as any ever published in this period. He portrayed the Council of Twelve as the nucleus of an "Aristocratic party," an aristocracy of office and of wealth, but wanting an adequate aristocracy of talent. From the floor of the Assembly, he once called the former Speaker S. B. Robie "a Barnacle on the bottom of the ship of State"; the next day Robie's enemies painted, over the mantelpiece of the anteroom leading into the Assembly room itself, a sign reading "Sir Simon Barnacle." The hostility between the two dated back to Robie's acceptance of the Master of the Rolls appointment, an office Young had opposed as totally unnecessary. The "Barnacle" incident resulted in Robie's refusal to shake Young's hand, producing an angry exchange of letters and a challenge from the incensed Young to a duel. Through the intervention of Judge Brenton Halliburton none took place.[29]

As part of the great division of counties that was one of the few significant achievements of the former Assembly, old Sydney County was divided into Guysborough and Sydney (later to be renamed Antigonish) Counties, each with two representatives. In the face of three local candidates coming forward for the new Sydney County and an equal number for Guysborough, Thomas Dickson could see no political future in trying to run again as non-resident. Young, however, determined to offer for one of the Sydney seats, saying it was an election to be decided on political principles, different from any that taken place in the past. Notwithstanding Young's reformist credentials, the feeling in Antigonish was running strongly that it should now be represented by residents. Young found himself opposed by the lawyer Alexander McDougall who had attended Pictou Academy with Young's son George Renny, and the merchant James Wilkie. The poll opened on the first Monday of December 1836. There was little canvassing by candidates and the polling went forward rapidly. At the end of the day McDougall led with 248, followed by Wilkie's 161. Young was last with 124 votes. At the close of poll on Tuesday, Young had not only fallen behind the leading McDougall by 272, but, worse still, was 91 votes behind

Wilkie. Not until then did he realize he was heading for an ignominious defeat. Up to now Bishop William Fraser had not intervened directly, but on Tuesday night there was a meeting of Young's chief supporters at the Bishop's residence. What happened next morning is described in the second quote introducing this section. For the next three days, Young's agents scoured the countryside, bringing men on foot from twenty and thirty miles away who had never witnessed an election before to vote "for the Bishop." They were told that unless they voted for Young, their bishop would "be degraded in the dust." For this Young obtained 175 votes, while Wilkie could just manage another 54 before resigning when Young surpassed him by 30 votes. Still Young never came close to catching McDougall, who amassed another 204 to top the poll with a remarkable 736 votes. All three candidates were of the Kirk. Fraser's intervention to save Young from "political extinction" was based on loyalty to a friend, and in a certain hubris when he came to believe that Young's defeat could be interpreted as a weakening of his influence over his people.[30]

Young attended the 1837 session before dying quietly at his Willowbank farm on the outskirts of Halifax. His election a year earlier was the last for a non-resident, and the last time Antigonish County did not have at least one Catholic representative. Wilkie did not offer, perhaps because two Roman Catholics came forward to contest for Young's seat. Of Irish Catholic parentage, Richard James Forrestall had come from Halifax as a boy with his mother, on the death of his father and his mother's remarriage to Robert Henry. He had attended the grammar school maintained by the Reverend Thomas Trotter before he established himself as a merchant. His opponent was another Catholic merchant, twice the age of the youthful Forrestall. From Kilkenny in Ireland, George Brenan did not arrive until the middle of the 1830s. On the birth of his twin girls, Bishop Fraser and the Reverend Colin Grant became their sponsors, so he did not lack for religious respectability. Forrestall won by 80 votes and entered the Assembly described as a young gentlemen of liberal principles and amiable manners, connected by religion with the mass of his constituents, and with family ties to the leading interests of the county.

Meanwhile, in the newly created Guysborough County, the feeling was equally strong that there should be no more non-residents. William Frederick DesBarres, now with a well-established practice in Guysborough town, was prepared to embark on a legislative career at the behest of his father-in-law. In fact, Thomas Cutler died within a month of the election and DesBarres assumed the mantle of leadership for the Cutler compact. John Joseph Marshall, grandson of Joseph and nephew of John George, also became a candidate. The thirty-year-old Marshall had gone through grammar school and chosen not to enter a profession, but to make his living as the keeper of a general store. The thought of having both county members coming from Guysborough town brought forth the candidacy of the Sherbrooke merchant Hugh MacDonald. It turned out not to be much of a contest; DesBarres easily led the poll, followed by MacDonald well behind. Marshall was a far distant third. Having gone to the Halifax Grammar School and articled with Lewis Morris Wilkins, DesBarres had close ties to Tory Halifax, but he was never to be more than a moderate Tory. By the last session before the 1840 election he had openly stated his belief in the need for constitutional reform. During the 1839 and 1840 sessions, MacDonald and DesBarres were successful in having £3,800 appropriated to complete the road from Halifax through the Musquodoboit Valley to Sherbrooke and on to Guysborough. In honour of the great event, MacDonald purchased the first carriage in Sherbrooke. The Guysborough County election of 1840 turned out to be a curious affair, for the poll was not moved from Guysborough; not unexpectedly, after two days of polling, DesBarres and Marshall were elected virtually unanimously.

The contrast with Antigonish, where Bishop Fraser's behaviour bordered on the eccentric, could not have been more extraordinary. McDougall decided not to re-offer, and it was generally expected that Forrestall and Brenan would go in without a contest. Then Forrestall's half-brother, the twenty-three-year-old William Alexander Henry decided to run. William Alexander had attended the Reverend Thomas Trotter's grammar school before studying law with MacDougall, and had just been admitted to the bar. After the first day of polling, the "Family Compact" of the two half-brothers led Brenan by a small margin. It was stormy the next day and voters coming in from the country sought shelter in the open houses of the candidates. To their consternation they found that Brenan, at the urgings of his bishop who had taken up the cause of temperance, had no drink to offer. At the open house of the brothers "everything was as abundant as the ocean." So after enjoying the brothers' hospitality, these voters went to the hustings where they pushed the majority for Forrestall and Henry to 100 votes over Brenan. The gap widened by 200 votes on the third day. Another stormy day followed, and many stayed home. Among his own age group Henry, a well-known sportsman, was highly popular. Some fifty of his fellows now voted. Few of them likely had freehold and the whole election was turning into a farce. On the morning of the fifth day, when Brenan was about to resign, Bishop Fraser mounted the hustings. He had earlier pledged not to interfere or to influence the election, and so he had waited until the last before giving his vote. In a highly agitated manner, he proceeded to reprimand all those who had voted for the two brothers: they had extremely disappointed him and if he had had 1,000 votes he would have used them to ensure against their election. But his fury was even more aroused against the "Galphers" (as he termed those who had frequented the brothers' open house): they would, he exclaimed, "gulp down the Gulph of St. Lawrence if it were Rum they had betrayed their country, and sold their votes for Rum, Brandy and Wine and would sacrifice their consciences, their Queen and their God at the same shrine." He then gave a single vote for Brenan who immediately resigned.[31]

When Henry took the oaths at the beginning of the 1841 session, he became the youngest member up to this time to sit in the Assembly. He had embarked on a political and judicial career that would see him become one of the drafters of the British North America Act, and be among the first judges appointed to the Supreme Court of Canada. His first significant intervention in the House was to move a resolution calling for compulsory assessment for local schools. His motion gained the support of no more than twelve members, but some twenty years later, as Attorney General, he would be foremost in pushing through free school legislation.[32] On the college question, Henry was more supportive of funding than either DesBarres or Forrestall, but in 1843, when it became a party issue, he voted with his fellow Reformers in opposing further grants to Acadia and other sectarian colleges.

Funding for sectarian colleges and party loyalty both played the most minor of roles in the 1843 elections for the two counties. Within Sydney County the losing party in the last election was determined that this time the "Family Compact" of brothers should be defeated. For this purpose George Brenan again offered, and all temperance principles were forgotten. Patrick Power also offered. A recent arrival from Waterford in Ireland, he had established himself as a merchant in Antigonish. The poll first opened at Malignant Cove, where after three days of quiet polling Henry led, followed by Power, Brenan and Forrestall in that order. From the totals it seems that there was mostly single voting for candidates, with individual popularity being the only issue. Henry, for example, had more than twice the number of votes as had his brother, and the same was nearly true for Power over Brenan. The single voting pattern became most evident by the time the polling concluded at Tracadie, where Forrestall resigned with a meagre 47 votes as compared to his brother's leading total of 326. The first day of polling, on a Saturday at the Antigonish courthouse, saw no disorder, but Henry's margin was much reduced. Although Forrestall was Catholic, William Henry had been brought up in his father's Presbyterianism. On the Monday, the cry was taken up by supporters of Brenan and Power: "Vote for your Religion." Power mobilized a force, led by a piper, of reportedly 500 partisans (few, however, were freeholders), and wholesale and violent intimidation of Henry's voters began. By the end of the day, Brenan and Power had polled three times the number of voters as had Henry. This had given Brenan a substantial lead over Henry, who dropped to third place, nine votes behind Power. The next morning about 100 of Power's supporters stationed themselves in and around the courthouse and forcibly seized the passageways up to the hustings. When the sheriff finally closed the poll, Power had a margin of five votes over Henry, giving him the second seat.

Although every one of the 1,150 freeholders polled could have voted for two candidates, just one-third of them did so, with the remainder voting for a single candidate. This was as good an indication as any that there had been little if any voting along party lines. Henry protested the result to the floor of the House but the election was not voided, probably because the Assembly felt that Henry's supporters had not been entirely innocent of the same behaviour as those of Power; the fact that on the final day, when the the intimidation of voters was at its worst, Henry polled 125 to Power's 121 votes was perhaps evidence enough of this. Although thwarted by the Assembly, Henry succeeded in having Power charged with giving five shillings to an elector for his vote. Power claimed that he gave the money because the individual had devoted much time in canvassing for him. A special jury found Power guilty of bribery and awarded Henry, as plaintiff, £100 in damages. The *Acadian Recorder* caustically headed the story of the trial "Enormous Damages." It held that trying the charge was tantamount to a second trial because the Assembly had already dealt with it.[33]

For the Guysborough election, there was also no sign of party voting. There was much ill feeling over the influence and control still exercised by the Cutler Family Compact and this likely accounts for the candidacy of William Heffernan, a Guysborough farmer. He was the first Methodist to run in a district that had been an Anglican preserve from the beginning. Hugh MacDonald once more came forward in the hope that the electorate would see fit to select a representative from each district, rather than two from Guysborough. For him to succeed, he had to do well at the Sherbrooke poll and make a strong showing at Guysborough. Although he led the Sherbrooke poll with 117 votes, DesBarres and John Joseph Marshall were just a few votes behind him. At the Guysborough courthouse, MacDonald polled only 17, while DesBarres and Marshall received 189 and 124 votes. The surprise was Heffernan who came ominously close to defeating Marshall for the second seat.

Although the party affiliation of their representatives had not greatly concerned the freeholders of Sydney and Guysborough, they had returned three liberals in DesBarres, Power and Brenan, and in Marshall a lone Tory. Power, however, proved to be a less committed Reformer than believed. During the 1844 and 1845 sessions he could be found on the liberal side on most recorded votes. Then, in 1846, he broke party ranks on a major issue, the disqualification bill. Introduced by John Joseph Marshall, its purpose was to disqualify any officer connected with the customs, excise and post office departments from sitting in the Assembly. Marshall had already conceded that true responsible government meant party government, but had argued that the elements of party were not to be found in small, colonial Nova Scotia; according to Marshall, its population needed to be six times greater and forty times as intelligent as it was then. Marshall intended his bill to be a direct challenge to what he called the "corner stone of responsible government" — the direct accountability of heads of government departments to the majority in the Assembly. As the Reformers rose to defend what was for them a vital constitutional principle, the bill brought forth much passionate debate. But a number of them saw it differently. Speaking after the Tory barrister and collector of excise for Hants County, James DeWolf Fraser, an irate Power rose and exclaimed: "Send lawyers to this House, and they will take care to make offices for themselves." Power went on to decry government by heads of departments, because they would so feather their nests and gain so much influence that "The great horse Sampson would not be strong enough to drag them out." It was his opinion that the liberals were fighting for the offices with the large salaries: "Take away these, and you will take the tongue out of Responsible Government."[34] In the five recorded votes during the debate, Power and some other liberals voted with the Tories and ensured the bill's easy passage.

Power's conversion to Toryism was poorly received in Antigonish. When Joseph Howe came from campaigning in Guysborough for a public meeting in October 1846, Power was forced publicly to defend his conduct. Reportedly 800 to 1,000 gathered and so a platform was hastily erected in front of the courthouse. It was cold and windy. Howe spoke for two hours, but not even the eulogistic pen of the ever-present Richard Nugent could disguise the fact that he was exhausted and not in good form. Still, Power was no orator. He caused a near riot by attacking local individuals and trying to play on religious feelings. Once order was restored, a chastened Power limply claimed that all he wanted was to defend both his support for the disqualification bill and the government for its liberality to Catholics. It did him little good; a resolution was put to the meeting, expressing disapprobation of those members of the Assembly who "have grossly deceived their constituents" and have been "induced or corrupted to desert their party." A shocked Power, realizing that it was aimed at him, asked unbelievingly from the platform, "Will you pass it?" Such was the feeling against him that it passed unanimously.[35]

When he began his canvass for the 1847 election, Power discovered just how much his desertion from the liberals was ill-received. People believed that he had been bought with Tory gold: a chant "A rat a rat dead for a ducat, dead," followed him about the countryside. With Power's unpopularity and the decision of Brenan not to re-offer, likely because of age, the field was left open for Henry to re-enter the fray. A newcomer, twenty-six-year-old James W. MacLeod, also became a candidate. His candidacy was a watershed in Antigonish politics. His grandfather Neil MacLeod with his wife Mary had been among the families who had emigrated from the little island of Eigg in the Hebrides. They had come first to Pictou and then with other Catholic families moved to Antigonish. James MacLeod was the son of their son, John, and he had studied law, likely with Henry or Alexander McDougall, the member elected in 1836 and now in the Legislative Council. With simultaneous polling in place, Power could not engage in intimidating his opponents' voters as he had in 1843. In fact, he seems to have withdrawn just before the vote, for the *Cape Breton Spectator* reported that "the renegade Power" had declined the contest.[36] With the election of MacLeod, the Scottish

Catholics of Antigonish had for the first time one of their own, and the first member as well who had been born in the county.

In Guysborough, the liberals also triumphed by a handsome majority when DesBarres and Hugh MacDonald were elected and the "arrogant & bullying" John Joseph Marshall defeated. But representation of the county was not to be decided until two by-elections were held. The first was occasioned by the appointment of DesBarres to be Solicitor General; in the practice of the day, this required him to seek re-election. The redoubtable Marshall refused to allow DesBarres the courtesy of being re-elected by acclamation; the popular DesBarres doubled the vote on him. Within months, however, DesBarres accepted an appointment to the Supreme Court and another election had to be held. This time Marshall, whom the liberals believed they had put "on the shelf," was easily the winner over his liberal opponent.

John Young's victory in the election of 1836 had proved to be the last in which an outsider was even a candidate in either Sydney or Guysborough Counties until the twentieth century, when Guysborough was represented from 1945 to 1956 by an outsider, A. W. MacKenzie. On Cape Breton Island, the process of naturalizing its representation took considerable longer, as repealers and annexationists waged a two-decade struggle for the Cape Breton soul.

Repealers Versus Annexationists on Cape Breton Island

I have induced all to unite on one common ground that of effecting the Repeal ... And I hope that success may attend our efforts, and that no motive will be attributed to me, except the sole one which actuates me attachment to, and love of Cape Breton, "MY OWN, MY NATIVE LAND"
>   Post Election Card of Edward C. Brown, *Novascotian*,
>   26 November 1840

You are now by an Act of the Province the County of Inverness, with the right of returning two members in place of one ... The light of science has beamed upon you, and for the first time you have substantial bridges and well constructed and level roads ... and the liberality of the House has enabled you to set on foot an Academy.

Speech by William Young to the electors of Inverness County,
Novascotian, 14 November 1840

When Cape Breton's Chief Justice Archibald Dodd ruled in 1816
that a local tax on rum was illegal because the royal prerogative to
tax had been surrendered in 1763, he set in motion a chain of events
that led to the re-annexation of Cape Breton Island to Nova Scotia
in 1820.[37] The royal proclamation of 1763 had united the former
French colony of *Île* Royale to peninsula Nova Scotia. With the
creation of New Brunswick as a Loyalist haven in 1784, Cape Breton
was also made a separate colony, with its own Lieutenant Governor
and appointed Council. It was anticipated that an Assembly would
be called into being, but none ever was, and the island continued to
be ruled by ordinances passed by the governor in council. In ruling
as he did Archibald Dodd accepted the legal reasoning of a former
Attorney General, Richard Gibbons. In London the law officers of
the crown agreed with Dodd and Gibbons, but the Colonial Office
decided that the island was in too poor a condition to warrant an
Assembly. It chose instead to re-annex Cape Breton to Nova Scotia
by order in council. Thirty office-holders in Sydney lost their offices
and a repeal movement was born to bedevil island politics for the
next three decades.

Gibbons and the barrister Edmund Murray Dodd, son of the
pensioned-off former Chief Justice, stood for the two Cape Breton
seats in the 1820 election. Their opponents were Richard John
Uniacke Jr., son of the Old Attorney General, and Laurence
Kavanagh. Another graduate of King's College at Windsor, young
Uniacke had first arrived in Cape Breton in 1813 when his father had
successfully intervened to ensure his son succeeded the irascible
Gibbons as Attorney General. Young Uniacke did not remain long
in Cape Breton, as the salary and fees of the Attorney Generalship
did not meet his expectations; he returned to Halifax in 1817. He
now reappeared in the summer of 1820 to contest the election for the
first two representatives for Cape Breton. Uniacke, especially as a
non-resident, should have stood no chance against his avowed repeal
opponents, but that would only have been true if the poll had remained in Sydney; however, it had to be moved to Arichat, where
the Kavanagh family held sway, and the population was as much for
annexation as that of Sydney was against. One of the first English-
speaking families to settle on the island, the Irish-born and Catholic
Kavanaghs greatly prospered as fish merchants. On the death of the

father in a shipwreck, Laurence assumed control of the business. He soon proved to be an energetic and shrewd merchant, amassing a small fortune and creating a magnificent estate at St. Peter's; it was said that he owned three-quarters of the population of Cape Breton.[38] At the time he decided to run with Uniacke in the 1820 election, his ledger had 689 names in it, an appreciably greater number than the total of freeholders who would vote in the forthcoming election. At the Sydney poll, Uniacke and Kavanagh managed just 42 each, compared to Dodd's 210 and Gibbons' 139 votes. But at Arichat it was no contest. The Kavanagh family influence brought to the hustings 288 freeholders for the alliance of Kavanagh and Uniacke; poor Gibbons could get but one and Dodd did hardly better with 17 votes.

Although Dodd unsuccessfully protested Kavanagh's election, he made no mention in his petition that Kavanagh, as a Roman Catholic, could not take his seat in good conscience. For Kavanagh to take his seat, he had first to take the oath against transubstantiation, which all knew he had no intention of doing. It took two years of negotiations and the determination of Uniacke to force the issue to a decisive vote, which he did on 3 April 1823. His motion for Kavanagh to take the state oaths, except the declaration against popery and transubstantiation, passed by 21 to 15. The Nova Scotia House of Assembly had admitted the first English-speaking Roman Catholic outside of Quebec in British North America, and six years before the British House of Commons. Likely because he was unwell, Kavanagh seldom attended sessions. As a consequence, representation of Cape Breton's interests rested with Uniacke. An extremely handsome man and, like others of his family, a natural and witty orator, Uniacke is, however, remembered most for killing his opponent in the last fatal duel fought in Nova Scotia.[39] He saw his sojourn in the Assembly only as a form of dues payment for promotion within his chosen profession. Still, he used his influence, both in the House and at the Council table, to gain for Cape Breton the largest road vote next to Halifax County. In the dispute with the Council in 1830 over the fourpence tax on brandy, Uniacke was one of three assemblymen who upheld the Council's right to amend money bills. In this stance he had the added motivation of knowing that there was awaiting a Supreme Court vacancy, caused by the death of James Stewart. As soon as the session closed, and after S. G. W. Archibald had turned it down, the judgeship went to Uniacke; he became the first native Nova Scotian to sit on the Supreme Court.

Cape Breton had not seen the last of the Uniackes, for another son of the recently deceased Old Attorney General appeared as a candidate for the 1830 election. James Boyle Uniacke had gone through King's College before entering his father's law office and being admitted to the bar in 1823. His father had then dispatched him to finish his studies at the Inner Temple in London. Of Richard John Uniacke's six sons, James Boyle probably had the best mind and was certainly the finest orator. In two years' time, he would have the good fortune to marry an heiress, Rosina Jane Black. She was not noted for her beauty. During a debate in the Assembly on the importation of horses, Uniacke jocularly compared his own racing horses to John Young's farming breeds: Young retorted that Scotsmen like himself selected their horses "upon the same principle that some gentlemen select their wives not for their beauty but for their sterling worth."[40]

The thirty-year-old Uniacke was joined on the hustings by Kavanagh's son, also called Laurence, who had inherited his deceased father's business and ledger. They were opposed by Richard Gibbons and the Arichat merchant Thomas Edward Chandler Jr. The results of the Sydney poll are unknown, but presumably Gibbons led. As Chandler had his own ledger influence to throw into the fray, the Uniacke/Kavanagh alliance did not have matters all their own way in Arichat. In fact, the polling turned into a major brawl, when a "lawless and merciless mob of Irishmen," mostly from Newfoundland and unqualified to vote, tried to force their way into the hustings. In Halifax a report circulated of three killed and over fifty injured; apparently, however, only one man (by the name of Callaghan) died, though the injury total was not far off the mark. The polling ended with Uniacke well in the lead, followed by Kavanagh, just two votes ahead of Chandler, and 25 in front of Gibbons. For the first time, the poll moved to Port Hood in what was to become Inverness County. There Gibbons resigned while Chandler got 60 to Uniacke's 188 and Kavanagh's 88 votes, giving the latter two the election by a wide margin.[41]

That the one non-resident candidate, Uniacke, should score such a decisive victory can best be explained by the genuine popularity of the man, combined with an oratorical skill having a good leavening of ribaldry. Chandler and Gibbons were not yet done with Uniacke. They protested the election on, as it turned out, the valid grounds that Uniacke had no legally acceptable freehold on the island. Although at the opening of the Sydney poll, Uniacke claimed he had seventy-five acres, he refused to swear to it. The reason was not far to seek; for the election act required that a candidate or an elector had to have their property registered six months before the writ was issued. Uniacke had not contemplated running until his brother's elevation to the bench. The issuing of the election writs four months later made it impossible for him to qualify. Likely he had hoped to be returned without opposition, as his brother had been in the previous election. In fact, this was to happen in the succeeding by-election and for the next four general elections as well.

If the violence at Arichat achieved nothing else, it gave added impetus to members of the Assembly to increase the representation for Cape Breton, so that its number of seats bore somewhat greater relation to its population compared to mainland constituencies. The result was the 1832 Act, which increased the Cape Breton County representation by one seat, and gave single seats to Sydney and Arichat Townships. In the succeeding by-elections, Edmund Murray Dodd and the Halifax lawyer and leading Catholic layman, Laurence O'Connor Doyle, took the two township seats unopposed. In Doyle's case, he had been looking for a constituency to gain entrance into the House. He had decided on Arichat rather than Cape Breton County, because, as he said: "I would be equally honored by representing the only Catholic Township in the Province, as by representing the largest County."

In Sydney, it was presumed that the new seat for the county would go unopposed to Richard Smith, the general manager for the General Mining Association's mines in the Sydney area. An Englishman and graduate of the Royal School of Mines, Smith had first come to Pictou in 1827 in the employ of the General Mining Association. He had established the G.M.A.'s coal mining operations in Pictou. Three years later he came to Sydney for the same purpose. To enter the Assembly, John Young had been forced to seek a seat for Sydney County as a non-resident. His son William (well-established in a legal career that was to lead to the chief justiceship of the province and a knighthood) determined to follow his father into the House by the same route. By rights he should have stood no chance against the resident Smith. Moreover, Smith had the massive financial backing of the General Mining Association (the election cost Smith a reputed £3,000, though Young later claimed £7,000). But the thirty-three- year-old Young, again following the strategy of his father, made an alliance with the Reverend Alexander MacDonell (sometimes MacDonald), the Catholic priest for the Scottish settlers rapidly settling the western half of the island. William's marriage into the Halifax Tobins, one of the most prominent Catholic families in the province, made him additionally acceptable as a "brither Scot." Presumably, this political marriage of convenience had the blessing of Bishop William Fraser, under whom MacDonell had studied, for he certainly made no move to dissolve it.[42]

Smith's spending in this election became legendary. There were open houses in every part of Sydney Township and an organized paid band of thirty to forty men, dressed with green scarves and white aprons, to accompany him everywhere he went. As his clerk, he chose the seventeen-year-old law student James McKeagney, and for his inspector the native-born Cape Breton repealer, Edward Brown. Young managed to entice none other than Richard Gibbons to abandon the cause of repeal temporarily and act as his clerk. There must have been a falling-out between Gibbons and Edmund Dodd — they had been related since 1824 as the result of old Justice Archibald Dodd's marriage to Gibbons' mother — for Dodd acted as Smith's "commander-in-chief." Sheriff John Fuller opened the poll on 12 November and the polling continued for six days. At Dodd's instigation the cry was "Down with Nova Scotians." The final total for the Sydney poll of 394 for Smith to Young's minuscule 7 votes told all about the preferences of Sydney freeholders. Both sides knew that matters would be different at Arichat and prepared for battle. Smith brought with him his gang of miners and had the backing of both Kavanagh and Uniacke (who came up from Halifax) as part of the effort to ensure Young's defeat. With the former candidate, Thomas Edward Chandler, throwing his influence to Young and with Laurence O'Connor Doyle campaigning for him to gain the Catholic vote, Young more than doubled the vote over Smith. Young would have likely done even better if it had not been for the intervention of the Reverend brothers, Henry and Patrick McKeagney, on behalf of Smith.

Of Irish birth and ordained in Quebec and Antigonish respectively, the two priests were the elder brothers of James McKeagney, Smith's clerk. Both had avidly embraced the repeal cause.[43] Although Henry's parish was Sydney, he had come to Arichat to vote and was the first at the hustings to give his choice for Smith, in what he intended would be a signal for all good Catholics to follow. The first to climb the hustings at the Port Hood poll and vote for Young was the Reverend Alexander MacDonell; 277 of his Highlanders followed their priest in due order. With the totals now standing 511 for

Young and 3 less for Smith, clearly the Cheticamp poll would decide the issue. It is unknown whether Alexander MacDonell went to Cheticamp, but a number of his flock accompanied Young, collecting numerous fellow Highlanders at the Margarees. It is, however, likely that at this point Smith sent word to Sydney to bring more of his miners as reinforcements for what was shaping up as a battle royal. Young took the first day's polling 23 to Smith's 22 votes, increasing his lead to 4. For what was to happen next day, the best explanation seems to be that Young became convinced that Smith had in reserve a greater number of voters than himself. Young determined on desperate measures. Well before the poll was to open next morning, in a concerted and planned assault and urged on by "inflammatory speeches" by Young, some 150 of his Highlanders armed with cudgels seized the hustings. When Smith's men found themselves excluded from the hustings, Father Henry McKeagney led them in an assault but by mid-morning they had to admit defeat. Forty-nine of Young's supporters now voted. Any of Smith's who dared to come forward were forcibly kept at bay until the sheriff, in connivance with Young, closed the poll at noon, declaring Young the victor.

In the folklore of Cheticamp and the Margarees there is the tradition that, when confronted by Young's Highlanders, the Acadians of Cheticamp went home for their muskets and were joined by the Irish in the area to resist the "Scottish invasion"; also, that at this junction Smith's reinforcements from Sydney arrived. Whatever strands of truth may lie in this tradition, it seems fairly clear that a violent clash between the two forces was narrowly averted when the victorious party, carrying the triumphant Young on their shoulders, left the hustings to go to Young's open house. Their route followed a corduroy road through a bog. Here Smith's men gathered for an ambush, but were seen by some of Young's own men, including his brother George, who called to William: "Let us head our men: we should be the first to fall today."[44] Supposedly, Henry McKeagney realized that Young's men meant to force their way through. He rushed among the ranks of Smith's forces pleading with them not to open fire, as they were armed. His timely intervention, joined by that of the Acadian priest, Julien Courteau, resulted in Smith's men allowing the opposing party to pass through. The reputed numbers engaged, 2,000 for Young and 1,500 for Smith, were likely much exaggerated, but there were certainly hundreds involved. Only 3 freeholders from Cheticamp voted and they supported Smith. Another 80, mostly Acadians, were never polled, but in all likelihood they would have

Lochaber Lake, County Sydney, Nova-Scotia
Drawn by William Moorsom, engraved by J. Clark for *Letters from Nova Scotia*,
published by Colburn & Bentley, London 1830.

voted for Smith. If Young's Highlanders had not seized the hustings
when they did, Smith would have won the election. This belief, and
the opinion that Young was more responsible for the violence than
Smith, caused a shocked Assembly to overturn the result and give
the election to Smith. As for Henry McKeagney's involvement, it
was part of a pattern of both clerical and political behaviour of such
a scandalous nature that it led to Bishop William Fraser permanently
suspending him from his parish duties in 1840. Unbowed as ever,
McKeagney held onto the possession of his church, claiming he had
simply resigned his spiritual duties, while denying he had ever been
suspended. His successor had to go to Chancery Court eventually to
gain possession of the church and and its lands from McKeagney.[45]
The people of Sydney, nonetheless, would long revere Henry
McKeagney as the builder of St. Patrick's Church (today a provincially registered heritage property), as a fierce opposer of annexation
to Nova Scotia, and as a superb horseman.

   For Cape Breton freeholders the overturning of Young's election
turned out to be a Pyrrhic victory, because Smith returned to England
after one session in the House. Not wishing for a repetition of the
Cheticamp violence, the Assembly never called for a by-election,
leaving Kavanagh, Uniacke and Doyle to represent Cape Breton's
interests until a general election was called in December 1836. Although the 1836 election was hotly contested on the mainland, there

was no reflection of this on the island. Young went in unopposed, as did Uniacke as the single member for Cape Breton County, Doyle for Arichat and Kavanagh for the new seat of Richmond County. Sydney Township alone saw the feeblest of election contests, with Dodd so overwhelming Gibbons that the latter resigned after a day's polling, when the best he could do was two votes. Whatever the original cause of the falling-out between them, it had degenerated into a permanent feud. At a victory dinner for Uniacke and Dodd, both spoke out, however, against continued annexation of the island to Nova Scotia. Dodd's speech especially brought on great cheering when he called for Cape Breton to have the privilege of legislating for itself, as did all other colonies in the British Empire.

Out of its five representatives, Cape Breton Island was now to have in the House three non-residents, four lawyers, and in Dodd one out-and-out repealer. Of these Uniacke, Kavanagh and Dodd were Tories, and Young and Doyle, Reformers. Cape Breton's political configuration changed, and dramatically and permanently so, when Uniacke came to the conclusion that the British government had accepted the necessity for a new colonial constitution in which the executive should be responsible to the majority in the Assembly. Although his apparent sudden embracing of constitutional reform took his contemporaries by surprise, the beginning of his conversion went back at least to his autumn 1838 meeting with Lord Durham and his reading of the Durham *Report*. Uniacke's public change of mind was precipitated by the 1839 despatch of the colonial secretary, Lord John Russell, to Governor Sir Colin Campbell, instructing him to remove his Executive Councillors when public policy dictated. Uniacke's conversion became official when on 12 February 1840 he voted with the majority for Howe's motion of non-confidence in the Executive Council. He then resigned from the Council, to which he had been appointed with Dodd two years earlier. Dodd did not appear in the House for the vote and did not resign his Council seat.

Uniacke's apostasy brought little retribution from his own class, to which he belonged by reason of family, education and marriage. He made it difficult for the Tories to attack his decision, by giving as his reason that he believed the British government had granted a new constitution; consequently, he could not but hold to his first political principle that he would never withdraw his "humble support from the Parent State."[46] When Uniacke renounced the Tory cause and—out of loyalty to the mother country—went over to the Reformers, he showed a touch of real political shrewdness. Reformers elsewhere were being taunted with disloyalty in the aftermath of the 1837 Rebellion in Upper and Lower Canada. His Cape Breton constituents, however, cared little for Uniacke's constitutional views; for them the issues of his non-residency and his uncertain stand on repeal were for the first time being debated in the public press. A correspondent, SMOOTHSTONE, was scathing in denouncing Uniacke's non-residency: "If our county member will bring his money, his horses and retinue into our Country, and identify his interests with ours ... Then will the splendid talents he possesses ... entitle him to our confidence and support." Another letter writer and avowed Tory, TOWN PUMP, argued instead that Uniacke had great influence in the Assembly—"more power in Halifax than all the Cape Bretonians put together"—and this was sufficient reason in itself to re-elect him.[47]

Well before the poll opened for the 1840 election, a call went out to freeholders to hold a public nomination meeting. Gibbons got a motion passed unanimously, that in the opinion of the meeting Cape Breton had men residing within itself capable of representing her interests. But Dodd pushed through Uniacke's nomination. Both men believed that Uniacke's unopposed re-election was now certain. They, however, underestimated the depth of feeling for repeal which, if anything, had grown stronger and was more passionately felt. Edward Brown, a long-standing native of the town and repealer, had seconded Gibbon's motion at the nomination meeting. The day before a public meeting called to debate the political union with Nova Scotia, Brown decided to become a candidate. Uniacke was now going to have to deal directly with the mounting agitation against annexation, or face an expensive and no doubt violent contest, if not actual defeat. His address, according to the *Cape-Breton Advocate,* "For manly and stirring eloquence, there were passages worthy of the best days of British Oratory." He began by stating that he supported dissolution of the union with the mainland, though he was frank in saying that he believed it would not be productive of the benefits anticipated.

Uniacke held the legal opinion that the 1820 annexation by order-in-council had been simply constitutionally wrong; consequently, the people of Cape Breton should have the right to have their case heard in the highest tribunals of the realm. In this, he was on solid legal ground and the political benefits were obvious. But Uniacke went further and used the opportunity to expound presciently on the need for a federal union of the British North American colonies in which Cape Breton would be a member separated from Nova Scotia. It was through a federal union, embracing all the colonies, that British North Americans would have self-government, growth and prosperity such as they saw to the south of them in the United States. They would be bound to the mother country by ties of love and affection. Before the dissolution of the meeting Uniacke pledged £250 in aid of sending delegates to England to further the cause of repeal; it was by far the largest amount pledged. The *Cape-Breton Advocate* reprinted his speech and distributed it throughout the island.[48]

Although a substantial sum, £250 was considerably less than a contested election would have cost Uniacke. It was with this foremost in mind that, on the day before the poll was to open, Dodd called on Edward Brown. If assured that Uniacke would advance the cause of repeal, Brown agreed to resign from the contest. The next day at the hustings, as agreed, Brown withdrew in order to avoid the evils of a contest. Gibbons voiced the only opposition to the arrangement. In an emotional speech, rambling to the point of incomprehensibility, he implored freeholders to continue the contest and go forward with the election. How he expected this to happen with no candidate in opposition to Uniacke was unrecorded. Nor was Gibbons prepared to challenge Dodd again, and so he also was unopposed for the township.

If Dodd, the conservative, could be instrumental in having the liberal, Uniacke, re-elected, party loyalty was clearly not an issue in Sydney Township. So too in Richmond County, party loyalty mattered little. For the first time a public nomination meeting was held that unanimously called for a local candidate to be chosen. The choice for the county member fell on William Clarke Delaney. A lawyer from Great Village in Colchester County, Delaney had established a practice in Arichat in 1822. The meeting postponed a decision on the township representative to allow for negotiations with the sitting member, Laurence O'Connor Doyle. After his arrival at Arichat, Doyle found such a strong feeling for a local candidate that he gracefully declined to offer again. In his stead, a merchant, Henry Martell, came forward and was unopposed. Martell was Catholic and Delaney an Anglican; the inference is that there was an understanding reached whereby Richmond would be represented by both a Protestant and a Catholic.

But the freeholders of the county were not to be allowed to so arrange their own affairs. James McKeagney served notice that he would be a candidate for the county seat. As we have already noted, as a young Sydney lawyer McKeagney had received his electoral baptism as clerk to Richard Smith in the 1832 by-election, in which his two clerical brothers, Henry and Patrick, had taken such prominent roles. Patrick was still pastor for the mission in the area of St. Peter's. He now called on his flock to support the candidacy of his younger brother, who began an active canvass among Richmond Catholics. McKeagney, of course, was an outsider at a time when the feeling was running strongly for local candidates, but he vowed to become a permanent resident of Arichat. A wild pugnaciousness marked the character of all the McKeagney brothers and the forthcoming election held in late November and early December of 1840 brought it once more to the fore.

The McKeagney brothers had not foreseen that the Arichat Catholics were not about to break the understanding reached with their Protestant neighbours. Although McKeagney campaigned as a Reformer, both Martell and Doyle, though Reformers themselves, supported Delaney, a Tory. Worse still for McKeagney's chances, the curé of Arichat, Jean-Baptiste Maranda, seems also to have made clear his preference for Delaney. The consequences for McKeagney were fully evident by the end of the Arichat polling, when Delaney went ahead by 111 votes. When the poll opened at St. Peter's, McKeagney, now desperate for votes, engaged in arguably the most disgraceful recruitment of voters so far, bringing to the hustings paupers, vagrants, minors, non-residents, strangers from the United States, and Indians last seen pitching their tents on the beaches of Dartmouth and paddling in Halifax regattas. All these people were told by McKeagney that they could take the freeholder's oath. Men armed with bludgeons and flails intimidated Delaney's voters and eventually seized the hustings. Martell was physically and verbally assaulted as one who had "sold his soul" and "betrayed his religion" by not voting for McKeagney.[49] When the poll finally closed, McKeagney was six votes ahead and declared elected.

The Assembly showed no hesitation in voiding the election and ordering a by-election which was held in July 1841. Once again, Delaney took the Arichat poll, with only 2 of the 158 Protestants polled voting for McKeagney, while 130 Catholics were for Delaney. When the St. Peter's poll opened, Delaney had a lead of over 100 votes. There was no repetition of the previous recruitment of voters and Delaney won with a fair majority. McKeagney blamed the Reverend Jean-Baptiste Maranda for being the "CHIEF ENGINE" of his defeat by conducting an active canvass and by using the most hostile invective from the pulpit against him. McKeagney wrote the *Nova-*

scotian that the whole affair had caused him a great depression.[50] He failed to tell his readers that a few weeks before the by-election Bishop William Fraser had finally acted to move his brother Patrick, by having him exchange parishes with Courteau at Cheticamp. Maranda was delighted to have Courteau as a neighbour, though he thought him "little suited to make up for the foolish acts of Paddy McKeagney."[51]

The increasing population in Inverness resulted in an additional seat for the county in time for the 1840 election. The Halifax Tories thought that they saw an opportunity to get elected one of their own party, and perhaps even unseat William Young. For this little bit of naïveté, they settled on the Halifax barrister Alexander Primrose, whose chief political attributes were being of Scottish birth and being the son of a Presbyterian minister. During the public nomination meeting at the Port Hood courthouse, Young produced the deed for Primrose's freehold qualification, pointing out that it had been registered a month and two days too late for it to be valid for his candidacy. Primrose should have resigned then and there and gone back to Halifax, but he persisted in the apparent belief that he could win with a 150-vote majority because the Irish and Acadians would vote overwhelmingly for him. The Reverend Alexander MacDonell then nominated Young. In his acceptance speech (an excerpt from which is quoted at the beginning of this section), Young extolled the benefits of Inverness as part of Nova Scotia. After also nominating another lawyer, James Turnbull of Arichat, the meeting adjourned for a public dinner given for Young with MacDonell in the chair. When the poll opened on 25 November, Young immediately forced to a decision the issue of Primrose's qualification; when faced with perjuring himself, Primrose refused to take the candidate's oath. After taking seven votes and letting the poll remain open the required hour, the sheriff declared Young and Turnbull duly elected.

Nowhere else in the province did the 1843 election result in fewer contests than in Cape Breton. Dodd, Uniacke and Young all were returned unopposed. With an open display of partiality by his friend and former business partner, Sheriff John Fuller, Martell easily disposed of Charles Harrington to retain Arichat. With Delaney too crippled from gout to re-offer, Turnbull determined to run for the single Richmond seat, giving up his Inverness seat to James McKeagney, who went in unopposed. Turnbull likely expected to be unopposed also, but Charles Harrington, like Turnbull a lawyer and an Anglican, became a candidate; for the second time in the same general election Harrington was defeated by a wide margin. Cape Breton freeholders had sent to the Assembly all lawyers, except for Martell; one Tory in Dodd, with the remainder all Reformers; three Anglicans, two Catholics and one Presbyterian. Of the six elected, half of them were non-residents—Uniacke, McKeagney and Young, all lawyers.

In the conservative administration of Attorney General J. W. Johnston, Dodd succeeded to the Solicitor Generalship. The others were in opposition, which McKeagney found extremely frustrating. He and Young could not get an appointment for a single magistrate or even a school trustee of their choice. It was during the 1845 session that from the opposition benches Uniacke made one of his most powerful speeches, denouncing Governor Lord Falkland for virtually proscribing Joseph Howe from again entering the Executive Council because of the personal vendetta between the two men. This was, claimed Uniacke, the first instance of proscription in Nova Scotia; he would "never yield to the exercise of power, unsanctioned by law no man, however high his rank, or pure his nature, can be trusted no freedom or rational liberty can be secured—to be governed by the will, and not the law, is tyranny." But it was the deeply cutting lashing he gave Johnston, the real author of the offending dispatch, that must have rankled the most among his own class: the last line sums up the bitter thrust when he accused the learned Attorney General of not caring "a curse for his victims as long as he retains power."[52]

In the 1847 election, Uniacke for the fourth time was unopposed. It was not, however, until nomination day that the conservative candidate, Nicholas Martin, withdrew. His withdrawal came after Uniacke promised to work for increased representation for Cape Breton. That Martin, a long-standing repealer, raised the question of increased representation, and not that of separation from Nova Scotia, lay in the Privy Council decision of the year before. It had ruled against the repealers and their cause. On nomination day, the real battle of words was not between the candidates, but between Dodd and the editor of the highly partisan liberal *Cape Breton Spectator,* Richard Huntington. The Tories were livid at the treatment Dodd had been receiving from the Spectator and had been boasting that Huntington would never dare to show himself on nomination day. They were mistaken. After all the other speakers had finished, Huntington came forward to reply to Dodd's allegations against his paper and to uphold the principles of the liberal party. He was shouted down by the sprigs of Sydney "nobility," assisted by their fathers, stable boys and shoe-blacks. In the end it mattered little, for on the 5th of August Dodd triumphed by a large majority over a weak liberal challenge from W. H. Munro; he too had been an avid repealer.

It was also an easy victory for the Tories in the Richmond County constituency. The primary reason lay in the by-election held a year earlier on the death of Turnbull. With Martell, the sitting member for Arichat, a Catholic, Turnbull by right should have been succeeded by another Protestant. Instead Arthur Brymer, a merchant from St. Peter's and a Catholic, chose to run as a liberal. Charles Harrington came forward as the Protestant candidate and also as a liberal. Brymer won by 32 votes, but many Arichat Catholics and Protestants stayed away from the hustings in disapproval. A few days before the polls opened for the 1847 election, Brymer died and Harrington went in unopposed. According to past practices, Martell should have gone in also without a contest, but he found himself opposed by Isaac LeVesconte, a member of one of the Protestant French, Jersey Islander merchant families who held such a stranglehold on the fishing industry off Cape Breton and in the Gulf of St. Lawrence. LeVesconte could bring to the polls a substantial ledger influence, which explains the closeness of the result; Martell won by a bare two votes. His victory, however, meant a return to the previous accommodation of dividing representation between a Catholic and a Protestant.

Religion was also a factor in the Inverness contest. The Tory cry of a Catholic Ascendancy in Nova Scotia found some resonance among the Presbyterians of Inverness. They were prepared to support John Tremain, a Port Hood lawyer and a Protestant, whose nomination was orchestrated from Halifax in another vain attempt to oust Young. Young's popularity was such that he led the poll with 1,043 votes out of the 1,160 voters polled. The real battle was for the second seat between McKeagney, as the sitting member, and Peter Smyth. Of Dublin birth and a Catholic, Smyth had established himself as a successful merchant at Port Hood. As a non-resident and unable to use religion against Smyth, McKeagney did surprisingly well to come within 109 votes of Smyth. In Smyth, Inverness had elected its first resident Catholic member. But not until 1868 did the county send to the Assembly a member born or even raised in Inverness. The 1851 census recorded 2,413 heads of households. Of these less than half voted in 1847, evidence that hundreds of families had no registered freehold tenure to the lands they were occupying.

In the 1847 election the freeholders of Cape Breton Island had sent to the Assembly, that would usher in responsible government, four liberals to two conservatives, four Protestants to two Catholics and four lawyers to two merchants. Of the six elected, two, Uniacke and Young, were non-residents.

The later the Scottish immigration to Pictou, Antigonish and Cape Breton Island, the longer it took to have resident members. In the case of Pictou, the struggle for residency was won when Edward Mortimer entered the Assembly in 1799. After that date the only non-resident was George Renny Young, whose candidacy as a Reformer and a Kirkman was the key to dividing the Kirk/Tory vote. Antigonish got its first resident member in 1806, but then from 1818 to 1836 turned to Thomas Dickson and John Young to represent its interests. On Cape Breton, however, the pattern of electing non-residents continued well into the third quarter of the nineteenth century.

The desire of non-resident lawyers to find Assembly seats delayed the process of naturalizing representation. This was especially true for Cape Breton, which, in electing nine lawyers between 1820 and 1847, sent more of this profession to the Assembly than even Halifax County from 1758 to 1847. Moreover, six of these nine were non-resident in their constituencies; four—the two Uniacke brothers, William Young and Laurence O'Connor Doyle—were from Halifax. A major reason for their success in getting elected was the ability of these lawyers to form local alliances of mutual interests. The lawyers gained the seats in the Assembly they so avidly sought; in turn, Cape Breton, and also Antigonish, got far stronger representation of their interests than would likely have been the case if only local candidates had been elected. The notable examples of these mutually satisfactory alliances were: Richard John Uniacke and the seating of Lawrence Kavanagh; James Boyle Uniacke and his leadership in finally having the 1820 annexation order ruled on by the Privy Council; and William Young's relationship with the Reverend Alexander MacDonell and the desire, above all else, by the settlers of Inverness County for roads and schools.

Chapter 10

Nova Scotian Politicians and the Achievement of Reform

In every class there was too great an inclination to look to the Legislature for assistance, instead of projects being carried forward into effect on their merit ... That [the] House represented the whole Province, and would regulate general interests better than Local Societies. These might be expected to combine their influence, and bring it to bear against the power of the House in the arrangement for duties and other matters. The scheme would tend to increase the system of exclusiveness which already prevailed in the Province to an extent scarcely known in any other part of the British Dominions.
Herbert Huntington, *Novascotian*, 25 March 1841

It is indeed generally admitted that in the present condition of the country one college might suffice ... But this appears to be out of the question. We Baptists are so stubborn, we can never consent to become Episcopalians [Anglicans] or Presbyterians as the sine qua non of obtaining the advantages of a College; we cannot perceive that our brethren of other Denominations are more pliable in this respect than ourselves ....
Silas Tertius Rand, *Christian Messenger*, 11 December 1840[1]

When all the polls around the province closed at five o'clock on the evening of 5 August 1847, the Reformers had triumphed over the Tories by 29 to 22 seats. Although the Tories delayed resigning until defeated in a vote of confidence in January 1848, and the Reformers did not finally assume office until 2 February, Nova Scotians had elected their first responsible government. No longer could a colonial governor select his own advisers. He had now to appoint to the Executive Council only those recommended to him by the leader of the victorious party. It was the end for the old Council of Twelve, centre of power for successive oligarchies, with its control over patronage. Moreover, the members of the new Executive Council became departmental heads. The old Council became a ministry responsible for its conduct to the elected representatives of the people.

The 1847 election was unlike any other Nova Scotia had experienced. Instead of lasting for weeks, simultaneous polling had made it possible to hold it everywhere in the province on the same day. Although there were ten petitions disputing election results, only that for Kings County made any mention of voter intimidation; the other nine charged returning officers either with partiality or with not following the new act correctly. Although an insufficient number of vote totals have survived to be certain, it seems that a significantly higher proportion of freeholders voted than ever before. Aside from the convenience of having so many polling stations, their very number made it impossible for candidates and their agents to challenge the eligibility of anywhere near the number of voters as in the past. Many must have voted who in previous elections would have been objected to and turned away. By having polling take place on a single day and at dozens of polling stations, the Simultaneous Polling Act had at long last swept away open houses and removed the chief cause of the drunkenness that accompanied so many past elections.

The drunkenness greatly contributed to the general rowdiness found at many elections and to the violent intimidation of voters at some of the most fiercely contested. Where battles royal took place for control of passageways, what usually happened was that one party, generally by some strategem, early gained possession; the best the opposing party could then do was to try and force the more hardy of its voters through to the candidates' platform, where the sheriff could take their votes. In the process there was much shouting, shoving and punching. But in these running battles sheer physical exhaustion often soon overtook one or both parties. This made it possible to restore order and to return to regular voting. When these battles occurred, the passageways were certainly not pleasant places, but there is no record of any man being killed in them. The two recorded deaths—at Pictou and Arichat during the 1830 election— happened away from the hustings; in the case of the death at Pictou, by an assault on an opposing candidate's open house. There were elections in which there was planned, wholesale, violent intimidation of voters. Among the worst cases were the 1832 Cape Breton by-election, in which William Young defeated Richard Smith by seizing the hustings at Cheticamp, and the St. Peter's poll during the 1840 Richmond County election, involving supporters of James McKeagney. In general, however, most elections, especially in the older smaller townships, passed off with no more disturbance than that caused by drunken rowdyism associated with open houses.

The 1847 election had all the hallmarks we have come to expect of a struggle for office between two political parties. Although in the 1843 election Joseph Howe and Attorney General J.W. Johnston had acted as though they were already leaders of political parties, by 1847 there was no question. For both parties large public nomination meetings had replaced the traditional speeches by candidates from the hustings. Public meetings in packed halls, sometimes lasting a day or more, had also become the major forum for electioneering. In the past, there had been much opposition to the personal canvassing of freeholders in their homes by candidates and their agents. Opponents accused such canvassers of making promises, using the ledger and courting to buy votes in the secrecy of the elector's abode. Instead of canvassing for weeks before an election, it was held that candidates should simply make public pledges of conduct in their election cards and on the day of the election speak to freeholders from the hustings. With elections now fought between two parties, all such gentlemanly notions disappeared. They were replaced by unabashed canvassing for weeks before an election and open bribery of electors with rum, tobacco and other desirables. Newspapers had become important forums for political debate, though by the 1840s all were highly partisan in their affiliation. Unquestionably, the better newspapers, and the most widely-read, were for the Reformers. This gave them a decided advantage which their Tory opponents could never overcome, even when driven to establish, for the 1847 election, their own newspaper in the *Standard and Conservative Advocate*.

Parties also meant political organization on an entirely different and greater scale. As early as 1806, Halifax freeholders had requested that before an election the sheriff hold a public meeting to nominate candidates. Their intention, of course, was to select candidates who would be unopposed and thus avoid the evils of a contest. By the mid-1830s, these had become large public meetings of freeholders, providing a platform to vent anger at the oligarchic control exercised through the Council of Twelve. Once party lines were more clearly drawn, the Tories and Reformers in Halifax held separate nomination meetings. Out of these meetings arose committees of freeholders who took over from candidates of their parties the tasks of raising money, arranging for open houses and bringing electors to the hustings; in short, they assumed the responsibility for the organization and direction of campaigns. The wide margin of the Reformer victory over the Tories in the four Halifax seats in 1847 can in good measure be attributed to the more broadly-based Reformer election committee and its far superior organization in the country districts.

For the 1847 election, Halifax Tories alone reputedly spent between £10,000 and £15,000. There was also heavy Tory spending in Annapolis County, and both parties continued a pattern of fighting costly elections in Pictou. The Reformers undoubtedly spent less than the Tories, though they seemed to have had ample funds to uphold their cause. However, in some counties spending may have been less than in previous elections because of the demise of open houses. A highly speculative estimate is that the 1847 election cost the two parties together somewhere between £20,000 and £30,000. If the spending was within this range, it was not a dramatic increase; the costs of fighting elections had been steadily rising since the 1820s. The first election in which expenditures were in the hundreds of pounds was the 1823 Halifax Township by-election. In his victory over John Young, Charles Rufus Fairbanks had behind him most of the ledger influence and wealth of the Halifax gentry class. Stephen DeBlois had the same backing when he defeated Beamish Murdoch in the 1830 Brandy Election. Murdoch claimed the election cost him personally £1,500; DeBlois and his friends likely spent much more.

But it was in the same election at Pictou that candidate expenses exceeded anything known before. The open houses of the eight candidates contesting for the four Halifax County seats were kept open for six days and nights, providing rum, food and lodgings for hundreds of supporters. Although William Young's claim that the 1832 by-election for a Cape Breton County seat cost Richard Smith and the General Mining Association £7,000 is far too high to be believed, nonetheless, it was a dramatic example of how costly fighting elections had become. The expense, however, for most elections in the 1830s was still within the low hundreds of pounds; for many of the old township seats it remained far less. Still, after the 1836 election, the rise in the proportion of merchants elected and the decline in the number of farmers reflected the increasing costs for fighting elections. Not only proportionally were farmer-assemblymen becoming fewer, but by the 1847 election, of the eleven farmers elected, just four were successful in county elections. The remaining seven were almost all from the oldest townships having the smallest number of freeholders.

The evidence is clear that the merchant class everywhere in the province paid the cost of elections. In Halifax there was in place an organized system of collecting for elections. For the Tories, much of the money raised came probably, directly or indirectly, through the Halifax Banking Company. The extent of financial involvement in elections of two of its most prominent bankers, Samuel Cunard and Enos Collins, is unknown, but they may well have been the largest contributors to the Tory cause. Both were members of the Council of Twelve and both were exceptionally wealthy men (by 1830 Cunard was believed to be worth £200,000 and Collins was well on his way to becoming one of the richest men in North America). Cunard was the more politically active of the two. Before his appointment to the Council in 1830, Cunard had sought in 1826 to enter the Assembly as a member for Halifax County, but had withdrawn on the morning of the poll to let the sitting members go in without a contest. Cunard and Mather Byles Almon certainly had a major hand in the failed attempt to force the Halifax merchant, John Steele, on the unwilling freeholders of Guysborough and Antigonish in 1820 and 1824. They may as well have been behind the even more inept attempt to unseat William Young in Inverness.

Mather Byles Almon (made president of the Bank of Nova Scotia in 1837) seems to have been the chief agent for raising funds for the Tories. His appointment by his brother-in-law, Attorney General J.W. Johnston, to the Executive and Legislative Councils in 1843 may be the first recorded instance in British North America of a party fund-raiser receiving his political reward. Unlike the contemporary Canadian Senate, however, there were no hefty salaries and pensions attached. In the case of the Reformers, William Stairs was the most likely person to have performed the same task as Almon. It was Stairs who managed the "Howe Fund," created for Howe to draw upon as he needed cash. This fund was certainly in existence by 1846 and probably earlier.

Elsewhere in the province, election fund-raising was best organized in Pictou, and at an early date. Both parties saw Pictou elections as extensions of Halifax battles and money flowed accordingly. Within Pictou, the Reformers probably had more of the county's wealth on their side, chiefly because of George Smith. Smith likely carried much of the expense for his own and others' elections in 1830, 1836, and particularly the costly 1843 election against Martin Wilkins. It is reasonable to suppose that the expense of these elections contributed to Smith's financial difficulties, which began in 1838 with his borrowing of £5,800 from Samuel Cunard, and his descent into total bankruptcy; by the time of his death in 1850 he was penniless. In Annapolis County, Judge Thomas Ritchie acted as the Tory fund-raiser and chief organizer. Presumably, the Halifax money backing Attorney General J.W. Johnston's 1843 and 1847 campaigns flowed through him. It is unknown if Amos "King" Seaman contributed to the Reformer cause in Cumberland, but it would have been in character. Although an arch Tory in his political beliefs, James Shannon Morse had a hand in the challenge mounted in 1836 by Gaius Lewis and Andrew McKim to unseat Alexander Stewart. The campaign against Stewart had all the marks of being well-organized and -funded. Morse played a major role and provided much of the money to petition the Assembly on behalf of McKim in the effort to have Stewart's election voided. Morse was a lawyer. Increasingly lawyers, if not candidates themselves, acted as agents for candidates. Robert Barry Dickey and Jonathan McCully in Cumberland and Silas Leander Morse in Annapolis are three examples of this. As a seventeen-year-old articling student, James McKeagney received his electoral baptism as clerk to Richard Smith in the violent 1832 Cape Breton by-election. It is impossible to be more precise about election funding in this period. What can be said, with some certainty, is that the amounts involved could be substantial and their collection and expenditure were made in a systematic and accountable manner.

Nova Scotians did not begin to think of their politics in terms of party until the widespread feeling arose in the 1830s that the province was being corruptly and grossly misgoverned by a clique of powerful office-holders, wealthy merchants and ambitious lawyers. The depression and currency debacle of the mid-1830s played a formative role in channeling the anger among Halifax freeholders into a party bent on reform. In Annapolis County, though, the Tory/Baptist alliance, the presence of J.W. Johnston and the heavy expenditure of money raised from Halifax Tories provided the sinews of a well-organized and -funded Tory party. The Tory and Reformer party organizations which arose in Pictou mirrored the governing structures for both the Kirk and the Secessionist Churches. Within this structure, congregations selected their own ministers and elected elders who together in sessions were the governing authorities for congregations. But Presbyterian polity was also hierarchic, with congregations associating within presbyteries made up of ordained ministers and an equal number of elders. Just how closely church and party organization could be allied can be glimpsed from the process by which the Tories decided before the 1843 election to refuse the offer of Reformers to have two Tories and one Reformer elected unopposed. The decision was made by a meeting at New Glasgow of delegates elected by freeholders at separate meetings called around the county. It seems that each Kirk congregation could elect and send a set number, as they did for presbyteries.[2] Only in Pictou County did political parties reach a level of organization that involved the formal meeting of elected delegates to decide party policy.

Elsewhere, parties often replaced rival family compacts. In Guysborough, for example, the Marshalls became Tories and the Cutlers (with W.J. DesBarres' adherence to the reform cause) Reformers. The Chipmans in Kings County became Reformers and the DeWolfs, Tories. For Shelburne, the surviving poll books allowed us to chart the growth of parties out of factions. Their origin lay in the determination of leading Anglicans and Kirkmen to keep, as their preserve, Shelburne's representation in the Assembly. The rancorous public feuding between Alexander Stewart and his brother-in-law, James Shannon Morse, became inseparably entwined with the division of Cumberland County along party lines. In Cape Breton, the conservative and liberal parties mirrored the divisions between Repealers and Annexationists. Those for repeal of the 1820 union with Nova Scotia became Tories; as support for repeal was concentrated in the Sydney area, so too was it true for the Tories. Richmond and Inverness Counties were solidly for continued union with the mainland; in 1847 they elected three liberals to a sole conservative. What is fascinating was how swiftly and how completely party loyalty came to absorb all these older local rivalries, feuds and divisions.

Moreover, in their voting along party lines, Nova Scotians seemingly ignored almost entirely such traditional divisive issues as the animosity of the western counties, especially Annapolis, towards the eastern region. Annapolis, Kings and Queens voted Tory, as did Colchester and Cumberland. But the Reformers took by far the majority of seats in Shelburne, Yarmouth, Hants and Lunenburg, so the western counties divided fairly evenly. The Reformers took ten of the thirteen seats from Pictou through to Sydney. Their success, however, was not based on exploiting any regional loyalty, but on Tory weakness. Although the Marshall family of Guysborough was Tory and Edmund Dodd survived on the old Repeal vote in the Sydney area, elsewhere the Tory attempts at interjecting candidates from Halifax were miserable failures. The chief cause lay in the inability of these outside candidates to form mutually advantageous local alliances. The success of John Young in cementing such alliances with Thomas Cutler and Bishop William Fraser and that of his son, William, with the Reverend Alexander MacDonell, were in striking contrast to Tory failures.

In also capturing all four Halifax town and county seats in 1847, the Reformers destroyed even the pretence that mercantile and Tory Halifax could ever create a majority in the Assembly favourable to its commercial ambitions. Country members had always expressed much ill feeling towards Halifax, but the real clash of interests was between the agricultural districts and those whose economic life-blood lay in the fishery and foreign trading. This clear division of economic interests can best be seen in the voting in the Assembly on the issue of support for native farmers. Cumberland, Pictou, Annapolis, Kings, Hants and Antigonish were the counties whose members most consistently, over five decades from the 1780s to the 1840s, voted in favour of protection for agriculture. On no question did members from these counties fight more tenaciously than for high duties on the importation of American flour. Their strongest opposition came from members of Queens, Lunenburg, Shelburne, Yarmouth, Digby and Cape Breton Counties, where farming was at best a secondary occupation to earning a living from and on the sea. Those from Halifax town and county tended to adopt an ambivalent attitude on the question. Their desire to secure favourable votes from country members on other issues caused such Halifax merchants as Stephen DeBlois, William Lawson and Henry Cogswell to vote as many times for agricultural protection as they did against. Halifax's members, however, showed where their true interests lay when it came to measures to support the fishery and to oppose any increases in general duties. It was the standing complaint of Halifax that nine-tenths of the provincial revenue came from duties collected from its merchants and that nine-tenths of this was spent outside the capital. On these two matters, there was a natural alliance of mutual interest between mercantile Halifax and the merchant-assemblymen, particularly from the south shore counties.

Where mercantile Halifax and its natural allies parted was over free ports. Halifax sought a privileged position among Nova Scotian ports within the closed trading system of the British Empire.[3] It sought to be the North American entrepôt for supplying the West Indies with lumber, fish and agricultural products. To achieve its commercial destiny as an entrepôt, the merchants of Halifax had to be able to draw into the port, for re-export at the cheapest price, the products demanded in the West Indies, whether they originated in Nova Scotia and its neighbouring colonies, or from the United States.

This was equally true for those merchants in the outports, but they laboured under the added disadvantage of not having the privileges of free ports. Britain moved from 1822 onwards to dismantle the old closed trading system of her empire and to replace it with the freedom for the colonies to trade as their commercial interests dictated. In the end, as we have seen, the outports gained, over the opposition of Halifax, the status of free ports. For Nova Scotia and the other British North American colonies, that freedom could not be fully exploited until the 1854 agreement for reciprocity (a form of free trade) in natural products with the United States. Still, the freeing of trade by imperial acts removed from Nova Scotian politics the issues of agricultural protectionism and special privileges for the port of Halifax.

After the outports gained the status of free ports by the early 1840s, neither the conservatives nor the liberals could be said to have stood for any particular economic interests. In the four sessions of the last Assembly before the 1847 election, there were no more than half a dozen recorded votes on such traditionally contentious questions as support for fishery. Moreover, in none of these votes was there any indication of voting along party lines. On a bill to give encouragement to the seal fisheries, the members from the fishing districts, led by James Boyle Uniacke, united in support of the measure, but it went down to defeat by a majority composed of such notable Tories and Reformers as Joseph Howe, Herbert Huntington, J.W. Johnston and Robert McGowan Dickey. It is, therefore, no wonder that in the 1847 election there was no perceptible division between the parties on economic issues. The Tories, for example, captured twelve of the fourteen seats in the predominantly farming counties of Cumberland, Colchester, Annapolis and Kings, while taking all three Queens County seats. The Reformers took both seats in Antigonish County, in which most electors earned their living from the land, and also in neighbouring Guysborough, where most were fishermen. Within Halifax County, the Reformers were able to hold the vote of both the farmers of the Musquodoboit Valley and of the fishermen of St. Margaret's Bay, while defeating the Tory challenge for the votes of the shopkeepers and tradesmen of the capital for the two Halifax Township seats.

Overall, in make-up the Assembly elected in 1847 differed little from previous Assemblies. In 1847 merchants and lawyers combined were seventy per cent of those elected. Moreover, both parties proportionally had very similar numbers of merchants, lawyers and farmers. In addition, however, the Reformers had on their benches four who had other occupations, notably including Joseph Howe and Herbert Huntington. Over and above their larger numbers, the Reformers had the advantage in superior legal talent. Other than J.W. Johnston, none of the Tory lawyers elected had demonstrated the abilities of William Young, James Boyle Uniacke or W.F. DesBarres. But where the profile of the two parties diverged significantly was in their religious breakdown. Overall, Anglicans and Church of Scotland still accounted for over forty per cent of those elected, but among the Reformers, Presbyterians and Roman Catholics outnumbered Anglicans and Church of Scotland fourteen to nine, with Baptists, Methodists and a Lutheran accounting for the remaining six out of the twenty-nine elected. Even in Pictou, where the Tories should have expected to take at least two of the three seats, this time the Reformers had so split the Kirk vote that instead it was they who had taken two of the three seats. The Tories failed to get elected one Roman Catholic. The cry of a Catholic Ascendancy had solidified their support in Colchester, Cumberland, Annapolis, Queens and Kings Counties, where they had taken fourteen of the sixteen seats. But it had failed in Halifax; the Reformers had taken the two township seats as well as the two for the county. The Catholic vote ensured liberal victories for the two Antigonish seats and four of the six seats on Cape Breton Island.

It was not until the 1843 election, and again in 1847, that religion became a significant factor in Nova Scotian politics. Until then, it had operated solely as a local influence on elections. The causes in each case and the form that the influence took varied greatly. In Halifax Township, Lunenburg and Shelburne, it was a matter of Anglicans treating the representation as their preserve. Of the twenty-nine individuals elected for Halifax Township from 1758 through to 1847, twenty were Anglicans, and another three were of the Church of Scotland. When the Methodist, Hugh Bell, won in 1835, his unopposed victory was not only salient for the cause of reform, it also finally broke forever the Anglican grip on the township seats. The Anglican hold on Lunenburg's representation was never broken, with twenty of the twenty-four elected for the township and county being Anglicans. Even when the Reformers took all three seats in 1847, two of the victorious were Anglicans. In Shelburne, however, the overthrow of the Anglican and Church of Scotland dominance over the county's representation heralded its turning to reform. In contrast, the intervention in the 1836 Cumberland election by the

Covenanter, the Reverend Alexander Clarke, against the candidacy of the Scotch Baptist preacher, Andrew McKim, had no major political consequences within or without Cumberland County. It remains, nonetheless, an extraordinary episode; it was evidence, if any more was wanting, of the passions aroused when clergymen openly intervened in elections.

Nowhere in Nova Scotia did clergy intervene more blatantly or with more lamentable consequences than in Pictou County. The quarrelling between Kirkmen and Seceders would have confined itself to Pictou if it had not been for the issue of public funding for Pictou Academy. The controversy during the 1820s and 1830s over grants for Pictou Academy fused religion and politics with an unparalleled intensity and violence. If support for Pictou Academy had been solely a matter of equality for Dissenters, the opposition of a few, but powerful, High Church Tories on the Council, and of ministers of the Church of Scotland, in all likelihood could have been overcome. But the demand by the supporters of the Academy for college status and for a permanent grant (as had been done in 1789 for the Anglican Kings College at Windsor) raised the whole thorny question of public funding for colleges.

We have already noted how such members as John George Marshall of Guysborough resolutely opposed any funding for academies or colleges, when the need was so great for common schools in the country districts. Within the Assembly, it was this issue that caused the most variance of opinion. Although, as expected, the Presbyterian members were the academy's chief sponsors, they were unable to gain wholehearted support for their cause from other Dissenters. The Baptists were lukewarm at best. Among the Methodist members, more than half voted against funding, with the Sargents of Barrington and William Holland from Annapolis particularly opposed. In fact, it was the Anglicans in the House who ensured that resolutions for funding passed. Moreover, such leading Anglican members as James Shannon Morse, William Lawson, William Rudolf and Joseph Freeman could nearly always be found voting on the side of the academy.[4] The main opposition came from Church of Scotland members, led by Alexander Stewart, though among the academy's strongest supporters was his bitter rival and fellow religionist, Charles Rufus Fairbanks. Opponents in the Assembly, moreover, knew that a majority of the Council was determined to thwart any designs for a permanent grant and college status. Attempts over three decades failed to reconcile Kirkmen and Seceders. The academy finally ceased being a political issue when its founder, the Reverend Thomas McCulloch, overborne by the animosities aroused (and to which he made his contribution), accepted in 1838 the offer to become the first president of Dalhousie College.[5] The struggle over the status and funding of Pictou Academy was a forewarning of what a heady mixture could be religion, colleges and politics.

The question of funding Dalhousie College did not bring forth the same intensity of emotion as Pictou Academy because no religious denomination had a major stake in its existence. In large measure Dalhousie was the creation of its namesake. When Lord Dalhousie arrived as Governor in 1816, he was shocked and affronted to find King's College closed to Dissenters (not until 1829 did King's remove from its statutes the requirement of its graduates to subscribe to the Thirty-nine Articles of the Church of England). He determined to establish a college on the Scottish model open to all sects and to all classes of society. Funds (derived from customs duties collected during the War of 1812 at Castine, Maine) were fortuitously available to begin the erection in Halifax of a building on the Grand Parade (on the site where today stands City Hall), but insufficient to complete it. A further grant of £1,000 from a reluctant Assembly, followed by a loan of £5,000 from the Assembly, allowed for the building's completion by 1823. The college itself, however, never opened its doors to students in this period. The major reasons were a board of governors who were apathetic, if not downright hostile to the institution; lack of funding; and the failure of attempts to bring about a union of Dalhousie and King's.[6] Dalhousie should have had broad support. But again, as with Pictou Academy, there was much opposition from country members in the Assembly; they saw all the money for the college being spent in Halifax, while the needs of common schools were ignored in favour of colleges. The strongest opposition came from members from Lunenburg, Queens, Shelburne and Annapolis. Outside of Halifax, in fact, the only consistent supporters were the Yarmouth members, Samuel Poole and Herbert Huntington. Dalhousie suffered from being a college few Nova Scotians really wanted.

Those in the Assembly who did favour Dalhousie could not have been more divided in their reasons. Joseph Howe and Herbert Huntington were among the very few who sincerely believed in its founding ideal. But the most support for Dalhousie came from some Anglicans and adherents of the Church of Scotland. Such Anglicans as Richard John Uniacke Jr. sought a union of King's and Dalhousie as salvation for a faction-ridden and impoverished King's. Those of the Church of Scotland hoped to secure a dominant position in the college's administration, whatever the view of its founder, who was Church of Scotland himself. In the Assembly votes, by far the most support for completing the building and opening the college came from members belonging to the Church of Scotland; John Young, for instance, never failed to give his vote in favour of the college. Many Anglicans, however, either opposed the idea of uniting King's and Dalhousie, or feared (probably rightly) that King's could not survive a successful Dalhousie. Where in the case of Pictou Academy a majority of Anglicans were supportive, they were generally found in opposition to Dalhousie. Neither the Presbyterians nor the Methodists in the House ever showed much enthusiasm for Dalhousie.

During 1835-36 there was another effort to bring about a union of King's and Dalhousie to create one provincial university. It was as unsuccessful as the previous attempts. Moreover, Dalhousie fell under the control of the Church of Scotland. Although the Reverend Thomas McCulloch assumed the presidency in 1838, all other professors had to be of the Church of Scotland. Of all the other denominations, the Baptist members in the Assembly had given the most support to Dalhousie, for its ideal of a college open to all religions. When they found that none but those of Church of Scotland could be professors, the Baptists immediately set about establishing Acadia. Halifax Catholics followed with St. Mary's. In 1841, overwhelming majorities in the Assembly passed bills for the incorporation of both colleges. But these were the last occasions of such unanimity on the college question.

There had always been, understandably, much unhappiness with the permanent grant, dating from 1789, for the Anglican King's College. Now the Assembly was faced with requests for equal grants from three more sectarian colleges—Dalhousie, Acadia and St. Mary's. The opposition initially came from an uneasy alliance of advocates for a single non-denominational college and from those who were against funding any colleges. In the most confusing sequence of votes in this period, on 7 and 8 March 1842, a majority made up nearly equally of Reformers and Tories approved grants for Dalhousie, Acadia and St. Mary's. But in the 1843 session the Reformers determined to oppose further funding. Under the pressure of voting along party lines, the majority of 1842 disintegrated. There were still some Tories who were not prepared to give up their long-standing opposition to grants, and likewise some Reformers their support for continued funding. A resolution of 24 February 1843 that funds of the province were unequal to any more than moderate support of sectarian colleges attempted a compromise. Seven Tories sided with twenty-one Reformers to defeat it decisively. Only four Reformers and all Baptists—Samuel Chipman, his cousin Samuel Bishop Chipman, Ichabod Dimock and Gaius Lewis—voted with seventeen Tories for the resolution. Then a month later, on 28 March, came the one-thirty in the morning vote on Joseph Howe's move to adjourn the House because he feared the passage of a resolution sanctioning continued funding. At great personal cost the Chipman cousins abandoned their previous wholehearted support for Acadia and joined their liberal brethren in opposition to further grants. Among the Reformers only Dimock and Lewis still voted with the Tories. Of the Tories only Stephen Fulton, Robert McGowan Dickey and William Clarke Delaney refused to heed the call of party. Howe's resolution carried by a single vote.

In forcing the Assembly to deal with the question of public funding of sectarian colleges as one of political principle, the Reformers ensured that the division would be along party lines. Probably unwittingly, they made Tories out of many Baptists. These Baptists felt as passionately about Acadia as the Reverend Thomas McCulloch and his fellow Seceders had about Pictou Academy. Kirkmen and Seceders were already divided along religious lines, so by the 1830s the quarrel over Pictou Academy had greatly contributed to turning Seceders into Reformers and Kirkmen into Tories. In the 1840s, with the future of Acadia believed to be at stake, many Baptists turned to the Tories, led by one of their own, Attorney General J.W. Johnston. By far the largest concentration of Baptists was in Hants, Kings, and Annapolis. In the 1843 election, the Tories took ten of the twelve seats in these counties and went on to win the election, as we know, by a single seat. More than any other factor the Tory/Baptist alliance cost the Reformers the 1843 election.

No such controversy as the funding of colleges was the cause for turning Roman Catholics into liberals by the 1847 election. Rather, it was the result of unrelated circumstances, with a good leavening of pure chance. In the case of the Scottish Catholics of Antigonish and Inverness Counties, it was no more than the desire of John Young and his son, William, to gain seats in the Assembly. Both Bishop William Fraser and the Reverend Alexander MacDonell recognized that it could be years before a resident Scottish Catholic would be elected. Meanwhile, "brither" Scots in the Youngs, though Protestants, would best serve the interests of their flocks. In this they were correct and in the process gave the liberals a firm hold on the allegiance of Scottish Catholics. However, the interventions in elections by Fraser, especially after he became Bishop for Nova Scotia in 1827, exceeded prudence. His opposition in the 1840 election to the half-brothers Richard Forrestall and William Alexander Henry was downright bizarre and remains inexplicable. Although the very wildness of Henry McKeagney's behaviour in Cape Breton elections, and his refusal to accept Fraser's authority, demanded dismissal from his priestly duties at Sydney in 1840, there was no denying there was more than a touch of hypocrisy in Fraser's action. On the other hand, Fraser had to deal with the intrigues of the Halifax Irish Catholic "faction," who actively encouraged McKeagney in his defiance of Fraser's authority.[7] Although by the 1840s Irish Catholics numbered no more than one in ten of the 60,000 Catholics in Nova Scotia, their political loyalties and aspirations proved to be of far greater consequence for Nova Scotian politics in the middle of the nineteenth century than those of the Scottish and Acadian Catholics.

We have noted in the two chapters on Halifax the rise in the importance of the Irish Catholic vote in the capital's elections. In the 1830 Halifax Township election, much of what little support Beamish Murdoch could muster came from Irish Catholics. There was a natural alliance between the Halifax Irish Catholics, with their aspirations for economic and social betterment, and the Reformers who sought the overthrow of the ruling oligarchy. When, however, in the Halifax Township election of 1843, the Reformers passed over Laurence O'Connor Doyle and nominated two Protestants, the alliance broke down. The result was that the Irish vote stayed home or went to the Tory, Andrew Mitchell Uniacke. As the 1847 election approached, the Tories had every reason to believe that their candidates could once more gain sufficient of the Irish Catholic vote to hold their one seat, if not do better. But in January of 1847 a newspaper war broke out between the Tory *Times* and the Roman Catholic newspaper the *Cross*. The Great Famine or Hunger was then sweeping Ireland and bringing untoward starvation and misery. Edward Ward of the *Times* raised the spectre of thousands of destitute and famished Irish arriving on the shores of Nova Scotia.[8] A Catholic Ascendancy in Protestant Nova Scotia would be the result. It is doubtful that leading Tories had a hand in Ward's fear-mongering, but they chose to take up the cry of a Catholic Ascendancy to rally Protestants to their party. Whatever the misgivings of the Halifax

Irish Catholics about the liberals, who in the past had demonstrated much hostility towards them over the Irish Repeal Movement, in 1847 they voted ninety-five per cent for the liberals.

Although it goes beyond the chronological bounds of this book, it is worthwhile to chart into the 1850s the course of sectarian politics and the Halifax Irish. The 1850s was, within the English-speaking world, a decade of widespread anti-Irish and anti-Catholic feelings. In England, it took the form of a Protestant opposition to the re-establishment of a Catholic Church hierarchy, five hundred years after the English Reformation. In the United States, it was opposition to further Irish Catholic immigration into what was still a predominantly Protestant society. In Nova Scotia, the fear of further Irish immigration, and reaction to the openly expressed anti-British sentiments held by some Halifax Irish, fueled anti-Irish and anti-Catholic prejudices.

Joseph Howe's relations with Irish Catholics in Halifax always had a tension to them. In the mid-1850s, this relationship turned into violent hostility and the worst sectarian warfare the province was ever to know.[9] The precipitating cause was bound up with Howe's misguided venture during 1854 to recruit men in the United States for service in the British forces fighting in the Crimea. A number of leading Halifax Irish opposed the Crimean War and were openly vehement in their anti-British feelings. Howe was accused of luring Irishmen to Nova Scotia on the pretence of their working on the construction of the Halifax-to-Windsor railway, but actually for enlistment. A drunken brawl among railway workers between Scottish Presbyterians and Irish Catholics proved to be the spark for open sectarian warfare. It led directly to a complete breach between Howe and Halifax Irish Catholics. The leading critic of Howe's Crimean War misadventure was William Condon, a provincial civil servant. When the liberal government, under the premiership of William Young, felt it had no choice but to dismiss Condon for so prominently involving himself in politics, the government fell in 1858 on a vote of confidence. Among the eight Catholic liberals who went over to the conservatives were François Bourneuf, Henry Martell, James McKeagney and Peter Smyth—all assemblymen who had entered politics during the previous decade in the cause of reform. So had William Alexander Henry, one of the two Protestants to cross the floor. He did so on the grounds that he refused to be part of an alliance for the prosecution of the Catholic or any other body, though some called him self-seeking. Howe became the leader of a Protestant Alliance, which played a major role in the liberals regaining power in the 1859 election.[10] Once they were in power, the anti-Catholic sentiments, earlier so violently expressed, largely disappeared.

As the Irish Catholics in 1847 had deserted the Tories with their cry of a Catholic Ascendancy, the liberal-inspired Protestant Alliance drove them in the 1859 election into the conservative party. Not until 1871 was there again in the Assembly a liberal Roman Catholic from Halifax. Although religion was to remain a potent factor in Nova Scotian politics, the sectarian warfare of the 1850s was never to be repeated. For those constituencies with substantial numbers of both Protestants and Catholics, the practice, which first appeared in the Cape Breton election of 1820, of dividing representation between the two denominations became the norm.

By 1847 the Tories knew in their hearts that the old order was finished. However much they detested the thought, a constitutional re-ordering was inevitable. Such Tories as Andrew Mitchell Uniacke and John Clarke Hall believed that responsible government was by then established in all the British North American colonies. They readily accepted that when executive councillors lost the confidence of a majority in the Assembly, they must resign. What they claimed they could not accept was that a party with a simple majority of seats should have all the patronage of government at its disposal. Nor could they accept that this patronage extended to heads of government departments. In practical political terms, the Tories could not have realistically campaigned against responsible government in principle. The best they could do was to charge the liberals with wanting nothing more than offices for themselves. When the Tories took up the cry of a Catholic Ascendancy, it was no more than a belated attempt to distract the populace from the issue of full responsible government as presented by the liberals. There was unquestionably a certain desperation to the Tory strategy for the 1847 election campaign, but it came closer to success than suggested by the outcome of twenty-nine liberals elected to twenty-two Tories.

In going into the campaign the Tories had every reason to believe that the three Lunenburg seats would continue to be theirs as they had really been since 1830. Without Howe's spirited campaigning and the vicious infighting among Lunenburg Tories, it was highly doubtful that the liberals could have taken the three seats. The Tories could also have expected again to take four of the five Hants County seats, conceding to the Reformers only Newport Township, represented by Ichabod Dimock. As we saw in Chapter 4 on Hants County, Joseph Howe had bested Lewis Wilkins and Benjamin Smith in a public debate in 1844 and put the Tories on the defensive. However, Wilkins and Smith could probably have hung onto the two county seats if it had not been for James DeWolf Fraser, the sitting Tory for Windsor, embarrassing them over the parish bill. Wilkins and Smith only lost by 40 votes and in 1851 the Tories recaptured the two county seats and also Falmouth Township to give them once more four of the five seats. If the Tories had held the Lunenburg and Hants seats, they would have won the 1847 election by twenty-eight to twenty-three seats for the liberals.

Responsible government would still have come, as it did for all British North America. But Nova Scotian Reformers did not just want a new constitution, they were determined to overthrow the old oligarchic order that had governed Nova Scotia since the founding of Halifax in 1749. In this they succeeded, and as Howe said, "without a pane of glass being broken."[11] Rough as Nova Scotian politics in this period could be, calls to violence and revolution were never heard. Both Reformers and Tories shared a common conservative ethos.

In the creation of this conservative political culture, the Loyalists were a formative force. Much has been written on the conservative ideology of the American Loyalist: his belief that there could be no true freedom or liberty without order and due respect for the law, and his insistence that the inevitable excesses of popular democracy had to be counterbalanced by the powers of the executive branch of government, which derived their legitimacy from the prerogatives of the crown.[12] The patrician class of Loyalists came to Nova Scotia with an imbued fear of unbridled democracy; many because of their loyalty had had horrifying experiences of mob violence. The French Revolution hardened these Loyalists, and such non-Loyalists as Attorney General Richard John Uniacke, in their almost fanatical opposition to republicanism and to any signs of popular democracy. Although the Loyalists elected in 1785 wasted no time before challenging the presiding clique of office-holders they found comfortably ensconced around Governor John Parr, and a number of Loyalists became supporters of the country party during Sir John Wentworth's governorship, Loyalists could mostly be found voting on the side of the government and the appointed Council when it came to clashes over the constitutional division of powers. Moreover, their influence went well beyond their numbers. Nearly half of the fifty-five Loyalists elected came from the professional class of lawyers and office-holders who had close ties to government. In religion, forty-five of these first-generation Loyalist-assemblymen were Anglicans, further strengthening the presence of that denomination in the Assembly. The ascendancy they gained over the offices of government and appointments to the bench markedly deepened the already conservative character of provincial society and politics.

The opposition to reform found among the first generation of Loyalists, however, did not continue into the second. Among the thirty-six sons of Loyalists who became members of the Assembly were numbered such leading Reformers as Joseph Howe, Herbert Huntington, William Stairs and Gaius Lewis. All eight, though, of the sons of Loyalists who were lawyers, including J.W. Johnston, became Tories. Those of the merchant class divided almost equally in their party loyalty. But the wealthiest among them were Tories—notably the Sargent brothers of Barrington, Stephen DeBlois of Halifax and Stephen Thorne of Bridgetown—and they proved to be among the most opposed to reform. In religion, three-quarters of them continued in the Anglicanism of their fathers. In their voting in the Assembly, those favourable to reform outnumbered those opposed by a margin of two to one. In their pursuit of reform, however, they remained true to the conservatism of their fathers—they were conservative reformers.[13]

After the prosperity of the war years and the defeat of Napoleon, Nova Scotia entered a period of prolonged economic depression, punctuated by severe fluctuations in prices, wages and international trading.[14] There were also serious crop failures in 1815/16 and 1833/34, and in Cape Breton the "Great Famine" of the 1840s. Although the 1820s witnessed acute economic distress, especially among Halifax merchants, there was no concerted attempt to challenge the control exercised by a few wealthy merchants and office-holders. When John Young was rash enough to stand for election for Halifax Township in 1823, on a platform of reconciling town and country interests, mercantile Halifax put up Charles Rufus Fairbanks to oppose him. The campaign they waged against Young lacked for neither money nor sheer beastliness. Young, as we saw, resigned on the fourth day of the election. Beamish Murdoch's defeat at the hands of Stephen DeBlois in the Halifax Township election in 1830 showed again just how malicious and ruthless the old order could be when openly challenged.

It is not until the deeply felt and widespread distress of the mid-1830s that we can observe a direct connection between economic conditions and the rise of a party committed to reform and the overthrow of the oligarchic rule of Halifax notability. Increasingly, Nova Scotians began associating their distressed condition with misgovernment by, in Thomas Forrester's phrase, the "wealth and interest" that so pressed upon the people. Forrester expressed his rage from the chair of the meeting of Halifax freeholders that nominated another Halifax merchant, Hugh Bell, to stand in the 1835 Halifax Township by-election in clear opposition to the "aristocracy" of the town. Bell, as we know, was unopposed; in the general election a year later he and Forrester took both Halifax Township seats. The rage of Halifax freeholders found a resonance around the province. In Kings County, Augustus Tupper called on his fellow farmers to break the "chains of oppression and misrule." In neighbouring Hants, the newspaper editor, E.K. Allen, fanned public anger in the same cause, while calling on freeholders to sign petitions for relief against "the oppressors grasp." In Cumberland, the distress caused by crop failures gave rise to the candidacies of Andrew McKim and Gaius Lewis, as representatives of the farming interest, in a concerted effort to defeat Alexander Stewart. The 1836 election put Nova Scotia on the road to reform, though the obstacles were to prove greater than the Reformers imagined.

To start with, there was the whole electoral system of the day, which favoured the continuance of oligarchic rule. The requirement for freeholders to have registered, six months before an election, whatever property they voted on restricted the franchise. The smaller the number of freeholders, the easier for candidates of local family compacts and those with large ledgers at their disposal to get elected. The most restrictive franchises were in the agricultural townships of the central and western counties and in Cape Breton. In the case of Cape Breton, the cause lay in the high numbers of Scottish immigrants who arrived after all the best land was taken and became squatters on the backlands, finding what work they could from their better-off neighbours. For the largely New England Planter settled townships, the cause seems to have been directly related to a fairly substantial and apparently propertyless labouring and tenantry class that found employment with a class of well-to-do farmers. Amherst was the exception in having nearly all its heads of families eligible to vote, but that was likely because it drew its labourers from outside the township boundaries, mostly from around Minudie. Although there were exceptions in the pattern, such as in Hants County, the central and western counties voted Tory.

The existing evidence does not allow us to be certain, but the franchise or suffrage was considerably less restrictive in the trading and fishing townships of the south shore than in the agricultural townships. From Lunenburg to Digby the numbers of freeholders voting probably ranged from two-thirds to three-quarters of the heads of families. There were exceptions, such as when John Heckman defeated the aging Edward James in the 1826 Lunenburg Township election. Just 226 voted, out of 1,100 heads of families in the township. This low number may have been because James resigned early when faced with certain defeat. In most of these townships, there was also a merchant class which used its ledgers without constraint to influence elections. Where this merchant class was strongest—Lunenburg, Queens, Barrington and Argyle—the Tories did well; where it was weakest—Yarmouth, Digby and Shelburne—these townships voted Reform.

The most restrictive suffrage by far operated in Halifax town, where just one-fifth of the heads of households were eligible to vote. The other four-fifths were almost all tenants of a small moneyed class of property owners. Moreover, the ledger influence that could be brought to bear at the hustings exceeded that of anywhere else in the province. The small numbers of freeholders and the ledger influence available allowed the mercantile and office-holding notability to control the township elections until Hugh Bell's election in 1835, followed by his and Forrester's victory in the 1836 election. The rage they felt against the "wealth and interest" turned them into Reformers. They, and other middling merchants who followed them, brought to the cause of reform money and organization. The results were evident enough in the 1840 Halifax Township and County elections when the Reformers recruited hundreds of Musquodoboit farmers to seize the passageways at the hustings. They beat the Tories at their own game in the roughest election Halifax was to know.

Elsewhere in the province, Pictou stands out as the county where the franchise was the least restrictive; generally in elections three-quarters of the heads of families voted. This was primarily because there was no landowning class, and because many of those who might have been forced onto backlands as squatters moved on instead to Antigonish and Cape Breton. In Pictou, however, the extended nature of the franchise benefitted the Tories more because Kirkmen outnumbered Seceders. In fact, the Tories encouraged fathers to sub-divide their lands so that their sons could vote.

Although it was the Tories, under J.W. Johnston, who introduced the Simultaneous Polling Act just before the 1847 election, the Reformers benefitted more from the increased numbers voting. But it was part of the process of the inevitable widening of the franchise as both parties vied in succeeding elections for votes. After the defeat of the Tories in 1847, Johnston went so far as to advocate universal suffrage, an elective legislative council, and elective municipal government.[15] Universal suffrage, however, did not come until 1920 and the Legislative Council was not abolished until 1928. The rotten system of local government by appointed justices of the peace was swept away by the County Incorporation Act of 1879, though not without much resistance.

In the first quote at the beginning of this concluding chapter, Herbert Huntington spoke of the "system of exclusiveness" that prevailed in Nova Scotia to an extent scarcely known elsewhere in the British dominions. He was speaking in opposition to a bill that had as its purpose the distribution of an equal sum (£75) to each county for local agricultural societies, to expend as they saw fit. A few others like William Young joined him in opposing the bill because there was no requirement for farmers to make any contribution themselves. In short, the money distributed in this manner would do nothing to encourage improved farming practices; the bill was a means of placating the farming interest. But Huntington's opposition went further and deeper when he questioned the inveterate tendency of every class in Nova Scotian society to look to the Assembly for assistance, such as the farmers were doing, instead of exerting themselves to bring about desired improvement in their own well-being and that of the province as a whole. He feared local interests were combining to impose their will without regard to any notion of the general good. The system of exclusiveness of which he complained was the ingrained disposition of Nova Scotians, and their politicians, to exclude from the consideration of public policy any but a concern for local or special interests.

Nowhere was this exclusiveness more obsessive than in the intense bargaining among members that took place for the annual road moneys. But reform of this, the most wasteful and inefficient system for building roads that could have been devised, proved to be beyond the realm of practical possibility. The same parochialism, reinforced by sectarianism, made it impossible for the Assembly to create a system of publicly funded common schools, though it was recognized that two-thirds of Nova Scotian children were growing up in ignorance. Compulsory assessment did not come until 1864; in some of the rural areas there was violent resistance against the resulting taxation. In the second quote, the Baptist minister Silas Tertius Rand reflected that one college was all that Nova Scotia required, but he agreed that it was out of the question. He was prescient; though there was another attempt between 1876 and 1881, it succumbed to the same forces of sectarianism that had prevailed before. Inseparable from the system of exclusiveness which Huntington so decried was the corrupting influence of patronage appointments on the workings of government. In fact, what had first drawn Huntington into politics was the corruption and partisanship of the Yarmouth magistrates he witnessed as a young man. Only by a complete reform of government and an end to oligarchic rule could, he believed, the evil be remedied.

The triumph of Reformers in the 1847 election ensured the demise of the old order and inaugurated full responsible government. Constitutional reform was achieved. But with it came the struggle of parties for power and, with victory at the polls, the spoils of office. The system of exclusiveness, with its enfeebling parochialism of special interests and insidious dependence upon patronage as an instrument of party government, remained to frustrate vision in the creation of public policy and energy in the pursuit of good government.

Notes On Databases And Sources

The story of early Nova Scotian politicians has as its research base three major databases which have been analysed and correlated using computer programmes. The largest database is biographical for the 437 members of the Nova Scotian Assembly who were elected from the first election in 1758 to and including those elected in the 1847 election. It consists of eighteen fields of information for each member—birth and death dates; place of birth; education; occupation; religion; age on election; Loyalist or son of Loyalist; year elected; county represented; resident or not in constituency; militia rank on election; whether justice of the peace on election or appointed during time in Assembly; offices held on election; offices received during or shortly after time in Assembly; reason, if seat vacated; last year in Assembly; and total years in Assembly.

The primary published source for the vital statistical information, and also often for education, religion, occupation and offices, was *The Legislative Assembly of Nova Scotia 1758-1983: a biographical directory,* edited and revised with painstaking accuracy by Shirley Elliott, and published by the Government of Nova Scotia in 1984. I have followed Shirley Elliott's spellings of MLA names. The other chief published source used was the biographies appearing in the volumes of the *Dictionary of Canadian Biography*. The Dictionary is a remarkable national achievement and deserves to be more widely used than appears to be the case. Allan Marble's *Nova Scotians at Home and Abroad: Biographical Sketches of over Six Hundred Native Born Nova Scotians* (Lancelot Press, Windsor, N.S., 1977) was also of service. The value of the county histories, published and unpublished, varied greatly. The most useful were W.A. Calnek and A.W. Savary, *History of Annapolis County* and A.W.H. Eaton, *The History of Kings County*. Among the manuscript sources most researched were the MG1 collection of individual and family papers in PANS, the 1790s poll tax returns and the censuses for 1827 (incomplete), 1838 (complete except for Cumberland County and parts of Cape Breton), 1851 (only for Halifax, Kings and Pictou Counties), and 1871 (complete). Aside from the usual information expected in searching deeds and wills in the county registries, these records proved an excellent source for occupations and the financial affairs of individuals before and at death.

It was surprising how much biographical information was available and in such a wide variety of sources. There are three fields of information, however, that deserve special comment—education, occupation and religion. The research into the level of education of MLAs proved to be most unrewarding. In Chapter 1, I have attempted to draw some general conclusions from the very limited material found. I am convinced that many more than for whom I have documentary evidence attended King's College

School (as opposed to the College) and especially the Halifax Grammar School during the time from 1790 to 1819 when the Reverend George Wright was headmaster. In the 1830s and 1840s at the great public meetings in Halifax called to nominate candidates, speakers would mention that many of their former classmates were present and would sometimes refer to them. From these comments, I have inferred that, for instance, Beamish Murdoch and Joseph Howe were among those who attended this school, though there is no direct documentary evidence. I also believe that the attendance at this school of William Frederick DesBarres and John George Marshall was part of a pattern in which parents from outside the capital sent their sons to reside with relations in Halifax, so they could obtain a grammar school education. I suspect that George Wright taught more future MLAs than any other teacher of this period.

On the question of definition of occupation, I have divided MLAs into four main categories—those in the professions, farmers, merchants, and others who ranged from blacksmiths and other tradesmen to half-pay officers, mariners, newspaper editors and surveyors. As discussed in Chapter 1, most Nova Scotians gained at least some of their livelihood from the land. Those whom I have called farmers, such as Shubael Dimock of Hants County or William Holland of Annapolis, were engaged solely in farming; included, however, are those like Simon d'Entremont of Argyle and Peter Spearwater of Shelburne who called themselves farmers, but earned part of their livelihood from the seasonal inshore fisheries. Those who engaged in any form of mercantile activity, whether as storekeepers, traders, shipbuilders, or were involved in commerce of any sort, I have classed as merchants. Some — for example Samuel Chipman of Cornwallis — were substantial marshland farmers, but as an MLA it was the extent and use of his ledger that was of the greater interest and he was classed as a merchant. Among the professionals elected, almost all were lawyers. The exceptions were two medical doctors—William Baxter of Cornwallis and John Bolman of Lunenburg—and a few early office-holders like James Bulkeley, the provincial secretary in the 1790s.

The determination of religion for many MLAs proved a challenging task. For those elected before 1800, and particularly prior to the arrival of the Loyalists, it was not too difficult. They were either Anglicans or Congregationalists with the occasional exception such as the Quaker John Hicks of Annapolis. Also because so many were Halifax residents and the records of St. Paul's and St. Matthew's churches so complete, it was usually possible to sort out Anglicans from Dissenters, except for a number of country members. For the later period, the 1827 and 1851 censuses give the religion of the heads of households. Where there was no other source or conflicting evidence, I have used the 1871 census if the MLA was still alive (or in a few cases his widow). But the main sources have been church records, particularly congregational minutes and subscription and pew lists. The high number of MLAs who turned out to be Anglicans was a surprise, especially for the period from 1820 onwards. I may have made some Anglicans out of Dissenters, but where there was doubt in my mind, I either listed them as belonging to one of the Dissenting denominations or as religion unknown.

There were fifty-two MLAs for whom I had to list their religion as un-known. The aim, of course, was to have been able to discover the religion of MLAs at the time of their election. This was not always possible, but for statistical purposes the results, I believe, are reasonably accurate.

A software programme, called FRAMEWORK 4, was used to do the correlation sorting — for example, of the fields of occupation and religion. This provided a breakdown of the religious affiliation of lawyers, farmers and merchants. In other cases, straight tabulations were done such as for the number of MLAs who were justices of the peace or militia colonels at the time of their election. There are, of course, numerous correlations that might be done with this biographical database. For this book on early politicians, I have selected those I felt most relevant and worked them into the text.

The second major database created was for the voting record of MLAs on twenty-six selected legislative issues. Broadly, these can be grouped into issues involving the Assembly's powers and constitutional relationship to the executive branch of government; the administration of justice, for example, on opposition to the inferior courts of common pleas; such economic questions as free ports, banks and assistance to agriculture; and education, including sectarian colleges and compulsory taxation for schools.

Not until 1785 did the Assembly begin recording in its Journals how members voted in the House on divisions. By no means were all the votes by members recorded. The House rules provided that any member could call for a recorded vote. Other than, presumably, when a member called for a recorded vote, I have been unable to discover any pattern as to why some votes were recorded and others not. Recording votes was a fairly lengthy process. On divisions, the ayes went to one side of the room and the nays to the other. The clerk of the House then wrote down the names. Although the Journals present an orderly picture of House proceedings, unrecorded hours of debate and divisions could pass between a motion and a final recorded vote. There was much bargaining for votes among assemblymen and they were open to all kinds of designing influences and the formation of temporary alliances of interest. Still, members were free of party discipline and could vote as their personal views and constituency interests dictated. It was with this context in mind that the voting record database was created and used as evidence of voting patterns.

The creation of the voting record database involved selecting 330 Assembly votes, where they were judged to be of a substantive nature or a matter of principle, as opposed to purely procedural. These 330 votes were broken down into twenty-six issue fields as noted above, ranging from how individual members voted on the constitutional power of the Assembly over money bills and whether the inferior courts of common pleas should be abolished, to such specific measures as grants to Pictou Academy. For each of these 330 votes, it was recorded whether each member voting was in support or in opposition—that is, voted either "yes" or "no." For example, between 1785 and 1847 there were thirty-seven recorded votes on the question of support for agriculture. Each time a member voted, either for or against protection, this was tabulated as a yes or no vote. The yes and no votes were totalled for all members who voted during their years in the

Assembly on the issue of protection. Alexander Lackie Archibald, for instance, voted fifteen times in favour of assistance to agriculture and three times against while the member for Truro from 1830 to 1843. As the member for Yarmouth from 1835 to 1847, Reuben Clements voted seventeen times against and never for. Many, such as Charles Budd, who sat for Digby, voted back and forth on the question; in his case, Budd voted seven times against compared to five occasions when he supported assistance. Then, there were those who had the opportunity to vote only once on the question while in the Assembly. To deal with this variation in voting patterns, a simple numerical code was designed to allow for cross tabulations of voting preference with the biographical database. The code developed was as follows:

CODE	DESCRIPTION
01	members marginally in favour (ratio of 2 to 1 or less in the "yes" category, or where 2 votes only are tabulated in the "yes" and none in the "no" categories)
02	marginally opposed (ratio of 2 to 1 or less in the "no" category, or where 2 votes only are tabulated in the "no" and none in the "yes" categories)
03	strongly in favour (ratio of more than 2 to 1 in votes in the "yes" category)
04	strongly opposed (ratio of more than 2 to 1 in votes in the "no" category)
05	equivocal (equal numbers of "yes" and "no" votes)
06	voted once in favour
07	voted once against

These code numbers (01 to 07) for those of the twenty-six fields on which a member voted at least once, were entered into a database which already included the biographical fields of education, occupation, religion, Loyalist, county represented, and offices. This enlarged database was done on dBASE III Plus and analysed using SPSS/PC+ (Statistical Package for the Social Sciences). This allowed for cross tabulations of coded voting preferences with the biographical data. Again, using support for agriculture as an example, the cross tabulation showed that, of the sixty-one farmers who voted on the issue from 1785 to 1847, thirteen were marginally in favour, two marginally against, seventeen strongly in favour, seven strongly opposed, twelve equally for and against, three voted in favour once and seven against once. The same cross tabulation was done for other occupations and by county to see where the most regional support lay for agricultural protection. Moreover, where the results did not seem to conform to other evidence or it seemed desirable to investigate further, this was easily done. For instance, among the seven farmers who were strongly opposed was Simon d'Entremont of Argyle; he voted seven times against and never for, which conforms to his statements in the House opposing a central board of agriculture.

Similarly, numerous cross tabulations were done for such other issues as yes or no for banks, inferior courts of common pleas or sectarian colleges and so on. As with the biographical database, I incorporated into the text only those results I felt most relevant. I tried to work them into the story of early Nova Scotia politicians without burdening the reader with too many statistics. Also, most importantly, readers should understand that cross tabulation results are used solely as general indicators for patterns over time of political behaviour. The results showed, for example, that the clash of interests between town and country was not so much between Halifax and the rest of the province, as between the agricultural townships and those where the fishery and trading were their economic lifeblood. This, in fact, is not a particularly original conclusion, but the statistical analysis does demonstrate how deep and continuous was the cleavage over time. The voting patterns become especially complex from the 1830s onwards, as members increasingly found themselves under pressure to vote along party lines. Readers are well advised to turn to Professor J. Murray Beck's biography *Joseph Howe: Conservative Reformer 1804-1847*, where he has brilliantly analysed in great detail the votes in the Assembly for the 1830s and 1840s.

The third major database consists of a series of small databases, listing by county and township for each election all the known candidates and the poll results. Where possible, the poll results were listed by location of polls. For each candidate were also listed his occupation, religion and family relationship to other politicians of the period. Newspaper election reports and RG5, Series E, Election Writs, PANS were the two main sources for poll results. Until the 1830s, most poll results appearing in Halifax newspapers came from travellers arriving in the capital. After the 1830s, it became common for partisans of individual candidates or parties in the counties to send letters to the editors giving results, while taking the opportunity to comment on the election and the candidates. The law required sheriffs to return the writs with the names of those candidates declared elected. Often sheriffs included such additional information as the names of the other candidates and their vote totals, the locations to where the poll had been moved, and the number of days the poll had remained open. Using these two sources it was possible to create a fairly comprehensive record of poll results for elections from 1799 onwards. For the earlier period, the best generally achieved was to determine whether or not there had been a contested election.

Disappointingly, little surviving manuscript material was found on elections. The papers of S.G.W. Archibald (MG1, Vol. 89, PANS); S.B. Robie (MG1, Vol. 793, PANS); Bliss Family Papers (MG1, Vols. 947-962, PANS); and John Young (MG1, Vols. 983-987B, PANS) all contain letters concerning elections, but their number proved to be few. Newspapers of the day remain the principal source for Nova Scotian elections.

The research material used for the introductory sections to the chapters, as seen through the eyes of an imaginary traveller, came from both contemporary sources of the period and from recent studies of historical geographers. For those contemporary to the 1830s, my chief source was Volume II of Thomas Chandler Haliburton's *An Historical and Statistical Account of Nova Scotia,* published by Joseph Howe in 1829. During his rambles around Nova Scotia in the early 1830s, Howe had with him Haliburton's *Account.* A compilation of Howe's *Western and Eastern Rambles: Travel Sketches of Nova Scotia* has been edited by M.G. Parks (1973). In places, I have used Howe's comments from this edition as a corrective to the reports of Haliburton's correspondents from around the province. For the background to Haliburton's undeniably promotional account of Nova Scotia of his day, readers may wish to refer to M. Brook Taylor's "Thomas Chandler Haliburton as a Historian," in *Acadiensis,* Vol. XIII, No. 2, Spring 1984, pp. 50-68. An anthology of excerpts from writings of travellers, who visited Nova Scotia between the founding of Halifax and Confederation, can be found in Marjory Whitelaw's editing of *Letters from Nova Scotia,* published by Oberon in 1986.

As the endnotes show, I have incorporated into the chapters' introductory sections some of the conclusions and data from the literature of historical geographers, principally from the work of Graeme Wynn of the University of British Columbia and a number of his former students. There is, however, no recent or comprehensive economic history for Nova Scotia, particularly one that deals with the subject of credit in the eighteenth and nineteenth centuries. For a framework, I have used Julian Gwyn's "A Little Province Like This," published in *Canadian Papers in Rural History,* Volume VI, in 1988.

It is my intention to deposit in the Public Archives of Nova Scotia printed copies and the computer disks for the databases created. The chapters in this book are much reduced from the original drafts which contain far more detail, especially for the eighteenth century, than could appear in the published versions.

Endnotes

Chapter 1

1. The history of the acts and regulations for Nova Scotian elections and the franchise can be found in a number of sources. The most comprehensive is J. Murray Beck's *The Government of Nova Scotia* (University of Toronto Press, Toronto, 1957). See also, in particular, John Garner, *The Franchise and Politics in British North America 1755-1867* (University of Toronto Press, Toronto, 1969), Chapters 2 and 14; and my "To Promote the Purity of Elections: The Conduct of Elections from Representative to Responsible Government," *Collections* of the Royal Nova Scotia Historical Society, Vol. 43, pp. 49-72.

2. Those under twenty-one years of age or Roman Catholic were specifically excluded from voting under the 1758 regulations. In the case of the latter, though the 1789 act regulating elections proclaimed "liberty of conscience," it was difficult for Catholics to own freehold, unless they took an oath rejecting any form of papal temporal authority or civil jurisdiction. Not until an act of 1826 repealed this special oath did Catholics begin voting in substantial numbers.

3. *Times,* 19 December 1843. Stairs' petition is in RG5, Series P, Vol. 8A, No. 70, Public Archives of Nova Scotia (hereafter PANS). The proceedings of the scrutiny were not tabled by Sheriff John James Sawyer until 6 March 1844. The House ignored them, not proceeding further with Stairs' petition.

4. *Journals of the House of Assembly* (hereafter *JHA*), 14, 15, 20, 21, 22, 24 and 27 February and 3 March 1812.

5. See Sheriff Benjamin DeWolf's report of the scrutiny, which lists by name the women who had the necessary property qualifications and voted, RG5, Series E, Vol. 2, PANS.

6. *JHA*, 20 November 1806 and RG5, Series E, Vol. 2, PANS.

7. Thomas McCulloch to S.B. Robie, c. 1820, MG1, Vol. 793, Part II, No. 75, PANS.

8. See also a statistical overview of the Nova Scotian bench by Clara Greco, "The Superior Court Judiciary of Nova Scotia, 1754-1900: A Collective Biography" in Philip Girard and Jim Phillips, eds., *Essays in the History of Canadian Law,* Vol. III (published for the Osgoode Society by the University of Toronto Press, 1990), pp. 42-79.

9. W. Moorsom, *Letters from Nova Scotia and New Brunswick; Comprising Sketches of a Young Country* (London, 1830), p. 288.

10. For a good description of a merchant's ledger, see Rusty Bittermann, "Farm Households and Wage Labour in the Northeastern Maritimes in the Early 19th Century" in *Labour/Le Travail,* No. 31, Spring 1993, pp. 16-17. The article is also a good analysis of the myth of the independent yeoman farmer in the literature of the Maritime Provinces.

11. *The Old Judge or, Life in A Colony* (London, 1849), Vol. I, pp. vi-vii.

12. Rusty Bittermann, Robert A. MacKinnon, and Graeme Wynn, "Of Inequality and Interdependence in the Nova Scotian Countryside, 1850-1870" in the *Canadian Historical Review,* Vol. LXXIV, No. 1, March 1993, pp. 17 and 36. They concluded that there were large inequalities in material circumstances of mid-nineteenth-century Nova Scotian lives. The evidence from elections in the first half of the century certainly supports this conclusion.

13. For a description of the lower courts, see Sandra Oxner, "The Evolution of the Lower Courts of Nova Sco-

tia" in Peter Waite, Sandra Oxner and Thomas Barnes, eds., *Law in a Colonial Society: The Nova Scotia Experience* (The Carswell Company, Toronto, 1984), pp. 59-79.

14. This figure is derived from a cross tabulation of votes for and against increased jurisdiction for justices of the peace, inferior courts and higher courts by merchants, lawyers and farmers. In the case of justices, for and against votes were tabulated for nine recorded divisions in the Assembly. In those votes, 36 merchants and 17 lawyers voted. Examples of voting by merchants are: the wealthy Pictou merchant, Edward Mortimer, voted four times for justices and summary trials and just once against; and Samuel Poole of Yarmouth voted five times for and never against. See NOTES ON DATABASES AND SOURCES at end of book.

15. "An Autobiography of John Young. aet. 21," *Nova Scotia Historical Review*, Vol. 12, No. 2, 1992, pp. 125-33.

16. *Novascotian*, 1 April 1841.

17. The breakdown of members elected from 1758 to 1847 by religion is as follows:

Anglicans	197
Baptists	25 (24 after 1800)
Church of Scotland	23
Congregationalists	45 (only one after 1785)
Lutherans	2
Methodists	32
New Lights	4 (see below)
Presbyterians	41
Quakers	2
Roman Catholics	14
Unknown	52
Total	437

Of the four I have classed as New Lights, Joseph Barss and Snow Parker were members of the Reverend John Payzant's New Light Congregationalist Church in Liverpool. The other two were Loran DeWolf of Windsor and Nathaniel Marsters of Onslow Township. Marsters was, however, likely already a Baptist by the time of his election in 1806.

18. For the opening of the 1841 session Charles Dickens was present and wrote his impressions in his *American Notes*, remarking that "it was like looking at Westminster through the wrong end of a telescope," so closely did the Nova Scotian procedures follow those of the British House of Commons. *American Notes and Pictures from Italy* (Oxford University Press, London, 1957), pp. 21-22. The first edition appeared in 1842.

Chapter 2

1. For Joshua Mauger and his "party" see John Bartlet Brebner, The Neutral Yankees of Nova Scotia: A Marginal Colony during the Revolutionary Years [1937], The Carleton Library No. 45 (McClelland and Stewart, Toronto, 1969), pp. 15-16 and index; see also Donald Chard, "Joshua Mauger," *DCB*, Vol. IV.

2. For what follows see John Bartlet Brebner, *The Neutral Yankees of Nova Scotia, op. cit.*, pp. 54-76.

3. For Day and his Assembly career I have relied upon Brebner's *Neutral Yankees of Nova Scotia*, pp. 199-200, and index. Also see Wendy Thrope, "John Day," *DCB*, Vol. IV.

4. *An Essay of the Present State of the Province of Nova Scotia ... by a Member of Assembly* (Halifax, c.1774), p. 5.

5. For Monk in this period see Barry Cahill, "James Monk's Observations on the Courts of Law in Nova Scotia, 1775," *UNB Law Journal*, Vol. 36, 1987, pp. 131-35.

6. What follows relies on James Monk's "Observations on the measures pursued in, and of Political progress of, the business transacted in the present sessions of General Assembly — Made December 10th, 1775," William Inglis Morse Collection, Vaughan Memorial Library, Acadia University. I am indebted to Edith Haliburton, Special Collections Librarian, for providing me with a copy. For the provenance of this document, see Barry Cahill, "James Monk's Observations on the Courts of Law in Nova Scotia, 1775," *op. cit.*, p. 136, footnote 28.

7. For the St. Paul's connection, see the various biographical sketches in Reginald Harris, *The Church of Saint Paul in Halifax, Nova Scotia:*

1749-1949 (The Ryerson Press, Toronto, 1949).

8. For Blowers, see Phyllis Blakeley, "Sampson Salter Blowers," *DCB*, Vol. VII.

9. *Nova Scotia Gazette and Weekly Chronicle*, 25 October and 1 November 1785 and Allan Dunlop, "James Brenton," *DCB*, Vol. V.

10. For the Loyalists in the Sixth Assembly, see Neil MacKinnon, *This Unfriendly Soil: The Loyalist Experience in Nova Scotia, 1783-1791* (McGill-Queen's University Press, Kingston and Montreal, 1986), pp. 118-36, and Margret Ells, "The Development of Nova Scotia, 1782-1812," unpublished Ph.D. thesis available in PANS, pp. 110-34.

11. The principal source for the "judges' affair" in 1787 and 1788 is *Extracts from the proceedings of His Majesty's Council February 21 & 28, 1788 in reference to complaints of improper and irregular administration of justice in the Supreme Court of Nova Scotia* (Halifax, 1788).

12. Donald Chard, "Charles Morris," *DCB*, Vol. VI, and *Nova Scotia Gazette and Weekly Chronicle*, 26 February 1788.

13. *Royal Gazette and Nova Scotia Advertiser*, 29 January 1793 and MG1, Vol. 424, No. 16, PANS.

14. Brian Cuthbertson, *The Old Attorney General: A Biography of Richard John Uniacke* (Nimbus, Halifax, 1980), pp. 29-36.

15. Fulton to Edward Mortimer, 19 October 1799, printed in the *Colonial Patriot* of Pictou, 6 November 1830.

16. S. Buggey, "Edward Mortimer," *DCB*, Vol. V.

17. Charles Morris to the Rev. James McGregor, 17 October 1799, McGregor Correspondence, Letter LXXIX, United Church, Maritime Conference Archives, Halifax, N.S.

18. James Fraser to McGregor, 25 November 1799, McGregor Correspondence, Letter LXXX, Maritime Conference Archives. Fraser was very much tied to the governing order and was Church of Scotland.

19. Mortimer to McGregor, 28 November 1799, McGregor Correspondence, Letter LXXXII, Maritime Conference Archives.

20. Petition by Pyke, 22 April 1800, RG5, Series A. Vol. 7, No. 61, PANS.

21. *Weekly Chronicle*, 23 July and 17 August 1801.

22. For biographies see Israel Longworth, *Life of S.G.W. Archibald* (Halifax, 1881) and J. Murray Beck, "Samuel George William Archibald," *DCB*, Vol. VII.

23. Jane Hollingworth Nokes, "William Lawson," *DCB*, Vol. VII.

24. As quoted in Marjory Whitelaw, ed., *The Dalhousie Journals* (Oberon Press, 1978), 28 March 1818, pp. 77-78.

25. As quoted in Andrew Robb, "John George Pyke," *DCB*, Vol. VI.

26. Allan Dunlop, "John Albro," *DCB*, Vol. VII.

27. Cogswell to John Sargent, 21 December 1799, MG1, Vol. 797B, NO. 29, PANS; also see David Sutherland, "Henry Hezekiah Cogswell," *DCB*, Vol. VIII.

28. The best study of Nova Scotian currency and finance remains that of J.S. Martell, "A Documentary Study of Provincial Finance and Currency 1812-36," *Bulletin of the Public Archives of Nova Scotia*, Vol.II, No.4 (PANS, Halifax, 1941).

29. *Acadian Recorder*, 14 March 1818.

30. *Acadian Recorder*, 21 March and 4 April 1818.

31. Marjory Whitelaw, ed., *The Dalhousie Journals, op. cit.*, 2 April 1820.

32. *Ibid.*, 14 April 1820.

33. *Halifax Journal*, 15 May 1820 and *Acadian Recorder*, 20 May 1820.

34. Edward Blanchard to William Young, Truro, 20 May 1820, MG2, Vol. 731, PANS.

35. *Acadian Recorder*, 20 May 1820.

36. Supplement to the *Halifax Journal*, twelve o'clock, 22 May 1820.

37. *Acadian Recorder*, 27 May 1820.

38. Julian Gwyn, " 'A Little Province Like This': The Economy of Nova Scotia under Stress, 1812-1853." In Donald H. Akenson, *Canadian Papers in Rural History*, Vol. VI, p. 197.

39. David Sutherland, "Charles Rufus Fairbanks", *DCB*, Vol. VII.

40. *Acadian Recorder*, 16 August 1823.

41. Young printed a handbill "To the Fishermen of the Township of Hali-

fax" in which he stated and refuted these "misrepresentations," MG2, Vol. 728, No. 523, PANS.
42. *Ibid.,* No. 531.
43. *Ibid.,* No. 524.
44. *Free Press,* 6 and 16 September 1826.
45. *Halifax Journal,* 15 September 1823.
46. Elisha DeWolf to William Young, 11 November 1823, MG2, Vol. 731.
47. Elisha DeWolf to William Young, 9 September 1823, MG2, Vol. 731.
48. MG2, Vol. 728, No. 712, PANS.
49. *Acadian Recorder,* 6 May 1826 and *Free Press,* 9 May 1826.
50. *Acadian Recorder,* 17 June 1826.
51. *Observations upon the Doctrine, Lately Advanced, That His Majesty's Council have no constitutional Power to Control Individual Appropriations, or to Amend or Alter Money Bills ... Pictou Academy* (Halifax, 1828). The pamphlet was undoubtedly written by Halliburton.
52. Wallace to Young, 26 December 1826, MG2, Vol. 729, No. 855.
53. *Colonial Patriot,* 9 January 1830. The editorial was filled with sarcastic, venomous attacks on individual members of the Council. During the forthcoming session copies of the paper were dumped in the Assembly on the mornings of publication.
54. The best and most detailed discussion of the Brandy Election remains that of Gene Morrison, "The Brandy Election of 1830," *Collections* of the Nova Scotia Historical Society, Vol. 30, pp. 151-83. See also my "Place, Politics and the Brandy Election of 1830," *Collections* of the Royal Nova Scotia Historical Society, Vol. 41, pp. 5-19.
55. Nathaniel White to Cornelius White, 16 April 1830, MG1, Vol. 955, No. 1232, PANS.
56. *Novascotian,* 15 and 23 September 1830. The term "notability" is David Sutherland's, which he defines as the merchant inner elite, "The Merchants of Halifax, 1815-1850: A Commercial Class in Pursuit of Metropolitan Status" (unpublished Ph.D. Thesis, University of Toronto, 1975), p. 100.
57. J. Murray Beck, "Jotham Blanchard," *DCB,* Vol. VI.

58. David Sutherland, "John Leander Starr," *DCB,* Vol. XI.
59. *Novascotian,* 15 September 1830.
60. *Novascotian,* 23 September 1830; see also J.D.W. White to his brother Nathaniel, 17 September 1830, MG1, Vol. 955, No. 1237, PANS.
61. *Novascotian,* 22 September 1830.

CHAPTER 3
1. For the debate over the incorporation of the Bank of Nova Scotia, see David Sutherland, "The Merchants of Halifax," *op. cit.,* pp. 211-16.
2. See J. Murray Beck, "Jotham Blanchard," *DCB,* Vol. VII.
3. See J. S. Martell, "A Documentary Study of Provincial Finance and Currency 1812-36," *Bulletin of the Public Archives of Nova Scotia,* Vol. II, No. 4 (PANS, 1941).
4. *Novascotian,* 11 December 1833.
5. The petition was the result of a public meeting at which, among others, Lawson, Fairbanks and DeBlois spoke, all giving differing opinions on the causes of and solutions to the currency crisis. See *Novascotian,* 22 January 1834.
6. J. Murray Beck, *Joseph Howe: Conservative Reformer,* Vol. 1 (McGill-Queen's Press, Kingston and Montreal, 1982), pp. 123-24, and the *Novascotian,* 20 March 1834.
7. The petition was printed in the *Novascotian,* 2 April 1834.
8. *Novascotian,* 26 February 1834.
9. *Novascotian,* 26 November 1835, as quoted in J. Murray Beck, *Joseph Howe, op. cit.,* p. 150.
10. The meeting was reported by Howe in the *Novascotian,* 26 November 1835.
11. *Ibid.*
12. Letter XI, *Acadian Recorder,* 15 October 1836.
13. Letter IX, *Acadian Recorder,* 24 September 1836.
14. The *Novascotian* of 17 November 1836 carried a full report of the public meeting and various letters relating to it. All quotes are from this number.
15. *Novascotian,* 30 November 1836. Joseph Starr earlier had recommended that members should be selected without personal canvass or expense and by prior gatherings of

freeholders. *Acadian Recorder*, 16 July 1836.

16. Maitland to Goderich, 6 June 1831, private dispatch, as quoted in Martell, "A Documentary Study," *op. cit.*, p. 300.
17. *Acadian Recorder*, 11 February 1837.
18. J. Murray Beck, *Joseph Howe, op. cit.*, p. 187.
19. *Novascotian*, 13 and 20 February 1840.
20. "Mercurial" is David Sutherland's aptly descriptive term for Forrester, see "The Merchants of Halifax," *op. cit.*, p. 230. For the Masons' Hall meeting, see *Novascotian*, 6 November 1840.
21. *Acadian Recorder*, 7 November 1840.
22. *Novascotian*, 29 October 1840.
23. *Novascotian*, 12 November 1840.
24. *Novascotian*, 21 January 1841.
25. See David Sutherland, "William Stairs," *DCB*, Vol. IX. For what follows I have relied almost entirely on this biography. The idea of the succession from Lawson to Forrester then to Stairs is mine however.
26. See J. Murray Beck, *Joseph Howe, op. cit.*, p. 257 and note No. 81.
27. *Novascotian*, 17 April 1843. As quoted in Beck, *Joseph Howe, op., cit.* p. 258.
28. The principal source for the quarrel between Howe, the Reformers and Halifax Irish Catholics is the newspapers of the day. The origin and outcome is analysed in Beck, *Joseph Howe, op. cit.*, pp. 262-64, and Terrence Punch, *Irish Halifax: The Immigrant Generation, 1815-1859*, Ethnic Heritage Series, Vol. V, (Saint Mary's University, Halifax, 1981), pp. 40-45.
29. *Morning Post*, 23 November 1843.
30. *Times*, 28 November 1843.
31. *Times*, 5 December 1843. The totals were later revised to McNab 775, Uniacke 633 and Stairs 606. See also Terrence Punch in *Irish Halifax, op. cit.*, pp. 44-45. A breakdown of voters would appear as below:

Candidate	Plumpers	Split Votes Reformers	Split Votes Uniacke/Ref	Totals
McNab	8	581	186	775
Stairs	14	581	11	606
Uniacke	436	n/a	197	633

The total number voting was given in the *Times* as 1,236 and can be confirmed by adding together the split votes for reformers of 581, the total plumpers of 458 and the 197 split votes for Uniacke/Reformers, for a grand total of 1,236 individual voters.

32. *Times*, 9 January 1843.
33. Mather Almon to S. B. Robie, 30 November 1843, MG 1, Vol. 793, No. 187, PANS.
34. For Doyle, see Charles Bruce Fergusson, *DCB*, Vol. IX and Terrence Punch, "Larry Doyle and Nova Scotia" in *Talamh An Eisc: Canadian and Irish Essays*, edited by Cyril J. Byrne and Margaret Harry (Nimbus, Halifax, 1986), pp. 166-79.
35. *Times*, 19 December 1843.
36. See Beck, *Joseph Howe, op. cit.*, pp. 274-77.
37. *Novascotian*, 17 February 1845.
38. *Ibid.*, 24 February 1845.
39. *Standard and Conservative Advocate* (hereafter *Standard*), 29 June 1847.
40. See Terrence Punch, *Irish Halifax, op. cit.*, pp. 45-46.
41. David Sutherland, "The Merchants of Halifax," *op. cit.*, pp. 403-4.
42. *Standard*, 7 May 1847.
43. *Ibid.*, 14 May 1847.
44. MG1, Vol. 200, No. 22A, PANS.
45. *Morning Post*, 9 June 1847, and *Novascotian*, 14 June 1847.
46. For the conservative use of ledger influence and the class aspect, see David Sutherland, "The Merchants of Halifax," *op. cit.*, pp. 403-4.
47. The broadside is in the Akins Library, AK F107 H13V, PANS. In what follows I have used David Sutherland's analysis of the broadsheet for merchant voting and Terrence Punch's analysis of religious voting: see "Merchants of Halifax," *op. cit.*, pp. 405-6; and *Irish Halifax, op. cit.*, p. 46.

48. A copy of Watt's letter to the Moderator of the Sessions, 10 September 1847, is in MG1, Vol. 3362, No. 12, PANS.
49. *Standard,* 6 August 1847.
50. David Sutherland, "Merchants of Halifax," *op. cit.,* p. 406.
51. Below is a correlation of the 1847 voting numbers by party for Halifax in the township election, as given in the broadsheet, with data from the 1851 census, showing percentage of heads of families who voted, and number of mechanics and merchants (the only two occupations recorded) living in each ward in 1851. The merchant classification included storekeepers. The wealthy lived mostly in wards one and two. In ward one, for example, there were 18 conservatives with estates valued at £1,000 or more and another 11 whose estates were between £500 and £1,000, whereas there were just three liberals whose estates were valued at over £1,000 and another seven between £500 and £1,000.

Ward	Voters	Families	Mechanics	Merchants
One	Cons 84	23%	123	109
	Libs 51			
Two	Cons 60	20%	81	41
	Libs 41			
Three	Cons 53	18%	524	20
	Libs 73			
Four	Cons 22	24%	184	139
	Libs 65			
Five	Cons 116	20%	421	110
	Libs 165			
Six	Cons 61	32%	151	29
	Libs 62			

The final totals for the township gave McNab 873, Doyle 818, Uniacke 676 and Grassie 655.

52. *Acadian Recorder,* 7 August 1847.
53. The data come from a town census done in 1791 and from the 1851 Provincial Census. For the 1791 census see Thomas Beamish Akins, "History of Halifax City," *Collections* of the Nova Scotia Historical Society, Vol. VIII, p. 103, and for the 1851 census see RG1, Vol. 451, PANS.

CHAPTER 4

1. For a recent history of the building of the dyke, see Brent Fox, *The Wellington Dyke: A History of the Canard River Dyke System* (Kings County Historical Society, Kentville, 1990). Marjory Whitelaw also kindly provided information from a manuscript she has prepared on the Wellington Dyke.
2. Debra McNabb, "Land and Families in Horton Township, N.S., 1760-1830" (M.A. Thesis, University of British Columbia, 1986), p. 72.
3. See *ibid.,* p. 82. Although the poll tax returns are not a precise count of heads of households, let alone freeholders, it serves as the best indicator that we have of the number of potential freeholders, that is those adult males who might have owned sufficient property to qualify as electors. The poll tax returns for Horton, Cornwallis and Aylesford Townships for 1791 total 591 individuals; say another 100 for Parrsborough, for which no records survive, and you have a county total of around 700.
4. The petition was reproduced in *JHA,* 12 February 1812. It is three pages long. In his charges against Crane, Chipman goes into much detail on the methods used by Crane to qualify voters without, in fact, transferring property.
5. *Free Press,* 4 March 1817.
6. RG1, Vol. 289, no. 48, PANS.
7. *Free Press,* 23 March 1819.
8. *Acadian Recorder,* 4 July 1818.
9. *Halifax Journal,* 26 June 1820. Hunt's speech was taken down verbatim by a "By-Stander" on 22 June. A transcript or copy of Hunt's letter to freeholders, which I attribute to Hunt, is in the Chipman family papers, MG1, Vol. 189, No. 138, PANS.
10. Beamish Murdoch, *History of Nova-Scotia or Acadie, op. cit.,* Vol. III, p. 99, and Lord Dalhousie's Journal, 1817, 6 October, transcript, MG1, Vol. 1776, PANS.
11. Crane wrote a lengthy detailed article "On Diking" for the *Acadian Recorder,* 27 February 1819.

12. Matthew Richey records in his *Memoir of the late Rev. William Black ...* (Halifax, 1839), p. 179: "through the mercy of God, Mr. Crane did not die. In his last affliction he was led to meet God with whole heart." Richey was writing of Crane not having a conversion experience until on his deathbed, for in 1817. On the formation of a Methodist Missionary Society, Crane appears as one of the stewards for Horton.

13. For what follows I have relied on a letter of William Allen Chipman to S. G. W. Archibald explaining the reasons for his defeat. The letter is dated 24 June 1826, see MG1, Vol. 89, No. 61, PANS.

14. *Novascotian,* 17 and 23 November 1836

15. *Novascotian,* 23 April and 10 September 1840.

16. "Common Sense" in the *Novascotian,* 1 October 1840.

17. *Times,* 21 November 1843. The *Times* argued that while Howe was an Executive Councillor, Falkland gave him control of patronage. The paper listed the appointments that went to Reformers and friends of Howe, including the registrar of probate for Kings County, which went to Samuel Chipman's nephew, William Henry Chipman.

18. *Christian Messenger,* 13 October 1843.

19. *Novascotian,* 20 November 1843. Pleasant Valley was near present-day Berwick.

20. *Times,* 21 March and 21 November 1843. The Chipman family (including the Whiddens) had held the office of sheriff from 1801 to 1838. In 1843, members of the Chipman family occupied the offices of prothonotary, chief magistrate, clerk of the sessions, collector of customs, judge of the inferior court and register of probate, as well as William Allen and Samuel being justices of the peace.

21. The claims against his estate nearly exceeded its value, including a still-outstanding mortgage of £470 with the Halifax Banking Company that almost certainly dated back to heavy borrowing in the 1820s for the building of the great Wellington Dyke, for which William Allen was one of the commissioners. For Chipman's indebtedness caused by the building of the Wellington Dyke, see his letter to S.G.W. Archibald, 24 June 1826, MG1, Vol. 89, No. 61, in which he asks Archibald to intervene with James Forman (the cashier of the bank) about the debt.

22. *Times,* 15 December 1843.

23. *JHA,* 28 March 1845 and RG5, Series P, Vol. 8A, No. 95; and Vol. 9, No. 12, PANS. Benjamin refused to pay the fees for a scrutiny demanded by Johnson and transferred all his personal and real property to his son, so that it would not be worthwhile to sue him. See RG5, Series P, Vol. 8A, No. 64, PANS.

24. *Novascotian,* 1 April 1844.

25. *Ibid.*

26. *Novascotian,* 26 May 1845.

27. The story is reproduced in John Duncanson, *Falmouth: A New England Township in Nova Scotia 1760-1965* (Mika Facsimile of the 1965 edition, Belleville, Ontario, 1990), p. 157.

28. *Novascotian,* 22 June 1845. Also see Judith Tulloch, "William Cottnam Tonge," *DCB,* Vol. VI, and my *The Loyalist Governor* (Petheric Press, Halifax, 1983), pp. 114-25.

29. For Wentworth's correspondence on Tonge and his use of patronage, see Margaret Ells' "Governor Wentworth's Patronage," *Collections,* NSHS, Vol. 25, pp. 49-73.

30. Gerald S. Graham, "The Gypsum Trade of the Maritime Provinces: Its Relation to American Diplomacy and Agriculture in the Early Nineteenth Century," *Agricultural History,* Vol. 12, No. 3 (July, 1938), p. 210.

31. *Free Press,* 23 March 1819.

32. *Ibid.,* 16 March 1819, and *Acadian Recorder,* 20 March 1819.

33. As quoted in Marjory Whitelaw, ed., *The Dalhousie Journals* (Oberon Press, 1978), p. 64.

34. *Acadian Recorder,* 20 January 1820, and *Novascotian,* 2 April 1825, as quoted in David Sutherland's "Merchants of Halifax, 1815-1850," *op. cit.,* p. 147.

35. As quoted in J. Murray Beck, "William Henry Otis Haliburton," *DCB,* Vol. VI.

36. *Acadian Recorder,* 31 October 1829. The English statute was 2 Geo. II, cap. 24 (1729). In 1817 the Assembly undertook a major revision of the acts regulating elections (57 Geo. III, cap. 7). Section 6 stated that any person or persons convicted of bribery at elections should suffer "all the penalties prescribed by the Laws of England, for such offences." For the petition to the Supreme Court, see Beamish Murdoch, *Epitome of the Laws of Nova Scotia,* Vol. 1 (Halifax, 1832), p. 71. In neither the Supreme Court records nor the newspapers have I found mention of the petition or its final disposition. The case, but not the petition, is noted by John Garner, *The Franchise and Politics in British North America 1755-1867, op. cit.,* p. 181.

37. William Blowers Bliss to Lewis Bliss, 14 April 1831, MG1, Vol. 1599, PANS.

38. See Lois Kernaghan, "Lewis Morris Wilkins," *DCB,* Vol. XI.

39. Petition of Joseph Dill, 4 March 1833, RG5, Series P, Vol. 4, No. 65. See also Deane White to his brother Cornelius, 2 February 1833, MG1, Vol. 955, No. 1312, PANS.

40. *Acadian Recorder,* Letter VIII, 17 September 1836.

41 *Hants & K[ings] Gazette,* 31 March, 16 June and 21 July 1834.

42. *Acadian,* 7 February 1834.

43. This story of Wilkins' decision to run as a Howite liberal comes from Charles Rohan "Parliamentary Portraits, Painted with Pen and Ink," *Acadian Recorder,* 26 April 1856. Rohan despised Wilkins for his ambition and political opportunism. I am indebted to Lois Yorke for giving me the reference to his letter. See also "Lewis Morris Wilkins," *op. cit.*

44. *Novascotian,* 16 and 26 February 1844. Young's reply to the organizers was reproduced in the *Novascotian,* 28 July 1845, in the report of the Falmouth meeting, which was chaired by Young's old opponent, John Manning.

CHAPTER 5

1. Jonathan Hoar to Thomas Hancock, 12 November 1759, Hancock Papers, Box 9, Folder 4, New England Historical and Genealogical Society. I am grateful to Ms. Brenda Dunn of the Canadian Parks Service for bringing this letter to my attention.

2. For what follows on the election, see W.A. Calnek and A.W. Savary, *History of Annapolis County* (originally published in 1897, Mika reprint, 1980), pp. 344-57; A.W. Savary, *Supplement* (Toronto, 1913, Mika reprint, 1980), pp. 37-40; "Poll Book for the County of Annapolis, 1786," *Nova Scotia Historical Review,* Vol. 1, No. 2, 1981, pp. 106-24; petition of Robert Tucker, RG5, Series A, Vol. 1b, No. 153, PANS; *The Royal Gazette and the New Brunswick Advertiser,* 27 December 1785 and 28 February 1786; and controverted elections, RG5, Series E, Vol. 1, PANS.

3. *JHA,* 23 June 1786.

4. David Seabury to Captain Geo. Cornwall, 14 December 1785, MG1, Vol. 2616, No.1, PANS.

5. W.A. Calnek, *History of Annapolis County, op. cit.,* p. 356.

6. For Barclay, Howe and Millidge, see Judith Tuloch, "Thomas Barclay," DCB, Vol. VI; and for Millidge, see Carol Ann Janzen, "Thomas Millidge," *DCB,* Vol. V.

7. See George DeLancey Hanger, "The Life of Loyalist Colonel DeLancey," *Nova Scotia Historical Review,* Vol. 3, No. 2, pp. 39-56.

8. As quoted in Lois Kernaghan, "Alexander Howe," *DCB,* Vol. V.

9. The speeches are recorded in Beamish Murdoch, *History of Nova Scotia,* Vol. III (Halifax, 1867), pp. 67-68.

10. *Ibid.,* p. 92.

11. Proceedings of the House of Assembly, *The Nova-Scotia Magazine,* May 1790, pp. 382-83.

12. For Moody, see Susan Shenstone, "Loyalist Squire, Loyalist Church," *Nova Scotia Historical Review,* Vol. 3, No. 2, pp. 71-88, and Stuart R.J. Sutherland, "James Moody," *DCB,* Vol. V.

13. There were three generations of Phineas Lovetts. The first Phineas (1711-1801), who was MLA 1770-74, married (1) Hannah Merriam and (2) Beulah Morse; a son

Phineas (1745-1828) married Abigil Thayer and they had sons Phineas (1772-1841) and James Russell (1781-1864). It was the third Phineas who married Margaret Rutherford in 1800. Winniett's return for the election has Phineas Lovett Jr. as the candidate. As Phineas Lovett I was dead, I believe that the "junior" must have referred to the third generation son and not to Phineas Lovett II as given in Shirley Elliott's *The Legislative Assembly of Nova Scotia.*

14. Nathaniel White to his father Gideon, 23 November 1815 and 11 January 1817, MG1, Vol. 953, Nos. 1023 and 1039, PANS.

15. The examination of Major R. Hutchinson before the bar of the Assembly, 24 March, as reported in the *Acadian Recorder,* 27 March 1819 and RG5, Series P, Vol. 1, No. 57, PANS. The poll book for the election is Nos. 29 and 30.

16. W.A. Calnek, *History of Annapolis County, op. cit.,* p. 416. It is uncertain what Calnek, or more likely Savary, meant by "extraordinary tact," but in 1819 the Lovett family estate at Round Hill had been sold and there was a resulting court case in which Phineas Lovett and his father were defendants.

17. See reports for the western and eastern districts of Annapolis County in *Bulletin of the Public Archives of Nova Scotia: A documentary study of early educational policy,* Vol. 1, No. 1 (Halifax, 1937), pp. 7-13. Peleg Wiswall was the author of the report of the western district which accounts for its eccentric phrasing; nonetheless, it provides a remarkable insight into the actual state of education in the 1820s and the attitude of such men of classical education as Wiswall to the apparent ignorance they found around them.

18. Joseph Warner, Letter VIII, *Acadian Recorder,* 17 September 1836.

19. Part of the poll book, dated 14 July 1824, has survived in MG1, Vol. 714, No. 10, PANS.

20. *Colonial Patriot,* 21 March 1828.

21. Thomas C. Haliburton, *History of Nova Scotia,* Vol. II, pp. 17-18. The biographical literature on Haliburton is vast. The *DCB* by Fred Cogswell in Vol. IX has a good overview of the man and the literature.

22. The itemized invoice has survived for the Sissaboo poll in which Wiswall and Ritchie account with Cereno Upham Jones for the costs of the open house. MG1, Vol. 2421, No. 17, PANS.

23. *Novascotian,* 30 September 1830.

24. For this contest see an "Extract of a Letter," dated Annapolis, 13 October, *Novascotian,* 20 October 1830 and a reply addressed to Mr. Howe, *Novascotian,* 17 November 1830.

25. The business of the store burning and its effects on Ruggles' mental stability are recorded in Calnek, *History of Annapolis County, op. cit.,* pp. 408-9. Both Calnek (Savary) and the *Acadian Recorder,* 26 November 1831, say the burning was unconnected with the election. Aside from an act of revenge, the arsonist may have had in mind the destruction of Ruggles' ledgers. Certainly settling his estate was complicated by the fire. His total estate came to £10,183 (with interestingly another $22,976 held in New York) and the debts were rated good, bad and doubtful. Even ten years later the estate was not settled and was still owed £3,875.

26. The first petition with one thousand signatures is dated 28 February 1833 and the second is undated but filed with those for 1833. The petitions are in RG 5, Series P, Vol. 4, Nos. 62 and 79, PANS.

27. *Novascotian,* 23 November 1836.

28. Calnek (Savary) gives the background to the 1836 county election, *History of Annapolis County, op. cit.,* pp. 286-87.

29. *Ibid.,* p. 436.

30. *Novascotian,* 3 December 1840.

31. *Novascotian,* 21 January 1841.

32. The poll book has survived in RG 5, Series E, Vol. 20, PANS. See also petition by Delap's supporters in RG 5, Series P, Vol. 8, No. 48, PANS and the counter petition, No. 58, by Thorne's friends.

33. *Novascotian,* 1 April 1841.

34. For the biographical details on Johnston I have relied extensively on David Sutherland's excellent article in the *DCB,* Vol. X. The suc-

ceeding quotes are all from this source.

35. MG1, Vol. 2, No. 154, PANS.
36. This is David Sutherland's view. See his *DCB* article, *op. cit.*
37. *Christian Messenger,* 21 and 28 July 1843.
38. *Christian Messenger,* 17 November 1843.
39. W. A. Calnek, *History of Annapolis County, op. cit.,* pp. 445-46. Calnek stated that the Baptists were bitterly divided and the majority supported Chipman; Savary has a note stating he always supposed the opposite and this is borne out by the final vote totals.
40. *Novascotian,* 6 November 1843. I hold the opinion that a good many of the similar letters that appeared in the *Novascotian* and other papers at this time were authored for party purposes; it is doubtful in this case if the author was either a Tory or an Anglican.
41. See David Sutherland, "J.W. Johnston and the Metamorphosis of Nova Scotia Conservatism" (unpublished M.A. thesis, Dalhousie University, 1967), p. 106, for a description of this election. The "granite" story comes from the *Times,* 6 February 1844.
42. *Times,* 12 December 1843.
43. David Sutherland, "J.W. Johnston and the Metamorphosis of Nova Scotia Conservatism," *op. cit.,* p. 170. The thesis is particularly good in describing the anti-Catholic aspects of the conservative campaign, pp. 170-71.
44. *Novascotian,* 12 July 1847, as quoted in *ibid,* p. 171.
45. *Novascotian,* 14 January 1841. See also the issue for 3 December 1840.
46. J.-Alphonse Deveau, "Anselm-François Comeau," *DCB,* Vol. IX.

CHAPTER 6
1. See Winthrop Pickard Bell, *The "Foreign Protestants" and the Settlement of Nova Scotia* (University of Toronto Press, Toronto, 1961), pp. 533-39; petition of Ferdinando John Paris to the Board of Trade, 27 January 1758, CO 217, Vol. 16, PRO. Bell's book, of course, is the pre-eminent source for the settlement of Lunenburg.

2. See A. A. MacKenzie, "Sebastian Zouberbuhler," *DCB,* Vol. IV.
3. For Knaut see J. Murray Beck, "Philip Augustus Knaut," *DCB,* Vol. IV.
4. See J. Murray Beck, "John Creighton," *DCB,* Vol. V.
5. See J. Murray Beck, "Dettlieb Christopher Jessen," *DCB,* Vol. V.
6. For Wilkins, see Phyllis R. Blakeley, "Lewis Morris Wilkins," *DCB,* Vol. VII.
7. Edward James to John William Schwartz, 18 January 1792, and James to Richard Bulkeley, 25 January 1792, RG1, Vol. 248, PANS. Although he had a farm, James seems to have lived entirely on his half-pay and later what he could take in fees as a justice of the peace.
8. See petitions by Schwartz and James, RG5, Series A, Vol. 7, 20 February 1800, PANS.
9. Joseph Pernette to Garrett Miller?, 18 March 1805, MG1, Vol. 584 and petition of Miller, RG5, Series A, Vol. 13, 2 December 1806, PANS.
10. Lott Church to the Freeholders of Lunenburg, *Acadian Recorder,* 24 June 1826. His letter, which was dated the same day as the newspaper, is a good example of how newspapers were increasingly politically important outside of Halifax.
11. See Creighton's letter to Joseph Parke of New Dublin, 31 August 1830, MG1, Vol. 605, Folder No. 1, PANS.
12. *Novascotian,* December 1836; petition of Lott Church and others, RG5, Series P, Vol. 6, No. 121; Garrett Miller to the Rev. Thomas Shreve, 23 January 1837, MG1, Vol. 605, Folder 2, PANS and *JHA,* 3 March 1837.
13. *Morning Chronicle,* 28 October 1845. For Howe's campaigning in Lunenburg and its role in the liberal victory, I am indebted to J. Murray Beck, who kindly sent me a draft of his analysis of the 1847 election in Lunenburg County.
14. See D.C. Harvey, ed., *The Diary of Simeon Perkins 1780-1789* (Toronto, 1958), p.xxx.
15. *Ibid.,* 14 March 1787, p. 362. For Alexander Brymer's wealth and in-

fluence, see Barry Cahill, "Alexander Brymer," *DCB*, Vol. VI.

16. Simeon Perkins to Samuel Hart, 14 March 1793, reproduced in Charles Bruce Fergusson, ed., *The Diary of Simeon Perkins 1804-1812* (Toronto, 1978), p. 430.
17. Charles Bruce Fergusson, ed., *The Diary of Simeon Perkins 1790-1796*, 4 March 1793, p. 214, and Perkins to Sampson Salter Blowers, 13 March 1793, reproduced in *The Diary of Simeon Perkins 1804-1812*, p. 429.
18. For the bill see RG5, Series U, Vol. 2, 1797, PANS.
19. Simeon Perkins to Capt Patrick Doran, 9 April 1798, reproduced in *The Diary of Simeon Perkins 1804-1812*, p. 454-55 and Perkins to Uniacke, April 25, p. 455.
20. As quoted in C. Bruce Fergusson, "Simeon Perkins," *DCB*, Vol. V.
21. Charles Bruce Fergusson, *The Diary of Simeon Perkins 1797-1803* (Toronto, 1967), 5 March 1801, p. 288. As soon as young Cochran was called to the bar from Lincoln's Inn, the British government appointed him Chief Justice of Prince Edward Island and in 1803 made him a judge of the Upper Canada Court of King's Bench; he drowned a year later while crossing Lake Ontario. Consequently, if he had been elected, he would have had to resign his seat immediately to take up his Prince Edward Island appointment.
22. *Novascotian*, 15 March 1826.
23. For the Barry Affair, including Gough's letter, see "Reminiscences of Our Native Land," reprinted in the *Liverpool Advance*, 19 and 26 April, 6 and 31 May 1899 and found in the T.B. Smith Genealogies, MG1, Vol 819, PANS.
24. As quoted in John Grant, "Zenas Waterman," *DCB*, Vol. XI; see also Waterman Collection, MG1, Vol. 933, No. 2, PANS.

CHAPTER 7
1. Clifford K. Shipton, ed., *Sibley's Harvard Graduates* (Boston, 1975), Vol. XVII, 1768-1771, p. 430.
2. At his death in 1804, Utley's real and personal estate, including money owed him, was £467 of which £323 was in outstanding debts from 76

individuals. Yarmouth County Probate Records.
3. The *Yarmouth Herald and Western Advertiser* (hereafter *Yarmouth Herald*), 9 January 1897.
4. J.R. Campbell, *A History of the County of Yarmouth* (St. John, 1876), p. 84.
5. G.S. Brown, *Yarmouth, Nova Scotia* (Boston, 1888), p. 50. Brown says incorrectly that Clements retired from the field at the pleading of Poole; in fact, Poole petitioned the Assembly, see *JHA*, 15 November, and 4,6 and 11 December 1830.
6. *Yarmouth Herald*, 9 January 1897.
7. I am most grateful to Peter Crowell, the Municipal Historian of the District of Argyle, for providing me with much material on Argyle and for reading the section on the township.
8. There is no full biography of Huntington, but see A. A. MacKenzie, "Herbert Huntington," *DCB*, Vol. VIII.
9. *Novascotian*, 10 February 1836.
10. *Yarmouth Herald*, 13 November and 23 December 1836.
11. *Ibid.*
12. *JHA*, 1 March 1836.
13. Louis Comeau, "Simon D'Entremont," *DCB*, Vol. XI and his obituaries in the *Yarmouth Herald*, 15 September 1886 and the *Presbyterian Witness*, 18 September 1886, p. 301.
14. *Novascotian*, 28 March 1840.
15. As quoted in A. A. MacKenzie, "Herbert Huntington," *op. cit.* Unless otherwise noted this paragraph is based on his *DCB* article.
16. *Novascotian*, 3 December 1840.
17. *Novascotian*, 1 April 1841.
18. *Christian Messenger*, 28 July 1843. Huntington was not wanting in political courage, but he had difficulty in dealing with Johnston's charges that Huntington and the others had not dealt fairly with the Executive Committee of the Baptist Educational Committee when it had petitioned the Assembly.
19. For the speeches of Clements, Huntington and Cook see the *Yarmouth Herald*, 29 November 1843.
20. *Ibid.*, 2 August 1847.
21. *Ibid.*, 5 August 1847.

22. This election is described in Edwin Crowell, *History of Barrington Township, Shelburne County, Nova Scotia 1604-1870, with a Biographical and Genealogical Appendix* (Yarmouth, 1923), pp. 296-98.

23. For biographical information on Sargent see H.L. Doane, *The Barrington Sargents* (Truro, N.S., 1916), and AO 12, Vol. 105/82 and AO 13, Bundle 49, Public Record Office, London.

24. As quoted in Phyllis R. Blakeley, "John Homer," *DCB*, Vol. VII.

25. John Homer, Esq., *A Brief Sketch of the Present State of The Province of Nova-Scotia, with a project offered for its relief* (Halifax, N.S., 1834).

26. *Acadian Recorder*, 24 March 1832.

27. As quoted in Phyllis R. Blakeley, "John Homer," *op. cit.*

28. Thomas Geddes to John Sargent, 1 and 27 December 1836, MG1, Vol. 1130, Nos. 7-14, PANS.

29. For the election, see Marion Robertson, *King's Bounty: A History of Early Shelburne* (Nova Scotia Museum, Halifax, N.S., 1983), pp. 169-70.

30. Both sides blamed Sheriff James Clarke. See James Clarke to Gideon White, 3 February and 9 March 1786, MG1, Vol. 949, Nos. 400 and 404, PANS. The totals for the County election were Leckie 601, McNeil 593, Ross 526 and Stanhope 507.

31. *JHA*, 14 March 1789. See also The Proceedings of the House of Assembly, *The Nova-Scotia Magazine*, pp. 304-5.

32. Jared Chipman to Gideon White, 28 March 1818, MG1, Vol. 953, PANS.

33. Jared Chipman to Gideon White, 4 July 1820, MG1, Vol. 954, No. 1107, PANS.

34. Gideon White to John Sargent, 26 April 1801, MG1, Vol. 797B, No. 30, PANS.

35. The poll book for this election is in the White Family Papers, MG1, Vol. 954, No. 1158, PANS. The 1827 Census for Shelburne Township has the religion and occupation of heads of households, most of whom can be classed as freeholders. With the aid of a computer, the data from the poll book and the census

were correlated to determine the degree of religious voting. The same was done for occupations but the results showed no pattern of voting by occupation for either candidate.

36. Nathaniel White to his brother Cornelius, 4 September 1824, MG1, Vol. 954, No. 1159, PANS.

37. The poll book for the 1826 election has also survived and a similar analysis done as for the 1824 election, and the two results then compared. The 1826 poll book is in RG5, Series R, Vol. 9, PANS.

38. "Reminiscences of Our Native Land," *op. cit.*, p. 40.

39. *Ibid.*, pp. 50-56.

40. Nathaniel White to his brother Cornelius, 16 April 1830, MG1, Vol. 954, No. 1232, PANS.

41. The poll book for the 1836 election is in RG5, Series R, Vol. 23, PANS.

42. *Novascotian*, 27 February 1840

43. *Novascotian*, 24 December 1840.

44. The poll book for the 1840 election is in RG5, Series E, Vol. 19, PANS.

45. *Novascotian*, 24 December 1840.

46. *Novascotian*, 16 February and 16 March 1846.

CHAPTER 8

1. Robert MacKinnon and Graeme Wynn, "Nova Scotian Agriculture in the 'Golden Age': A New Look" in Douglas Day, ed., *Geographical Perspectives on the Maritime Provinces* (Saint Mary's University, Halifax, 1988), p. 51.

2. For this aspect of the Cumberland or Eddy Rebellion, see Ernest A. Clarke, "Cumberland Planters and the Aftermath of the Attack on Fort Cumberland" in Margaret Conrad, ed., *They Planted Well: New England Planters in Maritime Canada*, (Acadiensis Press, Fredericton, New Brunswick, 1988) pp. 42-60.

3. The extent of Roach's ledger influence can be partially judged from a surviving account which shows that in 1811 he was owed £2,252 by 128 individuals in the Bay Verte area alone. MG1, Manuscript File, Thomas Roach, PANS.

4. Roach described the plan to S.B. Robie, dated 7 August 1818, MG1, Vol. 793, No. 28, PANS.

5. For biographies of Stewart, see that by the Honourable Charles J. Townsend (a grandson), "Life of the Hon-

orable Alexander Stewart, C.B." in
Collections of the Nova Scotia Historical Society, Vol. XV, pp. 1-114, and that of J. Murray Beck, "Alexander Stewart," *DCB*, Vol. IX.

6. *Colonial Patriot*, 21 May 1828.
7. *Hants' & King's County Gazette*, 31 March 1834.
8. For the political career of Andrew McKim, see James Smith, "Andrew McKim, Reformer," *The Nova Scotia Historical Quarterly*, Vol. 8, No. 3, September 1978, pp. 225-242.
9. *Novascotian*, 2 November 1836 and 4, 11, and 19 January 1837. For the verse, see James Smith, "Andrew McKim, Reformer," *op. cit.*, p. 228.
10. See Eldon Hay, "The Reverend Alexander Clarke and the Cumberland Covenanters," *Nova Scotia Historical Review*, Vol. 112, No. 1, 1992, pp. 96-118. Scottish Covenanters had never accepted the 1690 church and state settlement arrived at during the reign of William and Mary. Consequently, Covenanters had refused to vote in elections, to take an oath in the name of the king, or to hold any office where such an oath was required. Since the publication of his article, Professor Hay and I have had considerable correspondence on Clarke's political intervention; in voting Clarke was prepared to face excommunication from his church. In 1847 the Irish Synod of the church struck Clarke from its roll and the following year Clarke joined the more liberal and American New School Synod.
11. The following analysis by religion and residence of this election is based on the surviving county poll book in RG 5, Series R, Vol. 25, PANS. The voter list is correlated with the Cumberland County 1827 census return; the census for the county in 1838 has never been located, though the summary exists.
12. Dickey had joined the Covenanters or Reformed Presbyterians in 1828 and remained a faithful member until his death. In the strict sense Logan was likely not a member, but quite possibly an adherent; he was certainly a Presbyterian. My thanks to Professor Eldon for this distinction.

13. *Novascotian*, 10 April 1838. For the "Character of Andrew McKIM, Esqr." see the *Novascotian*, 31 December 1840.
14. *Novascotian*, 9 March 1837.
15. *JHA*, 24 March 1840.
16. "Character of Andrew McKIM Esqr.," *op. cit.*
17. *Times*, 12 December 1843.
18. For Howe's foray into Cumberland, see *Novascotian*, 14, 21 and 28 October 1844; *Morning Post*, 23 November 1844; and *Times*, 22 October 1844. The report in the last by A Subscriber is probably the most accurate; the reports by Richard Nugent in the *Novascotian* are suspect.
19. To the Farmers of Cumberland, signed ALPHA PI, *Acadian Recorder*, 31 July 1847.
20. As quoted in Donald Chard, "Mariot Arbuthnot," *DCB*, Vol. IV.
21. Letter XI To the Freeholders of Nova Scotia, *Acadian Recorder*, 15 October 1836.
22. As quoted in Israel Longworth, *Life of S.G.W. Archibald* (Halifax, N.S., 1881), pp. 115-20.
23. *Novascotian*, 30 November 1836.
24. The Petition of A. Peppard and others, February 1837, RG5, Series P, Vol. 6, No. 86, PANS.
25. Parliamentary Portraits, *Acadian Recorder*, 5 July 1856.
26. See P. B. Waite, "Gloud Wilson McLelan," *DCB*, Vol. VIII.
27. *Novascotian*, 27 February 1840.
28. *Novascotian*, 3 December 1840.
29. *Ibid.*
30. *Novascotian*, 6 May, 12 August and 14 October 1841, and *Pictou Observer*, 25 January 1842.
31. Letter from Colchester in the *Novascotian*, 27 November 1843.
32. *Novascotian*, 25 March 1841, and A. A. MacKenzie, "Herbert Huntington," *DCB*, Vol. VIII.
33. MG1, Vol. 1729, No. 62, n.d. but watermark reads 1842, PANS. This petition was signed by farmers residing in New Annan, Earltown and Tatamagouche.
34. *Novascotian*, 23 October 1843.
35. *Yarmouth Herald*, 29 July 1847.
36. McLelan to Joseph Howe and William Young, February 1850, MG1, Vol. 183, No. 48, PANS. He is giving advice on the liberals sending

agents to each county to give an hour or two schooling on getting deeds recorded before the next election. As well, he recommends that liberals should go from house to house and make a list of those friendly to the party who could be made freeholders.

CHAPTER 9

1. The poem was written in Gaelic and fairly widely distributed in Scotland. He lies buried in Glenbard Cemetery, Antigonish County, a provincially registered heritage property. For attitudes to emigration/immigration, see D. Campbell and R. A. MacLean, *Beyond The Atlantic Roar* (Carleton Library, No. 78, 1974), pp. 7-34.
2. The basic source remains *Immigration To and Emigration From Nova Scotia 1815-1838,* prepared by J. S. Martell and published by PANS in 1942. The figure of 17,500 is taken from Stephen J. Hornsby's *Nineteenth-Century Cape Breton: A Historical Geography* (McGill-Queen's Press, Montreal & Kingston, 1992), p. 45. Where Cape Breton agriculture and settlement are concerned I have drawn liberally on Hornsby's first-class work. For the second quote that begins this chapter, see MG 100, Vol. 174, No. 34, PANS.
3. Alan R. McNeil, "A Reconsideration of the State of Agriculture in Eastern Nova Scotia, 1791-1861" (unpublished M.A. thesis, Queen's University, 1985), p. 65. For what follows on the state of agriculture in Pictou and Antigonish Counties, I have relied extensively on this work.
4. Robert MacKinnon and Graeme Wynn, "Nova Scotian Agriculture in the 'Golden Age': A New Look," op. cit., p. 55.
5. *Ibid,* p. 91.
6. See Kenneth Donovan, " 'May Learning Flourish': The Beginnings of a Cultural Awakening in Cape Breton During the 1840s" in Kenneth Donovan, ed., *The Island: New Perspectives on Cape Breton History, 1713-1990* (University of Cape Breton Press, Sydney, 1990), pp. 89-112.
7. See an Account of Receipts & Expenditures of Monies Subscribed for Mr. Thomas Dickson's Election, February 1838, MG1, Vol. 324, No. 299, PANS. In the original manuscript for his *History of Pictou County,* George Patterson states on page 182 that McKenzie was a man of superior talents, but his life did not manifest a high standard of ministerial conduct. He died a few weeks after the election. The manuscript copy of Patterson's *History* is in the University of King's College Library, Halifax. I am grateful to Allan Dunlop for pointing out the reference to McKenzie.
8. Petition of Abraham Patterson, 17 February 1840, RG5, Series GP, Vol. 1, No. 93, PANS.
9. *Mechanic and Farmer,* Pictou, 25 November 1840.
10. *Ibid.,* 2 December 1840.
11. As early as 1828, Smith borrowed £2,500 from Samuel Cunard, but repaid him by 1835. The details of the second loan from Cunard for £5,802 can be found in the Chancery Court records, RG36, Vol. 1434, PANS. For the £4,292 worth of debts, see Pictou County deeds, Book 26, p. 414. Smith was able to discharge most of this sum and also a further loan from S.G.W. Archibald for £128. What may have precipitated Almon's decision to sue for the remainder due him (£2,309) was his discovery that apparently some of property for which he held the mortgage was also mortgaged as collateral for Smith's other debts.
12. As quoted in J. Murray Beck, "George Renny Young," *DCB,* Vol. VIII.
13. *Acadian Recorder,* 14 November 1843. See also Lois K. Kernaghan, "Martin Isaac Wilkins," *DCB,* Vol. XI.
14. *The Eastern Chronicle,* Pictou, 28 December 1843, provided a complete analysis of the vote. A total of 2,689 out of about 3,400 of the estimated heads of householders were polled, a high number compared to other counties.
15. See TO THE PRESBYTERIANS OF PICTOU TOWNSHIP from a Presbyterian, *Eastern Chronicle,* 29 November 1843.

16. For this election battle see RG5, Series P, Vol. 9, Nos. 55, 56, 57 and 59, all petitions to the Assembly, and a reprint from the *Eastern Chronicle* that appeared in the *Novascotian,* 24 March 1845.
17. For one of few surviving itemized lists of election expenses, see MG1, Vol. 324, No. 299, PANS. Everything from provisions, candles, and flags to the payment of servants is listed.
18. See Young to James D. B. Fraser, 26 January 1847, MG1, Vol. 324, No. 283, PANS.
19. See Judith Tulloch, "Thomas Cutler," *DCB,* Vol. VII.
20. A. C. Jost, *Guysborough Sketches and Essays* (Kentville Publishing, Kentville, N.S., 1950), p. 199. Jost's chapter "The Political History of Guysborough County," pp. 184-205, is excellent.
21. See Judith Tulloch, "Joseph Marshall," *DCB,* Vol. VII.
22. This story is recorded in the Reverend D. J. Rankin's *A History of the County of Antigonish Nova Scotia* (MacMillan, Toronto, 1926), p. 16.
23. Marshall describes the "providential" series of happenings in his *Personal Narratives; with Reflections and Remarks* (Halifax, 1866), pp. 37-40. See also C. E. Thomas, John George Marshall, *DCB,* Vol. X.
24. For Fraser's clerical career see David B. Flemming, "William Fraser," *DCB,* Vol. VIII.
25. The story of this election can be found in John Young to his wife, Antigonish, 28 July 1824, MG2, Vol. 728, No. 639, and Sydney County Election, 1825, RG5, Series R, Vol. 7, PANS.
26. Petition to Thomas Dickson and John Young, 2 March 1825 found with *ibid.*
27. Thomas Cutler to John Young, 24 April 1826, MG2, Vol. 729, No. 800, PANS.
28. *Colonial Patriot,* 21 May 1828.
29. See "Memorandum of a conversation held today January 20, 1831 at Willowbank between the Honourable Judge Halliburton and John Young" in MG2, Vol. 729, No. 861, PANS.
30. The phrase "political extinction" was used by Longworth in his *Life of S. G. W. Archibald, op. cit.,* p. 122.
31. See a letter from Antigonish, dated 28 November 1840 and entitled "Family Compact Among The Radicals," in the *Times,* 15 December 1840.
32. See Phyllis Blakeley, "William Alexander Henry," *DCB,* Vol. XI.
33. For this election see Henry's petition, RG5, Series P, Vol. 8A, No. 74, PANS, and the *Times,* 26 December 1843. For the bribery conviction of Power, see the *Acadian Recorder,* 26 July 1826. The trial was held before the judges of the Supreme Court while on circuit. A record of the trial has not survived; one has for another trial involving Power involving a suit for debt, but there seems to be no connection between the two trials.
34. *Novascotian,* 23 February 1846.
35. *Novascotian,* 12 October 1846.
36. *Cape Breton Spectator,* 21 August 1847.
37. See Robert Morgan, "Separatism in Cape Breton 1820-45" in *Cape Breton at 200: Historical Essays in Honour of the Island's Bicentennial 1785-1985,* edited by Kenneth Donovan (University College of Cape Breton Press, Sydney, 1985), pp. 41-51. This is the chief study of the repeal movement and Cape Breton separatism and I have relied on it extensively.
38. See R. J. Morgan, "Laurence Kavanagh," *DCB,* Vol. VI.
39. See B. C. Cuthbertson, "Richard John Uniacke," *DCB,* Vol. VI.
40. Duncan Campbell, *History of Nova Scotia* (Montreal, 1873), p. 231. See also J. Murray Beck, "James Boyle Uniacke," *DCB,* Vol. VIII.
41. For this election see A. A. MacKenzie, *The Irish in Cape Breton* (Formac, Antigonish, 1979), p. 68, *Novascotian,* 21 October 1830, and J. D. W. White to his brother Cornelius, 20 October 1830, MG1, Vol. 955, No. 1242, PANS.
42. For Alexander MacDonell see A. A. Johnston, *A History of the Catholic Church in Eastern Nova Scotia,* Volume II, 1827-1880 (St. Francis Xavier University Press, Antigonish, 1971), page references as given in index.

43. For the election and the McKeagney brothers, see Robert Morgan, "Separatism in Cape Breton," *op. cit.*, p. 43; A. A. Johnston, *A History of the Catholic Church in Eastern Nova Scotia, op. cit.*, pp. 126-29 and other page references in index; A. A. MacKenzie, *The Irish in Cape Breton, op. cit.*, pp. 68-69; and RG5, Series E, Vol. 20, which contains the poll book, among other documents tabled with the select Assembly committee charged with investigating the election.

44. This comes from James D. Gillis, *The Great Election* (North Sydney, n.d., but c.1910), p. 11.

45. Chancery Court, RG36, No. 1398, PANS. McKeagney had the backing of a core of Catholics in Sydney and, more importantly, of the Irish Catholic "faction" in Halifax in their running battle with Bishop Fraser. See David Flemming, "William Fraser," *op. cit.*

46. As quoted in J. Murray Beck, "James Boyle Uniacke," *op. cit.*

47. *Cape-Breton Advocate*, 21 October 1840.

48. *Cape-Breton Advocate*, 4 and 11 November 1840. Richard Huntington, editor of the *Advocate*, supported Uniacke, though a non-resident, because he was for reform.

49. Petition of William C. Delaney, prepared by his attorney, L. O'Connor Doyle, 3 February 1841, RG5, Series P, Vol. 8, No. 57, PANS. The petition makes no mention of the presence of either Henry or Patrick McKeagney, but the fact that Bishop William Fraser removes the latter for becoming entangled in political affairs shortly after the election is evidence enough of his involvement; the bringing in of the Indians to vote was likely his doing. In the case of Henry, it seems too out of character for him not to have come to the aid of his brother.

50. Letter from McKeagney to the Freeholders of Richmond County, *Novascotian*, 12 August 1841.

51. As quoted in A. A. Johnston, *op. cit.*, p. 129.

52. The speech was printed in pamphlet form and circulated. A copy is in MG 100, Vol. 7, No. 8, PANS.

CHAPTER 10

1. Letter by Silas T. Rand in the *Christian Messenger*, 11 December 1840. He describes the results of a trip into Cumberland County to raise funds for Acadia College. I am indebted for the quote to Dorothy May Lovesey's *To Be A Pilgrim: A Biography of Silas Tertius Rand, 1810-1889* (Lancelot Press, Hantsport, N.S., 1992), p. 25. Dr. Lovesey notes that Rand came to dislike these "begging excursions."

2. When George Renny Young first arrived in Pictou to seek the reform candidacy for one of the two county seats, he began his campaign at Barney's River. Before speaking to freeholders there, he met with the resident Kirk minister to receive his blessings for the meeting. The freeholders were all of the Kirk and presumably of the minister's congregation. After hearing Young, they elected delegates to attend the New Glasgow meeting. Moreover, they instructed the delegates to advocate compromise. If no compromise was reached, they were to separate from the Kirk party. *Novascotian*, 15 January 1844.

3. The crucial importance of the West Indian trade to Nova Scotia and Halifax especially is analysed in Julian Gwyn, " 'A Little Province Like This': The Economy of Nova Scotia Under Stress, 1812-1853" in *Canadian Papers in Rural History*, Volume VI, edited by Donald H. Akenson (Langdale Press, Gananoque, 1988), pp. 192-225 and see concluding paragraphs p. 222.

4. Although as a group Anglicans were only marginally in favour of Pictou Academy, their support was critical because, of the number of individual members recorded as voting on the issue, close to half were Anglicans. The cross tabulations by religion for those whose voting on the question showed that they were strongly or at least marginally in support are:

Presbyterians—18 of the 20 who voted
Anglicans—39 of the 59 who voted
Baptists—8 of the 13 who voted
Church of Scotland—4 of the 12 who

voted
Methodists—5 of the 14 who voted
  Among the highest totals recorded were for Thomas Dickson and William Lawson, who voted 9 times in support and never against. James Shannon Morse voted 7 times in favour and once against. Charles Rufus Fairbanks voted 7 times in support and never against. The arch enemy of both Morse and Fairbanks, Alexander Stewart, voted 6 times in opposition and never for.

5. On Pictou Academy I have greatly simplified what was an extraordinarily complex story. The complexities are exceptionally well handled by Susan Buggey and Gwendolyn Davies in their jointly written article on Thomas McCulloch for the *DCB*, Vol. VII.

6. The story of the founding of Dalhousie and its failure to open are dealt with by D.C. Harvey in his usual forceful style in three articles in the *Dalhousie Review*, Vol. XVII: "The Dalhousie Ideal," No. 2, July 1937, pp. 131-43; "Early Struggles of Dalhousie," No. 3, October 1937, pp. 313-26; and "From College to University," No. 4, January 1938, pp. 411-31. Harvey himself believed deeply in the ideal of Dalhousie as a non-sectarian provincial college. He saw its failure as a consequence of sectarianism. He did not examine the political implications of the admixture of religion and colleges, other than on page 420 of "From College to University," where he notes that the Baptists turning to the Tories (the remnants of the Family Compact) "threatened to split the reform party at the very moment when unity was imperative." He was forced to conclude that the people of Nova Scotia were not ready for a non-sectarian college and "that they were capable of strong effort on behalf of any educational institution only when stirred by appeals to both the higher passions of self-sacrifice and the lower passions of religious rivalry." Substitute "sectional, regional or special interest or advocacy groups" for "religious" and nothing has changed.

7. See David B. Flemming, "William Fraser," *op. cit.*

8. See Terrence Punch, *Irish Halifax, op. cit.*, pp. 45 and 46.

9. See *ibid.*, pp. 48-68, and J. Murray Beck, *The Politics of Nova Scotia* (Four East Publications, Tantallon, Nova Scotia), Vol. 1, pp. 143-49.

10. In his biography of Howe, J. Murray Beck argues that Howe's motivation in forming the Protestant Alliance lay in his immense loyalty to Britain and his profound distrust of organized religion. See *Joseph Howe: The Briton Becomes Canadian 1848-1873* (McGill Queens, 1983), p. 121.

11. *Novascotian*, 5 July 1847.

12. A recent study, and one of the best, is Janice Potter, *The Liberty We Seek: Loyalists Ideology in Colonial New York and Massachusetts* (Harvard University Press, 1983).

13. This, of course, is taken from the subtitle to Beck's *Joseph Howe: Conservative Reformer 1804-1848*, Vol. I, *op. cit.*

14. See Julian Gwyn, " 'A Little Province Like this:' " *op. cit.*, p. 194.

15. See J. Murray Beck, *The Politics of Nova Scotia, op. cit.*, p. 135.

Index

Acadia College 76, 77, 82, 107, 111, 155, 158, 160, 173, 196, 232, 300, 301
Acadian (Halifax) 123
Acadian Recorder (Halifax) 24, 28, 46, 47, 48, 50, 53, 56, 60, 66, 67, 73, 75, 89, 111, 118, 122,146-47, 150, 188, 199, 210
Acadians 26, 32, 40, 102, 131, 146-47, 150, 151, 158, 159, 160, 188, 194, 198, 207, 227, 239, 250, 269, 278, 302
Agricola (John Young) 47, 50
Agriculture, protection of 50, 96, 100, 236, 239, 252, 295
Albro, John 45, 46, 48
Allan, John 218
Allen, K.E. 122, 307
Allison, James 124, 125
Allison, John 97
Allison, Joseph 69, 98, 124
Almon, Mather Byles 81, 82, 88, 109, 154, 254, 256, 262
Amherst Township 16, 217, 292, 307; elections by year, 1785, 219; 1793, 219; 1799, 220; 1802, 220; 1806, 9, 220; 1811, 220; 1818, 221; 1820, 221; 1830, 224; 1836, 225; 1840, 231; 1843, 232; 1847, 234-35
Anglicans 22, 23, 26, 91, 96, 157, 207, 209, 213, 227, 294, 297, 300, 306
Annand, William 25, 68, 70, 72, 74, 75, 80, 81, 85
Annapolis Academy 145
Annapolis County 129-30, 131-32, 148-49; elections by year, 1759, 132; 1783, 132; 1785, 133-34; 1786, 135; 1793, 137; 1799, 138; 1806, 138; 1808, 139; 1811, 139-40; 1818, 140; 1820, 141; 1824, 141; 1826, 144; 1829, 146, 1830, 146-47; 1836, 149-50; 1840, 1843, 156; 1847, 157
Annapolis Royal 130, 131, 132
Annapolis Township 129, 130, 131-32; elections by year, 1759, 132; 1784, 132; 1785, 133; 1793, 137; 1799, 138; 1806, 139; 1808, 139; 1818, 141; 1820, 141-42; 1830, 147; 1836, 149; 1840, 155-53; 1843, 155-56; 1847, 157
Antigonish, town of 249
Antigonish County, see Sydney County
Aplin, Joseph 199

Arbuthnot, Mariot 235
Archibald, Alexander Leckie 239, 242, 244, 245
Archibald, Charles Dickson 144, 238
Archibald, Elizabeth (Dickson) 237
Archibald, Matthew 236
Archibald, Samuel 235
Archibald, Samuel George William 12, 43, 44, 47, 48, 52, 53, 55, 56, 57, 58, 59, 61, 65, 66, 67, 75, 76, 118, 143, 223, 229, 237, 239, 240, 241, 242, 243, 246, 274
Archibald/Dickson Connection 238, 245
Argyle Township 188, 189, 191, 192, 193; elections by year, 1836, 194; 1840, 194-95; 1847, 198
Arichat Township 276; elections by year, 1832, 276; 1836, 280; 1840, 282-83; 1843, 284; 1847, 286
Assembly, composition of 10-14, 22-24; 1836, 25, 1847, 296-97
Assembly, General, First to Fifteenth 1, 24, 25, 26, 29
Assembly, representation in 2-3, 10, 25, 30, 31, 69, 276
Attorney General, office of 13, 33, 37, 54, 273
Aylesford Township 95, 96

Bailey, Reverend Jacob 132, 133
Baker, Edward 9
Baker, William 220
Ballaine, John 260, 261
Bank of Nova Scotia 62, 69
Banks 46, 62, 63, 82, 118, 142, 193
Baptists 22, 26, 78, 107, 126, 156, 157, 158, 160, 196, 204-05, 244-45, 297, 298, 301; see also Tory/Baptist Alliance
Barclay, Thomas 34, 37, 133, 134, 135, 136, 145
Barney's River 255
Barrington Township 188; elections by year, 1785, 199; 1790, 199; 1793, 199; 1799, 200; 1818, 200; 1820, 200; 1826, 201; 1830, 202; 1836, 203; 1840, 203; 1843, 203-04; 1847, 204

Barry, John Alexander 57, 58, 59, 189, 208, 209-12, 214
Barry, Mary 208, 210
Barry, Robert 207
Barss, Edward 185
Barss, James 14, 184
Barss, John 14, 182, 187
Barss, Joseph 14, 182
Baxter, William 99
Bayard, Robert 101
Bayard, Samuel 139
Beckwith, Mayhew 106, 108, 109, 110
Bee (Pictou) 251
Belcher, Andrew 41, 42, 179
Belcher, Benjamin 97, 98
Belcher, Jonathan 30
Bell, Hugh 25, 66, 67, 68, 69, 71, 72, 76, 90, 124, 297, 307, 308
Benjamin, Perez 104, 105, 106, 108, 109, 110
Bent, John 233
Bent, William White 233, 234
Bingay, James 192, 206, 207
Binney, Jonathan 29, 31
Bishop, Samuel 103
Black, "Bishop" William 181, 208
Black, Martin Gay 208
Black, Rosina Jane 275
Black, W. A. 81
Blackadar, Henry 57, 58, 59, 253, 255, 257, 258
Blacks 75, 81, 87, 88, 90, 153
Blanchard, Edward 238
Blanchard, Jotham 57, 58, 59, 64, 65
Bliss, William Blowers 21, 121, 122
Blowers, Sampson Salter 33, 34, 36, 37, 38, 45, 54, 61, 121, 122, 175, 178, 242
Bluenoses 16, 133
Board of Trade 1, 30, 31,
Bolman, Charles 172
Bolman, John 166, 167, 175
Bounties 50, 183, 201-02, 239, 261, 271
Bourneuf, François 160, 303
Bowman, William 125
Brandy Election, 1830, 54-58, 61, 64, 85, 191, 223, 238, 264-65, 274, 291; see also by constituency
Brenan, George 266, 267, 268, 269
Brenton, James 34, 136, 205
Brewer, Joseph 205
Bribery 7, 51, 120, 139, 269, 290
Bridgetown 129-30
Brightman, George 111
Brown, Edward 110, 272, 277, 281
Brown, Paul 203
Browne, Winthrop 199

Brymer, Alexander 178
Brymer, Alexander (cousin of above) 178
Brymer, Arthur 286
Budd, Charles 147, 150, 151, 158, 160
Bulkeley, James Freke 36
Butler, John 29, 32, 33

Callahan, Robert 178
Campbell, Colin 206, 207
Campbell, Colin, junior 208
Campbell, Donald 247
Campbell, John 185, 186
Campbell, Robert 30
Campbell, Samuel 141, 142, 144
Campbell, Sir Colin 25, 64, 70, 71, 72, 105, 108, 152, 172, 173, 195, 230, 241, 280
Campbell, William 103
Cape-Breton Advocate 250, 281, 282
Cape Breton County elections by year, 1820, 273-74; 1830, 9, 275; 1832, 4, 276-79; 1836, 279-80; 1840, 281-82; 1843, 284, 1847; 285-86
Cape Breton Island 6, 16, 17, 307; annexation question, 273, 281, 285, 287
Cape Breton Spectator 271, 285
Card, William 127
Catholic Ascendancy, cry of 86, 157, 234, 286, 297, 302
Central Board of Agriculture 47, 50, 116, 142, 195-96
Chancery Court 19
Chander, Thomas Edward junior 275, 277
Chandler, Samuel 236
Chandler, Sheriff Joshua 230
Cheever, Reverend Israel 177
Chester Township 165, 169, 170
Cheticamp 249, 278-79, 289
Chief Justice, office of 18, 37, 55, 56, 64
Chipman family compact 108, 111
Chipman, George 104
Chipman, Jared 99, 207
Chipman, John 109
Chipman, Major 147
Chipman, Reverend William 107
Chipman, Robert 107
Chipman, Samuel 103, 104, 105, 106, 107, 108, 110, 111, 301
Chipman, Samuel Bishop 22, 106, 107, 153, 154-58, 301
Chipman, William Allen 15, 98, 99, 100, 101, 102, 103, 183, 207, 260
Chipman, William Henry 107, 108
Christian Messenger 107, 155, 288, 299
Church of England 124, 127, 231, 299

Church of Scotland 22, 23, 24, 26, 91, 207, 209, 213, 248, 251, 258, 293, 294, 297, 298, 300
Church, Charles Lott 169, 170, 171, 172
Civil list 63, 64, 66, 70
Clare Township 131, 152; elections by year, 1840, 159-60; 1843, 160; 1847, 160
Clarke, Reverend Alexander 226, 227, 298
Clarke, Sheriff James 205-06
Clements Township 130, 131
Clements, Reuben 191, 193, 195, 196, 197
Cochran, Felix 121, 124
Cochran, John 121, 122
Cochran, Terence 121
Cochran, Thomas 176, 180, 181
Cochran, Thomas junior 181
Cochran, William 34, 36, 39, 41, 42, 43, 44, 180, 181
Cocken, Alexander 213, 214
Cogswell, Henry Hezekiah 45, 46, 47, 48, 50, 61, 295
Colchester County 67, 239; elections by year, 1836, 239-40; 1840, 241-42; 1841, 242; 1843, 245; 1847, 245-46
Colchester District 36, 37, 38, 40, 43, 47, 216-17;   for elections see Halifax County
Colchester/Halifax Axis 236, 237, 239, 246
Colleges, sectarian 76-78, 106, 107, 125, 126, 154, 155, 156, 173, 185, 196, 232, 233, 244, 245, 299-301; see also by name of college
Collins, Benajah 177, 178, 179, 180
Collins, Enos 14, 54, 55, 61, 92, 208, 224
Collins, George 182
Collins, Hallet 179
Colonial Patriot (Pictou) 54, 55, 56, 57, 223, 248, 264
Common schools 107, 234, 261, 298
Comeau, Anselm-François 159
Condon, William 303
Congregationalists 22
Conservative political culture 305-06
Conservatives, see Tories
Controverted elections, see Elections, controverted
Convention with United States, 1818, 116
Cook, Caleb 197, 198
Corberrie 150
Cornwall, Thomas 134
Cornwallis Township 94-95; elections by year, 1785, 97; 1793, 98; 1799, 98; 1811, 99; 1818,100-01; 1826, 102-03; 1830, 103-04;1840, 106; 1843, 108; 1847, 110
Cornwallis, Edward 161

Council (to 1838)1, 18, 23, 26, 29, 54-55, 61, 64, 105, 113, 145, 155, 193, 223, 224, 225, 264, 265, 288
Council of Twelve, see Council (to 1838)
County Party 38, 42
Courteau, Reverend Julien 278, 284
Courts, see by name
Covenanters, Reformed Presbyterian 96, 226, 227, 235
Cox, James 206
Crane, Jonathan 6, 97, 98, 99, 100, 101, 102
Crane, Joseph 106
Crawley, Edmund 77, 78, 226
Creelman, Samuel 245
Creighton, John 165, 168
Creighton, John (son of above) 165
Creighton, John (son of above) 176, 171, 172, 173, 174, 175
Crop failures 46, 99, 225, 306
Cross (Halifax) 86
Crowe, John 238, 242, 244, 245, 246
Crowell, Paul 203, 204
Crowell, Thomas 208, 209, 212,
Cumberland County 217, 218; elections by year, 1759, 218; 1785, 219; 1786, 219; 1793, 219; 1799, 219-20; 1806, 220; 1811, 220; 1818, 220-21; 1820, 221; 1826, 222-23; 1830, 223-24; 1836, 225-27; 1840, 230, 31; 1843, 232; 1847, 234-35
Cumberland Rebellion 218-19, 235
Cumberland Township 218
Cunard, Samuel 61, 223, 254, 256, 262
Cunningham, John 260
Customs fees 117, 118
Cutler family compact 259, 267, 294
Cutler, Maria 13
Cutler, Robert 261, 263
Cutler, Thomas 259, 260, 261, 262, 263, 264, 266, 294

d'Entremont, Benoni 194
d'Entremont, Philippe Mius 194
d'Entremont, Simon 26, 151, 194, 195, 198
Dalhousie College 76, 142, 145, 196-97, 299, 300
Dalhousie, Lord 44, 46, 47, 102,299
Danks, Benoni 218
Day, John 97
Day, John (son of above) 30, 31, 32 91
Dean, Ephraim 177, 178
DeBlois, Stephen 57, 58, 67, 239, 291, 295, 306
DeLancey, James 136, 137, 138, 219
DeLancey, Stephen 132, 133, 135, 136
Delaney, William Clarke 282, 301

Delap, James 147, 148, 150, 151, 153
Denison, Gurden 97
Denison, Sherman 97, 103
Denominational colleges, see Colleges, sectarian
Denoon, Hugh 52
Denson, Henry Denny 97
DesBarres, J.F.W. 164
DesBarres, William Frederick 12-13, 264, 267, 268, 270, 272, 294, 297
Deschamps, Issac 34, 97, 136, 164, 206
DeWolf, Benjamin 111, 117
DeWolf, Benjamin (son of Loran) 119, 120, 121, 123
DeWolf, Elisha 52, 98, 100, 101
DeWolf, Elisha (son of above) 103, 104
DeWolf, James Ratchford 182, 183, 184, 187
DeWolf, Thomas Andrew Strange 104, 105, 106, 108, 109, 110
Dickey, Robert Barry 224, 228, 233, 293
Dickey, Robert McGowan 224, 228, 229, 230, 231, 232, 233, 234, 235, 296, 301
Dickson, Charles (of Horton) 97
Dickson, Charles (of Onslow) 235, 236, 237
Dickson, Joseph 244, 245
Dickson, Robert 239
Dickson, Thomas 12, 57, 237, 242, 244, 252, 253, 261, 262, 264, 265, 287
Dickson, William 237, 238
Digby County 152, 158; elections by year, 1840, 159; 1843, 160; 1847, 160
Digby Township 130-31, 132; elections by year, 1785, 133; 1793, 137; 1799, 138; 1806, 138; 1818, 140-41; 1820, 141; 1830, 147; 1836, 151; 1840, 158-59; 1843, 160; 1847, 160
Dill, David 121, 122
Dill, Joseph 122
Dimock, Daniel 173, 174
Dimock, Icabod 125, 126, 128, 301, 305
Dimock, Shubael 113, 114, 115, 116, 117, 120, 121, 128
Disputed elections, see Elections, controverted
Disqualification bill 270-71
Dissenters 22, 23, 119, 127, 270, 298, 299
Dixon, Charles 219
Dixon, Thomas 9
Dixon, Thomas Law 220
Doane, Samuel Osborn, school run by 201
Dodd, Archibald 273
Dodd, Edmund Murray 77, 273, 274, 276, 277, 280, 281, 282, 284, 285, 286, 294
Doggett, John 175
Doucett, Anselm 146, 147, 150

Doyle, Lawrence O'Connor 81, 82, 84, 86, 276, 277, 279, 280, 282, 287, 302
Drunkenness, see Elections, drunkenness
Duels 12, 36, 38, 66, 154, 265

Eddy, Jonathan 218
Education, level of 20-22, 24
Elder, John 124
Election, first in 1758 1, 29, 164, 165, 218
Elections, by year listed by constituency and year
Elections, conduct of 1-2
Elections, cost of 4, 5, 13, 58, 90, 121, 146, 242, 251, 252, 255, 257, 276, 291
Elections, controverted 8-10
Elections, drunkenness at 4, 5, 9, 289
Elections, intimidation & violence at 4, 5, 9, 73-75, 171-2, 215, 253, 256-57, 263, 269, 275, 278-79, 283, 289-90
Elections, nominations of candidates 5, 43, 46, 65, 67, 72, 86, 88, 290
Elections, numbers voting 4, 16, 29, 33, 35, 198
Elections, role of religion in 89, 124, 156, 209, 213-15, 226, 242, 251, 252, 254-56, 258, 297-98, 301-04; see also clergy by name
Elections, scrutinies of 7-8, 81, 99, 141, 147
Embree, Samuel 219
Ernst, George 174
Executive Council (after 1838) 65, 71, 79, 83, 105, 195, 253, 288, 304

Fairbanks, Charles Rufus 12, 50, 51, 52, 53, 56, 61, 62, 63, 65, 66, 91, 229, 262, 291, 298
Fairbanks, Samuel Prescott 12
Falkland, Viscount 72, 78, 82, 83, 84, 196
Falmouth Township 93, 94; elections by year, 1775, 112; 1799, 113; 1830, 120; 1836, 124; 1840, 125; 1843, 125-26; 1847, 127-28
Family compacts 10, 14, 15, 24, 26 27, 111, 128, 166, 175, 177, 182, 186, 204, 267, 268, 294
Fancy, George 173
Farmers, class of 17, 26, 105
Fillis, John 34, 91
Finucane, Bryan 34
FitzRandolf, Joseph 148, 149
FitzRandolf, Robert 137, 138
Flemming, James 240, 244, 245
Flemming, William 238, 242
Foreign Protestants 29, 161
Forman, John 192, 193
Forrestall, Richard James 266, 267, 302, 308

Forrester, Thomas 25, 65, 67, 68, 70, 71, 72, 73, 74, 75, 76, 90, 307
Forshner, Andrew 220, 221
Foster, Robert 218
Francklin, Michael 29, 32, 33
Fraser, Bishop William 262, 264, 266, 267, 268, 277, 279, 294, 301, 302
Fraser, James 40
Fraser, James D.B. 256, 257
Fraser, James DeWolf 126, 127, 128, 270, 305
Fraser, Simon 261
Fraser, William 118, 122
Free Church 258
Free ports 100, 116, 123, 171, 193, 224-25, *Free Press* (Halifax) 52, 53, 56
Freeholders, creating of 6, 98, 99, 254
Freeholders, eligibility 5-7, 89, 92, 98, 100, 151, 153, 178, 220, 227, 238, 265, 307-09
Freeman, Elisha 176
Freeman, Joseph 182, 183, 184, 187, 210
Freeman, Nathan 179
Freeman, William (of Liverpool) 180, 181
Freeman, William (of Amherst) 219
Fuller, Sheriff John 284
Fulton, James 36, 37, 38, 39, 40, 41, 236
Fulton, Stephen 230, 233, 234, 235, 301

Gage, Thomas 32, 199
Gamaliel 50
Gambould, Richard 199
Gates, Henry 152, 153, 155-56
Geddes, James 192-93
Geddes, Thomas 203
General Mining Association 250, 276, 291
General Sessions of the Peace 18, 20
Gerrish, Benjamin 176
Gesner, Arahram 17
Gesner, Henry 104
Gibbons, Richard 273, 274, 275, 277, 280, 281, 282
Gladwin, Henry 68
Glasgow University 26
Gleneg, Lord 70
Goudge, Henry 123, 124, 125
Gough, Patrick 183, 184
Government House 38
Gracie, George 206
Grammar schools 202
Grant, Reverend Colin 263, 266
Grant, Robert Patterson 258
Granville Ferry 130
Granville Township 129-30; elections by year, 1785, 133; 1793, 137; 1799, 138; 1806, 138; 1818, 141; 1820, 141; 1830,

147-48; 1831, 148; 1836, 150-51; 1840, 153; 1843, 156; 1847, 157
Grassie, George 46, 48, 49, 91
Grassie, Thomas 85
Gray, James 85, 86
Guysborough County 265; elections by year, 1836, 266-67; 1840, 267; 1843, 269-70; 1847, 272
Guysborough Township 249
Gypsum trade 114, 115, 116, 123

Haliburton, Thomas Chandler 16, 122, 144-46
Haliburton, William Otis 19, 115, 117, 118, 119, 128, 144
Halifax Banking Company 14, 62, 124, 208, 292
Halifax County 36; elections by year, 1759, 29; 1761, 29; 1765, 30; 1770, 30; 1785, 33-34; 1788, 39; 1793, 4, 36-37; 1799, 38-41; 1800, 41; 1806, 43-44; 1818, 44; 1820, 46-48; 1825, 52; 1826, 53; 1830, 56-59; 1836, 67-69; 1840, 72-75; 1843, 78-82; 1847, 85-90
Halifax Grammar School 12, 21, 57, 67, 73, 76, 222, 260, 267
Halifax Journal 48
Halifax Township 2, 5, 308, elections by year, 1765, 30; 1773, 30; 1785, 33-34; 1793, 36-37; 1799, 41; 1801, 42; 1806, 5, 42; 1818, 45; 1820, 48-49; 1823, 50-52; 1826, 53; 1830, 56-58; 1835, 65-66; 1836, 67-69; 1840, 72-75; 1843, 3-4, 8, 78-82; 1847, 85-90
Hall, James 141
Hall, John Clarke 106, 107, 109, 110
Halliburton, Brenton 42, 54, 55, 61, 265
Hamilton, Alexander 212
Hants & Kings Gazette (Windsor) 122
Hants County 93-94, 308, elections by year, 1785, 111; 1793, 112; 1799, 113; 1806, 106; 1820, 117; 1824, 119; 1826, 119-20; 1827, 120; 1830, 121-22; 1836, 123-24; 1840, 124-25; 1843, 126; 1847, 127-28
Harrington, Charles 284
Harris, James 103, 104
Harris, Sheriff John 256
Hart, Samuel 179
Hartshorne, Lawrence 36, 37, 39, 40
Hartshorne, Lawrence (son of above) 20, 52, 57, 58, 59, 85
Harvard College 20, 209
Harvey, Sir John 84, 85, 245
Hatton, Henry 251, 252, 254
Heckman, John 169, 170, 171, 172, 173, 174, 308

Hector 247
Heffernan, William 270
Henry, Robert 266
Henry, William Alexander 267, 268, 269, 271, 302, 303
Hill, John Thomas 262, 264, 265
Hill, John Thomas 262, 264, 265
Hinselwood, Archibald 165
Hoar, Jonathan 132
Holdsworth, James Bourne 151, 158, 159, 160
Holland, William 150, 151, 152, 298
Holmes, John 251, 252, 253, 255, 257, 258
Homer, John 21, 188, 199, 201-02
Homer, John William 203, 204
Horton Township 94; elections by year, 1785, 97; 1793, 98; 1799, 98; 1806, 96; 1811, 99; 1818, 100-01; 1820, 101; 1826, 103; 1830, 103-04; 1840, 106; 1843, 108; 1844, 109; 1847, 110
Houses of entertainment, see Open houses
Howe, Alexander 133, 134, 135, 136, 137
Howe, John 42
Howe, Joseph 12, 25, 27, 64, 65, 66, 68, 69, 71, 72, 73, 74, 75, 76, 77, 78, 80, 81, 82, 83, 84, 85, 86, 87, 88, 90, 93, 106, 108, 112, 114, 127, 147, 152, 186, 229, 242, 271, 285, 290, 292, 296, 299, 303, 304, 305, 306
Huestis, Robert 207
Hughes, John 140, 141
Humphrey, James 206
Hunt, William 101
Huntington, Herbert 21, 25, 76, 77, 192, 193, 194, 195, 196, 197, 198, 243, 244, 245, 288, 296, 297, 299, 306, 309, 310
Huntington, Richard 285
Hustings 2
Huston, Hugh 212, 213
Hutchinson, Foster 42

Indians 158-159, 283
Inferior Court of Common Pleas 18, 19, 20
Inglis, Bishop Charles 208
Inglis, Bishop John 54, 127, 233
Inspectors, at elections 2
Instant freeeholders, see freeholders
Inverness County 7-8, 284; elections by year, 1840, 284; 1843, 284; 1847, 286
Irish Catholic vote 40, 53, 73, 74, 76, 78, 79, 81, 82, 89, 302-04
Irish, Edward 260

James, Benjamin 133, 137
James, Edward 166, 167, 168, 169, 171, 175, 308

Jeffery, Thomas 65
Jeffrey, Matthew 194
Jessen, Dettlieb Christopher 166, 167
Johnny Bluenose 16
Johnson, William 106, 107, 108, 109
Johnston, James William 9, 77, 82, 83, 84, 88, 106, 146, 154-58, 232, 323, 290, 293, 296, 297, 306, 309
Johnston, John 146, 148, 149, 196, 197
Johnstone, John 9
Jones, Cereno Upham 144
Judges' affair 34, 35, 136-37, 206
Justices of the Peace, office of 18,19

Kaulbeck, Sheriff John Henry 172
Kavanagh, Lawrence 22, 119, 142, 273, 274, 287
Kavanagh, Lawrence (son of above) 275
Kedy, John 174
Keith, Alexander 73, 74
Kempt, Sir James 53, 118, 143, 191
Kenny, Heman 199
Kent, James 41
Kentville 94
Kidston, Richard junior 45
Killam, Thomas 197
King's College School 21
King's College, Windsor 20, 21, 26, 76, 77, 93, 145, 156, 244, 273, 275, 299, 300
Kings County 94-96; elections by year, 1783, 97; 1785, 97; 1793, 98; 1799, 98; 1806, 98; 1811, 99; 1818, 100-01; 1820, 101; 1826, 102-03; 1830, 103-04; 1836, 104-05; 1840, 106; 1843, 108; 1847, 110
Kirkmen, see Church of Scotland
Knaut, Philip 164, 165, 166, 167

Labouring class 14, 17, 98, 238
Langille, Peter 173
Larkin, John 194
Lawrence, Charles 1, 29, 161, 163, 175, 218
Lawrence, Elisha 97
Lawson, William 43, 44, 46, 57, 58, 59, 64, 67, 68, 69, 237, 295, 298
Lawson, William junior 85, 88
Lawyers 11-13, 17, 19, 22, 23, 26, 52, 53, 67, 69, 90, 101, 106, 122, 250, 270, 287, 293, 296, 306
Ledger influence 14, 15, 24, 26, 57, 73, 87, 92, 96, 104, 108, 109, 151, 153, 157, 172, 182, 195, 201, 219, 220, 234, 262, 298, 307, 308
Legge, Francis 31, 32, 41, 42
Legget, John 260
Legislative Assembly, see Assembly

Legislative Council (after 1838) 64, 65, 69, 70, 195, 309

Lent, Arahram 192

Lent, James 191, 192

Leonard, Samuel 97

LeVesconte, Isaac 286

Lewis, Gaius 25, 225, 226, 227, 229, 230, 231, 232, 234, 293, 301, 306, 307

Liberals, see Reformers

Liverpool Township 14, 17, 161-62, 176; elections by year, 1761, 175-76; 1775, 176; 1785, 177; 1787, 178-79; 1793, 179; 1799, 181; 1811, 182; 1818, 182; 1820, 182; 1826, 183; 1830, 184; 1836, 184-85; 1840, 185; 1843, 185; 1847, 186

Loan offices 100

Logan, Isaac 239, 240, 246

Logan, Thomas 228, 232, 234

Londonderry Township 216, 235; elections by year, 1785, 236; 1793, 236; 1799, 236; 1826, 238; 1836, 240-41; 1840, 241-42; 1843, 244-45; 1847, 245-46

Lord Durham's *Report* 152, 195, 280

Louisbourg 1

Lovett, James Russel 141, 147, 149

Lovett, Phineas III 141-2, 144

Lovett, Phineas junior 138, 139, 141

Loyalist ascendancy 33, 306

Loyalists 2, 6, 10, 16, 20, 22, 23, 33, 34, 35, 37, 54, 95, 129, 132, 134, 135, 166, 188, 204, 219, 259, 273, 305-06

Lunenburg County 161-63; elections by year, 1759, 164; 1773, 165; 1785, 165-66; 1793, 167; 1799, 167; 1806, 168; 1818, 169; 1820, 169-70; 1826, 170-71; 1830, 171; 1836, 171-72; 1840, 173; 1843, 173-74; 1847, 174-75

Lunenburg Township 2, 29, 161-62; elections by year, 1759, 164; 1783, 165; 1785, 165-66; 1793, 167; 1799, 167; 1818, 169; 1826, 171; 1830, 171; 1836, 172; 1840, 173; 1843, 174; 1847, 174-75

Lusby, Thomas 219, 220

Lutherans 162, 297

Lyle, John 203

MacDonald, Adjutant 260

MacDonald, Hugh 267, 270, 272

MacDonell, Reverend Alexander 276, 277, 278, 284, 287, 295, 301

MacKay, George 125, 126, 126

MacKay, John 120

MacKenzie, A.W. 272

MacKenzie, Reverend Hugh 226

MacKinnon, John 207

MacKinnon, Ranald 191, 192

MacLean, Bard John 246, 247

MacLean, Hector 112

MacLeod, James W. 186, 271

MacLeod, Neil and wife Mary 271

Magistrates 18, 20

Maitland, Sir Peregrine 54, 56, 64, 69

Maranda, Reverend Jean-Baptiste 283, 284

Marchinton, Philip 177

Marshall, John George 9, 99-100, 237, 259, 260, 261, 262, 298

Marshall, John Joseph 267, 270, 272

Marshall, Joseph 259, 260

Marshall, Samuel 190

Marsters, Nathaniel 236, 237, 238

Martell, Henry 282, 284, 285, 286, 303

Martin, Nicholas 285

Mauger party 29, 30, 31, 32, 33

Mauger, Joshua 29, 32

McCulloch, Reverend Thomas 12, 21, 223, 248, 252, 254, 299, 300

McCully, Jonathan 228, 230, 231, 234, 293

McCurdy, Daniel 236

McDougall, Alexander 265

McDougall, John 127

McFarlane, John 234

McGregor, James 253

McGregor, Reverend James 39, 40, 41

McHeffey, William 124

McKeagney, James 277, 282, 283, 286, 289, 293, 302, 303

McKeagney, Reverend Henry 277, 278, 279, 283, 302

McKeagney, Reverend Patrick 277, 278, 279, 283

McKenna, Gilbert 212, 213, 214

McKenzie, Reverend Kenneth John 252

McKim, Andrew 225-57, 228, 229-31, 293, 298, 300

McLelan, Gloud Wilson 25, 77, 240, 241, 243, 244, 245

McMonagle, John 9, 113, 114

McNab, James 8, 72, 73, 74, 75, 78, 79, 80, 87 88, 89, 108

McNab, Peter

McNamara, John (school of) 21, 140

McNeil, Charles 205

McQueen, Sheriff David 2, 262, 263

McQueen, Reverend Archibald 253

Mechanic and Farmer (Pictou) 254

Merchants, class of 1, 13-15, 17, 19, 23, 25, 26, 29, 31, 89, 90, 91, 250, 296, 308

Methodists 22, 26, 96, 209, 213, 226, 227, 235, 270, 297, 298, 300

Mignowitz, Henry 174

Militia officers 11

Mill Village 162

Miller, Garrett 165, 168, 170, 171, 172-3
Millidge, Thomas 133, 135, 136, 138
Money bills1 8, 42, 76
Monk, George 9, 113
Monk, James 31, 32, 33
Moody, E.W.B. 197
Moody, James 137, 138
Moore, Daniel 14, 109, 110
Moorsom, William Captain 14
Morning Chronicle (Halifax) 232
Morning Post (Halifax) 79, 218
Morris, Charles 18
Morris, Charles III (son of above) 35, 39, 40, 41, 49, 61, 91, 167
Morris, John Spry 61
Morse, James Shannon 221, 222, 223, 224, 226, 227, 228, 293, 294, 298
Morse, Silas Leander 153, 293
Mortimer, Edward 12, 38, 39, 40, 44, 46, 47
Morton, John (of Cornwallis) 102, 103, 105
Morton, John (of Digby) 147, 151
Morton, Lemuel1 06
Moser, Nicholas 126, 128
Mott, Henry 86, 88, 90
Munro, W.H. 286
Murdoch, Beamish 53, 56, 57, 58, 91-92, 102, 223, 229, 238, 291, 304, 306
Murray, Robert 258

Nesbitt, William 29, 31, 32, 33, 242
New Dublin Township 165, 172
New England Planters 2, 10, 16, 93, 94, 95, 129, 132, 138, 161, 188, 307
New Glasgow 255, 294
New Lights 141, 236
Newcomers 133
Newport Township 93-94, 133; elections by year, 1799, 113; 1820, 117; 1826, 120; 1830, 120-21; 1836, 123-24; 1840, 125; 1843, 126; 1847, 128
Newton, Charlotte Ann 12
Newton, Henry 178
Newton, Joshua 180, 185
Nimrod 108
Northern District of Queens County 184, 185
Northrup, Jeremiah 112, 113
Nova Scotia Royal Gazette (Halifax) 42
Nova Scotia Packet (Shelburne) 206
Novascotian (Halifax) 13, 24, 25, 64, 68, 72, 78, 81, 84, 108, 109, 110, 112, 114, 127, 147, 152, 152, 153, 172, 196, 213, 214, 225, 232, 231, 235, 273, 283, 288
Nugent, Richard 78, 81, 232, 240, 259, 271, 272

O'Brien, William 117, 120, 121, 123, 124

Office-holders, class of 25, 29, 31, 91, 306
Oldcomers 131, 135
Oligarchy 18, 25, 31, 32, 33, 54, 56, 57, 61, 169, 171, 176, 192, 215, 307, 310
Onslow Township 37, 40, 216; elections by year, 1785, 236; 1793, 236; 1799, 236; 1806, 236; 1818, 237; 1820, 238; 1826, 238; 1840, 242; 1843, 244-45; 1847, 245
Open houses 45, 75, 79, 290
Open voting 2, 4, 15
Owen, Charles 174
Oxley, George 219, 220, 221, 222
Oxley, Joseph 222
Oxley, Stephen 223
Oxner, John 169, 170

Palmer, Henry 125
Paper currency, see Treasury notes
Parish bill 127, 305
Parker, Snow 181, 182
Parliamentary grant 18
Parr, John 33, 36, 180, 210, 205, 206, 305
Parrsborough Township 95
Party fund raising 292-93
Patronage 14, 19, 24, 304, 310
Patterson, Arahram 251, 252
Patterson, Robert 39
Patterson, Sarah Ann 252
Payson, Jonathan 139
Payzant, Lewis 125, 126
Pearson, Thomas 236, 237
Perkins, Simeon 5, 161, 175, 176-82
Pernette, Joseph 164-65, 168
Pictou Academy 21, 57, 145, 252, 254, 261, 264, 298, 301
Pictou County 67, 239, 251; elections by year, 1836, 251; 1838, 252; 1840, 253-54; 1843, 254-55; 1847, 258
Pictou District 36, 37, 38, 39, 40, 43, 59, 247-49
Pictou Observer 255
Pictou Township elections by year, 1836, 251; 1840, 254; 1843, 255-56; 1845, 256-57; 1847, 258
Planters, see New England Planters
Plumpers 3, 4, 53, 58, 74
Political parties, formation of 293-94
Poll books 2, 3, 4, 7, 9, 135, 241
Poole, Samuel Sheldon 189, 190, 191, 299
Population numbers 2, 10, 16, 28, 60, 92, 132, 140, 204, 206
Portland, Duke of 37
Power, Patrick 268, 269, 270, 271
Presbyterians 22, 23, 26, 124, 227, 297, 300
Prescott, Charles Ramage 17
Prescott, Jonathan 166, 176

Preston, Reverend Richard 87
Prevost, Sir George 44, 115
Primrose, Alexander 284
Property qualification, see Freeholders, eligibility of
Protestant Alliance 303-03
Pryor, John 46, 48
Purdy, Elijah 232
Purdy, Henry 219, 220, 221
Pyke, John George 11, 34, 36, 39, 41, 44, 45, 136

Queens County 5, 161-63, 176-77; elections by year, 1765, 176; 1784, 177; 1785, 177; 1793, 179; 1797, 180; 1799, 180-01; 1801, 181; 1811, 182; 1818, 182; 1820, 182; 1826, 184-85; 1840, 185; 1843, 185; 1847, 186

Rand, Silas Tertius 288
Rawdon and Douglas Townships 94, 117
Redistribution, see Assembly, representation in
Reformers 25, 26, 70, 72, 73, 74, 76, 77, 78, 81, 83, 85, 88, 106, 152, 153, 156, 160, 173, 214, 229, 230, 231, 232, 240, 242, 243, 244, 251, 253, 254, 257, 280, 288, 290, 292, 293, 296, 297, 300, 301, 302, 304, 305, 306
Registrars of Deeds and Probate 6, 14, 18, 25
Religion, role in elections, see Elections, religion in
Responsible government 24, 25-26, 71, 83, 84, 86, 90, 110, 157, 213, 214, 229, 270, 288, 304-05, 310
Richmond County 280; elections by year, 1836, 289; 1840, 282-83; 1841, 283-84; 1843, 284; 1846, 286; 1847
Restricted franchise, see Freeholders, eligibility
Ritchie, John 132, 133
Ritchie, John William 149, 150
Ritchie, Thomas 115, 119, 119, 138, 139, 140, 142, 143-44, 209, 293
Ritchie, Thomas (cousin of above) 141
River Philip 216, 217
Roach, Thomas 219, 220, 221, 223
Roach, William Henry 140, 141, 142, 144, 146, 147, 147, 149-50
Road moneys 14, 15, 54, 55, 142-43, 149, 173, 193-94, 237, 238, 243, 245, 267
Robertson, Alexander 211
Robertson, Andrew 258
Robertson, John 142, 143
Robertson, William 139, 142

Robichaud, Frederick 26, 150, 151, 152, 159-60, 194
Robie, Simon Bradstreet 9, 12, 46, 47, 52, 54, 65, 67, 144, 154, 168, 220, 229, 236, 242, 265
Roche, Charles 208, 211, 121
Rogers, Samuel 218
Roman Catholics 22, 26, 29, 78, 297, 301
Roop, Sheriff Jacob 158
Ross, Hugh 257
Ross, John 242, 244, 245
Ross, Robert 205
Royal Gazette (Halifax)37
Royal William 248
Rudolf, Christopher 167
Rudolf, Francis Joseph 169, 170
Rudolf, William 170, 171, 172, 298
Ruggles, Timothy 141, 142, 144, 147, 148
Russell, Lord John 71, 72, 280
Rutherford, Henry 137, 138, 140
Ryder, John 14, 194, 195, 196, 197, 198

Sackville Township 218
Salter, Benjamin 36
Sanders, John 197
Sangster, James 127
Sargent, John 14, 168, 199-200, 208
Sargent, John (son of above)14, 203, 213, 293, 306
Sargent, William Browne 200, 201, 203, 298, 306
Sargent Winthrop 14, 124, 212, 213, 298, 306
Saxe Gotha 79, 80
Schools, compulsory assessment 142, 154, 196, 268, 310
Schwartz, John William 166, 167
Schwartz, Otto William 165
Scotch Irish Presbyterians 216, 218
Scots, settlement of 221, 247-48, 249
Scrutinies of elections, see Elections, scrutinies of
Seabury, David 133, 134, 135
Seaman, Amos "King" 227, 233, 293
Seceders 248-49, 252, 293, 298
Secret ballot 2
Seeley, Caleb 184
Shaw, Isaiah 138
Shaw, Joseph 148
Shaw, Moses 133
Shelburne County 193; elections by year, 1785, 204, 206; 1793, 206; 1799, 191, 206; 1805, 206; 1820, 207; 1826, 192; 1828, 192; 1830, 192-93; 1836, 212-13; 1840, 213-14; 1843, 214; 1847, 214-15
Shelburne Township 188; elections by year, 1785, 204-06; 1793, 206; 1799, 206;

1818, 207; 1824, 207-09; 1826, 209-10; 1829, 211; 1830, 212; 1836, 121-13; 1840, 213-14; 1843, 214; 1847, 215
Sherbrooke, village of 249
Sherbrooke, Sir John 44
Sheriffs, role at elections 2, 4, 5, 8, 14, 18 see also by name of sheriff
Sherlock, George William 177, 178, 179
Shey, William Henry 120
Shubenacadie Canal 56, 58
Shubenacadie River 216
Sigogne, Abbé 131, 146, 150, 160
Simultaneous polling 1, 5, 85, 90, 245, 258, 289, 309
Skinner, Stephen 206
Smith, Benjamin 123, 124, 126, 128, 305
Smith, George 47, 48, 54, 58, 59, 152, 237, 251, 252, 254, 255, 256, 292
Smith, James 236
Smith, Richard (of Cape Breton) 4, 276, 277, 278, 279, 282, 289, 291, 293
Smith, Richard (of Hants County) 119, 120, 121, 123, 124
Smith, William 124, 125, 176
Smyth, Peter 286, 303
Snow, Joshua 212, 215
Solictor General, office of 13, 37, 38, 54, 144
Song to America 247, 248
Sons of Liberty 199
Speaker of the Assembly 13, 24, 67, 75-76, 138, 144, 168
Spearwater, Peter 25, 212, 213, 214
Spirit of the Times (Sydney) 250
St. Andrew's Church, Pictou 252
St. John's Church, Lunenburg 164, 169, 175
St. Mary's College, Halifax 76, 196, 300
St. Matthew's Church, Halifax 89
St. Ninan's Parish 262
St. Paul's Church, Halifax 33, 36, 45, 142, 154
St. Peter's 283, 289
Stairs, William 7, 75, 76, 78, 79, 80, 81, 292, 306
Standard and Conservative Advocate (Halifax) 85, 89
Stanhope, Henry 205
Starr, John 102, 103
Starr, John Leander 57, 58, 59, 67
Star, Joseph 67
Steele, John 261, 262, 263, 264, 292
Sterns, Jonathan 34, 36, 37, 49, 92, 115, 167, 178
Stewart, Alexander 27, 64, 222, 223, 224, 225, 226, 227, 228, 229, 233, 238, 293, 294, 298, 307
Stewart, James 36, 38, 39, 40, 42, 54

Stewiacke River Valley 216
Strange, Thomas Andrew 35, 37, 137
Summary trials 19
Supreme Court 19, 221-22
Sydney County 265; elections by year, 1785, 259; 1793, 259; 1799, 259; 1806, 259-60; 1811, 260-61; 1818, 261; 1820, 261-62; 1824, 262-64; 1826, 264; 1830, 264-65; 1836, 265-66; 1837, 266; 1840, 267-68; 1843, 268-69; 1847, 271-72

Taylor, James 181
Taylor, John 138
Taylor, Joseph 178
Taylor, William Benajah 185, 186, 187
Temperance 5, 198, 267
Thomson, Charles Poulett 72
Thomas, Sarah Rachael 122
Thorne, Edward 138
Thorne, Stephen 150, 151, 152, 153, 154, 156, 157, 306
Times (Halifax) 72, 82, 86, 108, 161, 302
Tinkham, Sheriff 178
Tobin, James 61
Tobin, Michael junior 78, 86
Tonge, William Cottnam 38, 40, 41, 42, 112, 113, 114, 115, 167, 168, 200, 259
Tonge, Winkworth 14, 97
Tories 26, 70, 72, 73, 77, 78, 82, 87, 88, 185, 232, 241, 245, 251, 253, 254, 257, 288, 290, 292, 293, 296, 297, 300, 301, 304, 305
Tory/Baptist Alliance 77, 107, 106, 111, 152, 155, 157, 155, 158, 160, 185, 197, 245, 293
Tottie, John 211
Townsend, Reverend George 226
Treasury notes 45, 46, 61, 63, 100, 122
Trinty Church, Liverpool 186, 187
Trotter, Reverend Thomas 21, 263-54, 266, 267
Truro Township 59, 216; elections by year, 1785, 236; 1793, 236; 1799, 236; 1806, 237; 1811, 9, 237; 1818, 237; 1820, 238; 1826, 238; 1840, 242; 1843, 244-45; 1847, 245
Tucker, Sheriff Robert 134, 135
Tupper, Augustus 104, 106, 108, 307
Tupper, Reverend Charles 104, 226
Tupper, Samuel 47
Turnbull, James 284, 286
Twelve Resolutions 70, 105, 203

Uniacke, Andrew Mitchell 3-4, 8, 79, 80, 81, 84, 85, 86, 87, 89-90, 302, 304

Uniacke, James Boyle 9, 21, 70, 71, 75, 82, 83, 84, 108, 110, 275-76, 279, 280, 281, 282, 284, 285, 286, 287, 296, 297

Uniacke, Richard John 33, 34, 36, 37, 38, 50, 61, 180, 181, 305

Uniacke, Richard John junior 238, 273, 274, 286, 287, 299

Union of King's and Dalhousie Colleges 209-210

Universal suffrage 7, 309

Upham, Alexander 242, 244

Utley, Nathan 190

Van Buskirk, Jacob 192, 207, 208, 213

Vernon, Augustus 213

Voters eligibilty, see Freeholders, eligibility

Waddington, Samuel 34, 177

Walker, Thomas 139

Wallace River 217, 219

Wallace, Charles Wentworth 61

Wallace, Michael 34, 37, 38, 39, 40, 41, 54, 55, 61

Walsh, Bishop William 78

Ward, Edmund 53, 72, 302

Warner, Joe (John Young) 60, 66, 239-40, 243

Warwick, John 138, 140

Waterman, James 173

Waterman, Zenas 184, 185, 186

Watson, Samuel 203

Watt, John 89

Wellington Dyke 95

Wells, John 99, 101, 102, 103

Wells, Joseph 171

Wentworth, Sir John 36, 37, 39, 42, 44, 112, 113, 114, 115, 137, 168, 180, 200, 305

Whidden, John 106

White, Gideon 189, 199, 207, 208

White, Nathanie l56, 140, 208, 209, 210, 212

Whitman, Alfred 152, 153, 156, 157

Whitman, Edward 139

Whitman, Elnathan 149, 151, 152

Wier, John 238, 239, 241, 244

Wilkie, James 265, 266

Wilkins, Charles 34, 122

Wilkins, Isaac 205, 206

Wilkins, Lewis Morris 9, 13, 54, 67, 114, 122, 166, 168, 169, 175, 242, 260, 267

Wilkins, Lewis Morris (son of above) 121, 122, 124, 126, 127, 128, 305

Wilkins, Martin Issac 255, 256, 257, 258, 292

Wilmot Township 129

Wilson, Obediah junior 214

Windsor Township 17, 93, 96; elections by year, 1793, 9; 1799, 113; 1830, 121-22;

133, 122; 1836, 123-24; 1840, 124; 1843, 126; 1847, 127-28

Winniet, William 2, 140, 141

Wiswall, Peleg 139, 143, 146

Wolfville 94

Wollenhaupt, Casper 165, 167

Women voting 9, 152-53, 220

Woodbury, Foster 139

Yarmouth County 193; elections by year, 1836, 193-94; 1840, 195-96; 1843, 196-97; 1847, 197-98

Yarmouth Herald 189, 197, 198, 245

Yarmouth Township 17, 25, 188-89, 193; elections by year, 1785, 189; 1793, 190; 1799, 190; 1804, 190; 1811, 190; 1813, 191; 1818, 191; 1820, 191; 1826, 191; 1830, 191; 1835, 191; 1836, 193-94; 1840, 195-96; 1843, 196-97; 1847, 197-98

Yorkshiremen 218

Young, Elkanah 126, 128,

Young, George Renny 67, 84, 254-55, 257, 258, 265, 287

Young, John 28, 47, 50, 51, 52, 60, 66, 67, 75, 143, 239, 240, 243, 262, 263, 264, 265, 272, 276, 287, 291, 294, 301, 306

Young, William 4, 22, 25, 27, 50, 52, 122, 255, 263, 273, 287, 289, 291, 292, 294, 309

Young, William Mayhew 118, 127

Zouberbuhler, Sebastian 164, 165

Zwicker, Edward 173